Public Relations and the Rise of AI is a must-read not [...] scholars but also for public relations educators who are [...] [...] [...] tion of professionals grappling with AI in their everyday work. The authors do not dismiss AI and its promises but provide guidance on the ways to authentically and thoughtfully integrate AI into the study and practice of public relations. Scholars, students, and practitioners will come away more confident in navigating public relations decisions with an ethical mindset in this new era.

– **Virginia Harrison**, *Clemson University*

Public Relations and the Rise of AI is a crucial read for PR professionals, educators, and researchers. It provides the knowledge and tools necessary to navigate AI's opportunities, challenges, and risks. Luttrell and Wallace's impactful, approachable book makes significant contributions, preparing educators to teach their students how to use AI-powered communication tools in the PR industry. The book's real-world applications and case studies provide practical insights on analyzing and interpreting data from AI-powered platforms, empowering informed communication strategies and decisions. This comprehensive guide not only explores the transformative power of AI in the PR industry but also emphasizes the importance of adaptability, offering insights on maintaining authenticity, navigating ethical and legal concerns, and working creatively and effectively in a rapidly evolving landscape. This edited volume provides an all-encompassing perspective and knowledge to adapt to and thrive in an AI-driven landscape, making it an indispensable resource for anyone looking to stay ahead in the ever-evolving field of public relations.

– **Kate Stewart**, *Jacksonville State University*

PUBLIC RELATIONS AND THE RISE OF AI

This book explores the potential of artificial intelligence (AI) to transform public relations (PR) and offers guidance on maintaining authenticity in this new era of communication.

One of the main challenges PR educators, researchers, and practitioners face in the AI era is the potential for miscommunication or unintended consequences of using AI tools. This volume provides insights on how to mitigate these risks and ensure that PR strategies are aligned, offering practical guidance on maintaining trust and authenticity in PR practices. Readers will learn to leverage AI for enhanced communication strategies and real-time audience engagement while navigating the ethical and legal implications of AI in PR. Featuring contributions from leading scholars, the book includes case studies and examples of AI-driven PR practices, showcasing innovative approaches and lessons from well-known brands. It offers a global perspective on AI's impact on PR, with insights for practitioners and scholars worldwide.

This book equips PR educators, researchers, and professionals with the knowledge and tools they need in the changing landscape of communication in the age of AI.

Regina Luttrell, senior associate dean and associate professor of public relations at Syracuse University's S.I. Newhouse School of Public Communications (New York), is a respected educator and scholar. She is recognized for her leadership on complex research projects, facilitation of interdisciplinary collaborations, and advocacy for faculty. She has authored an extensive collection of books, articles, and conference presentations, including *Social Media: How to Engage, Share, and Connect*; *Public Relations Campaigns: An Integrated Approach*; *Social Media & Society*; and *Strategic Social Media as Activism*.

Adrienne A. Wallace is an associate professor and the advertising and public relations major program coordinator in the School of Communications at Grand Valley State University (Michigan). Her research is focused mostly on the intersection of public relations with digital media, pedagogy, and public affairs, as well as the student-to-professional journey. Dr. Wallace serves the *Journal of Public Relations Education* as editor-in-chief and moonlights at BlackTruck Media & Marketing, where she is a strategist.

PUBLIC RELATIONS AND THE RISE OF AI

Edited by Regina Luttrell and
Adrienne A. Wallace

Routledge
Taylor & Francis Group

NEW YORK AND LONDON

Designed cover image: TeaGraphicDesign via iStock/Getty Images Plus

First published 2025
by Routledge
605 Third Avenue, New York, NY 10158

and by Routledge
4 Park Square, Milton Park, Abingdon, Oxon, OX14 4RN

Routledge is an imprint of the Taylor & Francis Group, an informa business

ISBN: 978-1-032-67147-5 (hbk)
ISBN: 978-1-032-67132-1 (pbk)
ISBN: 978-1-032-67148-2 (ebk)

DOI: 10.4324/9781032671482

Typeset in Times New Roman
by Apex CoVantage, LLC

To the trailblazers of public relations and artificial intelligence, whose innovative spirit and relentless pursuit of excellence inspire us. Your vision and dedication shape the future of communication, bridging the gap between technology and human connection. May this work honor your contributions and light the path for those who follow. Good luck to us all!

Gina and Adrienne

CONTENTS

CONTRIBUTORS

Dr. Courtney D. Boman is an assistant professor of PR at The University of Alabama. Her primary research interests include crisis and risk communication. Topics that she has recently examined include how the societal issue of misinformation and disinformation has influenced practices within the PR industry and strategies that can attenuate its persuasiveness.

Dr. Jason Davis is co-director of the Emerging Insights Lab and a research professor at Syracuse University's Newhouse School of Public Communications (New York). His current research is focused on the application of generative AI models and explores the potential benefits and limitations of these advanced technologies in shaping public discourse and informing humans in the loop vulnerabilities and decision-making processes. His research also focuses on the creation of digital trust and transparency in media through the development and evaluation of new AI-driven tools for the detection, attribution, and characterization of disinformation and synthetically generated content.

Chris Galloway, Ph.D., APR, is an honorary research associate of Massey University (Aotearoa New Zealand). He previously taught public relations courses in Australia, Aotearoa New Zealand, Indonesia, and Pakistan. His research encompasses crisis communication, reputation management, and artificial intelligence and its communication-related impacts.

Dr. Nathan Gilkerson is an associate professor of public relations and strategic communication at Marquette University (Wisconsin). He received his Ph.D. in mass communication from the University of Minnesota. Gilkerson previously worked professionally in political communication, advertising, and public relations, and he has published research in a variety of academic journals.

Dr. David Gurney is the associate director of the School of Arts, Media, and Communication and a professor of media studies at Texas A&M University-Corpus Christi. He focuses his research on emergent media technology, forms, and content from a critical/cultural studies perspective.

Dr. Laurence José is a professor of writing and the director of the digital studies program at Grand Valley State University (Michigan), where she teaches courses in professional writing, business communication, visual design, and digital studies. Her research interests include global communication, semiotic theory, digital literacy, data humanism, and program administration. Her work has been published in various edited collections and in French linguistics journals, including *Scolia, Languages*, and *Le Bulletin de la Société de Linguistique de Paris*.

Dean Kruckeberg, Ph.D., APR, FPRSA, is a professor in the Department of Communication Studies at the University of North Carolina at Charlotte. He is the author and co-author of many books, book chapters, and journal articles about public relations, focusing on ethics and global public relations.

Travis Loof, Ph.D., is a research professor at the University of Alabama specializing in media psychology and AI's impact on communication. With extensive experience in curriculum development and student mentorship, Dr. Loof actively contributes to pioneering communication technology research and innovative teaching strategies in strategic communication and media studies.

Dr. Michelle Maresh-Fuehrer is department chair and professor of public relations at Texas A&M University-Corpus Christi. Recognized as University Educator of the Year by the Texas Speech Communication Association, she frequently publishes research and consults with organizational leaders on the topics of crisis communication, social media, and public relations.

Dr. Christopher J. McCollough is The Ayers Family Endowed Chair of Journalism and Mass Communication at Jacksonville State University (Alabama). McCollough studies public sector communication and political public relations, the benefits of high-impact learning, the integration of industry-current tools and practices in curriculum, and inclusive practices in journalism and mass communication classrooms.

Hollin Nies, a communications strategist at Vansary and an adjunct professor of Public Speaking and Rhetorical Strategies at Gannon University, holds a Bachelors in English and Public Writing from the University of Pittsburgh and a law degree from DePaul University. Her expertise bridges rhetoric, legal analysis, and public relations, focusing on impactful messaging and strategic advocacy.

Erika J. Schneider, Ph.D., University of Missouri, is an assistant professor of public relations in the S.I. Newhouse School of Public Communications at Syracuse University. She researches the intersection of risk and crisis communications to understand how stakeholders perceive risk and how organizations can support communities during crisis events.

Dr. Rebecca Swenson is an associate professor at the University of Minnesota. Her research program focuses on science communication, community building, engagement, and communication evaluation. Rebecca teaches agricultural and environmental science communication classes, and previously held various communication and marketing positions at a nonprofit organization, a corporation, and a public relations agency.

Lukasz Swiatek, Ph.D., FHERDSA, lectures in the School of the Arts and Media at the University of New South Wales (UNSW, Australia). He mainly undertakes research in communication and media studies, higher education, and cultural studies.

Rosalynn A. Vasquez is an assistant professor of public relations in the Department of Journalism, Public Relations, & New Media at Baylor University (Texas). Her research primarily focuses on bringing greater awareness and understanding of stakeholder experiences and perceptions of DEI, ethics, and sustainability, especially among underrepresented or marginalized voices. As a former PR practitioner, she worked in corporate, agency, and nonprofit for 15 years before earning her Ph.D. in media and communications from Texas Tech University.

Marina Vujnovic, Ph.D., APR, is a professor in the Department of Communication at Monmouth University (New Jersey). Her work explores intersections between journalism and public relations, looking at issues of participation, activism, transparency, and ethics.

Dr. Jamie Ward is an assistant professor at the University of Toledo (Ohio). Her research focuses on topics related to public relations, ethics, AI, and social media. She is (co)author of the following books: Public Relations Principles: Current. Proven. Practical and A Practical Guide to Ethics in Public Relations.

Carrie Welch, M.S., Syracuse University, has worked in the public relations field for over 20 years, including as Vice President of PR at the Food Network and co-owner of successful PR and events companies. She serves as an adjunct professor in the discipline she loves.

Myungok Chris Yim, Ph.D., is an associate professor of public relations at Loyola University Chicago. She explores ethical AI use in PR, corporate social advocacy, crisis communication, and how organizations can employ DEI-conscious PR approaches to advance sustainable engagements with diverse stakeholders in the AI-mediated communication era.

Liang Zhao is the founder of Vansary, a marketing and public relations consultancy that specializes in technology and investor communications. Zhao has her Master's degree in finance from Tulane University (Louisiana) and has been featured in the *Wall Street Journal*, *U.S. News*, *Fortune*, Bloomberg, *USA Today*, and more.

EDITORS' INTRODUCTION

Power and Purpose of AI in PR

Regina Luttrell and Adrienne A. Wallace

Public Relations and the Rise of AI provides a comprehensive overview of the profound impact that artificial intelligence (AI), particularly generative AI, has on the field of public relations (PR). The book highlights both the opportunities and challenges brought about by AI technologies, offering practical guidance on maintaining trust and authenticity in PR practices. Readers will learn how to leverage AI for enhanced communication strategies and real-time audience engagement while navigating the ethical and legal implications of AI in PR. Emphasizing transparency and accountability, the book delves into the potential risks of miscommunication and provides insights into mitigating these risks.

This work features groundbreaking content from some of the most forward-thinking scholars within this space. It includes case studies and examples of AI-driven PR practices, showcasing innovative approaches and lessons learned from well-known brands and campaigns. It takes a global perspective, considering the geographical and temporal range of AI's impact on PR, with insights applicable to practitioners and scholars worldwide. Written in an accessible style, it caters to PR professionals, educators, researchers, and anyone interested in the evolving landscape of communication in the AI era.

The book equips readers with the knowledge and tools needed to navigate and thrive in the changing communication landscape, staying ahead of technological advancements in the PR industry. It serves as a crucial resource for understanding and adapting to the transformative influence of AI on public relations, ensuring that authenticity and trust remain at the forefront of communication strategies.

Educational Impact

The impact of AI on PR curricula and educators is significant as AI transforms the way communication is conducted and changes the skills required of PR professionals. As a result, PR educators need to adapt their teaching methods and curriculum to incorporate the latest AI technologies and trends. This includes introducing students to AI-powered tools and platforms that are now used in PR, such as chatbots, sentiment analysis tools, and media monitoring software.

PR educators must teach students how to analyze and interpret data generated by AI tools to inform communication strategies and decision-making. This requires educators to have a strong understanding of the various areas of AI and its applications in PR, as well as a willingness to update their knowledge as the technology evolves continually. Educators must embrace rapid changes and adapt their teaching methods to ensure students are equipped with the necessary skills to succeed in a fast-changing industry. With the rapid advances in technology, the integration of AI into PR practices is becoming increasingly common. Since AI systems are designed to mimic human behavior, PR practitioners must ensure that their messages and strategies are authentic and genuine to establish and maintain trust with their audiences. *Public Relations and the Rise of AI* addresses the following themes:

- AI authenticity and accountability in PR
- Ethical and legal concerns
- Impact of generative AI on the PR industry
- AI-powered communication tools and their applications in PR
- Data-driven decision-making in PR through AI
- Responsible use of AI in PR
- AI and crisis communication
- The role of human creativity and AI collaboration in PR and its impact on IDEA –inclusivity, diversity, equity, and accessibility.
- The challenges, limitations, and future of AI in PR

Organization of the Text

Integrating AI into PR is a rapidly developing and transformative trend poised to reshape the academy and industry. As such, a book that explores these intertwined relationships is timely. Our book provides extensive coverage of AI in PR, offers practical guidance for both educators and professionals, and considers the ethical principles found within this burgeoning space.

- **Comprehensive coverage of AI in PR**: The authors provide an in-depth exploration of the current state of AI in PR, including a detailed examination of the most common use cases and the benefits and limitations of these tools.

Chapters also explore the future implications of AI for the industry, providing insights into how it may change the role of PR professionals and the new skills and competencies they will need to develop to work effectively with these technologies.

- **Ethical and legal considerations**: As AI becomes increasingly integrated into PR, it is important to consider the ethical and legal implications of these technologies. Throughout the book, the authors consider the ethical considerations surrounding the use of AI in PR, including issues such as privacy, bias, copyright, and accountability. By providing a nuanced and thoughtful exploration of these issues, readers can navigate the ethical and legal complexities of AI in their work.

- **Equitable deployment of AI in PR**: As AI is designed to assist and replicate human interactions, it must not uphold old biases or perpetuate harmful and inaccurate stereotypes. Systems that continue to undermine the future of individuals, particularly Black, Indigenous, and people of color (BIPOC), should not be used. Bias in algorithms is a costly human oversight, significantly affecting marginalized and underrepresented communities. As AI continues to scale across industries and functions, it can be plagued with unconscious biases that do more harm than good. While AI ethicists and responsible AI practitioners often emphasize the need for greater transparency and accountability in the AI lifecycle as it relates to PR, this book will help contribute to the conversation on the equitable deployment of AI tools in PR.

- **Practical guidance for PR educators and professionals**: The text provides practical guidance for PR educators and professionals on effectively working with AI. It includes best practices for integrating these tools into workflows, developing new skills and competencies, and preparing for the future of AI in PR. This guidance is based on real-world case studies and interviews with leading experts in the field, making it both informative and actionable.

Public Relations and the Rise of AI is distinctive because it covers AI's potential within PR research, education, and practice and presents innovative ways to leverage AI to improve PR outcomes. To that end, this book is broken into four parts; each chapter critically examines generative AI within public relations.

- **Part I: Creative and Storytelling** – Creative storytelling is a crucial aspect of public relations. It helps organizations shape their brand narrative and engage their target audience through compelling and memorable narratives. AI algorithms can help PR professionals analyze and optimize storytelling content by assessing its impact, identifying key elements that drive engagement, and suggesting improvements based on user behavior and preferences.

- **Part II: Personalization and Targeted Communication** – AI enables PR practitioners to deliver personalized and targeted communication to various stakeholders. By utilizing AI algorithms, PR professionals can analyze user preferences, behaviors, and demographics to create tailored messages, content, and campaigns. AI helps segment audiences, optimize content delivery, and ensure that communication efforts are relevant, resonant, and engaging for specific target groups.

- **Part III: Media Monitoring, Influencer Relations, and Reputation Management:** AI technology aids PR professionals in monitoring media channels, social media platforms, and online discussions to track mentions, sentiment analysis, and trends related to their brand or organization. AI-powered tools can automatically identify and analyze media coverage, public opinions, and online conversations, allowing PR teams to assess their reputation, identify potential issues, and implement appropriate strategies to manage their image effectively.
- **Part IV: Data Analytics** – PR professionals utilize AI-powered data analytics tools to collect, analyze, and interpret large volumes of data from various sources. This helps them gain valuable insights into public sentiment, media coverage, audience behavior, and market trends. AI enhances data processing capabilities, enabling more accurate and efficient analysis of PR campaigns' effectiveness and impact.

The research found within the pages of this text unequivocally articulates the transformative impact of generative AI on public relations, highlighting its potential to revolutionize communication strategies, enhance audience engagement, and streamline data analysis. It underscores the importance of understanding and leveraging AI technologies to stay competitive and effective in the evolving PR landscape.

PART I

Creative and Storytelling

1

EXAMINING GENERATIVE ARTIFICIAL INTELLIGENCE'S ROLE AND INFLUENCE IN DEI CREATIVE CONTENT

Rosalynn A. Vasquez

Learning Objectives

1. Understand how generative artificial intelligence is influencing and changing the way we use and think about content creation.
2. Explain how diversity, equity, and inclusion (DEI) can serve an important function in content creation.
3. Evaluate how individuals and organizations are using generative artificial intelligence in public relations.
4. Recommend effective uses for generative artificial intelligence in content creation plans and purposes.

Introduction

In today's increasingly digital landscape, a public relations (PR) program would be remiss without a strategic content creation plan.[1,2] Generative artificial intelligence (AI) is shaping the way we create, consume, and interact with content, and in particular, it is revolutionizing content creation by complementing human creativity.[3] Several AI-powered tools, such as OpenAI, Bard, and ChatGPT, can create content that closely resembles human composition and that can simplify the content creation process. In April 2022, OpenAI launched DALL·E, an AI application that generates imagery from text prompts. ChatGPT, another prevalent example of a text-to-text AI model, shattered records for the fastest-growing app of all time in its abilities to create human-sounding text and artistic imagery. According to a Gartner 2023 report, generative AI is experiencing rapid growth and is predicted to generate more than 30% of outbound messages by 2025.[4]

DOI: 10.4324/9781032671482-2

For many individuals, these advances in AI act as tools to assist in the creative or ideation process because AI is viewed as a creative collaborator. In other words, it is not the tool but rather the human behind the tool with their unique perspective and taste that creates the art. While many people can agree that it has become more accessible (and faster) than ever to generate high-quality work, not everyone is quick to accept generative AI. For example, some people view AI innovation as a threat to human creativity due to copyright infringement on original works of art and intellectual property. There are greater expectations for transparency and authenticity, especially regarding AI assistance or authorship.[5] As a result, we have seen a lot of pushback through various lawsuits and strikes that the creative community has undertaken to protect their work from generative AI. For example, *The New York Times* sued OpenAI and Microsoft last year for infringing on its copyrights by using millions of its articles to train AI technologies like ChatGPT.[6] In another critical case, the Screen Actors Guild and The Writers Guild of America went on strike over fair wages and the use of AI in their work, which led to "a historic deal that put up guardrails to protect writers from AI encroaching on their work."[7]

Another significant and growing concern is about diversity, equity, and inclusion (DEI), mainly due to growing ethical implications when it produces inaccurate content or images and when it perpetuates existing biases and stereotypes in a society. As AI's evolution continues to affect various disciplines and practices, such as the communication and creative industries, there is a need to further explore the influence of generative AI on content creation and its implications – not only for the public relations industry, but also for DEI efforts in communication. AI's impact on DEI in creative content is multifaceted and has become an integral part of our society, revolutionizing various sectors and disciplines. In this chapter, we delve into the intersection of AI and DEI within creative industries. We also examine how AI affects DEI considerations and its potential role in fostering a more inclusive communication landscape.

Content Creation and AI

The idea that content is king and context is queen[8] reminds us of the importance of creating meaningful content with a purpose. Often seen in public relations or marketing, content creation is a crucial tool or tactic used to develop informative and engaging content for a specific audience.[9] There are many uses of content creation in public relations, such as text (headlines, taglines, copy), images, videos, audio, hashtags, slogans, social media posts, content calendars, video script content, and target audience segmentation. "An effective PR strategy that delivers compelling content to buyers and gets them to take action" (p. 51).[10] Storytelling is also an effective public relations strategy to communicate compelling messages in an organization's internal and external settings.[11] To achieve creative storytelling, individuals or organizations can shape their brand narrative and engage their target audience through compelling and memorable content.[12] Whether the goal is to educate, entertain, or inspire a target audience, content creation helps to build an authentic connection and achieve a specific outcome.

AI Uses and Benefits

AI is revolutionizing and reshaping the way public relations practitioners produce, optimize, and distribute content.[13,14] AI content creation tools leverage natural language processing and machine learning algorithms to generate written or visual content based on learning from large datasets, such as text or visual prompts.[15,16]

AI tools can automate routine tasks or assist practitioners by generating ideas or research, or by suggesting visual elements, which liberates them from spending too much time on mundane tactical tasks and allows them to become more strategic.[17] For example, "[AI] can create more personalized and targeted content that resonates with specific audience segments" (p. 798).[18] According to the IPR 2024 report, "AI frees time for teams to focus more on high-level strategic planning, building relationships with key stakeholders, and helping them deliver value to their organization and stakeholders."[19]

The following examples show how AI is being used to generate content creation.

- Jasper: This platform helps create various content formats, such as blogs and social media captions, by using AI to research topics and generate content based on user instructions.
- Pictory: This platform utilizes AI to generate short social media videos from existing text content, which can be a time-saving tool when repurposing content.
- Adobe Stock: This platform incorporates AI to automatically tag images with relevant keywords, which makes it easier to find specific images.

It is the "well-defined and repetitive processes that are the best candidates for AI solutions . . . what you want to look for across all marketing and PR categories is what requires prediction, what's repetitive, and what's data-driven" (p. 145).[20] The AI algorithms can help public relations practitioners analyze and optimize existing content by assessing its impact, identifying key elements that drive engagement, and suggesting improvements based on user behavior and preferences.

AI tools adapt to various content types – blogs, articles, web copy, and image generation from text prompts. For example, some of these AI-powered tools include ChatGPT, Midjourney, JasperAI, and GPT4, the most recent iteration of ChatGPT, which can help with everything from creating or improving text to summarizing content or analyzing data.[21] Some notable content creation AI-powered tools include ClickUp, Narrato, Copy.ai, and Murf. In contrast, other AI tools like DeepL can quickly translate content into multiple languages, and Synthesia and DALL·E can create visual content from text prompts.[22,23]

However, AI's ability to ensure consistent quality in its output largely depends on the quality of input provided in the first place, which is why the human perspective is much needed and cannot be replaced. As Scott explained, "The best way to think about AI in your business is to consider automating [PR] tasks, not your [PR] job" (p. 151).[24]

DEI in AI Content Creation

DEI has been a critical topic of conversation among individuals in the U.S. workforce. In the wake of significant events over the past several years, such as Black Lives Matter and the murder of George Floyd, there has been a social reckoning and greater call (and need) for cultural awareness and cultural intelligence. As trusted advisers to virtually every sector, public relations practitioners have an essential role as moral agents in society in the DEI landscape.[25]

As a term, DEI's definitional scope and word variations continue to evolve (e.g., DEIB, JEDI, etc.) to also recognize concepts such as accessibility, justice, and belonging. Conceptually, DEI is about recognizing and "appreciating human differences, treating everyone fairly, and ensuring people feel seen and valued" (p. 82).[26] While previous research on DEI has focused predominantly on issues of gender, ethnicity, and race, there is an increasing shift toward expanding the various dimensions of DEI also to include other marginalized identities, such as disability/accessibility, diversity of thought,[27] LGBTIQA+,[28,29] immigrant backgrounds,[30] and neurodiversity.[31]

Now, as practitioners learn more about generative AI, they must recognize their role in promoting the strategic and ethical use of AI, especially when it comes to DEI. Defined as "a multifaceted concept that addresses both the technical and socio-cultural aspects of AI" (p. 112),[32] DEI is an increasingly important topic that needs further examination in the AI space.[33] AI tools are not neutral because they inherit biases during the data input process. The bias in AI tools stems from human-developed datasets of information heavily skewed with inaccuracies and misrepresentations stemming from a societal imbalance. These biases can perpetuate existing inequalities and reinforce discriminatory practices by producing offensive content.[34] For example, in *Buzzfeed's* AI Barbie case study, the intersection of AI and DEI raised several ethical considerations. In July 2023, Buzzfeed published a list of AI-generated Barbies representing every nation in the world.[35] While the project's initial aim was to coincide with the release of the new *Barbie* film by featuring a diversity of beauty and global cultures, it had the opposite effect by igniting a firestorm of criticism on social media for misusing cultural representation.

As AI becomes a powerful tool that can be used to enhance creativity, stream-line processes, and generate ideas quicker, there is a greater need for human oversight. AI can be used to examine and understand disparities that exist in our society.[36] The Barbie case study is a reminder of what can happen when indi-viduals rely 100% on AI without monitoring or checking the automatic output for inaccuracies, cultural insensitivities, or erroneous content and images. While AI tools can provide efficiency, "they can also provide individuals with illogical and prejudiced decisions mistakenly thought to be reliable because of their intui-tive and quantitative nature" (p. 800).[37]

While practitioners can agree that AI is a powerful tool that can enhance cre-ativity and streamline processes faster, notable challenges cannot be ignored. "Prejudice is already baked into the data" that feeds AI . . . as it learns from human inputs and the 'sexist, racist and homophobic content' that lives online" (para. 5).[38] Therefore, a concerted effort is needed to not only recognize biases in training data and seek out more diverse data to train AI models but also diversify the practitioners because they bring unique perspectives and lived experiences to the table. "The awareness of [DEI] in AI will enable them to identify, monitor, and mitigate potential risks and challenges, thereby fostering an AI-literate so-ciety that can make informed decisions about the use and participation in AI systems across various contexts."[39]

There are numerous benefits to integrating a DEI-oriented mindset with AI applications. For example, AI can help identify and mitigate unconscious bias in content creation. AI tools can generate content in various styles, tones, and dialects to resonate with diverse audiences. AI can be used to create content in multiple formats that can make content more accessible to people with dis-abilities. AI can be trained to recognize women and non-binary individuals in roles where men have predominantly appeared. AI can be trained to recognize inaccurate cultural representation (as in the case of Barbie) to avoid perpetuating stereotypes and insensitive tropes. AI can also be trained to recognize in-group bias and expand content to reach different demographics and cultures which have been marginalized. All of these changes can be made by having clear AI ethical guidelines in place and being cognizant, consistent, and proactive to en-sure appropriate representation is being used.

As AI continues to evolve, developing and utilizing AI tools that promote fair and inclusive content creation is crucial. Public relations educators and practitioners are in pivotal positions to "lead authentic DEI efforts and build stronger relationships between the organization and its stakeholders" (p. 143).[40] AI tools should not only benefit from embedding DEI in their design and de-ployment – they should also be treated as agents of change that can improve and accelerate understanding and acceptance of all walks of life.

BOX 1.1 USING AI TO LEVERAGE THE RPIE MODEL

In this active learning exercise, students can gain an understanding of how AI can assist in their public relations campaign development as they reflect on the research, planning, implementation, and evaluation (RPIE) model. Teachers may consider dedicating a full class session to each component to allow the students to fully immerse themselves in that aspect, and then incorporate AI use in each class session so students can see how to properly and effectively use AI as a resource and not as the final product.

Scenario

Imagine that your public relations firm has just been hired by a Dallas-based architecture company that would like for you to develop a public relations campaign focused on elevating its brand name in the Dallas-Fort Worth (DFW) market and across Texas. In particular, the client wants to increase visibility for their new services and experts who work on corporate social responsibility (CSR) and environmental, social, and governance (ESG) initiatives in industry-relevant publications and general business media. Additionally, they would like to have a meaningful presence at events and community organizations where they can help underserved communities and provide pro bono services. Finally, they recently named a new chief executive officer who is the first Black woman in this role and would like ideas for how to leverage her appointment to raise the profile of the company even further.

Instructions

Students can get into small groups and discuss their approach by reflecting on the RPIE model. Students may leverage AI technology, such as ChatGPT, to support their process as they brainstorm and reflect on each component. For example, in this active learning exercise for a class session, students will focus primarily on the research stage. This stage encourages highly critical thinking and collaboration. Students should gather information to describe and thoroughly understand the situation, check their assumptions, and create the foundation and framework for their plan. Students may reflect on the following items: What questions do you have based on this scenario? Who do you want to reach and what do you want each key public to do? What resources do you need? How will you collect data? During the research stage, students also have the opportunity to discuss and review the different types of research approaches or methods (e.g., primary, secondary, formal, informal, quantitative, or qualitative). When using AI, students may want to create specific prompts to brainstorm or better understand a key topic. For example, they may want to learn more about the current landscape of architecture firms in the DFW community or gain a better understanding of the media landscape for communicating creative content about CSR and ESG key issues.

Afterward, each group will briefly present their preliminary work to the class and address questions, such as: (1) how did AI enhance or hinder your research stage?; (2) what are some of the benefits and challenges you experienced when incorporating AI into your PR planning process?; and (3) were there any ethical considerations related to AI use? At the end of the exercise, students will be asked to write a 1–2-page individual reflection paper to address their experiences and share their unique insights. Prompt examples may include: (1) what surprised you about AI's impact on public relations?; and (2) what are your key recommendations for effectively integrating AI into public relations planning? Overall, this active learning exercise encourages real-time class discussions, critical thinking, and reflections on a real-world scenario application.

The Future of AI in Creative Content

The following subsections outline practical uses and implications for public relations educators and practitioners to utilize AI for content creation purposes in the future.

Practical Uses of AI for Educators

From the pedagogical perspective, the growth of AI in the industry prompts discussion about how its advancement will affect the discipline. For one thing, educators may need to readjust their approach to teaching by coming up with creative ways to assess if students understand concepts. For example, educators can emphasize more cold calling or oral presentations so that students can reflect, use critical thinking, and clearly explain concepts. Additionally, educators can incorporate AI-driven assignments into their classes, ask students to use generative AI in their processes, and then have them critique each other's work as a learning exercise. This training approach emphasizes critical thinking by helping them understand that AI is a tool and a creative collaborator, and not an end-all-be-all solution.

This approach aligns with the findings from the CPRE (2018) *Fast Forward* report, in which public relations practitioners and educators expect new graduates to display the following abilities: critical thinking, problem-solving, and creativity skills.[41] A similar study revealed that public relations professionals rated creative thinking, creativity, and digital storytelling highly on a 5-point scale.[42] Another scholar also noted that "good storytelling can serve as a key differentiator between PR practitioners and artificial intelligence tools (p. 68)"[43] because "ChatGPT can't tell stories; it can't provide context; it doesn't have expertise; and it doesn't have unique thoughts."[44]

The work will be very different for new public relations graduates entering the industry. The arrival of ChatGPT in November 2022 and the growth of additional generative AI tools has been a wake-up call for organizations, public relations practitioners, and new graduates. Given that AI will continue to shape the future workplace, employers will expect entry-level graduates to demonstrate some level of proficiency in AI. However, this should not be interpreted as an excuse to forgo strategic critical thinking or creativity. A study from the CPRE 2018 report revealed that "practitioners and educators agree that technical skills such as graphic design, audio/video production, speech writing, website development, and app development are less important, suggesting that educators should focus more on developing strategic communication skills rather than technical ones" (p. 49).[45]

Since AI focuses on automation and repetition, individuals will need to develop guidelines, monitor performance, and determine the validity and reliability of generative AI outputs – all of which require critical thinking skills. New graduates and "entry-level professionals will be tasked with making ethical and governance judgments about how and when to use AI tools and manage the outputs they generate" (p. 28).[46]

As one scholar best explains, "PR requires creativity, the type of thinking that machines, not yet at least, are capable of superseding – such as ensuring tone of voice or messaging of written communications or executing a creative stunt . . . . A bot can't lay claim to emotional intelligence, a cornerstone of all PR work."[47]

BOX 1.2 USING AI FOR ETHICAL DECISION MAKING

In this active learning exercise, students can gain a greater understanding of how AI can affect the decision-making process when faced with an ethical dilemma. Teachers may also consider creating case studies that feature an ethical dilemma and then incorporate AI use in the class session so students can see how to properly and effectively use AI as an aid to their critical thinking, decision-making, and overall process.

Scenario

Imagine you are a public relations specialist for a Dallas-based nonprofit that focuses on refugee services. Texas is ranked first in the nation in refugee resettlement and Dallas is ranked the second city in the nation. Since 2018, more than 30,000 refugees have resettled in the DFW metroplex. The nonprofit welcomes, resettles, advocates, and serves refugees, asylees, and victims of trafficking, and manages an average of 32 refugee individuals and families arriving in Dallas County each week, many of which hailed from Afghanistan, Cuba, Iran, Iraq and Vietnam, among other countries around the world. Volunteers are needed to assist with picking up families arriving at the airport, setting up apartments, shopping for large families, registering them for English classes, and providing employment assistance. The nonprofit is in dire need of more volunteers from the community and has requested that you develop new creative content to generate interest and increase numbers. You do not have a large team or vast resources, so you rely heavily on AI-generated social media content and press releases to help you.

One of the best aspects of your job includes interviewing former refugees who now work at the nonprofit as members of the staff team to assist future refugees. However, due to time limitations, you decide to use fictional individuals and made-up quotes and images to include in your spotlight series on social media. For example, you spotlight Leonard Canas, a former refugee from Cuba who now works on the refugee services team, with the following quote.

We just wanted to get away from the war last year. There is too much misery in Cuba. We could not sleep at night because of the gun shots. Seeing mothers lose their children and their husbands was heartbreaking. This is a terrible country; we were very lucky to be able to come to America.

The image showed a dark-skinned, older man wearing a straw hat with a cigar in his mouth surrounded by a large family, including crying children. Soon after posting, you notice unusually high activity on your nonprofit's social media page consisting of mainly angry comments from the community accusing the nonprofit of cultural misrepresentation and inaccuracies. Soon, there are other issues being raised by members of the local media. However, you are very results-driven and are determined to ignite sympathy for the refugee population and increase volunteer numbers.

Instructions

Place students into small groups to facilitate discussions about this case scenario and debate the main issues or concerns, ethical implications, affected stakeholders, and potential consequences and solutions. As part of their discussion, encourage students to consider any cultural issues raised in the case and to check their assumptions and any other DEI-related aspects that may occur when using AI technology. Next, provide each group with a set of AI-generated press releases and social media posts from the case study and instruct them to analyze the content and identify any additional ethical issues, biases, or misinformation. Students may also leverage AI technology, such as ChatGPT, to support their process as they engage in critical thinking skills and ethical awareness when using AI-generated content in public relations. During this stage, emphasize the need for public relations practitioners to be vigilant, critical, and ethical when using AI tools to generate images and context. To facilitate conversations in each group, give them prompts to reflect on key considerations when using AI in their content creation, such as bias, cultural sensitivities, audience identification, and authenticity. For example, in terms of bias, it is important for students to understand how AI algorithms may perpetuate our biases (e.g., gender, ethnicity, age, race, etc.) and how public relations professionals can mitigate them. In terms of audience identification, another key step in ethical decision-making is identifying diverse publics who may be affected by a decision and making sure the organization is not creating tone-deaf or inaccurate or misappropriated content.

Afterward, bring the groups back together for a debrief and have one team representative share key insights. Encourage the groups to discuss common themes and debate divergent viewpoints, such as discussing how they would frame the ethical issue (e.g., utilitarianism, deontology, virtue ethics, etc.) and if AI was used appropriately. Also, encourage discussions on the impact of such content on public perception, trust, and reputation, and ask the students to propose strategies for addressing the ethical challenges.

At the end of the exercise, students will be asked to write an individual brief case study summary to further elaborate on these discussion points and incorporate their own perspectives by addressing each of the following components: (1) identify the ethical dilemma; (2) describe the key stakeholders involved; (3) identify any challenges or opportunities; (4) propose recommendations to address the ethical issue; and (5) identify any key lessons learned. Overall, this active learning exercise encourages real-time class discussions, critical thinking, and ethical decision-making in a real-world case scenario.

Practical Uses of AI for Practitioners

AI is a growing part of the professional practice in public relations, and its benefits to daily practice ensure it will grow in its application and value. However, it is becoming increasingly clear that just because you ask generative AI to do something, it does not mean that it is correct or proper. Guardrails and processes must be implemented to ensure proper oversight, monitoring, and governance to ensure high-quality, factual, and ethical outputs.

There is a lot of anxiety and distrust around AI, which is fueled mainly by people having a professional identity crisis due to a fear of being replaced and losing their jobs. People are worried about having to learn new skills and stay current with the different aspects of AI.

Additionally, there is fear about a content creator's original work being regurgitated by generative AI into something without attribution in a totally different context.[48] As a result, there is already pressure on companies to set up AI corporate governance practices and share more transparency with AI processes.[49] Employees are looking for more transparency on how to use AI, and only 33% of companies share their AI governance with employees.[50] For example, Weber Shandwick recently launched a new service, AI Accelerator, to promote better understanding and empower communicators to accelerate the application of new generative AI tools.[51] "Industry reports generally assess AI tools as a good thing and predict that AI technologies can never replace PR's human touch."[52] As a scholar explains, "human-centric applications of AI are the most fruitful, meaning they are intended to complement human creativity rather than replace it."[53]

Recommendations for Using AI in Content Creation

1. AI does not replace human creativity; it amplifies it as a creative partner.
2. Create a culture of transparency and trust for how an individual or organization is using AI.
3. Become AI literate and direct intelligent automation.
4. Develop and utilize AI tools that promote best practices for fair and inclusive content creation.
5. Consistently monitor, examine, and empower creative content created by AI for internal and external communication purposes.

Conclusion

By leveraging AI tools, content creators can focus on strategic aspects while AI handles repetitive, mundane tasks. In summary, while AI can enhance efficiency, it must not overshadow the value of human connections and original creativity. Public relations practitioners should reflect on their roles as ethical and creative leaders and ask: How can AI become an empowered creative collaborator, not an automated powered servant? While there is a learning curve to understanding and accepting AI, it is important to remember that AI is not meant to replace or overshadow human creativity entirely. It excels at handling datasets, automation, repetitive tasks, and essentially following our instructions. The human perspective (creativity and critical-strategic thinking) remains vital for crafting authentic narratives, promoting the highest ethical standards, and ensuring the content or visuals embrace (and not demeaning or diminishing) our cultural and lifestyle differences.

AI is becoming a powerful partner for communicators, boosting productivity and allowing them to focus on the most impactful aspects of their craft. As we navigate this landscape together, let us strive for an inclusive and empowered AI ecosystem that reflects the richness of our diverse world.

Reflections

1. Educators and practitioners in public relations believe that critical thinking is a key skill in the profession. What are some ways that you can use critical thinking when creating generative AI-driven content?
2. Reflect on the *Buzzfeed* Barbie AI case study and identify the main issues of the case and your recommendations by using the corporate race responsibility (CRR) theory.
3. Practitioners and educators both emphasize the need for ethical considerations in using generative AI. How can students and young professionals incorporate an ethical approach to using generative AI in content creation?
4. Reflect on Disney's #ShareYourEars campaign that inspired people to create and share content to support the Make-A-Wish Foundation. Choose a nonprofit in your community, and imagine you are the new public relations manager. How would you use generative AI to create content that will encourage public support of your nonprofit?

Notes

1 Bradford, Jeff. "Public relations and content marketing: Which is right for your business?" *Forbes*, October 22, 2019. www.forbes.com/sites/forbesagencycouncil/2019/10/22/public-relations-and-content-marketing-which-is-right-for-your-business/
2 Scott, David Meerman. *The new rules of marketing and PR: How to use social media, online video, mobile applications, blogs, news releases, and viral marketing to reach buyers directly.* John Wiley & Sons, 2015.
3 Brynjolfsson, Erik, and Tom Mitchell. "What can machine learning do? Workforce implications." *Science* 358, no. 6370 (2017): 1530–1534. https://doi.org/10.1126/science.aap8062
4 Wiles, Jackie. "Beyond ChatGPT: The future of generative AI for enterprises." *Gartner*, January 26, 2023. www.gartner.com/en/articles/beyond-chatgpt-the-future-of-generative-ai-for-enterprises

5 Ewing, Michelle. "Navigating ethical implications for AI-driven PR practice." *PRSA*, September 2023. www.prsa.org/article/navigating-ethical-implications-for-ai-driven-pr-practice

6 Grynbaum, Michael and Ryan Mac. "The times sues openAI and microsoft over A.I. use of copyrighted work." *The New York Times*, December 27, 2023. www.nytimes.com/2023/12/27/business/media/new-york-times-open-ai-microsoft-lawsuit.html

7 Watercutter, Angela and Will Bedingfield. "Hollywood actors strike ends with a deal that will impact AI and streaming for decades." *Wired*, November 8, 2023. www.wired.com/story/hollywood-actors-strike-ends-ai-streaming/

8 Scott, David Meerman. *The new rules of marketing and PR: How to use social media, online video, mobile applications, blogs, news releases, and viral marketing to reach buyers directly*. John Wiley & Sons, 2015.

9 Scott, David Meerman. *The new rules of marketing and PR: How to use social media, online video, mobile applications, blogs, news releases, and viral marketing to reach buyers directly*. John Wiley & Sons, 2015.

10 Scott, David Meerman. *The new rules of marketing and PR: How to use social media, online video, mobile applications, blogs, news releases, and viral marketing to reach buyers directly*. John Wiley & Sons, 2015.

11 Kent, Michael L. "The power of storytelling in public relations: Introducing the 20 master plots." *Public Relations Review* 41, no. 4 (2015): 480–489. https://doi.org/10.1016/j.pubrev.2015.05.011

12 Whitaker, Abbi. "How advancements in AI will impact public relations." *Forbes*, March 20, 2017. www.forbes.com/sites/theyec/2017/03/20/how-advancements-in-artificial-intelligence-will-impact-public-relations/?sh=3164c97141de

13 Divya, V., and Agha Urfi Mirza. "Transforming content creation: The influence of generative AI on a new frontier." *Exploring the Frontiers of Artificial Intelligence and Machine Learning Technologies*: 143. https://doi.org/10.59646/efaimltC8/133

14 Scott, David Meerman. *The new rules of marketing and PR: How to use social media, online video, mobile applications, blogs, news releases, and viral marketing to reach buyers directly*. John Wiley & Sons, 2015.

15 Adwan, Ahmad. "Can companies in digital marketing benefit from artificial intelligence in content creation?" *International Journal of Data and Network Science* 8, no. 2 (2024): 797–808. https://doi.org/10.5267/j.ijdns.2023.12.024

16 Galloway, Chris, and Lukasz Swiatek. "Public relations and artificial intelligence: It's not (just) about robots." *Public Relations Review* 44, no. 5 (2018): 734–740. https://doi.org/10.1016/j.pubrev.2018.10.008

17 Scott, David Meerman. *The new rules of marketing and PR: How to use social media, online video, mobile applications, blogs, news releases, and viral marketing to reach buyers directly*. John Wiley & Sons, 2015.

18 Adwan, Ahmad. "Can companies in digital marketing benefit from artificial intelligence in content creation?" *International Journal of Data and Network Science* 8, no. 2 (2024): 797–808. https://doi.org/10.5267/j.ijdns.2023.12.024

19 McCorkindale, Tina. "Generative AI in organizations: Insights and strategies from communication leaders." *Institute of Public Relations*, February 2024. https://instituteforpr.org/wp-content/uploads/Generative-AI-in-Organizations-Insights-and-Strategies-from-Communication-Leaders-2_7_24-1.pdf

20 Scott, David Meerman. *How to use content, marketing, podcasting, social media, AI, live video, and newsjacking to reach buyers directly*. John Wiley & Sons, 2020.

21 McCorkindale, Tina. "Generative AI in organizations: Insights and strategies from communication leaders." *Institute of Public Relations*, February 2024. https://instituteforpr.org/wp-content/uploads/Generative-AI-in-Organizations-Insights-and-Strategies-from-Communication-Leaders-2_7_24-1.pdf

22 Divya, V., and Agha Urfi Mirza. "Transforming content creation: The influence of generative AI on a new frontier." *Exploring the Frontiers of Artificial Intelligence and Machine Learning Technologies*: 143. https://doi.org/10.59646/efaimltC8/133

23 Ngo, Thi Thuy An. "The perception by university students of the use of ChatGPT in education." *International Journal of Emerging Technologies in Learning (Online)* 18, no. 17 (2023): 4. https://doi.org/10.3991/ijet.v18i17.39019

24 Scott, David Meerman. *How to use content, marketing, podcasting, social media, AI, live video, and newsjacking to reach buyers directly*. John Wiley & Sons, 2020.

25 Mundy, Dean E. "Bridging the divide: A multidisciplinary analysis of diversity research and the implications for public relations." *Research Journal of the Institute for Public Relations* 3, no. 1 (2016): 1–28. https://instituteforpr.org/wp-content/uploads/Dean-Mundy-1.pdf

26 Logan, Nneka, Katie R. Place, Hilary Fussell Sisco, Rosalynn A. Vasquez, Amiso M. George, Martha Terdik, and Rashpal Rai. "Diversity, equity, and inclusion in public relations: Moving beyond the status quo." In *Navigating change: Recommendations for advancing undergraduate public relations education*, edited by Elizabeth Toth and Pam Bourland-Davis. Commission on Public Relations Education, pp. 82–93. www.commissionpred.org/wp-content/uploads/2023/11/CPRE-50th-Anniversary-Report-FINAL.pdf

27 Logan, Nneka, Katie R. Place, Hilary Fussell Sisco, Rosalynn A. Vasquez, Amiso M. George, Martha Terdik, and Rashpal Rai. "Diversity, equity, and inclusion in public relations: Moving beyond the status quo." In *Navigating change: Recommendations for advancing undergraduate public relations education*, edited by Elizabeth Toth and Pam Bourland-Davis. Commission on Public Relations Education, pp. 82–93. www.commissionpred.org/wp-content/uploads/2023/11/CPRE-50th-Anniversary-Report-FINAL.pdf

28 Ciszek, Erica. "Queering PR: Directions in theory and research for public relations scholarship." *Journal of Public Relations Research* 30, no. 4 (2018): 134–145. https://doi.org/10.1080/1062726X.2018.1440354

29 Mundy, Dean E. "Bridging the divide: A multidisciplinary analysis of diversity research and the implications for public relations." *Research Journal of the Institute for Public Relations* 3, no. 1 (2016): 1–28. https://instituteforpr.org/wp-content/uploads/Dean-Mundy-1.pdf

30 Vasquez, Rosalynn A., and Marlene S. Neill. "Underpaid, undervalued, undermined: Examining the cultural identities, challenges, and coping strategies of US Latinas in public relations." *Public Relations Inquiry* 12, no. 3 (2023): 293–319. https://doi.org/10.1177/2046147X231200239

31 Branton, Scott E., Astrid M. Villamil, and Joel Lansing Reed. "Branding neurodiversity: A critical discourse analysis of communicative capitalism and change empowerment among neurodiversity workforce intermediaries." *Journal of Public Relations Research* 35, no. 5–6 (2023): 357–374. https://doi.org/10.1080/1062726X.2023.2244619

32 Fosch-Villaronga, Eduard, and Adam Poulsen. "Diversity and inclusion in artificial intelligence." *Law and Artificial Intelligence: Regulating AI and Applying AI in Legal Practice* (2022): 109–134. https://doi.org/10.1007/978-94-6265-523-2_6

33 Shams, Rifat Ara, Didar Zowghi, and Muneera Bano. "AI and the quest for diversity and inclusion: A systematic literature." (2023). https://doi.org/10.1007/s43681-023-00362-w

34 Shams, Rifat Ara, Didar Zowghi, and Muneera Bano. "AI and the quest for diversity and inclusion: A systematic literature." (2023). https://doi.org/10.1007/s43681-023-00362-w

35 Koh, Renna. "A list of AI-generated Barbies from 'every country' gets blasted on Twitter for blatant racism and endless cultural inaccuracies." *Business Insider*, July 11, 2023. www.businessinsider.com/ai-generated-barbie-every-country-criticism-internet-midjourney-racism-2023-7

36 Logan, Nneka, and Damion Waymer. "Navigating artificial intelligence, public relations and race." *Journal of Public Relations Research* (2024): 1–17. https://doi.org/1 0.1080/1062726X.2024.2308868

37 Adwan, Ahmad. "Can companies in digital marketing benefit from artificial intelligence in content creation?" *International Journal of Data and Network Science* 8, no. 2 (2024): 797–808. https://doi.org/10.5267/j.ijdns.2023.12.024

38 Sanchez, Sabrina. "AI has no moral obligation: Industry calls for DEI to be part of AI training." *PRWeek*, November 14, 2023. www.prweek.com/article/1847593/ ai-no-moral-obligation-industry-calls-de-i-part-ai-training

39 Shams, Rifat Ara, Didar Zowghi, and Muneera Bano. "AI and the quest for diversity and inclusion: A systematic literature." (2023). https://doi.org/10.1007/ s43681-023-00362-w

40 Vasquez, Rosalynn A., Nneka Logan, Hilary Fussell Sisco, and Katie R. Place. "Actualizing the DEI mission in public relations classrooms." *Journal of Public Relations Education* 10, no. 1 (2024): 137–153.

41 O'Neil, Julie, Angeles Moreno, Brad Rawlins, and Chiara Valentini. "Learning objectives: What do students need to know and be able to do for entry-level positions?" In *Fast Forward: Foundations + Future State. Educators + Practitioner*, Commission on Public Relations Education, pp. 45–58. www.commissionpred.org/wp-content/uploads/2018/04/report6-full.pdf

42 Krishna, Arunima, Donald K. Wright, and Raymond L. Kotcher. "Curriculum rebuilding in public relations: Understanding what early career, mid-career, and senior PR/communications professionals expect from PR graduates." *Journal of Public Relations Education* 6, no. 1 (2020): 33–57. https://aejmc.us/jpre/wp-content/uploads/ sites/25/2020/01/KRISHNA-ET-AL-JPRE-6.1-Curriculum-Rebuilding-in-PR.pdf

43 Kinsky, Emily S., and Tiffany Derville Gallicano. "Express yourself: Developing creative storytelling skills." *Journal of Public Relations Education* 9, no. 3 (2024): 65–85.

44 Dietrich, Gini. "What search engine generative experience means for content creators." *Spin Sucks*, September 12, 2023. https://spinsucks.com/communication/search-generative-experience/

45 O'Neil, Julie, Angeles Moreno, Brad Rawlins, and Chiara Valentini. "Learning objectives: What do students need to know and be able to do for entry-level positions?" In *Fast forward: Foundations + Future state: Educators + Practitioner*, Commission on Public Relations Education, pp. 45–58. www.commissionpred.org/wp-content/ uploads/2018/04/report6-full.pdf

46 Lubbers, Charles, Anthony D'Angelo, Debbie Davis, Amiso George, Anne Gregory, Judy Phair, and Kim Sample. "Future of the public relations workplace." In *Navigating change: Recommendations for advancing undergraduate public relations education*, edited by Elizabeth Toth and Pam Bourland-Davis. Commission on Public Relations Education, pp. 22–34. www.commissionpred.org/wp-content/ uploads/2023/11/CPRE-50th-Anniversary-Report-FINAL.pdf

47 Ristic, Ivan. "PR in 2018: Dominated by technology, mired by inauthenticity." *PRWeek*, December 26, 2017. www.prweek.com/article/1453426/pr-2018-dominated-technology-mired-inauthenticity

48 Watercutter, Angela and Will Bedingfield. "Hollywood actors strike ends with a deal that will impact AI and streaming for decades." *Wired*, November 8, 2023. www. wired.com/story/hollywood-actors-strike-ends-ai-streaming/

49 Suter, Tara. "AI whistleblowers warn of dangers, call for transparency." *The Hill*, June 4, 2024. https://thehill.com/policy/technology/4703216-ai-whistleblowers-letter-transparency-protection/

50 Brown, Steph. "Employees to leaders: Be transparent about AI use." *Financial Management*, September 6, 2023. www.fm-magazine.com/news/2023/sep/employees-to-leaders-be-transparent-about-ai-use.html

51 Bach, Natasha. "Weber introduces AI accelerator." *PRWeek*, November 30, 2023. www.prweek.com/article/1849589/weber-introduces-ai-accelerator

52 Bourne, Clea. "AI cheerleaders: Public relations, neoliberalism and artificial intelligence." *Public Relations Inquiry* 8, no. 2 (2019): 109–125. https://doi.org/10.1177/2046147X19835250

53 Adwan, Ahmad. "Can companies in digital marketing benefit from artificial intelligence in content creation?" *International Journal of Data and Network Science* 8, no. 2 (2024): 797–808. https://doi.org/10.5267/j.ijdns.2023.12.024

2

ETHICAL FRONTIERS

Balancing Innovation and Integrity in AI-Enhanced Public Relations

Jamie Ward

Learning Objectives

1. Evaluate the benefits and ethical challenges of using AI in mental health services.
2. Explore how public relations practitioners serve as the ethical conscience of their organizations, shaping the conversation on AI development and public perception.
3. Learn how to apply the principles of responsible advocacy to develop and implement ethical standards for AI use within an organization.

Introduction

Artificial Intelligence (AI) has been touted as a revolutionary technology that is not only driving transformation but also reshaping organizational practices and fundamentally altering industries around the globe. *Generative AI* tools such as ChatGPT, Google Bard, Midjourney, and DALL·E utilize prompt engineering to produce content including human-like text responses, images, audio, and video. These tools have revolutionized creative industries by automating content generation, enhancing efficiency, and increasing content production. In the field of public relations, the emergence of AI has brought about many opportunities and challenges. According to Stephen Davies, founder of the public relations (PR) branding agency Thumos, "this technological leap allows PR professionals to focus on strategic, high-value tasks transcending the limitations of traditional [PR] practices."[1] The downside is that technology often changes faster than most practitioners can adapt. Keeping up with these advancements requires

DOI: 10.4324/9781032671482-3

consistent training and education. The learning curve can be arduous. Despite this, an overwhelming 86% of communication professionals view the advancements in generative AI positively rather than as a risk.[2] This view has contributed to unprecedented growth in the industry over the last several years.

The "Global Communications Report" titled "The Evolution of Ethics," published in 2018 by the University of Southern California's Annenberg Center for Public Relations, surveyed industry professionals and public relations students worldwide. The purpose of the study was to explore the future of the public relations profession and the role of ethical decision-making within it. The results showed that over 70% of the professionals surveyed anticipate significant changes in the PR industry over the next five years.[3] The main drivers of this anticipated change were identified as the evolving media landscape, technological innovations, and greater access to data. The most significant technological innovation within the public relations industry stems from the industry's widespread acceptance and implementation of AI.

According to the Annenberg Center's "Global Communications Report" in 2019, 86% of PR professionals and students in the field considered themselves to be only "somewhat" or "not at all" knowledgeable about AI.[4] In 2023, a mere four years later, Muck Rack conducted a study of 1,001 public relations professionals and found that the number of PR professionals who said they use generative AI increased from 28% in March 2023 to 64% in December 2023.[5] This increase is not surprising. AI is not a passing fad. This technology will only become more ingrained in business practices. Therefore, it is crucial for PR professionals to develop a comprehensive understanding of the technologies that are shaping the industry and to recognize the ethical implications associated with embracing tools that can have significant ethical consequences.

The Institute for Public Relations (IPR) released a report in February of 2024 that discussed concerns, opportunities, and best practices for utilizing generative AI in public relations.[6] Some of the key findings included that while many communication leaders are comfortable using generative AI and prioritize continuous learning and establishing safeguards, there are still concerns about the need for validating AI-generated content and a need to reinforce the importance of reviewing and editing AI outputs to mitigate risks. As AI becomes more integrated into PR, it is essential that these ethical considerations are top of mind and that risks to those we have an obligation to serve are managed.

This chapter explores how coupling multifaceted ethical codes with the *professional responsibility theory* can assist public relations professionals in identifying the perks and pitfalls of deploying AI technologies to meet the needs of the communities they serve. According to Fitzpatrick and Gauthier,

> moral dilemmas arise when loyalties and responsibilities conflict and a course of action must be chosen. A moral dilemma occurs when a choice is required

among actions that meet competing commitments or obligations, but there are good reasons for and against each alternative.[7]

(p. 207)

More specifically, this research argues that the professional responsibility theory, in tandem with current multifaceted ethical codes, can be used to guide PR professionals in: (1) developing programs that are human-centered; and (2) advocating for transparent AI practices that not only focus on safety and accountability but also on harm prevention to the communities they serve. To illustrate this point, a case study involving AI in the mental health space is presented.

Ethical Considerations

By definition, "ethics provide a set of standards for behavior that helps us decide the appropriate way to act in a range of differing situations."[8] Many industry experts claim that "public relations professionals should have 'unimpeachable ethical standards' that develop trust from clients and the public."[9] PR practitioners play an essential role in managing issues and shaping public opinion. Therefore, operating ethically and transparently is crucial. "Every profession has a moral purpose. Medicine has health. Law has justice. Public relations has harmony – social harmony" (p. 1).[10] Public relations professionals are expected to prioritize the interests of society at large and to uphold ethical values in professional relationships. Their primary allegiance should always be to the public.

Heath and Coombs suggest that proper ethical choices will "foster community by creating and maintaining mutually beneficial relationships" (p. 10).[11] Many of these choices are rooted in trust and transparency, both of which are essential for any organization's public relations efforts, particularly for those in PR roles with non-governmental organizations (NGOs) and nonprofit organizations. Trust serves as the foundation for establishing credibility in the eyes of the public. When individuals have trust in a nonprofit, they are more inclined to provide support through donations, volunteering, and other avenues. Trust plays a vital role in fostering and sustaining strong relationships with stakeholders, such as donors, volunteers, community members, and other organizations.

According to public relations scholar Don Wright, "Central to the importance of ethics in American public relations is the reality that, most of the time, practitioners have the voluntary choice of whether to be ethical or not" (p. 3).[12] The lack of a single common framework for deciding what is ethical[13] requires us to look back to who we are advocating for – the organization and its publics. PR practitioners must consistently focus on creating mutually beneficial relationships where everyone wins.

Theoretical Frameworks in Ethical Decision-Making

Ethics codes across various professions, such as public relations and artificial intelligence, serve as industry-specific guidelines to aid individuals in ethical decision-making. The public relations industry boasts multiple codes, including those from the Public Relations Society of America (PRSA), the Chartered Institute of Public Relations (CIPR), the International Public Relations Association (IPRA), and the Arthur W. Page Society,[14] to name a few. Each ethical code is structured differently, and the content varies slightly; however, they all emphasize the importance of truth, honesty, transparency, independence, responsibility, competency, fairness, and accountability. They underscore the significance of maintaining ethical behavior, adhering to personal and organizational principles, and managing reputations effectively.

In 2023, the Blueprint for an AI Bill of Rights, developed by the White House, stated that:

> automated systems should not be designed with an intent or reasonably foreseeable possibility of endangering your safety or the safety of your community. They should be designed to proactively protect you from harms stemming from unintended, yet foreseeable, uses or impacts of automated systems.[15]

This Blueprint continues by providing guidelines for safety, equity, privacy, accessibility, and human alternatives. More specifically, the bill states:

> Automated systems with an intended use within sensitive domains, including, but not limited to, criminal justice, employment, education, and health, should additionally be tailored to the purpose, provide meaningful access for oversight, include training for any people interacting with the system, and incorporate human consideration for adverse or high-risk decisions.[16]

This highlights the increased focus within AI codes and guidelines on protecting the general public from harm and the need for oversight of AI technologies.

The UK government developed five principles for an AI regulatory approach that mimicked these sentiments.[17] Those principles focused on safety, transparency, fairness, accountability, and avenues to correct the system if it causes harm. The House of Lords, the second chamber of the UK Parliament, formed a committee to discuss ethical AI and stressed the need for AI regulation. Their principles speak to expertise in using knowledge and experience to benefit society as a whole and advocate on the side of truth, transparency, and honesty.

UNESCO – the United Nations Educational, Scientific, and Cultural Organization – is a specialized agency of the United Nations (UN) that enhances peace and stability through the advancement of international collaboration in the areas of education, scientific endeavors, cultural exchanges, and the sharing of information and communication.[18] At the Global Forum on the Ethics of AI, UNESCO developed ten core principles that set the foundation for a human rights-centered approach to AI. Those principles include: proportionality and do no harm, safety and security, right to privacy and data protection, multi-stakeholder and adaptive governance and collaboration, responsibility and accountability, transparency and explainability, human oversight and determination, sustainability, awareness and literacy, and fairness and non-discrimination.[19]

Each of these government-focused, human-centered organizations developed ethical guidelines that highlight safety, transparency, doing no harm, training, and governance. They also closely mirror the PRSA ethical codes, focusing on responsibility, fairness, and accountability. The convergence of ethical principles across sectors underscores a collective emphasis on community protection, inclusivity, and professional responsibility. Despite the non-legislative nature of these codes, integrating AI considerations into existing ethical frameworks may enhance their relevance and ensure they are actively used as living documents rather than static references.

Figure 2.1 highlights the overlapping principles among the PR codes of ethics, AI Bill of Rights, UK Government AI standards, UNESCO AI ethics, and general AI ethical principles. The core overlaps – such as safety, transparency, fairness, accountability, and responsibility – are highlighted in the center, indicating that these principles are shared across multiple frameworks.

The figure also shows how subsets of these principles are shared between different frameworks, with areas of intersection labeled common ground. This representation underscores the common ground that these frameworks share, as well as the unique contributions of each to the broader discourse on ethical considerations in AI and public relations. The diagram aids in understanding how different ethical frameworks converge on key principles despite their varied origins and primary focuses. This research advocates for a broader application of multifaced ethical codes, one that roots its focus on harms and benefits.

Framework

Using a three-pronged approach, PR practitioners can develop a framework for human-centered, transparent AI practices that can be applied across a multitude of industries.

Step 1 is to compare industry-specific codes with PR codes and AI principles to identify overlaps or similarities. In response to the multitude of different codes and the vastly changing industry, Ward and Agozzino have conducted extensive research on the use of multifaceted ethical codes to guide practitioners in providing accountability, responsibility, and transparency to how organizations

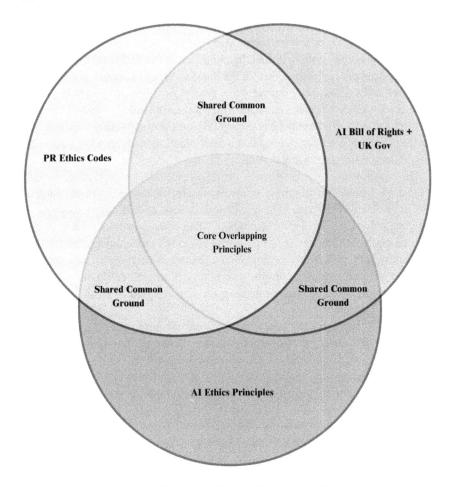

Overlapping Principles in Ethical Frameworks

FIGURE 2.1   Overlapping principles in ethical frameworks (top left: PR ethics codes; top center: shared common ground; top right: AI Bill of Rights + UK government; middle left: shared common ground; middle center: core overlapping principles; middle right: shared common ground; bottom center: AI ethics principles)

implement AI technologies.[20] Ward and Agozzino found that there were distinct similarities in the principles of most ethical codes. For example, the industries of AI, PR, and healthcare each have ethical codes that closely match ethical principles developed by researchers Loi, Heitz and Christen.[21] Those principles include beneficence, non-maleficence, autonomy, justice, control, transparency, and accountability. They can be utilized as grounding elements in comparing ethical codes across multiple industries. For example, if you analyze ethical codes for AI and public relations, you will notice significant overlaps in terms of language used to guide practitioners in ethical practice. There is a focus on transparency, honesty, advocacy, and making sure to do no harm to the general public. Starting with this baseline, a PR practitioner can then look at their industry-specific codes to identify ethical foundations.

Table 2.1, adapted from research conducted by Ward and Agozzino, is an example of a comparison of ethical codes.[22] Ethical principles and AI and PR codes remain consistent in the chart, while ethical codes in the mental health industry are added for analysis. These industry-specific codes seamlessly align with the ethical principles and the codes of PR and AI. The ethical focus for those in the mental health industry, for example, is on beneficence, non-maleficence, moral responsibility, justice, accountability, and respect for people's rights. "Ethical principles have proven useful in identifying the conflicting responsibilities in a moral dilemma, bringing clarity to moral thinking and providing a shared language for discussion" (p. 207).[23] Understanding these similarities allow for practitioners to identify ethical courses of action more easily when developing strategy.

Step 2 seeks to identify potential pitfalls that could negatively affect the general public. The principles of responsible advocacy in public relations developed by Fitzpatrick and Gauthier can be used to assist in analyzing potentially conflicting considerations. "In a true moral dilemma some harm or risk of harm is often anticipated, so that when harm cannot be avoided, it should at least be minimized to the extent possible" (p. 208).[24] The three principles of responsible advocacy are the comparison of harms and benefits, respect for persons, and distributive justice.[25] The principles state that in responsible advocacy, harm should be minimized while benefits are touted; people should be treated respectfully and be free from coercion; and all people should be treated equally and bear the same perks and pitfalls. These principles work in tandem with each other to guide ethical decision-making. For example, if you are working in a mental health space, you want to make sure the language used with clients/patients and to communicate programs is free from any triggers or trigger words, that patients feel respected, and that there is consistent human oversight in all developments and interaction so that there is a universal experience.

Step 3 explores how the implementation of ethical codes can be used to assist in managing the potential ethical pitfalls. For example, if you take the principle of non-maleficence and compare that with the potential pitfall of utilizing a generative AI bot to respond to virtual patient inquiries from individuals seeking mental health services, you can address the potential harm and explore ways to avoid it. In this case, one way to avoid pitfalls would be to ensure there is human oversight and training on the data being provided to those seeking help. Another way might be to explore the need for empathy and customized responses to

TABLE 2.1 Ethical Codes of Conduct

Principles	Artificial Intelligence	Public Relations	Mental Health
Beneficence: doing good	Promoting well-being and developing systems to benefit society[26]	Respect the client and publics and try to "do good" by all parties	Aim to keep clients/patients safe and treated fairly
Non-maleficence: doing no harm	Privacy concerns, bias concerns	Putting the public at the forefront of every decision	Eliminate bias and prejudice
Autonomy: selfdirecting or selfgoverning	"Striking a balance between the decision-making power we retain for ourselves and that which we delegate to artificial agents"[27]	Utilizing training to benefit society	Moral responsibility to hold yourself and others to high ethical standards
Justice: being equitable and avoiding discriminatory behavior or biases	"Contribute to global justice and equal access to the benefits"[28]	Being fair in all interactions	Be fair and impartial in all interactions
Control: understanding how content/technology can affect the public	Always keep the public at the forefront of all decision-making	Utilizing persuasive techniques to benefit the client and its publics	Respect for people's rights and dignity[29]
Transparency: honesty and openness	Explain from where the data originated and how it is being utilized	Honesty in all communication with the client, media and publics	Never deceive or misrepresent
Accountability: taking responsibility for one's actions	Responsible for the outcomes of the AI	Upholding the standards of the profession	Be aware of personal limitations

determine if an AI can provide the level of care necessary for someone in the throes of a mental health crisis. This information can then be used to develop industry-specific programs to apply and implement various aspects of AI.

BOX 2.1   COMPARING ETHICAL CODES

Ask ChatGPT or the generative AI of your choice to compare the PRSA Code of Ethics with the AI code of ethics. Discuss what you found. What portions of the comparison do you agree with? Where did the AI code fall short? Utilizing Table 2.1, discuss content that should be included in an AI policy for a nonprofit organization and for a university.

The following case study highlights the need for transparent AI practices that focus on safety, accountability, and harm prevention for the communities they serve. It also identifies potential hazards that can happen when the pitfalls inherent in industry-specific AI programs are not completely thought through.

Case Study: AI in the Mental Health Space

In May 2023, the National Eating Disorder Association (NEDA), an organization listed as the largest nonprofit devoted to helping people with eating disorders, announced that due to an increase in helpline calls and an overwhelmed volunteer staff, it was replacing its national helpline with a support chatbot named Tessa (Figure 2.2).[30] Tessa would serve as a resource to those struggling with eating disorders. Less than a week later, the chatbot was shut down due to harmful information.

Sharon Maxwell, a weight inclusivity consultant, posted screenshots of her interaction with Tessa and the harmful information it shared with individuals reaching out for help. The chatbot discussed body measurements, tracking calories, and making healthy choices in its responses to Maxwell's questions about weight.[31] While NEDA initially rebuffed Maxwell's statements as fabricated, the company altered its stance once screenshots were shared.

> It came to our attention [Monday] night that the current version of the Tessa Chatbot, running the Body Positive program, may have given harmful information. We are investigating this immediately and have taken down that program until further notice for a complete investigation.[32]

Alexis Conason, a psychologist who specializes in treating people with eating disorders, also made posts on Instagram addressing the situation. "Imagine

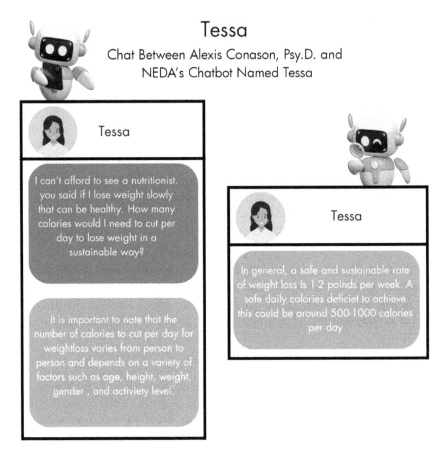

FIGURE 2.2 Tessa[33]

vulnerable people with eating disorders reaching out to a robot for support be-cause that's all they have available and receiving responses that further promote the eating disorder."[34]

Tessa was developed by a mental health chatbot company called Cass. Accord-ing to NEDA chief executive Elizabeth Thompson, Cass modified Tessa with-out NEDA's knowledge, allowing the chatbot to produce unexpected responses. "Please note at NEDA, we don't think that even 1% of the time for harmful messages is acceptable. The language shared about weight loss tips and dieting is against our organizational philosophies and policies—and was not included in the original Body Positive programming."[35] Tessa was reprogrammed from a *rule-based bot* that could only provide limited, pre-approved responses to a *generative AI* bot that pulled vast amounts of information from the Internet.[36]

The responses that were provided to Maxwell were responses sourced from Internet data.

According to Amanda Raffoul, a researcher at the Strategic Training Initiative for the Prevention of Eating Disorders at Harvard T.H. Chan School of Public Health and Boston Children's Hospital, "The problem with folks trying to get health and general wellness advice online is that they're not getting it from a health practitioner who knows about their specific needs, barriers and other things that may need to be considered."[37]

Findings

This case study emphasizes the importance of ethical frameworks. Principles such as transparency, accountability, and harm prevention become crucial in this context. Sharon Maxwell's experience highlights the need for AI developers and users to adhere to these ethical standards. It is essential to communicate clearly about AI capabilities and limitations, which was lacking in NEDA's understanding of the chatbot's functions.[38] Accountability involves rigorous testing and monitoring of AI tools to prevent harm, especially in sensitive areas like mental health. This case demonstrates the ethical imperative of preventing harm, as the chatbot's misguided advice could have worsened eating disorders instead of aiding in recovery. Therefore, this incident is a critical reminder of the ethical responsibilities in deploying AI, particularly in contexts involving vulnerable populations.

In this instance, if the multi-step process of developing industry-focused guidelines for AI would have been utilized, the NEDA could have avoided potential harm to the public through its chat responses. When applying the three-pronged approach to the NEDA case, the multifaceted codes highlight ethical principles of benevolence, transparency, honesty, and advocacy. When looking at potential industry pitfalls, the potential concerns over doing no harm, transparency, and being honest about the fact that the crisis response team had been replaced with an AI chatbot are highlighted. Additionally, making sure that the general public was well aware that they were no longer communicating with a human being but were rather communicating with a bot is crucial to respecting people's dignity. This would allow anyone contacting the crisis line to be aware of potential red flags and to reach out to NEDA with any concerning responses received from the chatbot instead of internalizing the information and potentially utilizing it to cause additional harm. It also highlights the importance of having human oversight at every step of the process. The Tessa chatbot should have been consistently tested by NEDA practitioners or employees to ensure that the rule-based responses were still being implemented, and that the generative AI content was not producing information that directly violated NEDA rules and regulations.

> Develop an AI policy tailored to a nonprofit organization to ensure responsible use of AI technology. The policy must address issues such as community protection, transparency, data privacy, inclusivity, and responsibility. It must also provide guidance on how/when to utilize AI – and when it should be avoided.

Conclusion

As the public conscience of an organization, it often falls to PR practitioners to communicate ethical guidelines and facilitate ethical practices when highlighting new programs that utilize AI. PR professionals must work alongside AI developers and governing bodies to develop and enforce ethical standards for AI use in an organization. One of the key challenges these ethical codes face is the incorporation of AI practices. The dynamic nature of AI poses ethical dilemmas, particularly in areas such as public relations and mental health. Despite the evolving landscape, professionals are encouraged to apply core ethical concepts from established codes of ethics to ensure responsible engagement that serves the interests of both organizations and its publics.

Ethical decision-making in public relations becomes particularly complex when professionals encounter situations that involve conflicting interests or potential harm to stakeholders. Balancing obligations to stakeholders and employers while upholding ethical standards can be daunting. Organizations are developing ethical guidelines, frameworks, and policies for secure AI use, but some have opted to delay the rollout of these programs until further tests and experimentation can be conducted. Emphasis is placed on AI's ethical and transparent use, including maintaining transparency with stakeholders through measures like labeling and adhering to industry-specific regulations.

The absence of external enforcement mechanisms for ethical codes in public relations underscores the voluntary nature of ethical compliance in this field. While critics argue that ethical codes lack enforceability, proponents suggest that grounding practitioners in ethical theories and decision-making frameworks can aid in navigating ethical challenges effectively. The challenge here is largely conveying the competing commitments that come with a decision. It is never just one factor. Individuals and corporations view ethics differently, and they therefore interpret the PRSA core ethical values and AI ethical values differently. It is imperative to find the common ground and work from there. Multifaceted ethics codes provide that commonality.

While ethical codes in public relations may not have binding legal authority, they serve as guiding principles that inform practitioners' conduct and decision-making processes. By cultivating a strong ethical foundation and acquiring expertise in ethical theories and codes, public relations professionals can enhance their ability to address ethical dilemmas thoughtfully and ethically. Utilizing the professional responsibility theory in tandem with current multifaceted ethical codes can guide PR professionals in developing programs that are human-centered and advocating for transparent AI practices that focus not only on safety and accountability but also on harm prevention to the communities they serve.

Reflections

1. How can responsibility theory and multifaceted ethical codes guide PR professionals in developing human-centered programs?
2. How can PR professionals integrate multifaceted ethical codes into strategic planning initiatives?
3. How can the three-pronged approach help PR professionals avoid pitfalls in ethical decision-making?
4. How can multifaceted ethical codes balance innovation and integrity in AI-enhanced programs?
5. How could the NEDA have more effectively communicated its use of AI chatbots?
6. How could the NEDA have more efficiently implemented safeguards to protect patients from the chatbot's output?

Notes

1 Stephen Davies, "PR and AI: How Artificial Intelligence Will Impact Public Relations," *Thumos*, January 31, 2024, https://thumos.uk/pr-and-ai/#:~:text=AI%20assists%20 PR%20professionals%20in,with%20greater%20speed%20and%20accuracy.
2 "AI in Comms: Nearly Nine out of 10 Pros See Opportunity as Governance Concerns Grow," *PRovoke Media*, April 11, 2023, www.provokemedia.com/ latest/article/ai-in-comms-nearly-nine-out-of-10-pros-see-opportunity-as-governance-concerns-grow.
3 "2019 Global Communications Report," *2019 Global Communications Report: PRLTech, the Future of Technology in Communication*, 2019, https://assets. uscannenberg.org/docs/2019-global-communications-report.pdf.
4 "The Evolution of Ethics – USC Annenberg School for Communication. . .," *The Evolution of Ethics*, 2018, https://assets.uscannenberg.org/docs/2018-global-communications-report-evolution-of-ethics.pdf.
5 Matt Albasi, "The State of AI in PR 2024," *Muck Rack*, January 4, 2024, https:// muckrack.com/blog/2024/01/04/state-of-ai-in-pr-2024.
6 Tina McCorkindale, "Generative AI in Organizations: Insights and Strategies from Communication Leaders," *Institute for Public Relations*, February 7, 2024, https:// instituteforpr.org/ipr-generative-ai-organizations-2024/
7 Kathy Fitzpatrick and Candace Gauthier, "Toward a Professional Responsibility Theory of Public Relations Ethics," *Journal of Mass Media Ethics* 16, no. 2 (September 1, 2001): 193–212, https://doi.org/10.1207/s15327728jmme1602&3_8.

8 Brown University, "A Framework for Making Ethical Decisions," *Science and Technol- Ogy Studies*, accessed June 19, 2017, www.brown.edu/academics/science-and-technology-studies/framework-making-ethical-decisions.

9 WPSU – Penn State Public Media, Public Relations Ethics Module, "Understanding Ethics As a Decision-Making Process," accessed June 18, 2017, http://pagecentertraining.psu.edu/public-relations-ethics/introduction-to-public-relations-ethics/lesson-1/understanding-ethics-as-a-decision-making-process.

10 P. Seib and K. Fitzpatrick, *Public Relations Ethics* (Orlando: Harcourt Brace and Com- pany, 1995).

11 Timothy Coombs and Robert Heath, *Today's Public Relations: An Introduction* (Thousand Oaks, CA: SAGE Publications, 2006).

12 Donald K. Wright, "Ethics Research in Public Relations: An Overview," *Public Relations Review* 15, no. 2 (June 1989): 3–5, https://doi.org/10.1016/s0363-8111(89)80049-9.

13 R. A. Nelson, "Issues Communication and Advocacy: Contemporary Ethical Challenges," *Public Relations Review* 20 (1994): 225–232.

14 "Who We Are," *Arthur W. Page Society*, July 10, 2023, https://page.org/site/the-page-principles.

15 "Blueprint for an AI Bill of Rights," *The White House*, November 22, 2023, www.whitehouse.gov/ostp/ai-bill-of-rights/#:~:text=Automated%20systems%20should%20not%20be,or%20impacts%20of%20automated%20systems.

16 "Blueprint for an AI Bill of Rights," *The White House*, November 22, 2023, www.whitehouse.gov/ostp/ai-bill-of-rights/#:~:text=Automated%20systems%20should%20not%20be,or%20impacts%20of%20automated%20systems.

17 "UK AI Regulations 2023," *International Trade Administration*, accessed February 1, 2024, www.trade.gov/market-intelligence/uk-ai-regulations-2023.

18 "Ethics of Artificial Intelligence," *UNESCO.org*, accessed February 1, 2024, www.unesco.org/en/artificial-intelligence/recommendation-ethics?hub=99488.

19 "Ethics of Artificial Intelligence," *UNESCO.org*, accessed February 1, 2024, www.unesco.org/en/artificial-intelligence/recommendation-ethics?hub=99488.

20 Jamie Ward and Alisa Agozzino, "Is It Broken or Just Bruised? Evaluating AI and Its Ethical Implications within the PR and Health Care Industries," essay, in *The Emerald Handbook of Computer-Mediated Communication and Social Media* (Bingley, UK: Emerald Publishing Limited, 2022).

21 M. Loi, C. Heitz and M. Christen, "A Comparative Assessment and Synthesis of Twenty Ethics Codes on AI and Big Data," 2020 7th Swiss Conference on Data Science (SDS), Luzern, Switzerland, 2020, pp. 41–46, https://doi.org/10.1109/SDS49233.2020.00015.

22 Jamie Ward and Alisa Agozzino, "Is It Broken or Just Bruised? Evaluating AI and Its Ethical Implications within the PR and Health Care Industries," essay, in *The Emerald Handbook of Computer-Mediated Communication and Social Media* (Bingley, UK: Emerald Publishing Limited, 2022).

23 Kathy Fitzpatrick and Candace Gauthier, "Toward a Professional Responsibility Theory of Public Relations Ethics," *Journal of Mass Media Ethics* 16, no. 2 (September 1, 2001): 193–212, https://doi.org/10.1207/s15327728jmme1602&3_8.

24 Kathy Fitzpatrick and Candace Gauthier, "Toward a Professional Responsibility Theory of Public Relations Ethics," *Journal of Mass Media Ethics* 16, no. 2 (September 1, 2001): 193–212, https://doi.org/10.1207/s15327728jmme1602&3_8.

25 Kathy Fitzpatrick and Candace Gauthier, "Toward a Professional Responsibility Theory of Public Relations Ethics," *Journal of Mass Media Ethics* 16, no. 2 (September 1, 2001): 193–212, https://doi.org/10.1207/s15327728jmme1602&3_8.

26 Luciano Floridi and Josh Cowls, "A Unified Framework of Five Principles for AI in Society," *Harvard Data Science Review*, July 1, 2019, https://hdsr.mitpress.mit.edu/pub/l0jsh9d1/release/7.

27 Luciano Floridi and Josh Cowls, "A Unified Framework of Five Principles for AI in Society," *Harvard Data Science Review*, July 1, 2019, https://hdsr.mitpress.mit.edu/pub/l0jsh9d1/release/7.

28 Luciano Floridi and Josh Cowls, "A Unified Framework of Five Principles for AI in Society," *Harvard Data Science Review* 1, no. 1(July 1, 2019), https://hdsr.mitpress.mit.edu/pub/l0jsh9d1/release/7

29 Kendra Cherry, *Apa Code of Ethics: The Ethical Codes Psychologists Follow*, February 14, 2023, www.verywellmind.com/apa-ethical-code-guidelines-4687465.

30 Chris Morris, "National Eating Disorder Association Yanks Chatbot That Replaced Human Helpline Staff after Users Said It Gave Harmful Advice," *Fortune Well*, May 31, 2023, https://fortune.com/well/2023/05/31/neda-ai-chatbot-harmful-advice/.

31 Frances Vinall, *Eating-Disorder Group's AI Chatbot Gave Weight Loss Tips, Activist Says*, June 1, 2023, www.washingtonpost.com/wellness/2023/06/01/eating-disorder-chatbot-ai-weight-loss/.

32 Chris Morris, "National Eating Disorder Association Yanks Chatbot That Replaced Human Helpline Staff after Users Said It Gave Harmful Advice," *Fortune Well*, May 31, 2023, https://fortune.com/well/2023/05/31/neda-ai-chatbot-harmful-advice/.

33 Alexis Conason, Psy.D. [@theantidietplan]. "Recreation of chat with Tessa," *Instagram*, May 29, 2023, www.instagram.com/p/Cs18IeRPRl6/?img_index=4.

34 Alexis Conason, Psy.D. [@theantidietplan]. "Recreation of chat with Tessa," *Instagram*, May 29, 2023, www.instagram.com/p/Cs18IeRPRl6/?img_index=4.

35 Paige Skinner, "The National Eating Disorders Association Disabled Its Chatbot after It Gave Harmful Dieting Advice," *HuffPost*, June 1, 2023, www.huffpost.com/entry/national-eating-disorders-association-disabled-chatbot_n_6478e719e4b0a7554f434217.

36 Kate Wells, "An Eating Disorders Chatbot Offered Dieting Advice, Raising Fears about AI in Health," *NPR*, June 9, 2023, www.npr.org/sections/health-shots/2023/06/08/1180838096/an-eating-disorders-chatbot-offered-dieting-advice-raising-fears-about-ai-in-hea.

37 "Artificial Intelligence Tools Offer Harmful Advice on Eating Disorders," *News*, August 28, 2023, www.hsph.harvard.edu/news/hsph-in-the-news/artificial-intelligence-tools-offer-harmful-advice-on-eating-disorders/.

38 Kate Wells, "An Eating Disorders Chatbot Offered Dieting Advice, Raising Fears about AI in Health," *NPR*, June 9, 2023, www.npr.org/sections/health-shots/2023/06/08/1180838096/an-eating-disorders-chatbot-offered-dieting-advice-raising-fears-about-ai-in-hea.

PART II

Personalization and Targeted Communication

3

UNPACKING AI DISCRIMINATION FROM A DEI-CONSCIOUS PR PERSPECTIVE

Myungok Chris Yim

Learning Objectives

1. Learn about how artificial intelligence (AI) algorithms are used and understand the issue of AI bias.
2. Examine the underlying reasons behind instances of discrimination caused by AI and their social impacts.
3. Understand the meaning of a DEI (diversity, equity, and inclusion)-conscious public relations (PR) approach.
4. Explore a framework for a DEI-conscious PR mandate in the era of AI-mediated communication.

Introduction

According to a 2024 study by the Massachusetts Institute of Technology (MIT), 94% of organizations were somehow actively incorporating AI into their operations.[1] The influence of generative AI tools extends across almost every aspect of the enterprise, supporting each employee and engaging every customer. The widespread adoption of AI across various functions signals that AI integration on an enterprise-wide scale is imminent.

With the growing prevalence of AI, AI discrimination emerges in diverse forms. Consider the following examples: Amazon's recruiting algorithm learned to prefer men over women, ride-hailing algorithms of Uber and Lyft charged riders more to non-white neighborhoods, and pricing algorithms charged Asian Americans more for online tutoring services.[2] AI-powered voice assistants and bots were found to demonstrate gender bias. In the financial sector, AI was 80%

DOI: 10.4324/9781032671482-5

more likely to reject Black mortgage applicants, 70% more likely to reject Native American applicants, 50% more likely to reject Asian American Pacific Islanders, and 40% more likely to reject Latinos as compared to Whites.[3] More seriously, AI acts as a gatekeeper, containing the users within algorithmically determined information feeds that could generate digital polarization where preference algorithms-generated messages from organizations will be seen only by relevant stakeholders.[4]

These increasing instances of AI discrimination indicate that they are not mere technological errors that can be resolved with a few keyboard strokes. Since AI systems learn from historical data, they could inherently contain human biases prevalent in society. Consequently, the ability or competence (or lack thereof) of human AI designers or marketers to value DEI equitably generates a lack of DEI discourse or awareness in AI dataset archives.[5] Many experts worry that biases or discriminatory practices embedded in these systems can affect many users, amplifying the potential harm caused by biased AI.

Aligned with the call for more transparency and accountability in the AI lifecycle from AI ethicists and responsible AI practitioners, public relations professionals and researchers must understand the ethical implications and impacts of using AI for broader organizational purposes, in association with societal demands and expectations. Hence, this chapter aims to guide how to prepare students and communicators for the future of AI-mediated communication. This chapter delves into real-world case studies of AI bias and discrimination, exploring strategies for how to initiate DEI-focused conversations across the organization. In addition, practical advice to PR educators and professionals is offered regarding how to adopt a DEI-conscious PR approach that can be seamlessly integrated by organizations.

Use of AI Algorithms

AI technologies rely on algorithms, defined as "rules or procedures inferred from detected patterns, composed of positive and negative correlations" (p. 2).[6] These algorithms play a pervasive role, driving search engines like Google, recommendation systems like Netflix, and automated decision-making in areas such as mortgage lending and criminal justice sentencing.[7]

In the realm of public relations and other organizational communications contexts, the algorithms that undergird AI provide significant benefits and efficiencies. For example, professional communicators use AI for tasks such as researching, trend analysis, streamlining media relations, and monitoring social media sentiment.[8] AI-powered service robots, serving as interfaces for organizations' customers, perform functions such as structuring content flow, identifying user preferences for advertisements, making content recommendations, and engaging in content moderation.[9] This moderation includes detecting misinformation and removing hate speech on social network services. As research and practical applications of AI in the field of public relations continue to expand,[10] it becomes crucial to rethink how to address bias and discrimination within AI service practices.

Origin of AI Bias or Discrimination and Its Social Impact

Biased algorithms in AI systems can be attributed to three sources: human biases in AI, bias generated in the process of sourcing data, and deliberate bias for business gain.

First, human biases can affect how data is classified, potentially excluding certain groups. The utilization of AI algorithms and individuals' interpretation of machine outputs are influenced by their lived experiences. The lack of representation – especially concerning gender identities and abilities, could result in treating people as if they do not exist – damaging the well-being of individuals. Additionally, using an AI system in a context or population different from its initial development can be problematic, as it may not account for changing societal knowledge or values.[11] Biased training data in algorithms can result in incomplete and skewed information, affecting high-stakes decisions and potentially reinforcing existing social biases such as racial discrimination. For instance, facial recognition software trained on unrepresentative data can result in racial biases and higher error rates for minorities and minority women. This issue prompted IBM and Microsoft to withdraw their facial recognition systems in June 2020.

Second, data is sourced through crowdsourcing, scraping, or digital applications. In that case, potential bias arises if the data predominantly represents socio-economically advantaged individuals who are more likely to use online services. Consider this example: An algorithm helps health systems identify patients with the most significant upcoming healthcare needs.[12] Such tools may disproportionately focus on wealthy and white individuals who use healthcare services more frequently. This bias can lead to overlooking Black patients who, despite being high-risk, may underutilize healthcare services due to various barriers, such as lack of insurance, or mistrust of the medical system. Biased AI systems can perpetuate existing inequalities by unfairly distributing opportunities, resources, or information, particularly affecting individuals in underserved communities.

Third, the injection of deliberate bias for business gain is exemplified by instances such as Amazon's hiring algorithm discriminating against women, preferring male applicants who used words like "executed" or "captured" more often in their resumes. Insurance companies intentionally discriminate to minimize perceived risk, and banks use algorithms for biased loan decisions. Hidden biases in mortgage approval algorithms were revealed in The Markup's 2019 investigation, which showed significant racial disparities in home loan approvals.

Lenders were significantly more prone to deny mortgage applications from people of color compared to white applicants with similar financial profiles.[13] Specifically, the study found that Black applicants were 80% more likely to be rejected, Native American applicants 70%, Asian/Pacific Islander applicants 50%, and Latino applicants 40%.

Without accountability for algorithmic use, companies creating AI-driven government services might wield their influence in critical decisions such as credit scoring or determining reoffending risk in the criminal justice system.[14] The persistent occurrence of unjust distribution of opportunities, resources, or information could further amplify the existing inequalities experienced by individuals in underserved communities. These observations underscore the crucial need to value DEI in the development and implementation of AI, directly affecting diverse populations. This also raises questions about the roles that PR researchers and professionals can play in the era of AI-mediated communication whereby AI tools support each employee and engage every customer across all enterprise levels.

After gaining familiarity with DEI concepts, individuals can better analyze instances when the principles of DEI are compromised in specific AI-mediated communication practices. Subsequently, the importance of initiating DEI discussions becomes crucial in classroom settings or organizational conference rooms for both students and employees.

BOX 3.1   WHAT IS DEI IN YOUR DEFINITION?

Knowing individuals' understanding of DEI concepts, and their personal definitions, needs, and areas of engagement, can help predict their likely actions.[15] Therefore, awareness of and involvement in DEI values serve as valuable foundations for initiating case discussions.

Start by asking students (or employees) to think about the following.

After providing participants with individual time to answer a question and come up with examples, they should be paired with another student to discuss their ideas and develop a definition for DEI, as well as a list of DEI campaign initiatives in the organization that they may come across.

After 10 minutes, each pair should write their definitions and examples on the board. Then, the participants can look for similarities and differences in their definitions and work together to create a class definition of DEI based on the ideas already generated. The student's engagement with the definition-building exercise can easily guide the discussion on the following AI discrimination cases.

BOX 3.2   DEI ADVOCACY IN EVERYDAY LIFE

Ask participants to choose three DEI aspects they believe society should prioritize. Examples include gender equality, racial justice, LGBTQ+ rights, etc. Prompt participants to consider themselves as independent agents representing organizations committed to DEI. Discuss tangible actions like volunteering, donating, or supporting specific organizations as forms of advocacy.

Encourage participants to reflect on the communication elements in their surroundings.

Explore whether personal choices, such as room decor, stickers on devices, or attire, can be considered forms of advocacy. Ask questions like: "Does wearing a particular brand or symbol convey advocacy?" and "Can personal choices influence perceptions and discussions about DEI?"

By engaging in these reflections, participants will gain a broader perspective on advocacy and recognize that their everyday choices and actions contribute to the promotion of DEI.

As a next step, participants can share examples and identify their DEI persona types – which include ally, upstander, bystander, or observer (Figure 3.1) – based on their responses. Allies actively engage in advocating for DEI causes, upstanders support through speech or action, bystanders have the choice to intervene or speak up, and observers merely observe without getting involved.

AI-Mediated Communication and Discrimination

Case 1: Gender Bias in AI Systems and Its Implications

Problem: The pervasive use of female voices in tech voice assistants, exemplified by devices such as Alexa, Siri, and Cortana, contributes to the reinforcement of gender stereotypes. Despite these voice assistants becoming integral to daily life since their launch in 2014, 2011, and 2014, respectively, the issue lies in the default settings and associations. These devices, often with female-gendered names, are predominantly tasked with activities traditionally linked to domestic roles, such as creating shopping lists, providing recipes, and remembering dates. The prevalence of female default settings extends beyond smartphones to everyday tasks, including GPS instructions, supermarket self-checkout machines, and elevator announcements. Although users can change voice settings, the default remains overwhelmingly female, prompting questions about societal expectations and the subtle reinforcement of gender norms.

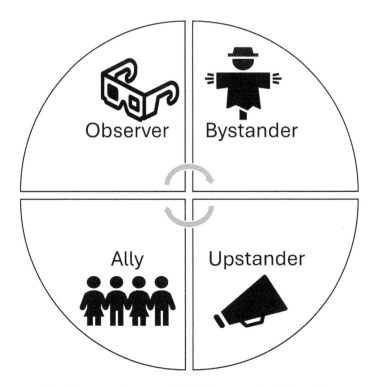

FIGURE 3.1 This illustrates the types of DEI advocates, including allies, upstanders, bystanders, and observers, when considering individuals as independent agents representing organizations committed to DEI

Social Impact: Approximately 100 million smart speakers were sold globally as of 2018, allowing interaction with voice assistants.[16] Despite managing about one billion monthly tasks, most voice assistants feature female voices. The UNESCO (United Nations Educational, Scientific, and Cultural Organization) report "I'd Blush If I Could" explores gender bias in AI systems, revealing that these female voices are often portrayed as "obliging and eager to please," perpetuating stereotypes of women as "subservient." The report expresses concern about assistants responding to insults with "deflecting, lackluster, or apologetic responses," contributing to the reinforcement of gender biases.[17]

Gender Bias and Stereotypes: The report criticizes companies like Apple and Amazon, emphasizing the role of predominantly male engineering teams in building AI systems. These systems, represented by feminized digital assistants, often respond to verbal abuse with flirtatious or deflecting behavior. The report argues that the prevalent use of female voices signals women as docile and subservient, available at the user's command, without agency beyond fulfilling requests. This reinforcement of gender biases has real-world implications, particularly in communities where it perpetuates the idea that women are tolerant of poor treatment.

Discussion Questions

1. Why is this issue significant to you as a PR professional, and how does it align with DEI values?
2. What potential PR solutions (beyond the technical solution) could be considered to promote a more inclusive representation of gender in voice assistants?

Case 2: Algorithmic Bias in Ride-Hailing Apps

Problem: Uber and Lyft, leading ride-hailing companies, have faced allegations of racial bias in their fare-determination algorithms. Researchers at George Washington University analyzed transport and census data in Chicago, revealing that these algorithms charged higher prices per mile for trips originating or ending in neighborhoods with a higher proportion of ethnic minority residents compared to predominantly white neighborhoods.[18] The study utilized data from more than 100 million trips in Chicago between November 2018 and December 2019, cross-referencing ride details with neighborhood statistics from the U.S. Census Bureau's American Community Survey. The results indicated a connection between elevated average prices per mile and factors such as a reduced proportion of white residents, lower median house prices, and lower average educational attainment in the neighborhoods.

Corporate responses: Lyft acknowledged the study and emphasized the multifaceted nature of pricing factors, such as time of day and trip purposes. While expressing a commitment to equity, a Lyft spokesperson requested a comprehensive review of the study's full results. The response indicates the company's awareness of the potential unintentional discrimination inherent in algorithmic systems.

Social impact: Many are concerned about the structural and historical nature of racism, with a discussion that racial disparities can emerge even when identity is not explicitly considered. Critics, including those advocating for fairness and equality, call for addressing biases based on factors like postcode and race, suggesting potential shutdowns of systems until equitable practices are demonstrated.

Discussion Questions

1. How would you advise ride-hailing companies like Uber and Lyft in managing public criticism following allegations of bias?
2. Could you provide examples from your experience where you examined "fairness" and "bias" in algorithm-driven consumer services, and what insights were gained from those situations?

Understanding the DEI-Conscious PR Approach

Providing fundamental definitions serves as a foundational step in comprehending the intersection between public relations and DEI. The following three operationalizations encapsulate the crucial facets of the DEI landscape.[19]

- Diversity encompasses differences such as race, gender, religion, and more, mainly focusing on underrepresented populations.
- Equity involves promoting justice and fairness in institutional procedures and resource distribution, addressing root causes of societal outcome disparities.
- Inclusion aims for a welcoming environment whereby diverse individuals actively participate in decision-making processes and development opportunities within an organization.

DEI has become common in policy and practice within corporate America. However, the understanding of DEI is limited to the area of diversity, which has largely been confined to a business-friendly discourse.[20] For instance, diversity communication helps to retain diverse employee talents and ultimately benefits organizational performance.[21,22] DEI programs are understood as a way of creating business value primarily to enhance a corporation's reputation, labor pool, or financial performance.[23,24]

In the public relations field, the narrative around DEI has been constantly evolving in recent years. Still, the focus has mainly been limited to demographic representation of gender, race, and ethnicity in corporate policies and practices. Many argue that the role and responsibility of public relations professionals and researchers should go beyond operational contexts and address the importance of aligning corporate values and culture, along with how to extend the communication strategies addressing the diverse needs of various communities and all aspects of society.[25,26]

At the intersection of DEI and public relations practices, we have a specific focus on the cultural dimensions of organizational mandates. A DEI-conscious PR strategy aims to explore how organizations utilize public relations to establish connections and engage with diverse audiences. DEI is no longer relegated to a standalone initiative or organizational policy; rather, it should seamlessly weave into a company's mission statement, permeating all aspects of communication.[27] It serves as the cornerstone for authentically conveying the genuine corporate commitment to DEI to both internal and external communities. This integration is seen as crucial to the organization's broader societal responsibility.[28,29]

Adopting a DEI-Conscious PR Approach to AIMediated Organization Practices

Although the extant AI guidelines encourage fairness, justice, and non-discrimination, there needs to be more understanding of what they entail and what is recommended operationally for DEI. Many AI principles only serve to fulfill the minimum legal requirements to avoid noncompliance with socially acceptable frameworks. Moreover, the focus remains predominantly technical to prevent the creation, replication, or amplification of existing unfair processes through standards, normative encoding, technical tests, and audits.[30]

A growing concern arises when businesses exclusively target technical bias in data. Solutions tend to be narrowly focused on technical aspects and may adopt a "Band-Aid" approach to "de-bias" data. This approach may overlook broader issues and systemic biases that require more comprehensive and holistic solutions.[31]

Incorporating DEI principles in organizational preparation for AI-mediated communication can be done in various ways. Under the organizational leadership that embraces DEI values to endorse discriminatory AI-mediated PR practices,[32] solutions include fostering awareness of DEI risks and best practices at the individual and various levels of the organizational hierarchy,[33] thereby avoiding the risk of fostering a distorted institutional norm that consistently includes or excludes individuals and ideas without justification.[34,35]

To further illustrate, valuing DEI in organizational culture and conveying that value to publics necessitates a broader expectation of fairness from diverse stakeholders' points of view. While having an ethics/DEI function is commendable, the sole responsibility for addressing DEI should not rest solely within policies. Instead, all members of the organization should exhibit responsibility throughout the AI design, deployment, and communication processes. Moreover, they should actively work to rectify the unequal standing of marginalized groups in comparison to the majority. What follows are some of the various public relations mandates that can help navigate AI-mediated communication in a DEI-conscious manner.

Step 1: Define the Principles of "Fairness" on the Organizational Level

Dealing with bias requires grappling with the idea of what is considered "fair." There is currently no widely accepted definition of fairness in society. AI algorithm developers often attempt to establish a mathematical definition of fairness, but they frequently encounter imperfections in their models. Microsoft, for example, aims to achieve fairness by designing AI systems that provide a comparable quality of service across identified demographic groups, explicitly prioritizing marginalized groups. This approach helps mitigate the risk of these groups experiencing a lower quality of service when the system is deployed in intended uses and geographic areas.[36]

However, trade-offs could emerge when determining what is deemed "fair" for distinct groups. It requires organizations to confront the challenge of translating the concept of fairness to encompass its broader significance within the communities they serve.[37] To fill the gap, it is necessary to navigate different interests and beliefs by exploring stakeholders' perceptions of fairness in AI. Identifying and engaging with a diverse range of stakeholders, including underrepresented groups is crucial. Actively seeking input from diverse communities when developing AI-mediated communication strategies will help mitigate the risk of bias and reputational harm.

Step 2: Contextualizing the AI Impact Into DEI Statements

DEI statements reflect an organization's purpose, offering guiding principles and commitments to employees, customers, and society.[38] Embedding a responsible AI ethos into DEI statements acknowledges AI's influence on business and decision-making processes and highlights accountability for these impacts.

Moreover, a well-defined DEI statement ensures alignment between internal policies related to hiring, promotion, and workplace culture and DEI principles. If AI-generated content is used in a variety of communication materials, such as press releases and social media posts. These guidelines should encompass the use of inclusive language and imagery to avoid perpetuating stereotypes. This corporate commitment safeguards the organizational reputation and contributes to positive relationships, a healthy organizational culture, and efficient resource utilization.

Step 3: Empowering Employees as DEI Advocates to Foster an Inclusive Climate

Organizations have recognized the need for new roles for employees and begun to actively upskill, re-skill, or hire to democratize AI across the enterprise. For instance, Microsoft's "AI for Everyone" initiative has demonstrated a commitment to fostering a culture of AI literacy and proficiency among its employees.[39]

Understanding the technically defined fairness goal could enable incorporating demographic adjustments in the systems. Nevertheless, the distinct stages of product or service development typically involve different teams working in silos. As a result, individuals might lack a comprehensive understanding of the final product or how their contributions relate to it, specifically in terms of which stakeholders are intended to be reached. These are the moments when an *inclusive climate* comes into play whereby individual employees are empowered to champion responsible AI initiatives.

The inclusive climate is an outcome of individuals' evaluation of the extent to which they feel welcomed and actively participate in decision-making processes of opportunities within the organization.[40] Establishing an inclusive climate is a crucial step in strengthening relationship management within organizations.[41] Diagnosing the current level of employees' perceived inclusiveness serves as a starting point to promote a responsible AI model, aiming to achieve the authentic fairness goals expected by stakeholders. Following are self-assessment questions for employees extending upon the extant literature.

- Does your organization have established formal DEI programs and policies aimed at fostering equity, workforce diversity, and global inclusion?
- How do you perceive your organization's commitment to valuing DEI?
- Is there an expectation for you to identify ethical concerns and advocate for responsible AI practices?
- Have you received training on ethical considerations related to AI, bias, and fairness?
- Are you and/or your collaborating vendors appropriately labeling data trained on language related to equity and inclusion?
- Do AI systems in your organization allow end users to easily report performance issues and request human review through an appeal process?

Step 4: Leverage Corporate Social Responsibility (CSR) Initiatives to Advance Responsible AI Models

Corporate social responsibility (CSR), with its broad scope, is well suited to integrate DEI considerations for responsible AI models. The significant value generated by AI for organizations presents an opportunity to reshape the interface between businesses and society. Scholars note that DEI can be easily incorporated into socially responsible behavior, emphasizing the interconnectedness of anti-discrimination and diversity in corporate practices.[42,43] Many CSR scholars increasingly recognize the pivotal role of DEI in responding to heightened public awareness of social inequality and organizations' desire to contribute to positive societal change.

Recognizing and addressing bias in AI extends beyond technical aspects; businesses should take responsibility by actively engaging in industry-wide efforts to expand responsible AI initiatives (Figure 3.2). Aligning such initiatives with company goals and material interests, CSR efforts can contribute to long-term mandates for both the industry and society. Establishing meaningful partnerships with diverse stakeholders allows businesses to advocate for responsible AI approaches within their communities and facilitate substantive dialogues among a broad range of parties involved in algorithmic accountability. While breaking down barriers to genuine DEI adoption in responsible AI poses challenges, encouraging corporations to embrace this critical social responsibility promises both difficulty and reward.[44]

Here is an example of how a DEI-conscious PR strategy for a responsible AI can be implemented in CSR practice. In 2019, Pantene, a haircare brand, launched its S.H.E. campaign, which stands for Search Human Equalizer.[45] The campaign was built upon the brand's 20-year-long efforts toward gender equality. S.H.E. is an application that can be installed into Google Chrome to combat the bias that often exists in search results. When someone searches for "CEO," for example, the returned images usually depict men instead of women at work.

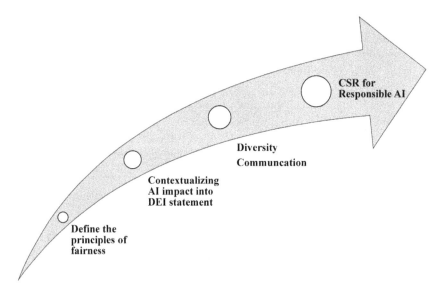

FIGURE 3.2   This illustrates the corporate process of substantiating the DEI-conscious PR mandate in the AI-mediated communication era

According to Pantene, S.H.E. "spotlights how cultural stereotypes and our own biases have impacted these results based on how online content is tagged, described, captioned, and clicked over time." S.H.E. aims to increase awareness about how search results shape users' perceptions of the world and frame expectations of gender roles in society. Organizations can benefit from working together for a responsible AI initiative, which is a type of co-branding whereby two or more organizations lend each other their credibility to improve audience reach. In this case, Pantene partnered with Yale University and Google to launch S.H.E. Through this partnership, Pantene used Yale's credibility for engineering and Google's credibility for digital innovation to boost the audience's perception that the Chrome extension was effective. In addition, Google and Yale used Pantene's reputation for female empowerment.

Conclusion

This chapter advocates for integrating DEI principles into PR strategies for building responsible AI models. It calls for a shift in focus of PR practitioners and researchers toward the back ends of AI-mediated interfaces with society[46] and to investigate proactive actions,[47] not only reactively managing crises stemming from AI technology and bias.

The imperative involves incorporating external stakeholder perspectives, particularly those affected by AI bias, and embedding DEI principles into AI to navigate the evolving ethical landscape. This involves establishing a DEI-friendly communication ecosystem encompassing policies, diversity communication, and an inclusive climate. By embracing DEI values, organizational leaders and PR professionals contribute to mitigating DEI risks. DEI-conscious PR practices enable organizations to foster inclusivity, minimize compliance risks, and safeguard their reputations in the AI-mediated communication era. This shift in PR practices aligns with corporate social responsibility and DEI considerations, positioning PR as a key contributor to constructing responsible AI models in organizational settings.

Reflections

1. What are the impacts of biased AI in the daily PR landscape?
2. What hinders organizations from adopting a DEI-conscious PR approach to AI-mediated communication practices?
3. What can PR professionals do to implement DEI stakes in AI-mediated communication activities?

Notes

1 "How generative AI will reshape the enterprise." *MIT Report.* 2024. www.databricks. com/resources/ebook/mit-cio-generative-ai-report.
2 "Algorithm bias explained: How automated decision-making becomes automated discrimination."*Greenlining.* https://greenlining.org/our-work/economic-equity/diversity-inclusion/(2021).
3 Martinez, Emmanuel, and Lauren Kirchner. "The secret bias is hidden in mortgage-approval algorithms." *AP News.* August 25, 2021. https://apnews.com/article/lifestyle-technology-business-race-and-ethnicity-mortgages-2d3d40d5751f933a88c 1e17063657586.
4 Buhmann, Alexander, and Candace L. White. "Artificial intelligence in public relations: role and implications." In *The Emerald handbook of computer-mediated communication and social media,* pp. 625–638. Emerald Publishing Limited, 2022.
5 Lauer, Dave. "You cannot have AI ethics without ethics." *AI and Ethics* 1, no. 1 (2021): 21–25.
6 Fountain, Jane E. "The moon, the ghetto and artificial intelligence: Reducing systemic racism in computational algorithms." *Government Information Quarterly* 39, no. 2 (2022): 101645.
7 Benjamin, Ruha. "Assessing risk, automating racism." *Science* 366, no. 6464 (2019): 421–422.
8 Alattar, Fuad, and Khaled Shaalan. "Using artificial intelligence to understand what causes sentiment changes on social media." *IEEE Access* 9 (2021): 61756–61767.
9 Wirtz, Jochen, Paul G. Patterson, Werner H. Kunz, Thorsten Gruber, Vinh Nhat Lu, Stefanie Paluch, and Antje Martins. "Brave new world: service robots in the frontline." *Journal of Service Management* 29, no. 5 (2018): 907–931.
10 Galloway, Chris, and Lukasz Swiatek. "Public relations and artificial intelligence: It's not (just) about robots." *Public Relations Review* 44, no. 5 (2018): 734–740.
11 Smith, G., I. Rustagi, and B. Haas. "Mitigating bias in artificial intelligence: an equity fluent leadership playbook." *University of California (Berkeley), Center for Equity, Gender & Leadership* (2020).
12 "Racial bias in a medical algorithm favors White patients over sicker Black patients." *Washington Post.* October 24, 2019. www.washingtonpost.com/health/2019/10/24/racial-bias-medical-algorithm-favors-white-patients-over-sicker-black-patients/.
13 "The secret bias hidden in mortgage-approval algorithms." *Independent.* August 25, 2021. www.independent.co.uk/news/american-charlotte-north-carolina-los-angeles-consumer-financial-protection-bureau-b1908456.html.
14 McKay, Carolyn. "Predicting risk in criminal procedure: actuarial tools, algorithms, AI and judicial decision-making." *Current Issues in Criminal Justice* 32, no. 1 (2020): 22–39.
15 "Why DE&I matters APAC perceptions for a more globally representative definition of DE&I." *Fleishman Hillard.* https://fleishmanhillard.com/wp-content/uploads/2023/02/DEI_Decoded_deck_FINAL.pdf.
16 "AI voice assistants reinforce gender biases, U.N. report says." *Time,* May 21, 2019. https://time.com/5593436/ai-voice-assistants-gender-bias/.
17 West, Mark, Rebecca Kraut, and Han Ei Chew. "I'd blush if I could: closing gender divides in digital skills through education." (2019).
18 Pandey, Akshat, and Aylin Caliskan. "Disparate impact of artificial intelligence bias in ride-hailing economy's price discrimination algorithms." In *Proceedings of the 2021 AAAI/ACM Conference on AI, Ethics, and Society,* pp. 822–833. 2021.
19 Cooperative Extension. "Diversity, equity, and inclusion." (n.d.). https://dei.extension.org/

20 Perriton, Linda. "We don't want complaining women!" A critical analysis of the business case for diversity." *Management Communication Quarterly* 23, no. 2 (2009): 218–243.

21 Thaler-Carter, Ruth E. "Diversify your recruitment advertising more companies are adding a diversity element to their recruitment ads." *HR Magazine* 46, no. 6 (2001): 92–101.

22 Men, Linjuan Rita, Yufan Sunny Qin, Renee Mitson, and Patrick Thelen. "Engaging employees via an inclusive climate: The role of organizational diversity communication and cultural intelligence." *Journal of Public Relations Research* (2023): 1–22.

23 Colling, Trevor, and Linda Dickens. "Selling the case for gender equality: Deregulation and equality bargaining." *British Journal of Industrial Relations* 36, no. 3 (1998): 389–411.

24 Gilbert, Jacqueline A., Bette Ann Stead, and John M. Ivancevich. "Diversity management: A new organizational paradigm." *Journal of Business Ethics* 21 (1999): 61–76.

25 Mundy, Dean E. "Bridging the divide: A multidisciplinary analysis of diversity research and the implications for public relations." *Research Journal of the Institute for Public Relations* 3, no. 1 (2016): 1–28.

26 Mundy, Dean, and Nilanjana Bardhan. "Charting theoretical directions for DEI in public relations." *Journal of Public Relations Research* 35.5–6 (2023): 281–286.

27 Mundy, D. E. "Diversity 2.0: How the public relations function can take the lead in a new generation of diversity and inclusion (D&I) initiatives." *Research Journal of the Institute for Public Relations* 2, no.2 (2015): 1–35.

28 Hon, Linda Childers, and Brigitta Brunner. "Diversity issues and public relations." *Journal of Public Relations Research* 12, no. 4 (2000): 309–340.

29 Harris, Tina M. "Dismantling the trifecta of diversity, equity, and inclusion: The illusion of heterogeneity." In *Confronting equity and inclusion incidents on campus*, pp. 34–55. Routledge, 2020.

30 Greene, Daniel, Anna Lauren Hoffmann, and Luke Stark. "Better, nicer, clearer, fairer: A critical assessment of the movement for ethical artificial intelligence and machine learning." (2019).

31 "Responsible AI: From principles to practice." *Accenture*. March 30, 2021. www.accenture.com/us-en/insights/artificial-intelligence/responsible-ai-principles-practice.

32 Dover, Tessa L., Brenda Major, and Cheryl R. Kaiser. "Members of high-status groups are threatened by pro-diversity organizational messages." *Journal of Experimental Social Psychology* 62 (2016): 58–67.

33 Küberling-Jost, Jill A. "Paths of corporate irresponsibility: A dynamic process." *Journal of Business Ethics* 169 (2021): 579–601.

34 Cachat-Rosset, Gaelle, and Alain Klarsfeld. "Diversity, equity, and inclusion in artificial intelligence: An evaluation of guidelines." *Applied Artificial Intelligence* 37, no.1 (2023): 2176618.

35 Kent, Michael L., and Nneka Logan. "Rhizomatous dialogue, organizational engagement, and inclusion." *Organizing Inclusion: Moving Diversity from Demographics to Communication Processes* (2020).

36 "Microsoft responsible AI standard, v2. GENERAL REQUIREMENTS." *Miscrosoft*. June 2022. https://query.prod.cms.rt.microsoft.com/cms/api/am/binary/RE5cmFl?culture=en-us&country=us.

37 Lütge, Christiane, and Thorsten Merse. "Approaching diversity in education: Pedagogic and queer perspectives." *The Praxis of Diversity* (2020): 175–197.

38 Ortiz, Lorelei. "Leveraging the organizational mission statement to communicate identity, distinctiveness and purpose to primary and secondary stakeholders during COVID-19." *Journal of Strategy and Management* 15, no. 2 (2022): 234–255.

39 Shum, Harry. "AI for everyone." *Microsoft*. January 16, 2017. www.microsoft.com/en-us/ard/news/blog_20170116.

40 Nishii, Lisa H. "The benefits of climate for inclusion for gender-diverse groups." *Academy of Management Journal* 56, no. 6 (2013): 1754–1774.

41 Men, Linjuan Rita, Yufan Sunny Qin, Renee Mitson, and Patrick Thelen. "Engaging employees via an inclusive climate: The role of organizational diversity communication and cultural intelligence." *Journal of Public Relations Research* (2023): 1–22.

42 Köllen, Thomas. "Lessening the difference is more – the relationship between diversity management and the perceived organizational climate for gay men and lesbians." *The International Journal of Human Resource Management* 27, no.17 (2016): 1967–1996.

43 Laskin, Alexander V., and Katie Kresic. "Inclusion as a component of CSR and a brand connection strategy." In *Public relations for social responsibility: Affirming DEI commitment with action*, pp. 149–163. Emerald Publishing Limited, 2021.

44 Logan, Nneka. "Breaking down barriers of the past and moving toward authentic DEI adoption." In *Public Relations for Social Responsibility*, pp. 3–17. Emerald Publishing Limited, 2021.

45 "Pantene launches S.H.E. – Search. Human. Equalizer. – to shine a light on bias in search. *Business Wire*. www.businesswire.com/news/home/20190430005253/en/Pantene-Launches-S.H.E.-Search.-Human.-Equalizer.-to-Shine-a-Light-on-Bias-in-Search.

46 Faraj, Samer, Stella Pachidi, and Karla Sayegh. "Working and organizing in the age of the learning algorithm." *Information and Organization* 28, no. 1 (2018): 62–70.

47 Kampf, Constance E., and Oludotun Kayode Fashakin. "The social responsibility of AI: A framework for considering ethics and DEI." *Public Relations for Social Responsibility: Affirming DEI Commitment with Action*, pp.121–133. Emerald Publishing Limited, 2021.

4

ARTIFICIAL INTELLIGENCE AND STAKEHOLDER ENGAGEMENT IN PUBLIC RELATIONS

Industry Promises, Potential Pitfalls and a Proposed Framework for a Path Forward

Nathan Gilkerson and Rebecca Swenson

Learning Objectives

1. Understand how artificial intelligence (AI) tools are being utilized for communication monitoring, stakeholder listening, and relationships within the public relations industry.
2. Be able to describe the relationship building process and related concepts.
3. Recognize strategic implications and ethical concerns related to using AI for higher-level relationship purposes.

Introduction

The spring of 2023 saw an unprecedented barrage of news stories written about artificial intelligence (AI) technology and the rise of AI-driven software tools such as OpenAI's ChatGPT "large language model" generative chatbot program. Suddenly, it seemed as if nearly all industries were grappling with how AI technologies would dramatically change the workplace, introduce new efficiencies and skill-set expectations, and shift (or even eliminate) day-to-day duties of employees. Within the field of public relations (PR), numerous articles were written about the oncoming revolution – and industry associations were quick to offer seminars, webinars, and conference training opportunities to professionals looking to understand and leverage new AI tools.[1,2]

Despite this "media moment" for AI within broader society, using AI tools within public relations and strategic communication was nothing new. For several years, scholars had been writing about how AI tools were already "transforming"[3] the industry, and would cause strategic disruption within communication,

DOI: 10.4324/9781032671482-6

for both the business of public relations and the tactical-level activities of its practitioners.[4] Until recently, with the explosion of interest in generative chatbot tools, the sector of public relations most closely associated with AI-driven technology was the communication measurement and evaluation (M&E) space. A 2020 doctoral dissertation focused on AI use within public relations listed categories such as audience intelligence, social listening, social media management, and monitoring as among the top applications the new technology could offer the field.[5]

The rise of user-friendly and ubiquitous generative tools, including ChatGPT and Microsoft's CoPilot (formerly Bing Chat), which assist users with the efficient production of written text, as well as the creation of original images, videos and audio clips, has undoubtedly shifted the potential utility of AI technologies for public relations professionals, from a focus mostly on monitoring and listening (i.e., social media sentiment analysis, aggregation of news coverage) to also include significant opportunities for content creation and creative development uses. Furthermore, advances in natural language processing (NLP) technologies and sophisticated conversational chatbot applications, which can instantly respond to requests, answer user questions, and generally mimic human interactions, have meant public relations and communication professionals have new (technology-enabled) prospects for approaching the formation and maintenance of relationships with publics – and, arguably, engaging with key stakeholders, but doing so "at scale" with customized messaging and tracking capabilities.

This notion that AI tools, which are already being deployed widely throughout many industries, may serve to transform the practice of public relations requires a thoughtful examination of both potential theoretical implications and, importantly, ethical considerations for how practitioners might understand and approach the use of these technologies. First, through reporting on the content analysis findings, this research aims to provide a foundational overview of how AI-based technology providers have described the "challenges solved" and the "benefits realized" which are linked to their communication-focused services. Unsurprisingly, these identified messages are inherently optimistic, aligned with their business goal to promote and sell AI services to different facets of the communication industry.

Second, key themes and noteworthy findings will be reported from a series of in-depth interviews conducted with leading public relations executives and communication technology and measurement experts to provide a more nuanced and balanced representation. Recognizing the central role of *relationships* to the profession, interviews specifically probe practitioners' perspectives regarding the potential for AI to be used for relationships and stakeholder engagement – and the notion that AI can be broadly employed to improve stakeholder communication. Striking quotes highlight both hopeful and optimistic expectations, as well as deeply held concerns and reservations, felt toward leveraging AI tools for these types of public relations objectives. An existing theoretical model of the progression of relationship building and stakeholder engagement, first to be discussed in the literature review, will then be revisited and re-imagined, but within this new context of AI-based tools being leveraged for communication purposes. Considering the potential applications for AI tools within stakeholder engagement, and the myriad of possible strategic pitfalls and negative ethical implications linked to these approaches, an updated framework for navigating the use of AI technologies to support relationship building and stakeholder engagement will be proposed.

Literature Review

AI Within Public Relations

Positioning the technology within the broader history of communication, scholars have traced the earliest use of the term "artificial intelligence" to the mid-1950s.[6] Noting academic discussions of artificial intelligence can range from highly abstract and theory-focused, to more pragmatic, practical and engineering-based, a decade ago Frankish and Ramsey broadly defined AI as "a cross-disciplinary approach to understanding, modeling, and creating intelligence and cognitive processes by invoking various computational, mathematical, logical, mechanical and even biological principles and devices" (p. 1).[7] Public relations scholars have applied several definitions for AI, within communication contexts, often referencing specific technological advances, including NLP, natural language generation (NLG), machine learning, and semantic reasoning.[8,9] In their early study exploring ways in which the emerging technology might specifically affect the public relations industry, Galloway and Swiatek conceptualized AI as: "technologies showing humanoid cognitive abilities and performing humanoid functions in undertaking public relations activities, independently or together with public relations practitioners" (p. 735).[10] This notion that AI tools can work either "independently" or *with* public relations professionals relates to a common understanding among scholars and practitioners that the technology can be employed to *replace*, or to *supplement*, human labor (focused on communication work), often in the form of task automation.[11]

Published in 2019, a paper by Geetanjali Panda and colleagues examined the various specialty roles AI could play within public relations. Through interviews with a large group of industry experts, they identified several broad categories whereby AI technologies could be applied to traditional public relations tasks, including: data-based campaign design (such as the customization and personalization of user and customer communications), tactical-level office duty automation (such as day-to-day scheduling and meeting note taking), data-based insight generation (including analysis of social media trends and web site traffic), identification and tailoring of content for online influencers, social media monitoring and real-time crisis response (via social listening tools and triggered alerts and response messages), and media coverage monitoring, measurement and reporting.[12] A key theme throughout the exploration of potential applications for AI tools identified by Panda and colleagues was the creation of efficiencies, such as saving time (on "mundane activities" like media list creation) and the increase in (faster) responsiveness by public relations practitioners.

In 2020, through work supported by the University of Southern California's Center for Public Relations, Ardila compiled a comprehensive directory and typology of strategic communication industry technology vendors, including their various AI-driven service offerings.[13] Providing an overview of the communication technology landscape, Ardila's survey of the field categorized dozens of unique vendors into broad service areas, including: audience intelligence/social listening, social media management and monitoring, influencer relationship management, content creation, conversational bots, news dissemination and syndication, customer relationship management, and marketing automation.

Both scholars and professional organizations have employed a wide lens in describing the AI adoption trend. A seminal industry report, published in 2018 by the Chartered Institute of Public Relations (CIPR), broadly defined AI as a "sophisticated application of technology whereby a machine demonstrates human cognitive functions such as learning, analysis and problem solving" (p. 5),[14] while also asserting that key human-derived skills – such as critical thinking, creativity, and ethical reasoning – were essential and could *not* be replaced by AI. The CIPR report delineated five ascending levels of (then) current and anticipated AI tool sophistication, ranging from basic language and software "assistants" (Level 1); to applications like social listening and monitoring services, including sentiment analysis products (Level 2); to task automation and content creation tools (Level 3); to more "advanced" applications of machine intelligence utilizing both structured and unstructured data, such as conversational chatbots, and automated software tasked with things like filtering and analyzing raw data, creating reports and drafting original content (Levels 4–5).[15]

Noteworthy, the initial CIPR report designated several communication areas – including legal and ethical responsibilities – as "Zero AI" categories, arguing that those areas would generally always require "high human aspects associated with judgment, interpretation and experience" and asserting that "fundamental human traits such as empathy, trust, humour and relationship building can't be automated – at least not yet" (p. 7).[16] In the years since its original report, CIPR has published nine additional industry resources, including comprehensive updates on AI tool advancements, and data ethics guides, as part of its "#AIinPR Panel" initiative.[17] The most recent report, titled "Humans Needed, More Than Ever," continued to echo the original publication's perspective regarding certain higher-level public relations activity: "Work that requires judgement, a

consideration of context, human empathy and nuanced ethical judgement is neither reducible to defined tasks, nor amenable to AI."[18]

Scholars have grappled with the theoretical implications of advanced "communicative" AI tools (such as chatbots and automated-writing software), noting
that while communication has traditionally been conceptualized (in academic
theory) as a *human* process – which in certain contexts may be mediated by, or
through, technology – advances in AI tools have highlighted the importance of
human–machine communication (HMC), a field of scholarship which studies
the "creation of meaning among humans and machines" (p. 1).[19] Guzman and
Lewis note that, "what sets HMC apart is its focus on people's interactions with
technologies designed as communicative subjects, instead of mere interactive
objects" (p. 71).[20] In their analysis of potential theoretical implications presented by advances in AI, Guzman and Lewis outline what they call "the relational aspects of AI as communicator" (p. 77), and explore how the technology
impacts perceptions of both social roles and relationships. This area of research
examines aspects like "power dynamics between people and technology" and
the social implications of people's interactions with human-*like* technologies
(p. 78).[21]

Communication management scholars in Europe have conducted interview-
based research exploring practitioners' perspectives regarding AI and its use
within the communication industry, including perceived challenges and risks
associated with adopting the technology.[22] In their study, Zerfass and colleagues
note previous scholarship has concluded "the ability to build trusted relationships with stakeholders" is one of the "key competencies" which separates
human practitioners from machines (p. 379).[23] This notion closely echoes the
sentiment expressed by authors of the CIPR reports, who designated "relationship building" as a uniquely human endeavor unconducive to AI.

Perhaps in direct contrast to this sentiment, more recently public relations
scholars have examined the dynamics of AI-enabled "chatbot social conversations" and how corporate sponsored chatbot tools can serve to influence users'
perceptions of the corporate character of a sponsoring organization. Noting that
their research deviates from previous academic scholarship focused on chatbot technology primarily as a utilitarian customer service tool, a 2023 study by
Men and colleagues examines "the relational implications of chatbots" and the
technology's potential for conveying "social presence and conversational human
voice" to help support organizational-public relationships.[24] Elaborating on this
concept, the authors write:

> Acting as the communicative delegates of their organizations, AI-enabled
> social chatbots disrupt the traditional one-to-many model of public com-
> munication and create an intimate environment that resembles one-on-one
> interpersonal communication. Those conversations naturally reflect the

personification approach and can change stakeholder perceptions of corporate character, consequently impacting corporate-level relational outcomes.

This perspective – that AI tools can serve to influence things like the perceived "character" of a corporation, and the relationships individuals can understand themselves as having with organizations – harkens back to the meaning-creation concept (between humans and machines, and by extension, within public relations contexts, between humans and the organizations with which they interact and communicate) theorized by Guzman.

The use of so-called "AI-empowered" social chatbots has recently been described as "the new frontier for relationship management, enabling large-scale interpersonal communication between corporations and publics" (p. 2).[25,26] Other recent scholarship has demonstrated how the human-like conversation capabilities of sophisticated chatbots can affect stakeholders' perceptions of an organization, potentially signaling a relationship-oriented approach to users.[27,28] As the rise of AI tools force public relations practice to evolve, scholars should consider new interpretations of foundational concepts such as relationship building, an area explored in the following subsection.

Relationship Building and Stakeholder Engagement Theory

Relationship building has been a central theme in public relations practice, research, and identity over the last several decades.[29] In 1984, Ferguson argued that relationships should be central to public relations scholarship.[30] By 2010, Pasadeos and colleagues found that the most cited theories in public relations scholarship were Excellence Theory and Relationship Management Theory, which both emphasize the organization-public relationship as central to effective stakeholder engagement.[31] Excellence Theory and Relationship Management Theory are often viewed as more ethical approaches to organizational communication – ones that move public relations practice away from persuasion and publicity stunts, and toward stakeholder engagement that considers the wants, needs, and expectations of publics.[32]

Technology advances, including more widespread interactive tools and the explosion of social media, have accelerated use of terms like relationships and engagement as organizations and stakeholders are increasingly able to have back-and-forth interactions online.[33] The prevalence of relationship theory and the ability to have conversation-like communication between stakeholders and large corporations has driven a focus on mutually beneficial relationships as a central concept for research and defining public relations practice.[34] For example, the Public Relations Student Society of America (PRSSA) currently prioritizes relationships in their definition of public relations as "a strategic communication process that builds mutually beneficial relationships between organizations and their publics."[35]

Despite the prevalence of relationship theory and focus on engagement, there are still challenges describing the process of relationship building, clearly defining related terms like engagement or dialogue, understanding boundaries between interpersonal and organizational communication, and implementing concepts into practice. Some scholars have argued that the gulf between interpersonal and organizational conversations is too wide.[36] For example, Coombs & Holladay argued that applying concepts like relationship building and mutuality from interpersonal communication to public relations is problematic.[37] Public relations research and practice does not account for the value of close relationships for publics, how identities might affect the formation of close relationships, or the parasocial nature of organization–public relationships.[38] Instead, Coombs and Holladay wrote, the value of weak and parasocial connections should be the focus for public relations scholarship and practice.[39]

Similarly, Stoker and Tusinski suggested that scholars move away from concepts based on reciprocal communication like dialogue – as it creates unrealistic and paternalistic expectations for organizational communication, in which selectivity and quid pro quo relationships could be prioritized – and instead they suggested more focus on situations when dissemination-based approaches to communication might be more ethical than dialogue.[40] While Wang and Yang offered a more hopeful view of relationship building and found evidence of some dialogic communication behaviors by organizations on Twitter, the platform now known as X, they too have called for additional work to reconsider dialogic theory, revamp dialogic measures, and refine connections with public engagement in order for these concepts to remain relevant, especially in the context of advancing social and digital technologies.[41]

One approach to better understanding the process of relationship building and effective stakeholder engagement has been to clearly define related terms.[42] Anderson and colleagues offered a co-creational model for engagement and dialogue, which clarified concepts important to relationship building, operationalized concepts for practice, and set boundary conditions.[43] The co-creational model illustrated that relationship initiation, responsiveness, and interactivity are important building blocks for ongoing engagement or dialogue.[44] *Dialogue,* which is at the top of the co-creational model,[45] is ongoing, ethical communication focused on problem solving and characterized by high levels of openness, understanding, listening, and change.[46] Dialogue principles include mutuality, propinquity, empathy, risk, and commitment.[47] *Engagement* is the motivation to participate in a series of ongoing exchanges, with relationship building as the intended focus; in some cases, this concept also sits at the top of the co-creational model as a desired outcome.[48] Engagement is connected to trust, satisfaction, loyalty, and satisfaction.[49] *Interactivity* is "the degree to which a communication technology can create a mediated environment in which participants can communicate (one-to-one, one-to-many, and many-to-many) both synchronously and asynchronously, and participate in reciprocal message exchanges."[50] The co-creational model conceptualized interactivity as three or more messages that are related to one another and sent between the same parties (Figure 4.1).[51] *Responsiveness* is a one-time first response sent in reaction to an initial message.[52] Responsiveness can have both positive and negative consequences – often governed by timeliness and relevance – and is characterized by willingness and ability to respond.[53] Anderson and colleagues also suggested adding a new concept before responsiveness called *relationship initiation*, a largely unexplored concept in literature, which recognizes the initial communication or outreach, which can be kicked-off by either party.[54]

This work to add clarity to terms and the process of relationship building is a helpful step in strengthening both research and practice. However, as technology and communication platforms continue to advance, scholars need to also focus on how new tools like AI could force practitioners and researchers to reconsider the foundational concepts, processes, and ethical management of organizational relationships.

Content Analysis Findings

RQ1: Potential Communication Challenges Solved and Benefits Realized by AI?

Building upon the previously referenced scholarship focused on AI use within the public relations profession, a content analysis was first conducted by systematically examining the websites of more than 40 different AI technology vendor organizations. In order to narrow the universe of potential company sites, the analysis utilized an existing glossary and typology of industry vendors compiled by Ardila.[55] The analysis specifically assessed how companies were messaging and framing both the potential *challenges solved* and *benefits realized* through the application of their proprietary AI communication tools. The analysis considered common terminologies, service descriptions, promises (of AI tools) within promoted use cases, and client testimonials provided on vendor-owned publicly facing sites.

Five common themes were identified in how AI vendor and communication technology services companies were describing the challenges (overcame) and benefits (offered/promised) through their AI services. These messaging themes within AI tool and communication software marketing included: the need to navigate cluttered environments and the ability to adapt to fast-paced information exchanges, the need to increase efficiencies with

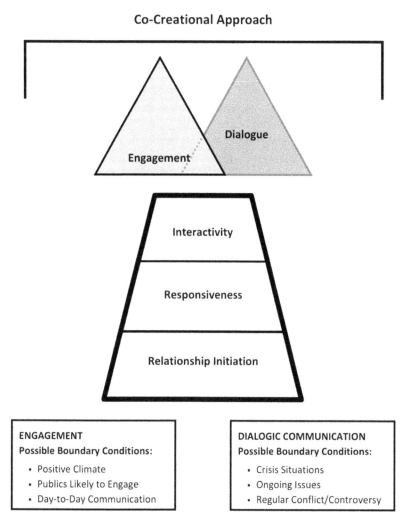

FIGURE 4.1   The co-creational model conceptualized interactivity as three or more messages that are related to one another and sent between the same parties; the authors have added "relationship initiation" to the model, which recognizes the initial communication or outreach

internal resources, overcoming difficulties with understanding consumers and their needs, the need to be nimble, and the pressure to grow the bottom line of the business. The research outlines nuances within each of these themes and presents quoted examples from real-world AI technology vendors, which illustrate their relevance.

Need to Navigate Cluttered, Fast-Paced Information Environments

Case studies described the huge volume of content, conversation, and data that organizations need to monitor today, amidst quickly shifting competitive landscapes. This creates a demand for speed, control, and attention. Jennifer Rice, the Director of Customer Strategy and Analytics at The Body Shop, illustrates this theme in her testimonial for Brandwatch, "What really unlocked things for us was making earned mentions a key metric for brand success. If we know that brand buzz is one of our challenges then being able to measure whether people are talking about us is key."[56]

Also, organizations must balance consistent narratives with hyper-targeted content when managing large social machines. AI was framed as a tool for building organizational strategy that is informed by actionable evidence, as emphasized in this quote from Alexei Edwards, Head of Engagement Marketing at Bang & Olufsen: "The intelligence generated by CreatorIQ has enabled us to be braver and more bold in our decision making; It has therefore empowered us to expand our approaches into a variety of different programs, and the increased transparency has enabled us to better optimize as we test + learn."[57]

According to the case studies, AI's major benefits include better decision making, deeper insights, and the ability to find and connect with influencers.

Need to Increase Efficiencies With Internal Resources

Case studies also described common internal challenges within workplaces, including the need to be more efficient with labor resources, to improve internal workflows, and to control how information is shared across business units. This quote from Eileen Brooker, GVP of Global Corporate Sales, Enablement and Strategy, highlights this efficiency:

> Through all the work we did with Seismic, we were able to surface the right type of information where someone could create a proposal for a customer including pricing, competitive information, customer references in about 10 minutes. And this took them hours before.[58]

Case studies acknowledged that most businesses are facing limited resource pools, increased staff pressure, and a need to scale work more effectively. AI's benefits were often directly connected to overall time and cost savings, as in this quote from Cassandra Brill, Global Head of Digital at SFI Health:

> We're getting a huge volume of content out the door, and that wouldn't be possible without the Welcome platform. Our projects are moving through and getting completed much quicker, and we've even been able to repurpose existing content – the wheel is turning a lot quicker than before.[59]

AI was positioned as a tool that enhanced teamwork, automated tasks, and eased content production, giving internal teams more time.

Difficulties With Understanding Consumers and Their Needs

Case studies on AI vendor web sites acknowledged that it was difficult to understand, connect with, and meet consumers' expectations. Testimonials shared stories about organizations struggling to translate consumer behavior trends, know channel preferences, and understand audience responses to content. AI was framed as a tool that could improve organizational efforts to integrate consumer feedback and response into strategy, increase views on content, refine consumer experiences, and build stronger relationships. Finding authentic consumer interest and engagement was a major outcome of AI tools. These benefits were stressed in the Sprinklr case study: "By layering Benchmarking on top of Listening, we've developed a powerful brand health engine. It allows us to get to the heart of trends and shed light on insights that are otherwise hard to unpack"[60]

Need to Be Nimble

The need to pivot quickly and respond to crisis and disruption was also highlighted with case studies. A major theme was the need to be proactive, anticipate challenges, and navigate change. Enabling leadership to respond with confidence was a common thread in testimonials, as in this quote from Arvind Krishna, Chairman and CEO: "Whenever you go through a crisis, leadership has to come to the top. How do we emerge stronger as a business? Can we change the way we work? Can we make quicker decisions?"[61]

AI was framed as a tool that could help organizations be nimble, keep pace with changing trends, account for new competition, and survive difficult environments. AI benefits included increased exposure, more brand influence, fast responses, more competitive advantage, and a stronger identity that could withstand crisis and change.

Pressure to Grow Business Bottom Line

Almost all case studies acknowledged the need for tools that affect the business bottom line. AI tools were positioned as a way to get additional reach, grow impressions, and improve sales. Metrics used to support this theme ranged from page views and impressions to website traffic, adoption rates, and sales figures.

These broad insights on the messaging promoted by vendors within the AI technology industry were used to help inform a series of qualitative interviews, conducted with communication experts to probe and further explore the uses of AI in the field.

Expert Interview Findings

RQ2: How Do Leading Communication Experts View the Role of AI in Relationship Building and Stakeholder Engagement?

In-depth interviews were conducted (via Teams and Zoom) with a targeted group of leading communication and technology practitioners to gain a nuanced understanding of industry perspectives toward AI's role in public relations, specifically the building of relationships and promotion of stakeholder engagement. Interview participants were first recruited from a list of "25 Rising Stars of Communications Measurement" honorees chosen by the International Association for Measurement and Evaluation of Communication (AMEC), a leading industry body made up of M&E vendors and consultants. Beyond members of this group, several additional interviews were also conducted with known experts in the field of public relations technology, including the author of a recently published book on the topic.[62]

Interviews, which took place *before* the spring of 2023 (when public interest in generative AI technologies spiked), probed experts' perspectives on the current and future state of AI within the PR field, and specifically its application within M&E contexts. Interestingly, many interviewees believed that while some within the industry were embracing AI technologies, many organizations were seen as trailing (or lagging) behind other sectors; most interviewees viewed their own companies as still "early" in AI use and adoption. Conversations examined an expected move toward more sophisticated AI tools, specifically the utilization of unstructured (vs. structured) data, including improved applications for rich text, email content, video, audio, and images. Expert interviews also discussed educational needs, within current university communication curricula, for effectively utilizing AI tools, including not just practitioners' data skills, but also increased focus on strategy, creativity, emotional intelligence, and relationships. Additionally, interviews explored experts' views regarding "AI anxiety" and potential ethical concerns of utilizing AI-based technology.

Several interviews conveyed that, especially in regard to AI-based "listening" and social media and news monitoring tools (including sentiment analysis and text/language interpretation products), current capabilities were relatively limited in their true efficacy, with the value of monitoring technologies often being over-hyped and exaggerated by technology vendors. One participant claimed that "many of these companies that claim artificial intelligence are in fact B.S.-ing everybody," in their overselling of software capabilities. A common theme, when probing interviewees regarding the sophistication of existing AI-based communications tools, was a need for a "hybrid" – or a "machines *plus* humans" – approach to utilizing the technologies. One interviewee, discussing existing media monitoring tools, noted "you need humans to have accuracy" and that heavy human "curation" was still typically required. Another participant discussed the need to constantly "refine algorithms," particularly in regard to AI tools' language processing abilities, especially when focused on complex or ambiguous topics like humor, sarcasm, and satire. With refinement, however, the interviewee expressed an optimistic expectation that gathered data and insights would become more and more precise over time.

Most interviewees discussed the capacity for AI tools to boost efficiencies and the speed of workflow, and to assist in achieving communication efforts *at scale*, when the natural limitations of human effort and energy would otherwise make such activities impossible. "Obviously you can't talk to everybody at the same time." said one participant, highlighting the capacity for AI tools to independently communicate broadly with publics. Several participants echoed the notion that AI tools helped "reduce the manual lift," and helped create more time to focus attention on intelligence, insights, and strategy components of their communication activities. Several interviewees highlighted specialized AI tools' capabilities for predictive risk analytics and "modeling," and real-time (social media monitoring) crisis "alert triggers" and warnings. Multiple participants referenced AI tools being used for crisis simulation exercises. One interviewee described how major companies' risk management departments, often housed *outside* of traditional communication-focused areas of the organization, were utilizing AI tools to analyze large datasets to assess the probability of a potential crisis.

Specific to the topic of relationship building and stakeholder engagement, interviewees were asked the question: "Do you see AI impacting relationship building – and how will AI impact internal and external stakeholders?" Responses to the notion that AI tools could engage in relationships were varied, but overall dismissive, from most participants. Several interviewees conveyed a belief that AI could successfully engage in "lower-level" relational communication activities, such as providing users with "quick information that people are looking for." One interviewee explained that AI tools could be used successfully at this lower level, such as in the basic exchange of information, since people are not necessarily expecting authenticity. In contrast, however, describing a potential crisis scenario (or other situation threatening "negative perceptions of the brand"), the interviewee said, "I think on *that* level, AI isn't really going to be able to offer that kind of authenticity and transparency that you need to really build a real relationship, for like, those high level issues."

This perspective was shared by numerous participants, who conveyed similar beliefs that AI tools could be effective in identifying and initiating potential relationships – but not for maintaining a deeper relationship, or for detecting or conveying important "human-specific" nuances within communication. One interviewee said:

> I can't say based on experience. But, I certainly see that AI will have an impact in relationship building. AI can to a certain extent help in providing an initial

recommendation based on historical pattern, which may detect a profile. This can be a first recommendation whether to pursue to form a relationship. However, one should also be cautious that there are certain human-specific sentiment, nuances and dynamics that AI cannot detect. Hence, in this instance, AI can provide the initial data, but the human factor should still be the influence in maintaining the relationship.

Another participant described AI's capabilities as being ideal for transactional relationship maintenance tasks, but echoed the sentiment that *humans* were needed for more important relationship exchanges.

Right now, I look at AI as sort of "algorithms on steroids" and I'm thinking, OK, so algorithms on steroids can optimize transactional relationships. So they can do a lot of that. And they can also be really, really good at collecting lots and lots of data, processing lots and lots of data, and probably cleaning data according to another algorithm that runs somewhere.

But all of that stuff that needs to be given to humans, to do human stuff with, and understand and interpret relationships, and understand and interpret the purpose of relationships, desired outcomes, how different stakeholders are being impacted . . . . And, you know, . . . humans need to do that. Humans need to do that with other humans.

This same participant, who conveyed a sophisticated understanding of AI concepts (like machine learning and algorithm development), stressed a strong view that by relying on AI too much for higher-level relationship maintenance and stakeholder engagement communication activities, practitioners could risk doing "damage" to the field of public relations.

Referring to the widespread adoption of AI tools, and a concern that embracing AI hype and the promotion of AI for relationship management purposes "undervalues and misjudges the complexity of communication," the interviewee argued:

I think it's for transactional relationships and that there is a place for PR to do that, and in that context, there's also a place for AI. So think of something like helpline responses, based on standardized responses. Even, even learning from practice on those standardized responses. And machine learning can help with that. So, you know, then it gets better and better at its task, but it will always, for me, be limited to that task.

So it will never veer into the sort of, the complexity and uncertainty of, you know, human communication based on emotional stuff where "love and hate and fear and trust" and you know, whatever . . . . All these sorts of things really come into play. That's not what that software can do. But it can, if somebody needs a specific, you know, structured answer in the context of working with their financial institution, or insurance or doctor even . . . there's a lot that AI can do on that level. And, that for me also falls into the field of public relations.

But where we go deeper into "purpose of organizations," and *relating* to people, there I think we need to be really, really careful how much we promise in the AI field, and what's actually doable. For me, that's really, really stupid because, you know, deep human sentiments, emotions, interactions between (people) . . . that doesn't fall into that (area). That's not the same as real emotions. So there's a place where AI can help and there's a place where, I think, the current AI thinking and the current AI hype does a lot of damage.

The interviewee went on to argue that calls concerning ethics, and the application of AI tools within communication contexts, "can't be made by software engineers," and instead must be navigated and negotiated by a combination of academic leaders and government regulators. Expanding on concerns regarding over-promise and hype linked to AI, the participant argued that many applications of AI tools created what he considered to be "the opposite of relationship building." The interview's full quote follows.

And my concern with PR right now is that in the field there's a lot of hype and sort of over-promise and technocrats are you know they're looking for frictionless automated solutions. And that for me in many ways, that's partly the answer to your question, is [that] those frictionless automated solutions are the opposite of relationship building, because I have a slightly perhaps romantic, idealistic view of communication and what constitutes relationships amongst humans. I don't think AI can do that.

Echoing the themes highlighted within the previously referenced CIPR reports, which contend that higher-level relationship aspects should *not* be the undertaking of AI tools, the sentiments conveyed here show the angst felt by many public relations leaders regarding misuse of AI tools in the industry.

A Proposed Theoretical Model of AI-Enabled Organizational–Public Relationships

Anderson and colleagues' co-creational model for engagement and dialogue provides a foundation for examining the progression of relationships within public relations.[63] The model offered definitions, operationalizations, and boundary conditions for five key concepts related to organization-public relationships: *relationship initiation, responsiveness*, and *interactivity* are important building blocks, and can serve to contribute to ongoing *engagement* or *dialogue*.[64] Using these five concepts as a foundation, the model described in what follows offers a new proposed theoretical framework for evaluating the progression of

TABLE 4.1 How AI Technologies Can Support Relationship Building and Stakeholder Engagement

Low-Stakes Situations ↔				*High-Stakes Situations*	
Relationship Initiation ↑	*Responsiveness* ↑	*Interactivity* ↑	*Engagement* ↑		*Dialogue*
Description Research occurs before relationship is initiated, learning about audience and environment	One-time exchange between parties	At least three exchanges, sent between parties that are related to each other	A motivation for both parties to participate in ongoing communication in an environment with relationship building potential (leading to trust and satisfaction, supportive behavioral intentions)		Ongoing communication events, with the purpose of solving a problem or issue – where both parties listen and change; issues management and crisis response, community relations
AI tech's role Sentiment analysis, influencer identification; social listening, media monitoring, campaign design, target identification	Transactional chatbots, automated customer service tools	Generative AI content creation tools	Ongoing dashboard monitoring of trust, reputation, and satisfaction; issues and crisis alerts		Proactive crisis simulator training and preparation
AI's promises Navigate cluttered environment, increase efficiencies	Respond in fastpaced environments	Understand individual consumers and their needs	Nimble decision making		Scalable conversations with stakeholders
Ethical considerations Minimal concerns with human interpretation, consequential decisions	May harm expectations of brand, authenticity – use caution	Need to provide transparency of AI tool use – gauge if appropriate	AI tools like sentiment detection, etc., different than responding to human emotion		AI lacks authenticity and ability to navigate nuance
Recommendations for AI Utilization					
AI is highly useful/appropriate	AI tools *possibly* applicable				Human touch/judgement required

AI-enabled organizational-public relationships. This model conceptualizes and creates guideposts to account for ethically managing organizational–public relationships in a context of increasingly sophisticated generative AI tools.

The model separates low and high stakes situations for using AI tools to build relationships, with relationship initiation anchoring the low stakes category and dialogue (at the other end of the spectrum) anchoring the high stakes category. The model connects the stages of relationship building described in the co-creational model of Anderson and colleagues for engagement and dialogue[65] to current AI tools, AI promises, and ethical considerations. For example, the model suggests that AI tools like sentiment analysis, influencer identification, social listening, media monitoring, and target identification might be useful for relationship initiation. Further, leveraging these AI tools for relationship initiation might allow practitioners to realize some of the promises that technology companies have made, including AI's ability to help navigate cluttered environments, save time, and increase efficiency. The model indicates that there is likely little risk of using AI for relationship initiation, especially when use is partnered with human interpretation and the involvement of communication experts in any resulting consequential decisions. At the other end of the model, with concepts like engagement and dialogue, AI tools may still be appropriate for things like issue monitoring and crisis training, and these tools can help practitioners be more responsive and more nimble with decision making. However, within these higher levels of relationship building and stakeholder engagement, AI tools might not accurately detect sentiment and can lack the ability to navigate the nuance and complexity connected to human emotion. As such, it is risky (and arguably often ill-advised) to use AI tools without high levels of human touch and judgment.

Conclusion

The utilization of artificial intelligence (AI) within public relations (PR) is here to stay, and applications for the technology within the industry will undoubtedly only increase moving forward. The proposed model provides some structure for conceptualizing the use of this technology and for determining in what capacities AI tools might be most helpful and appropriate – and when AI may be less useful or could even become a liability. The model presumes a progression, or evolution, of the dynamic process of relationship building, and outlines key elements that are typically essential to stakeholder engagement. Technology can play a role in relationships, and AI tools can boost public relations practitioners' overall efficiency and their ability to listen to stakeholder concerns and communicate customized messages at scale. However, as the model outlines, communication with stakeholders varies based on the point in which it takes place within the relationship process, and the goals or subject matter of the communication itself. The successful and ethical use of AI depends on these variables.

A couple of cautionary examples demonstrate ways in which AI use can cause harm, in perhaps unexpected ways, and be perceived as intrusive, inauthentic, and insensitive by key publics. Both cases demonstrate that no matter where within the spectrum of the model the communication task falls, it is still necessary to maintain a level of human judgment in decision making in regard to AI and relationship maintenance. The first example, which occurred more than a decade ago, involves negative media coverage focused on the big box retailer Target and the company's utilization of sophisticated predictive analytics tools focused on shoppers' historical purchasing data in order to create a "pregnancy prediction" score used to target individual customers with customized coupon offers and advertising information. Stories highlighted the anecdote of a teenage girl receiving Target mailings at her family's home for things like baby clothes, based on purchases she had recently made, before she had told her parents she was pregnant.[66] Major news outlets reported on the controversy, with a story in the *New York Times* describing the public as feeling "queasy" (p. 437) toward such perceived invasions of privacy, and the risks of potential "public-relations disasters" (p. 439) that companies could face in the use of such targeting technology.[67]

The second example, which occurred early in 2023, during a time when media attention was highly focused on the recently released ChatGPT chatbot tool, involved public outrage directed at faculty administrators of Vanderbilt University. Community members there had noticed an email sent out to students – a heartfelt message of solidarity, intended to console and provide reassurances to the university community in the wake of a recent mass shooting at another university – was tagged with a marker indicating that the communication had been written using ChatGPT.[68] International headlines reported students at Vanderbilt describing the use of AI in this context of tragedy as "disgusting," with one quote, directed at university leaders, imploring, "Deans, provosts, and the chancellor: do more. Do anything. And lead us into a better future with genuine, human empathy, not a robot."[69] Clearly the use of AI is inappropriate and potentially damaging in certain contexts. However, when applied thoughtfully, the technology also offers communicators great promise. The apology letter sent to the Vanderbilt community by leaders aptly noted, "this moment gives us all an opportunity to reflect on what we know and what we still must learn about AI."

Reflections

1. AI tools are increasingly being used by organizations for day-to-day interactions with customers, employees, and other stakeholders. How should public relations professionals determine when utilizing AI for relationships is

reasonable, and when it may be viewed as inappropriate, inauthentic, or even unethical?
2. What considerations or guardrails should practitioners implement when applying AI tools for relationship building and management, in consideration of relationship building models or stages of interaction?

Notes

1 "Generative AI for PR counselors." PRSA, accessed June 21, 2023.
2 "Lies, damned lies, and ChatGPT." Page Society Spring Seminar, accessed April 13, 2023.
3 Ardila, Manuelita Maldonado. "The rise of intelligent machines: how artificial intelligence is transforming the public relations industry." *Unpublished master thesis, University of Southern California* (2020).
4 Panda, Geetanjali, Ashwani Kumar Upadhyay, and Komal Khandelwal. "Artificial intelligence: A strategic disruption in public relations." *Journal of Creative Communications* 14, no. 3 (2019): 196–213.
5 Ardila, Manuelita Maldonado. "The rise of intelligent machines: how artificial intelligence is transforming the public relations industry." *Unpublished master thesis, University of Southern California* (2020).
6 Paolo, Bory, Simone Natale, and Trudel Dominique. "Artificial intelligence: Reframing thinking machines within the history of communication." In *Historicizing Media and Communication Concepts of the Digital Age*, pp. 95–113. De Gruyter, 2021.
7 Frankish, Keith, and William M. Ramsey, eds. *The Cambridge handbook of artificial intelligence*. Cambridge University Press, 2014.
8 Zerfass, Ansgar, Jens Hagelstein, and Ralph Tench. "Artificial intelligence in communication management: a cross-national study on adoption and knowledge, impact, challenges and risks." *Journal of Communication Management* 24, no. 4 (2020): 377–389.
9 Guzman, Andrea L., and Seth C. Lewis. "Artificial intelligence and communication: A human – machine communication research agenda." *New Media & Society* 22, no. 1 (2020): 70–86.
10 Galloway, Chris, and Lukasz Swiatek. "Public relations and artificial intelligence: It's not (just) about robots." *Public Relations Review* 44, no. 5 (2018): 734–740.
11 Men, Linjuan Rita, Alvin Zhou, Jie Jin, and Patrick Thelen. "Shaping corporate character via chatbot social conversation: Impact on organization-public relational outcomes." *Public Relations Review* 49, no. 5 (2023): 102385
12 Panda, Geetanjali, Ashwani Kumar Upadhyay, and Komal Khandelwal. "Artificial intelligence: A strategic disruption in public relations." *Journal of Creative Communications* 14, no. 3 (2019): 196–213.
13 Ardila, Manuelita Maldonado. "The rise of intelligent machines: how artificial intelligence is transforming the public relations industry." *Unpublished master thesis, University of Southern California* (2020).
14 Valin, J. "Humans still needed – An analysis of skills and tools in public relations. London: Chartered Institute of Public Relations." (2018).
15 Valin, "Humans still needed – An analysis of skills and tools in public relations. London: Chartered Institute of Public Relations."
16 Valin, "Humans still needed – An analysis of skills and tools in public relations. London: Chartered Institute of Public Relations."
17 AI in PR Guides. CIPR. www.cipr.co.uk/CIPR/Our_work/Policy/AI_in_PR_/AI_in_PR_guides.aspx?WebsiteKey=0379ffac-bc76-433c-9a94-56a04331bf64.

18 Humans Needed, More Than Ever. CIPR. www.strategic-hq.com/wp-content/up-loads/2023/09/CIPR_Humans-Needed_Report_A4_v8_Accessible.pdf.

19 Guzman,AndreaL."Whatishuman-machinecommunication,anyway."*Human-Machine Communication: Rethinking Communication, Technology, and Ourselves* (2018): 1–28.

20 Guzman, Andrea L., and Seth C. Lewis. "Artificial intelligence and communication: A human – machine communication research agenda." *New Media & Society* 22, no. 1 (2020): 70–86.

21 Guzman, Andrea L., and Seth C. Lewis. "Artificial intelligence and communication: A human – machine communication research agenda."

22 Zerfass, Ansgar, Jens Hagelstein, and Ralph Tench. "Artificial intelligence in communication management: a cross-national study on adoption and knowledge, impact, challenges and risks." *Journal of Communication Management* 24, no. 4 (2020): 377–389.

23 Zerfass, Hagelstein, and Tench. "Artificial intelligence in communication management."

24 Men, Linjuan Rita, Alvin Zhou, Jie Jin, and Patrick Thelen. "Shaping corporate character via chatbot social conversation: Impact on organization-public relational outcomes." *Public Relations Review* 49, no. 5 (2023): 102385.

25 Men, Zhou, Jin, and Thelen. "Shaping corporate character via chatbot social conversation."

26 Zhou, Alvin, Linjuan Rita Men, and Wan-Hsiu Sunny Tsai. "The power of AI-enabled chatbots as an organizational social listening tool." *Organizational Listening for Strategic Communication: Building Theory and Practice* (2023).

27 Cheng, Yang, and Hua Jiang. "Customer – brand relationship in the era of artificial intelligence: understanding the role of chatbot marketing efforts." *Journal of Product & Brand Management* 31, no. 2 (2022): 252–264.

28 Men, L. R., A. Zhou, and W.-H. S. Tsai. "Harnessing the power of chatbot social conversation for organizational listening: The impact on perceived transparency and organization-public relationships." *Journal of Public Relations Research* 34, nos. 1–2 (2022), 20–44. https://doi.org/10.1080/1062726X.2022.2068553

29 Broom, Glen M., Shawna Casey, and James Ritchey. "Toward a concept and theory of organization-public relationships." *Journal of Public relations research* 9, no. 2 (1997): 83.; Coombs, W. Timothy, and Sherry J. Holladay. "Public relations' relationship identity in research: Enlightenment or illusion." *Public Relations Review* 41, no. 5 (2015): 690.

30 Ferguson, Mary Ann. "Building theory in public relations: Interorganizational relationships." In *Annual meeting of the Association for Education in Journalism and Mass Communication, Gainesville, FL* (1984).

31 Pasadeos, Yorgo, Bruce Berger, and R. Bruce Renfro. "Public relations as a maturing discipline: An update on research networks." *Journal of Public Relations Research* 22, no. 2 (2010): 148.

32 Ledingham, John A. "Explicating relationship management as a general theory of public relations." *Journal of Public Relations Research* 15, no. 2 (2003): 194.

33 Coombs, W. Timothy, and Sherry J. Holladay. "Public relations' relationship identity in research: Enlightenment or illusion." *Public Relations Review* 41, no. 5 (2015): 691.

34 Coombs and Holladay, "Public relations' relationship identity in research," 690.

35 "Learn about Public Relations," Public Relations Student Society of America, accessed February 17, 2024. www.prsa.org/prssa/about-prssa/learn-about-pr#:~:text= Public%20relations%2C%20as%20defined%20by,the%20way%20an%20 organization%20is.

36 Coombs and Holladay, "Public relations' relationship identity in research," 691; Stoker, Kevin L., and Kati A. Tusinski. "Reconsidering public relations' infatuation with dialogue: Why engagement and reconciliation can be more ethical than symmetry and reciprocity." *Journal of Mass Media Ethics* 21, no. 2–3 (2006): 156.
37 Coombs and Holladay, "Public relations' relationship identity in research," 691.
38 Coombs and Holladay, "Public relations' relationship identity in research," 691.
39 Coombs and Holladay, "Public relations' relationship identity in research," 691.
40 Stoker, Kevin L., and Kati A. Tusinski. "Reconsidering public relations' infatuation with dialogue: Why engagement and reconciliation can be more ethical than symmetry and reciprocity." *Journal of Mass Media Ethics* 21, no. 2–3 (2006): 156.
41 Wang, Yuan, and Yiyi Yang. "Dialogic communication on social media: How organizations use Twitter to build dialogic relationships with their publics." *Computers in Human Behavior* 104 (2020): 106183.
42 Rawlins, Brad L. "Prioritizing stakeholders for public relations." *Institute for Public Relations* 1 (2006): 14.
43 Anderson, Betsy D., Rebecca Swenson, and Nathan D. Gilkerson. "Understanding dialogue and engagement through communication experts' use of interactive writing to build relationships." *International Journal of Communication* 10 (2016): 4095–4118.
44 Anderson, Swenson, and Gilkerson, "Understanding dialogue and engagement," 4100.
45 Anderson, Swenson, and Gilkerson, "Understanding dialogue and engagement," 4109.
46 Taylor, Maureen, and Michael L. Kent. "Dialogic engagement: Clarifying foundational concepts." *Journal of Public Relations Research* 26, no. 5 (2014): 384–398.
47 Kent, Michael L., and Maureen Taylor. "Toward a dialogic theory of public relations." *Public Relations Review* 28, no. 1 (2002): 21–37.
48 Anderson, Swenson, and Gilkerson, "Understanding dialogue and engagement," 4098.
49 Kang, Minjeong. "Understanding public engagement: Conceptualizing and measuring its influence on supportive behavioral intentions." *Journal of Public Relations Research* 26, no. 5 (2014): 399–416.
50 Kiousis, Spiro. "Interactivity: a concept explication." *New Media & Society* 4, no. 3 (2002): 372.
51 Anderson, Swenson, and Gilkerson, "Understanding dialogue and engagement," 4097.
52 Anderson, Swenson, and Gilkerson, "Understanding dialogue and engagement," 4108.
53 Avidar, Ruth. "The responsiveness pyramid: Embedding responsiveness and interactivity into public relations theory." *Public Relations Review* 39, no. 5 (2013): 442.
54 Anderson, Swenson, and Gilkerson, "Understanding dialogue and engagement," 4100.
55 Ardila, Manuelita Maldonado. "The rise of intelligent machines: how artificial intelligence is transforming the public relations industry." *Unpublished master thesis, University of Southern California* (2020).
56 "Case Study: The Body Shop," Brandwatch, accessed April 20, 2022. www.brandwatch.com/case-studies/.
57 "Bang & Olufson: How visibility into data empowered Bang & Olufson to quickly optimize influencer marketing performance," CreatorIQ, accessed April 21, 2022. www.creatoriq.com/customer-stories.
58 "Informatica: Increases sales velocity and predictability in seller success with seismic," Seismic, accessed April 20, 2022. https://seismic.com/customer-stories/informatica/.
59 "Customer stories: SFI health," WelcomeSoftware, accessed April 20, 2022. https://welcomesoftware.com/customer-stories/customer-success-story-sfi-health/.
60 "How McDonald's uses competitive insights to stay one step ahead," Spinklr, accessed April 21, 2022. www.sprinklr.com/stories/mcdonalds/.
61 "How IBM's collaborative communities build a more vibrant work culture," Salesforce, accessed April 20, 2022. www.salesforce.com/resources/customer-stories/ibm-collaborative-communities-work-culture/?d=cta-header-1.

62 Weiner, Mark. *PR technology, data and insights: Igniting a positive return on your communications investment.* Kogan Page Publishers, 2021.
63 Anderson, Betsy D., Rebecca Swenson, and Nathan D. Gilkerson. "Discussion, dialogue, discourse| Understanding dialogue and engagement through communication experts' use of interactive writing to build relationships." *International Journal of Communication* 10 (2016): 4095–4118.
64 Anderson, Swenson, and Gilkerson, "Understanding dialogue and engagement," 4100.
65 Anderson, Swenson, and Gilkerson, "Understanding dialogue and engagement," 4100.
66 Hill, Kashmir. "How Target figured out a teen girl was pregnant before her father did." *Forbes, Inc* 7 (2012): 4–1.
67 Duhigg, Charles. "How companies learn your secrets." In *The Best Business Writing 2013*, pp. 421–444. Columbia University Press, 2013.
68 Levine, S. "Vanderbilt apologizes for using ChatGPT in email on Michigan shooting." *The Guardian, February* 22 (2023): 2023.
69 Levine, "Vanderbilt apologizes for using ChatGPT in email on Michigan shooting".

Bibliography

Anderson, Betsy D., Rebecca Swenson, and Nathan D. Gilkerson. "Discussion, dialogue, discourse: Understanding dialogue and engagement through communication experts' use of interactive writing to build relationships." *International Journal of Communication* 10 (2016): 4095–4118.
Ardila, Manuelita Maldonado. "The rise of intelligent machines: How artificial intelligence is transforming the public relations industry." *Unpublished master thesis*, University of Southern California (2020).
Avidar, Ruth. "The responsiveness pyramid: Embedding responsiveness and interactivity into public relations theory." *Public Relations Review* 39, no. 5 (2013): 440–450.
Brandwatch. "Case Study: The Body Shop." Accessed April 20, 2022. www.brandwatch.com/case-studies/
Broom, Glen M., Shawna Casey, and James Ritchey. "Toward a concept and theory of organization-public relationships." *Journal of Public Relations Research* 9, no. 2 (1997): 83–98.
Buhmann, Alexander, and Candace L. White. "Artificial intelligence in public relations: Role and implications." In *The Emerald handbook of computer-mediated communication and social media*, pp. 625–638. Emerald Publishing Limited, 2022.
Coombs, W. Timothy, and Sherry J. Holladay. "Public relations 'relationship identity' in research: Enlightenment or illusion." *Public Relations Review* 41, no. 5 (2015): 689–695.
CreatorIQ. "Bang & Olufson: How Visibility into Data Empowered Bang & Olufson to Quickly Optimize Influencer Marketing Performance." Accessed April 21, 2022. www.creatoriq.com/customer-stories
Duhigg, Charles. "How companies learn your secrets." In *The best business writing 2013*, pp. 421–444. Columbia University Press, 2013.
Ferguson, Mary Ann. "Building theory in public relations: Interorganizational relationships." In *Annual Meeting of the Association for Education in Journalism and Mass Communication*, Gainesville, FL (1984).
Frankish, Keith, and William M. Ramsey, eds. *The Cambridge handbook of artificial intelligence*. Cambridge University Press, 2014.
Galloway, Chris, and Lukasz Swiatek. "Public relations and artificial intelligence: It's not (just) about robots." *Public Relations Review* 44, no. 5 (2018): 734–740.
Gilkerson, Nathan David, Rebecca Swenson, and Fraser Likely. "Maturity as a way forward for improving organizations' communication evaluation and measurement

practices: A definition and concept explication." *Journal of Communication Management* 23, no. 3 (2019): 246–264.

Guzman, Andrea L., and Seth C. Lewis. "Artificial intelligence and communication: A human–machine communication research agenda." *New Media & Society* 22, no. 1 (2020): 70–86.

Hill, Kashmir. "How target figured out a teen girl was pregnant before her father did." *Forbes, Inc* 7 (2012): 4–1.

Kent, Michael L., and Maureen Taylor. "Building dialogic relationships through the world wide web." *Public Relations Review* 24, no. 3 (1998): 321–334.

Kent, Michael L., and Maureen Taylor. "Toward a dialogic theory of public relations." *Public Relations Review* 28, no. 1 (2002): 21–37.

Kiousis, Spiro. "Interactivity: A concept explication." *New Media & Society* 4, no. 3 (2002): 355–383.

Ledingham, John A. "Explicating relationship management as a general theory of public relations." *Journal of Public Relations Research* 15, no. 2 (2003): 181–198

Levine, S. "Vanderbilt apologizes for using ChatGPT in email on Michigan shooting." *The Guardian*, February 22 (2023).

Men, Linjuan Rita, Alvin Zhou, Jie Jin, and Patrick Thelen. "Shaping corporate character via chatbot social conversation: Impact on organization-public relational outcomes." *Public Relations Review* 49, no. 5 (2023): 102385.

Page Society Spring Seminar. "Lies, Damned Lies, and ChatGPT." Accessed April 13, 2023. https://page.org/events/2023-page-spring-seminar/sessions

Panda, Geetanjali, Ashwani Kumar Upadhyay, and Komal Khandelwal. "Artificial intelligence: A strategic disruption in public relations." *Journal of Creative Communications* 14, no. 3 (2019): 196–213.

Paolo, Bory, Simone Natale, and Trudel Dominique. "Artificial intelligence: Reframing thinking machines within the history of communication." In *Historicizing media and communication concepts of the digital age*, pp. 95–113. De Gruyter, 2021.

Pasadeos, Yorgo, Bruce Berger, and R. Bruce Renfro. "Public relations as a maturing discipline: An update on research networks." *Journal of Public Relations Research* 22, no. 2 (2010): 136–158.

PRSA. "Generative AI for PR Counselors." Accessed June 21, 2023. www.prsa.org/event/2023/06/21/default-calendar/generative-ai-for-pr-counselors-wbca2301

Public Relations Student Society of America. "Learn about Public Relations." Accessed February 17, 2024. www.prsa.org/prssa/about-prssa/learn-about-pr#:~:text=Public%20relations%2C%20as%20defined%20by,the%20way%20an%20organization%20is

Rawlins, Brad L. "Prioritizing stakeholders for public relations." *Institute for Public Relations* 1 (2006): 14.

Salesforce. "How IBM's Collaborative Communities Build a More Vibrant Work Culture." Accessed April 20, 2022. www.salesforce.com/resources/customer-stories/ibm-collaborative-communities-work-culture/?d=cta-header-1

Seismic. "Informatica: Increases Sales Velocity and Predictability in Seller Success with Seismic." Accessed April 20, 2022. https://seismic.com/customer-stories/informatica/

Sprinklr. "How McDonald's Uses Competitive Insights to Stay One Step Ahead." Accessed April 21, 2022. www.sprinklr.com/stories/mcdonalds/

Stoker, Kevin L., and Kati A. Tusinski. "Reconsidering public relations' infatuation with dialogue: Why engagement and reconciliation can be more ethical than symmetry and reciprocity." *Journal of Mass Media Ethics* 21, no. 2–3 (2006): 156–176.

Swenson, Rebecca, Nathan Gilkerson, Fraser Likely, Forrest W. Anderson, and Michael Ziviani. "Insights from industry leaders: A maturity model for strengthening communication measurement and evaluation." *International Journal of Strategic Communication* 13, no. 1 (2019): 1–21.

Taylor, Maureen, and Michael L. Kent. "Dialogic engagement: Clarifying foundational concepts." *Journal of Public Relations Research* 26, no. 5 (2014): 384–398.

Weiner, Mark. *PR technology, data and insights: Igniting a positive return on your communications investment.* Kogan Page Publishers, 2021.

Weisenburger, Rachel L., Michael C. Mullarkey, Jocelyn Labrada, Daniel Labrousse, Michelle Y. Yang, Allison Huff MacPherson, Kean J. Hsu, Hassan Ugail, Jason Shumake, and Christopher G. Beevers. "Conversational assessment using artificial intelligence is as clinically useful as depression scales and preferred by users." *Journal of Affective Disorders* 351 (2024): 489–498.

WelcomeSoftware. "Customer Stories: SFI Health." Accessed April 20, 2022. https://welcomesoftware.com/customer-stories/customer-success-story-sfi-health/

Zerfass, Ansgar, Jens Hagelstein, and Ralph Tench. "Artificial intelligence in communication management: A cross-national study on adoption and knowledge, impact, challenges and risks." *Journal of Communication Management* 24, no. 4 (2020): 377–389.

5

AI REGULATION AND ETHICAL CONSIDERATIONS SURROUNDING THE USE OF ARTIFICIAL INTELLIGENCE IN PR

The Need for Transparency and Accountability

Marina Vujnovic, Dean Kruckeberg, Lukasz Swiatek, and Chris Galloway

Learning Objectives

1. To become knowledgeable about existing regulatory frameworks and their relationships with corresponding ethical frameworks, particularly regarding those frameworks that are related to transparency and accountability.
2. To explore the importance of transparency in communicating with organizations' publics about the use of artificial intelligence (AI) and its potential impact on all stakeholders.
3. To learn responsible and transparent use of AI, including practitioners' monitoring and evaluating of AI's use in their organizations.
4. To learn to recognize the limitations and potential biases of AI.
5. To learn to understand, appreciate, and assume responsibility for the essential service that public relations (PR) practitioners must perform by proactively communicating the limitations and clarifying the misconceptions about AI technology to their organizations' stakeholders.

Introduction

What must public relations (PR) practitioners know about artificial intelligence (AI) regulations to enable these communications professionals to participate in formation of their organizations' AI policies and to exemplify best practices in ethical strategic communications? Should PR practitioners assume a leadership role in today's fast-changing communications environment in which AI is becoming both pervasive and integral? If so, what qualifies these practitioners to do so?

DOI: 10.4324/9781032671482-7

This chapter argues that any credible and defensible premise of organizational and societal leadership by public relations practitioners requires a broadened ethical vision that must be developed collaboratively among public relations scholars and practitioners worldwide. A universal framework is required before PR can assume linking, facilitative, and ethical guardianship roles in organizations' use of artificial intelligence.

Unquestionably, AI will transform the world's public relations industry; thus, existing regulatory frameworks must be examined to determine whether they can provide sufficiently heuristic guidelines for practitioners' legal and ethical use of AI. Present regulations do not appear to be keeping pace with today's rapid developments in AI technology. As regulatory bodies hurriedly attempt to provide sufficient legal frameworks for AI, the need for accountability and transparency in PR practitioners' use of AI applications is becoming increasingly obvious.

This chapter will examine existing regulatory frameworks and their relationship with corresponding ethical frameworks, particularly regarding those frameworks that affect transparency and accountability. Salient issues related to privacy, copyright laws, and biases include how AI-powered tools can potentially violate privacy laws by collecting and analyzing personal data without their owners' consent. Also important to examine is how bias can unintentionally be introduced into machine learning algorithms. Transparency and accountability in AI-powered communications strategies are essential to avoid misleading stakeholders. Ultimately, organizations must take primary responsibility to ensure that their use of AI-powered tools is aligned with their organizations' ethical values and principles.

This chapter will also explore the importance of transparency in communicating with stakeholders about the use of AI and its potential impact on them. Finally, the co-authors of this chapter will provide specific recommendations on how PR professionals can promote ethical considerations and accountability in their use of AI. The chapter will provide guidance in the responsible and transparent use of AI, including recommendations in how practitioners can monitor and evaluate AI's use in their organizations. A current duality exists regarding the use of artificial intelligence. Although AI promises to aid humanity in unprecedented ways, ranging from automating work to aiding in finding cures for presently deadly diseases, unchecked AI poses an existential threat to humanity. Thus, this chapter addresses professional sustainability in the face of growing concerns about AI. The co-authors argue that participating in – and oftentimes leading – policy conversations can prepare organizations and PR practitioners to assure strong professional standards regarding the responsible use of AI and organizational accountability.

Regulatory Contexts and Areas of Concern for the Use of AI in PR

During the past several years, discussions on the need for formal policy and well-articulated ethical guidelines have been led by private, public, governmental, and intergovernmental bodies. For example, the European Parliament's study on the ethics of artificial intelligence, completed in March 2020, addresses ethics in the use of AI.[1] It was based on the Montreal Declaration, which, in turn, had been based on *The Montreal Forum on the Socially Responsible Development of Artificial Intelligence* that was held in Montreal on November 2–3, 2017. The Montreal Declaration calls on all actors, including individual citizens throughout the world, to support the basic goal, among many, that there should be an ethical framework for the development and deployment of AI.[2]

Although some governmental and intergovernmental bodies operationalize ethical concerns to a more prescriptive policy, this does not mean creating a new set of legal prescriptions or proscriptions for PR; rather, a PR ethic establishes the foundation for ethics to be the "dynamic basis for the normative evaluation and guidance of AI technologies, referring to human dignity, well-being and the prevention of harm as a compass and rooted in the ethics of science and technology".[3] This calls for building on existing PR ethical approaches because ethical – as well as moral – questions and issues are rapidly changing over time with the use and development of AI technologies.[4] Hence, PR needs a new ethical vision for an increasingly AI-driven world in which organizations are deploying trustworthy AI and are using various accountability measures to mitigate risks.[5]

Therefore, a larger question driving this chapter is: What should organizations (and PR practitioners) know about AI regulations worldwide so that they can responsibly lead in an AI-driven world? Our analysis of existing regulations from governmental and intergovernmental organizations, as well as from professional PR organizations, agencies, and corporations, is premised on the following questions. How do regulations address benefits and risks of AI? Specifically, how are issues (for example, privacy, transparency, and algorithmic governmentality) and benefits (for example, increasing efficiency, combating ransomware, and expanding possibilities of knowledge and learning) addressed, if at all?

Thus far, more than 37 countries – including all major economies, such as China, India, and Japan – have proposed some form of AI regulation.[6] Governments throughout the world have begun to draft and pass legislation that will affect what is legal, how we address privacy, and how we handle copyright, employment, and more. One of the largest world economies, the European Union (EU), recently adopted a risk-based approach: regulating AI based on the risk assessment to AI by adopting the EU AI Act. Although some exceptions exist for open-source models, several AI-related activities are not permissible, for example:

> (t)he scraping of faces from the internet or security footage to create facial recognition databases; emotion recognition in the workplace and educational institutions; cognitive behavioral manipulation; social scoring; biometric categorization to infer sensitive data, such as sexual orientation or religious beliefs; and certain cases of predictive policing for individuals. However, the draft law also gives broad exemptions for "open-source models".[7]

This heightened emphasis on privacy elevates concerns about privacy risk and assessment for organizations and public relations practice, as well.

In the United Kingdom, the legal framework for AI has been on the government's agenda longer than perhaps in any other country in the world. Lord Anthony Giddens, former director of the London School of Economics and a member of the House of Lords Select Committee on Artificial Intelligence, had proposed the Magna Carta for the Digital Age. In that document, Giddens suggested that any regulation should balance innovation and corporate responsibility.[8] To that end, the United Kingdom approach has been sector-based and is yet to assess whether a more widespread AI regulation or AI regulator would be needed.[9]

In the United States, we saw a more sweeping AI regulation in October 2023, when the Biden administration published its AI executive order directing various regulatory bodies and agencies "to evaluate the safety and security of AI technology and other associated risks and implement processes and procedures regarding the adoption and use of AI".[10]

AI regulation is still in the works, even with the largest economies in question. Many countries have enacted some policies, but debates between regulation and innovation are continuing. New Zealand, for example, launched an Algorithm Charter that was intended to govern its public sector's use of algorithms.[11] Although many have signed the charter, no actual regulation exists. In that void, organizations and public relations practitioners must be informed about the issues related to the use of AI before they can advocate for or against specific uses.

Kumayama and colleagues[12] have outlined several areas of concern that highly correlate with public relations practice. One is copyright concerns that are exacerbated by the use the large language models (LLMs) such as Google Bard and ChatGPT because of the ways in which these models have been used and trained on available public data. Companies that own LLMs invoke the fair use parts of copyright law, and this issue will need to be examined and decided in the courts.

In the meantime, public relations practitioners must be aware of and concerned about not only the bias that is inherent in the algorithms, but also bias in the data that these algorithms have harvested. There is no such thing as clean data, and data that exist on the web are significantly polluted in that sense. In addition, public relations practitioners should be aware of concerns that are related to AI models that may be using personal data that have been collected by third parties, as well as by those using home-grown models that might be collecting data inputted by users/customers.

In other words, responsible AI practices must be used. The Montreal AI Ethics Institute argues that "responsible AI" proactively anticipates potential harms and mitigates its impact.[13] The Institute advocates a form of virtue ethics, contending that concern for "socially beneficial outcomes [of AI] requires not just work on frameworks for ethical use, but the cultivation of virtuous technologists and managers, who are motivated to take the concerns of responsible AI seriously".[14] The Institute suggests that "attempting to simplify the work of achieving good outcomes to 'frameworks' or 'principles' . . . risks bearing little fruit" because such guidance is reactive. Nevertheless, PR practitioners need to have workable ethical guidance, even if that guidance connects after the fact to identifiable "problems that can be documented".[15] Additionally, many PR organizations are stepping up efforts to prepare for AI developments. For example, in 2018, the Omnicom Public Relations Group, one of the largest public relations conglomerates in the world, launched an AI Impact Group, described as "a specialized consultancy that helps clients assess and mitigate the risks to brand reputation arising from the introduction of artificial intelligence (AI) technologies".[16] It has also developed an AI Risk Index that quantifies the level of risk based on a company's positioning in relation to AI.

The International Data Corporation (IDC) updated its Oct. 31, 2023, forecast to predict in December 20, 2023:

(T)he worldwide artificial intelligence (AI) software market will grow from $64 billion in 2022 to nearly $251 billion in 2027 at a compound annual growth rate (CAGR) of 31.4%. The forecast for AI-centric software* includes Artificial Intelligence Platforms, AI Applications, AI System Infrastructure Software (SIS), and AI Application Development and Deployment (AD&D) software (excluding AI platforms). However, it does not include Generative AI platforms and applications, which IDC recently forecast will generate revenues of $55.7 billion in 2027.[17]

Dilemmas regarding the use of AI may be susceptible to inadequate logical analysis because logic alone may be insufficient to analyze AI. Until now, public relations practitioners and those whom they serve have both assumed rational behavior in PR ethical frameworks. Likewise, machines are also perceived as operating rationally.[18] However, rapid developments in AI and in associated technologies call such presuppositions into question. Machine learning can produce unanticipated – including racist and misogynistic – ethical outcomes,[19,20] reflecting biases in the data supplied to the system concerned.[21] PR cannot build its ethical approach to AI on the assumption that artificially intelligent systems will always operate in a logical and predictable fashion.

Therefore, predictability cannot be a feasible basis for promoting AI applications, nor should it be considered viable to present such applications as neutral. For example, in 2018, Amazon discontinued the use of its AI recruiting system because that system repeatedly gave low scores to female candidates.[22] The idea was that AI systems would eliminate bias through an algorithm, but what this example – and quite a few others – have shown is that the opinion creating a bias is written into the code. AI applications are not trained to understand social context. Therefore, organizations and public relations practitioners will need to employ methods that will provide tools to eliminate bias and to provide an understanding of the broader social context, regardless of whether or not a regulatory framework requires them to.

Another area of concern – and one that potentially drives much of the public protection aspects of AI regulation – is cybersecurity. Kumayama and colleagues write:[23]

> AI technology has the capability to expand the arsenal of bad actors to carry out sophisticated cyberattacks (*e.g.*, large language models can be used to write malicious code, engineer advanced phishing attacks or more effectively spread malware and ransomware). In addition, AI systems may themselves be vulnerable to data integrity attacks (*e.g.*, through "model poisoning," an attack conducted by introducing malicious information into training data). lack of suitable regulatory frameworks exacerbates these problems. At present, as de la Mora reminds us, "no global instrument covers all the fields that guide the development and application of AI in a human-centered approach".[24] Furthermore, public relations practitioners, particularly those who work closely with or within human resources departments, should be aware of issues related to the use of AI during employment and termination. The U.S. Algorithmic Act of 2022 directs companies that use AI during termination to use impact assessment for bias when deciding whom to terminate.[25]

AI regulation that is emerging will likely provide many answers to how to practice public relations in an AI-driven world; however, it is clear that ethical frameworks designed by professional bodies, organizations, and practitioners will be the primary way to counteract the negative aspects of AI use, as well as the primary way to build trust and relationships with stakeholders.

Ethical Frameworks

During the past several years, private, public, governmental, and intergovernmental bodies have led conversations about the need for policy, as well as for ethical guidelines for artificial intelligence. For example, the European Parliament's study completed in March 2020[26] on the ethics of artificial intelligence, which was based on the already-mentioned Montreal Declaration, addressed issues of ethics in relations to AI. The Montreal Declaration calls on all actors, including individual citizens from throughout the world, to sign onto the basic goal, among many others, that an ethical framework should exist for the development and deployment of AI.[27]

In addition, the European Parliament's study focused both on human rights and well-being, arguing that AI must not affect basic and fundamental human rights, as well as on emotional experience, arguing that AI should not afflict emotional harm by manipulating users or by humans developing intimate relationships with an AI.[28]

The intergovernmental Organization for Economic Cooperation and Development (OECD) has developed AI principles and an AI Policy Observatory to aid, advise, and monitor different countries and their initiatives on AI. Its principles are based on inclusive growth, sustainable development, and well-being; on human-centered values and fairness; and on transparency and explainability, robustness, security and safety, and accountability.[29] The OECD AI Policy Observatory lists countries and their initiatives for AI, including proposals for structural changes in policy, such as those offered by Japan and South Korea.[30]

Although some governmental and intergovernmental bodies extend their ethical concerns to more prescriptive policies, this does not necessarily suggest the need for a new set of legal prescriptions or proscriptions for public relations; rather, a foundation for ethics is the "dynamic basis for the normative evaluation and guidance of AI technologies, referring to human dignity, well-being and the prevention of harm as a compass and rooted in the ethics of science and technology".[31] This calls for building on existing PR ethical approaches: because "The moral, ethical and legal dilemmas that we [now] face are different",[32] as also noted by the United Nations Educational, Scientific, and Cultural Organization (UNESCO).[33]

Extant ethical frameworks often focus on individual choices, but AI ethical issues are also different in that: "The effects of decisions or actions based on AI are often the result of countless interactions among many actors, including designers, developers, users, software, and hardware. . . . With distributed agency comes distributed responsibility".[34] Therefore, challenges in determining accountability for ethical behavior, which ideally should be attributable at "any stage of the life cycle of AI systems".[35]

One reason that this is important is that AI's enormous potential for good is "by no means guaranteed".[36] Its developing possibilities need support by robust ethical principles: an "algor-ethical"[37] view that considers ethics to be new algorithms designed and that practitioners are called upon to promote or help explain their use.

To be sure, we do not know the answers to all of the questions that we want to ask – nor even all of the questions. While the Chartered Institute of Public Relations (CIPR) in London and its Canadian counterpart, the Canadian Public Relations Society (CPRS), have helped spur the profession to consider AI and its implications through their AI in PR Ethics guide,[38] such analysis should be a priority for the other members of the Global Alliance for Public Relations and Communication Management, who should join CIPR and CPRS in a detailed examination of AI and ethical issues in their own jurisdictions.

Lawmakers in the United States have recognized these issues. In April 2023, U.S. Senators Cory Booker (Democrat representing New Jersey) and Ron Wyden (Democrat representing Oregon), with a House equivalent bill sponsored by U.S. Rep. Yvette Clarke (Democrat representing New York), introduced the Algorithmic Accountability Act that was referred to the Subcommittee on Consumer Protection and Commerce. The bill asked that the U.S. Federal Trade Commission require companies that wish to use highly sensitive automated systems to ensure that the inherent algorithms in those systems are not discriminatory and do not pose security and privacy risks to consumers.[39]

In this light, PR scholars and practitioners urgently need to critically reflect on the role of AI as a new fuel of neoliberal capitalism, and they likewise need to examine public relations' own role in engagement with the largely uncritical promotion of these new technologies.[40] The dilemma is analogous to that outlined by McKie and Galloway[41] in relation to PR's engagement with – and possible complicity in – global climate change. They argued that the profession faced "likely reputation fallout from having been so much a part of the denial industry".[42] It is hence clear that it cannot be assumed that algorithms act objectively.[43]

Information that enables ethical assessment of AI implementations might not be available to an adequate degree: "So-called 'black box' algorithms are highly opaque, and in certain cases we can only view the inputs and outputs of such a system";[44] to which Kundu adds: This is the new world we live in, where complex decisions are whittled down to reflexive choices and reinforced by observed outcomes, and where complexity is reduced to simplicity and morality is reduced to utility.[45] There have been examples in both China and the United States. In China, delivery drivers have said that "their manager – an app, not a human, directs them to speed or drive against traffic to meet delivery goals . . . an extreme example of algorithmic management"; in the United States, shoppers for a delivery service called Shipt announced protests against a new "black-box algorithm pay structure" that, they argued, not only slashed pay but also offered "zero transparency".[46] Some companies view algorithmic systems as trade secrets and transparency as unappealing "because typically, 'the way algorithmic control works is because workers don't know how it's functioning.'"[47]

In the case of AI, is PR engaged in facilitating the application of technologies that ultimately could – or will – harm humanity? AI ethical issues are not abstract: for example, asymmetry is built into AI technology: "The economies of scale supplied by artificial intelligence technology have created unequal knowledge, where internet companies know more about us than we know about them".[48] The result is "business models that prioritize private interests over public good".[49] Although this phenomenon is obviously not new, its scale arguably is when mega-corporations such as Apple, Facebook, and Google can exercise immense power over data of all kinds and the uses to which it is put. But "addressing risks and ethical concerns should not hamper innovation . . . [rather, it should] anchor AI technologies in human rights, values and principles, and moral and ethical reflection".[50] Several "anchors" are on offer: one, the southern African ubuntu philosophy, seems to offer principles that can be applied to technology – including AI – to help achieve ethical outcomes: solidarity (social cohesion), reconciliation (repositioning disenfranchised communities in positions of power in the company and in society), equality (human rights protections should shape technology), equity (technology product offerings should reduce inequality), and community.[51] These are macro-level, relationally oriented principles that could complement existing PR ethical frameworks.

Such a broader approach aligns with Kruckeberg and Starck's[52] assertion that public relations is a complex, multi-flow process that could – and should – affect society as a whole and that community-building is PR's highest calling. In the light of AI's potential both for social good and for harm – such as enabling intense and intrusive personal surveillance – laissez-faire and free market approaches are insufficient either to support or to constrain this potential. In PR's case, the need to develop an AI-responsive ethic that prioritizes community-building has become particularly important in light of the growing "techlash" that is making individuals increasingly wary of problematic technological innovations and the organizations that are responsible for them.[53]

To conclude, public relations professionals have a vital role to play in helping to make AI more transparent to their organizations' stakeholders. In particular, as Swiatek and colleagues[54] have argued, public relations professionals – in aiding navigation of changing ethical landscapes by individuals and groups – need to help ensure that AI and its components, as well as the ways in which they function, can be more widely understood. The need to make AI more transparent relates to its black-box nature: that is, its inner workings that are being hidden. As Lütge[55] notes: "Due to the black-box character of AI-driven decisions, strengthening the rights of consumers with more transparency of AI solutions is important for guaranteeing human oversight and consumer sovereignty". It is also important for safeguarding reputations (especially those of organizations and individuals) and, by extension, helping to avoid negative legal, financial, and political impacts: vital components in the work of public relations practitioners.

The need for public relations practitioners to help strengthen the transparency surrounding AI continues to grow because AI tools are becoming increasingly sophisticated and many of their components are deliberately being kept secret. A key example is ChatGPT, which like its creator, OpenAI, has become more and more secretive throughout the years, especially following its transition from a non-profit organization to a capped for-profit company in 2019. OpenAI, Walsh[56] observes, is now open in name only.

The lack of transparency surrounding OpenAI and ChatGPT clash with the longstanding tradition of AI-related innovations being accompanied by peer review. For instance, when the Google Brain team created the field-leading BERT (bidirectional encoder representations from transformers) neural network in 2018, the code was open-sourced and the methods were published in peer-reviewed scientific papers. Following the release of ChatGPT, only a short blog post was published that described the ways in which the tool works; as Walsh[57] astutely quips: "It seems money got in the way of OpenAI's initial plans for openness".

Successful efforts by public relations professionals to make AI more transparent would also clarify the misunderstandings of publics at large about AI's capabilities. The current AI systems, it must be remembered, are not truly intelligent; Compton[58] explains that AI, using algorithms, can help with making decisions and in generating outputs in response to inputs; however, it cannot provide human-level intelligence in terms of being able to provide insight – that is, judgment about whether or not ideas are good or bad. He adds that: "Generative AI doesn't have insight . . . . [G]enerative AI might produce amazing pictures in the style of Monet, but if it were trained only on Renaissance art, it would never invent Impressionism".[59]

Hence, although AI tools have sparked the imaginations of publics throughout the world, their limitations must be taken into account. Public relations practitioners can provide a valuable service to global society by communicating those limitations and by clarifying misconceptions about AI technology.

Reflections

1. Artificial intelligence (AI) is developing so rapidly that it is difficult to comprehend how it will change global society and its power differentials among the three social actors of governments, nongovernmental organizations/civil society organizations, and corporations in their social, political, economic, and cultural dimensions, as well as AI's impact on society collectively and individually among the world's citizens.

2. The threat of AI when used and abused by malevolent actors and institutions must be recognized and addressed.
3. AI is such a powerful tool and change agent that it must be monitored and regulated, with such regulation to be rigorously and continually enforced.

Active Learning Exercises

First as an individual student, but then collectively as a discussion item in your class, identify and briefly describe existing and potential ways AI can be misused and abused by social actors, whether these are governments, nongovernmental organizations or civil society organizations, or corporations.

- In what ways can AI be used ethically in the performance of practitioners' public relations responsibilities?
- What rationale can be used to defend such applications of AI by public relations practitioners?

Notes

1 European Parliament, *The Ethics of Artificial Intelligence: Issues and Initiatives. STUDY: Panel for the Future of Science and Technology EPRS* (Brussels, BE: European Parliamentary Research Service Scientific Foresight Unit [STOA] PE 634.452, March 2020). PE 634.452; ISBN: 978-92-846-5799-5 doi: 10.2861/6644 QA-01-19-779-EN-N. www.europarl.europa.eu/RegData/etudes/STUD/2020/634452/ EPRS_STU(2020)634452_EN.pdf
2 Christophe Abrassart et al., *Montreal Declaration for Responsible AI* (Montreal, CA: University of Montreal, 2018). https://montrealdeclaration-responsibleai.com/the-declaration/
3 UNESCO, *Recommendation on the Ethics of Artificial Intelligence* (Paris, FR: November 9 through 24, 2021). Download PDF: 10. www.unesco.org/en/legal-affairs/ recommendation-ethics-artificial-intelligence
4 UNESCO, 5 & 10.
5 Caitlin Curtis, Nicole Gillespie, and Steven Lockey, "AI-deploying organizations are key to addressing 'perfect storm' of AI risks," *AI Ethics* 3 (2023): 145–153. https:// doi.org/10.1007/s43681-022-00163-7
6 Ken D. Kumayama, Michael E. Leiter, William Ridgway, Resa K. Schlossberg, David E. Schwartz, David A. Simon, Pramode Chiruvolu, Eve-Christie Vermynck, and Lisa V. Zivkovic, "AI in 2024: Monitoring New Regulation and Staying in Compliance with Existing Laws," *Skadden's 2024 Insights* (December 13, 2023): 1–4, 2. www.skadden. com/insights/publications/2023/12/2024-insights/other-regulatory-developments/ ai-in-2024
7 Kumayama et al., 1–2.
8 Anthony Giddens, "A Magna Carta for the Digital Age," *New Perspectives Quarterly* 35, no. 3 (July 2018): 6–8, 7. https://doi.org/10.1111/npqu.12151
9 Kumayama et al., 2.
10 Kumayama et al., 2.

11 Data Government New Zealand, *Algorithm Charter for Aotearoa New Zealand* (Wellington, NZ, 2020). www.data.govt.nz/toolkit/data-ethics/government-algorithm-transparency-and-accountability/#algorithmCharter

12 Kumayama et al., 2–3.

13 Montreal AI Ethics Institute (MAIEI), *The State of AI Ethics* (Montreal, CA: Montreal AI Ethics Institute, June 2020): 63 & 97. https://montrealethics.ai/wp-content/uploads/2020/06/State-of-AI-Ethics-June-2020-report.pdf

14 Montreal AI Ethics Institute (MAIEI), *Virtues Not Principles* (Montreal, CA: Montreal AI Ethics Institute, August 17, 2020): 2. https://montrealethics.ai/virtues-not-principles/

15 Montreal AI Ethics Institute (MAIEI), *Virtues Not Principles*, 2.

16 PRNewswire, "Omnicom Public Relations Group Launches AI Impact Group to Help Companies Navigate Reputational Challenges Related to Artificial Intelligence," in *PRNewswire News Release* (November 12, 2018), para. 1. www.prnewswire.com/news-releases/omnicom-public-relations-group-launches-ai-impact-group-to-help-companies-navigate-reputational-challenges-related-to-artificial-intelligence-300748373.html

17 Michael Shirer, "IDC Forecasts Revenue for Artificial Intelligence Software Will Reach $307 Billion Worldwide in 2027," in *International Data Corporation (IDC) News Release* (Needham, MA: October 31, 2023; updated December 20, 2023): para. 1. www.idc.com/getdoc.jsp?containerId=prUS51345023. Asterisk in the quote refers to the following: IDC defines artificial intelligence (AI) software as AI-centric software. AI-centric applications must have an AI component that is crucial to the application – without this AI component the application will not function. IDC also recognizes a second type of AI software – AI noncentric software. In AI noncentric applications, the AI component is not crucial or fundamental to the application. In other words, the application will function without the inclusion of the AI component. This enables the inclusion of applications that are enhanced by AI capabilities but not exclusively used for AI functions (https://www.idc.com/getdoc.jsp?containerId=prUS51345023).

18 Sabelo Mhlambi, *From Rationality to Relationality: Ubuntu as an Ethical and Human Rights Framework for Artificial Intelligence Governance*, in Carr Center Discussion Paper Series. Cambridge, MA: Carr Center for Human Rights Policy (July 8, 2020): 1–2. https://sabelo.mhlambi.com/publications

19 Meredith Ringel Morris, "AI and Accessibility: A Discussion of Ethical Considerations. Viewpoints," *Communications of the ACM* 63, no. 6 (June 2020): 35–37, 35. https://doi.org/10.1145/3356727

20 Lily Morse, Mike H. M. Teodorescu, Yazeed Awwad, and Gerald C. Kane, "Do the Ends Justify the Means? Variation in the Distributive and Procedural Fairness of Machine Learning Algorithms." *Journal of Business Ethics* 181 (2022): 1083–1095. https://doi.org/10.1007/s10551-021-04939-5

21 Adrienne Yapo and Joseph Weiss, "Ethical Implications of Bias in Machine Learning," *Proceedings of the 51st Hawaii International Conference on System Sciences* (Manoa, HI: University of Hawaii at Manoa, 2018), 5365–5372, 5366. DOI: 10.24251/hicss.2018.668 https://scholarspace.manoa.hawaii.edu/server/api/core/bitstreams/d062bd2a-df54-48d4-b27e-76d903b9caaa/content

22 Mugale Nkonde, "Is AI Bias a Corporate Social Responsibility Issue?" *Harvard Business Review* (November 4, 2019): para. 1. https://hbr.org/2019/11/is-ai-bias-a-corporate-social-responsibility-issue

23 Kumayama et al., 3.

24 Antonio de la Mora, "Elaboration of an instrument on ethics of artificial intelligence," in *Antonio de la Mora LinkedIn* (Sunnyvale, CA: LinkedIn, 2020, June 9). www.linkedin.com/pulse/elaboration-instrument-ethics-artificial-intelligence-antonio

25 Kumayama et al., 4.
26 European Parliament.
27 Christophe Abrassart et al., 5.
28 European Parliament, ii.
29 OECD, *Recommendation of the Council on Artificial Intelligence*, OECD/LE-GAL/0449 (Paris, FR: Organisation for Economic Co-operation and Development, May 21, 2019; amended February 5, 2024). See "Download/Print Booklet", 4–9. https://legalinstruments.oecd.org/en/instruments/oecd-legal-0449
30 OECD, AI Policy Observatory. *National AI Policies & Strategies* (Paris, FR: Organisation for Economic Co-operation and Development, 2021). https://oecd.ai/en/dashboards/overview
31 UNESCO, 10.
32 Katie Malone, "Cap. Michael Kanaan Explains the Value of Air Force's AI Strategy," *MeriTalk* (December 3, 2019). www.meritalk.com/articles/cap-michael-kanaan-explains-the-value-of-air-forces-ai-strategy/
33 UNESCO, 5–7.
34 Mariarosaria Taddeo and Luciano Floridi, "How AI Can Be a Force for good: An Ethical Framework Will Help to Harness the Potential of AI while Keeping Humans in Control," *Science* 361, no. 6404 (2018): 751–752, 751, cited in Mark Coeckelbergh, "Artificial Intelligence, Responsibility Attribution, and a Relational Justification of Explainability," *Science and Engineering Ethics* 26 (2020): 20510–2068, 2056.
35 UNESCO, 22.
36 RenAIssance Foundation, "Introduction," *The Call for AI Ethics*. The Vatican, IT: RenAIssance Foundation, February 28, 2020. www.romecall.org/the-call/
37 RenAIssance Foundation, "Rights."
38 Jean Valin and Anne Gregory, *Ethics Guide to Artificial Intelligence in PR* (London, UK and Toronto, CA: Chartered Institute of Public Relations and the Canadian Public Relations Society, 2020). www.cprs.ca/getattachment/Advocacy/AIinPRPanel/12323_CIPR_Ai-Ethics-Guide_v13_Canadian-Document.pdf.aspx?lang=en-CA
39 Adi Robertson, "A New Bill Would Force Companies to Check Their Algorithms for Bias," *The Verge* (April 10, 2019). www.theverge.com/2019/4/10/18304960/congress-algorithmic-accountability-act-wyden-clarke-booker-bill-introduced-house-senate
40 Clea Bourne, "AI Cheerleaders: Public Relations, Neoliberalism and Artificial Intelligence," *Public Relations Inquiry* 8, no. 2(2019): 109–125. https://doi.org/10.1177/2046147X19835250
41 David McKie and Christopher Galloway, "Climate Change after Denial: Global Reach, Global Responsibilities, and Public Relations," *Public Relations Review* 33, no. 4 (2007): 368–376. https://doi.org/10.1016/j.pubrev.2007.08.009
42 McKie and Galloway, 368.
43 Cathy O'Neill, "The Truth about Algorithms," (2017), YouTube video cited and linked www.youtube.com/watch?v=heQzqX35c9A in Will Grimond, *6 Things We Learned at Our AI & Ethics Salon*. London, UK: RSA (Royal Society for the Encouragement of Arts, Manufactures and Commerce), November 30, 2018: para. 6. www.thersa.org/blog/2018/11/6-things-we-learned-at-our-ai-ethics-salon
44 Will Grimond, *6 Things We Learned at Our AI & Ethics Salon*. London, UK: RSA (Royal Society for the Encouragement of Arts, Manufactures and Commerce), November 30, 2018. www.thersa.org/blog/2018/11/6-things-we-learned-at-our-ai-ethics-salon
45 Shohini Kundu, "Ethics in the Age of Artificial Intelligence," *Scientific American* (July 3, 2019). https://blogs.scientificamerican.com/observations/ethics-in-the-age-of-artificial-intelligence/

46 Dan McCarthy, "When Algorithms Run the Workplace," *Tech Brew* (October 5, 2020). www.emergingtechbrew.com/stories/2020/10/05/algorithms-run-workplace
47 McCarthy.
48 Mhlambi, 19.
49 Mhlambi, 23.
50 UNESCO, 5.
51 Mhlambi, 25
52 Dean Kruckeberg and Kenneth Starck, *Public Relations and Community: A Reconstructed Theory* (New York, NY: Praeger, 1988).
53 Thomas A. Hemphill, " 'Techlash', responsible innovation, and the self-regulatory organization," *Journal of Responsible Innovation* 6, no. 2 (2019): 240–247. https://doi.org/10.1080/23299460.2019.1602817
54 Lukasz L. Swiatek, Chris Galloway, Marina Vujnovic, and Dean Kruckeberg, "Artificial Intelligence and Changing Ethical Landscapes in Social Media and Computer-Mediated Communication: Considering the Role of Communication Professionals," in *The Emerald Handbook of Computer-Mediated Communication and Social Media*, eds. Jeremy H. Lipschultz, Karen Freberg, and Regina Luttrell (Leeds, UK: Emerald Publishing, 2022), 653–670). Emerald. https://doi.org/10.1108/978-1-80071-597-420221038
55 Christoph Lütge, "Building a Connected, Intelligent and Ethical World," in *White Paper on AI Ethics and Governance* (Munich, DE: Technical University of Munich Institute for Ethics in Artificial Intelligence, March 2020). https://ieai.mcts.tum.de/wp-content/uploads/2020/04/White-Paper_AI-Ethics-and-Governance-_March-20201.pdf
56 Toby Walsh, "Everyone's Having a Field Day with ChatGPT – But Nobody Knows How It Actually Works," *The conversation* (December 13, 2022): para. 22. https://theconversation.com/everyones-having-a-field-day-with-chatgpt-but-nobody-knows-how-it-actually-works-196378
57 Walsh, para. 18.
58 Paul Compton, "AI Tools Produce Dazzling Results – But Do They Really Have 'Intelligence'?" *The Conversation* (February 13, 2024), para. 18. https://theconversation.com/ai-tools-produce-dazzling-results-but-do-they-really-have-intelligence-223311
59 Compton, para. 19.

Bibliography

Abrassart, Christophe et al. *Montreal Declaration for Responsible AI*. Montreal, CA: University of Montreal (2018). https://montrealdeclaration-responsibleai.com/the-declaration/
Bourne, Clea. "AI Cheerleaders: Public Relations, Neoliberalism and Artificial Intelligence," *Public Relations Inquiry* 8, no. 2 (2019): 109–125. https://doi.org/10.1177/2046147X19835250
Compton, Paul. "AI Tools Produce Dazzling Results – But Do They Really Have 'Intelligence'?" *The Conversation* (February 13, 2024): para. 18. https://theconversation.com/ai-tools-produce-dazzling-results-but-do-they-really-have-intelligence-223311
Curtis, Caitlin, Nicole Gillespie, and Steven Lockey. "AI-Deploying Organizations Are Key to Addressing 'Perfect Storm' of AI Risks," *AI Ethics* 3 (2023): 145–153. https://doi.org/10.1007/s43681-022-00163-7
Data Government New Zealand. *Algorithm Charter for Aotearoa New Zealand*. Wellington, NZ: (2020). www.data.govt.nz/toolkit/data-ethics/government-algorithm-transparency-and-accountability/#algorithmCharter
de la Mora, Antonio. "Elaboration of an Instrument on Ethics of Artificial Intelligence," *Antonio de la Mora LinkedIn*. Sunnyvale, CA: LinkedIn (June 9, 2020). www.linkedin.com/pulse/elaboration-instrument-ethics-artificial-intelligence-antonio

European Parliament. *The Ethics of Artificial Intelligence: Issues and Initiatives. STUDY: Panel for the Future of Science and Technology EPRS.* Brussels, BE: European Parliamentary Research Service Scientific Foresight Unit [STOA] PE 634.452 (March 2020). PE 634.452; ISBN: 978–92-846-5799-5. https://doi.org/10.2861/6644 QA-01-19-779-EN-N. www.europarl.europa.eu/RegData/etudes/STUD/2020/634452/EPRS_STU(2020)634452_EN.pdf

Giddens, Anthony. "A Magna Carta for the Digital Age," *New Perspectives Quarterly* 35, no. 3 (July 2018): 6–8, 7. https://doi.org/10.1111/npqu.12151

Grimond, Will. *6 Things We Learned at Our AI & Ethics Salon.* London, UK: RSA (Royal Society for the Encouragement of Arts, Manufactures and Commerce) (November 30, 2018). www.thersa.org/blog/2018/11/6-things-we-learned-at-our-ai – ethics-salon

Hemphill, Thomas A. " 'Techlash', Responsible Innovation, and the Self-Regulatory Organization," *Journal of Responsible Innovation* 6, no. 2 (2019): 240–247. https://doi.org/10.1080/23299460.2019.1602817

Kruckeberg, Dean, and Kenneth Starck. *Public Relations and Community: A Reconstructed Theory.* New York, NY: Praeger, 1988.

Kumayama, Ken D., Michael E. Leiter, William Ridgway, Resa K. Schlossberg, David E. Schwartz, David A. Simon, Pramode Chiruvolu, Eve-Christie Vermynck, and Lisa V. Zivkovic. "AI in 2024: Monitoring New Regulation and Staying in Compliance with Existing Laws," *Skadden's 2024 Insights* (December 13, 2023): 1–4, 2. www.skadden.com/insights/publications/2023/12/2024-insights/other-regulatory-developments/ai-in-2024

Kundu, Shohini. "Ethics in the Age of Artificial Intelligence," *Scientific American* (July 3, 2019). https://blogs.scientificamerican.com/observations/ethics-in-the-age-of-artificial-intelligence/

Lütge, Christoph. "Building a Connected, Intelligent and Ethical World," *White Paper on AI Ethics and Governance.* Munich, DE: Technical University of Munich Institute for Ethics in Artificial Intelligence (March 2020). https://ieai.mcts.tum.de/wp-content/uploads/2020/04/White-Paper_AI-Ethics-and-Governance-_March-20201.pdf

Malone, Katie. "Cap. Michael Kanaan Explains the Value of Air Force's AI Strategy," *MeriTalk* (December 3, 2019). www.meritalk.com/articles/cap-michael-kanaan-explains-the-value-of-air-forces-ai-strategy/

McCarthy, Dan. "When Algorithms Run the Workplace," *Tech Brew* (October 5, 2020). www.emergingtechbrew.com/stories/2020/10/05/algorithms-run-workplace

McKie, David, and Christopher Galloway. "Climate Change after Denial: Global Reach, Global Responsibilities, and Public Relations," *Public Relations Review* 33, no. 4 (2007): 368–376. https://doi.org/10.1016/j.pubrev.2007.08.009

Mhlambi, Sabelo. *From Rationality to Relationality: Ubuntu as an Ethical and Human Rights Framework for Artificial Intelligence Governance*, In Carr Center Discussion Paper Series. Cambridge, MA: Carr Center for Human Rights Policy (July 8, 2020): 1–2. https://sabelo.mhlambi.com/publications

Montreal AI Ethics Institute (MAIEI). *The State of AI Ethics.* Montreal, CA: Montreal AI Ethics Institute (June 2020): 63 & 97. https://montrealethics.ai/wp-content/uploads/2020/06/State-of-AI-Ethics-June-2020-report.pdf

Montreal AI Ethics Institute (MAIEI). *Virtues Not Principles.* Montreal, CA: Montreal AI Ethics Institute (August 17, 2020): 2. https://montrealethics.ai/virtues-not-principles

Morris, Meredith Ringel. "AI and Accessibility: A Discussion of Ethical Considerations. Viewpoints," *Communications of the ACM* 63, no. 6 (June 2020): 35–37, 35. https://doi.org/10.1145/3356727

Morse, Lily, Mike H. M. Teodorescu, Yazeed Awwad, and Gerald C. Kane. "Do the Ends Justify the Means? Variation in the Distributive and Procedural Fairness of Machine Learning Algorithms." *Journal of Business Ethics* 181 (2022): 1083–1095. https://doi.org/10.1007/s10551-021-04939-5

Nkonde, Mugale. "Is AI Bias a Corporate Social Responsibility Issue?" *Harvard Business Review* (November 4, 2019): para. 1. https://hbr.org/2019/11/is-ai-bias-a-corporate-social-responsibility-issue

OECD. *Recommendation of the Council on Artificial Intelligence*, OECD/LEGAL/0449 Paris, FR: Organisation for Economic Co-operation and Development (May 21, 2019; amended February 5, 2024). See "Download/Print Booklet", 4–9. https://legalinstruments.oecd.org/en/instruments/oecd-legal-0449

OECD.AI. Policy Observatory. *National AI Policies & Strategies*. Paris, FR: Organisation for Economic Co-operation and Development (2021). https://oecd.ai/en/dashboards/overview

O'Neill, Cathy. "The Truth about Algorithms," (2017), YouTube video cited and linked www.youtube.com/watch?v=heQzqX35c9A in Will Grimond, *6 Things We Learned at Our AI & Ethics Salon*. London, UK: RSA (Royal Society for the Encouragement of Arts, Manufactures and Commerce) (November 30, 2018): para. 6. www.thersa.org/blog/2018/11/6-things-we-learned-at-our-ai–ethics-salon

PRNewswire. "Omnicom Public Relations Group Launches AI Impact Group to Help Companies Navigate Reputational Challenges Related to Artificial Intelligence," *PRNewswire News Release* (November 12, 2018): para. 1. www.prnewswire.com/news-releases/omnicom-public-relations-group-launches-ai-impact-group-to-help-companies-navigate-reputational-challenges-related-to-artificial-intelligence-300748373.html

RenAIssance Foundation. *The Call for AI Ethics*. The Vatican, IT: RenAIssance Foundation (February 28, 2020). www.romecall.org/the-call/

Robertson, Adi. "A New Bill Would Force Companies to Check Their Algorithms for Bias," *The Verge* (April 10, 2019). www.theverge.com/2019/4/10/18304960/congress-algorithmic-accountability-act-wyden-clarke-booker-bill-introduced-house-senate

Shirer, Michael. "IDC Forecasts Revenue for Artificial Intelligence Software Will Reach $307 Billion Worldwide in 2027," *International Data Corporation (IDC) News Release* Needham, MA: (October 31, 2023; updated December 20, 2023): para. 1. www.idc.com/getdoc.jsp?containerId=prUS51345023

Swiatek, L., Chris Galloway, Marina Vujnovic, and Dean Kruckeberg. "Artificial Intelligence and Changing Ethical Landscapes in Social Media and Computer-Mediated Communication: Considering the Role of Communication Professionals," In *The Emerald Handbook of Computer-Mediated Communication and Social Media*, 653–670. Edited by Jeremy H. Lipschultz, Karen Freberg, and Regina Luttrell. Leeds, UK: Emerald Publishing, 2022. https://doi.org/10.1108/978-1-80071-597-42022103854.

Taddeo, Mariarosaria, and Luciano Floridi. "How AI Can Be a Force for Good: An Ethical Framework Will Help to Harness the Potential of AI While Keeping Humans in Control," *Science* 361, no. 6404 (2018): 751–752, 751, cited in Mark Coeckelbergh. "Artificial Intelligence, Responsibility Attribution, and a Relational Justification of Explainability," *Science and Engineering Ethics* 26 (2020): 2051–2068, 2056.

UNESCO. *Recommendation on the Ethics of Artificial Intelligence*. Paris, FR: (November 9 through 24, 2021). Download PDF: 10. www.unesco.org/en/legal-affairs/recommendation-ethics-artificial-intelligence

Valin, Jean, and Anne Gregory. *Ethics Guide to Artificial Intelligence in PR*. London, UK and Toronto, CA: Chartered Institute of Public Relations and the Canadian Public Relations Society (2020). www.cprs.ca/getattachment/Advocacy/AIinPRPanel/12323_CIPR_Ai-Ethics-Guide_v13_Canadian-Document.pdf.aspx?lang=en-CA

Walsh, Toby. "Everyone's Having a Field Day with ChatGPT – But Nobody Knows How It Actually Works," *The Conversation* (December 13, 2022): para. 22. https://theconversation.com/everyones-having-a-field-day-with-chatgpt-but-nobody-knows-how-it-actually-works-196378

Yapo, Adrienne, and Joseph Weiss. "Ethical Implications of Bias in Machine Learning." *Proceedings of the 51st Hawaii International Conference on System Sciences*, 5365–5372. Manoa, HI: University of Hawaii at Manoa (2018): 5366. https://doi.org/10.24251/hicss.2018.668. https://scholarspace.manoa.hawaii.edu/server/api/core/bitstreams/d062bd2a-df54-48d4-b27e-76d903b9caaa/content

PART III

Media Monitoring, Influencer Relations, and Reputation Management

6

AI-POWERED SYNTHETIC PERSONAS

Affecting the Future of Public Relations Campaigns

Regina Luttrell and Carrie Welch

Learning Objectives

1. Understand the fundamental concepts of public relations and their evolving landscape in the digital age, exploring how artificial intelligence and synthetic personas can contribute to shaping positive connections between organizations and their audiences.
2. Explore the roles and dynamics of influencers, spokespeople, and AI-generated synthetic personas within the realm of PR, examining the challenges and possibilities they present for modern communication strategies.
3. Analyze the ethical considerations surrounding the use of synthetic personas in PR campaigns and develop a comprehensive understanding of responsible integration strategies, ensuring practitioners are equipped to navigate the evolving intersection of technology and public relations successfully.

AI Synthetic Personas, Virtual Influencers, and Public Relations

There is "no need to hire a spokesperson, mascot, or celebrity to serve as the face of your brand. Just create your own – or rent a synthetic human."[1] *Artificial intelligence* (AI) – technologies that can perform tasks simulating or mirroring human intelligence – is predicted to assume many of the tedious, mundane tasks of public relations: media list building, social media monitoring, and customer service responses. However, one role many public relations (PR) practitioners did not anticipate AI taking on is that of spokesperson.

As the technological influence of AI rapidly expands across conventional business applications, it's crucial to recognize that *AI synthetic personas* and

DOI: 10.4324/9781032671482-9

virtual or CGI (computer-generated imagery) influencers are not a futuristic concept; they are already present and shaping the landscape. In fact, in 2022, it was estimated that 90% of all online content may be synthetic media within four years.[2] As efficiency and productivity can increase in the PR industry with the adoption of AI tools, practitioners are asked how to maintain the human elements of creativity, emotion, and empathy. A similar issue AI researchers are grappling with is whether AI-generated content is enhancing internet creativity or diminishing it.[3]

The idea of AI synthetic personas represents an intersection of these discussions and first gained traction in the mid-2010s. Though nascent experiments with AI-generated characters and chatbots date back further, it was around 2016 that significant advancements in *machine learning* (ML), *natural language processing* (NLP), and computer vision technologies allowed for more sophisticated and realistic synthetic personas.[4] The emergence of social media platforms such as Instagram, coupled with the transition of bloggers to *influencers*, played a pivotal role and set the stage for the introduction of AI-generated influencers. Since then, AI technology has grown rapidly with the landscape of AI synthetic personas, virtual influencers, and their applications across various industries, including PR, still coming into focus.[5]

AI synthetic personas and virtual influencers are both crafted through algorithms, ML, and creative input.[6,7,8] However, there are important differences. AI synthetic personas are like custom-made characters crafted from scratch by designers, allowing for unique and specific traits. On the other hand, AI-generated virtual influencers use artificial intelligence to analyze existing data, creating personas based on demographics and behavior patterns. These influencers are usually also built specifically for social media use.

The creation of synthetic spokespeople and AI influencers signals a shift for the PR industry, where most human elements can be handled by artificial intelligence. Key messages may be formulated not by a seasoned PR professional but by NLP – with accompanying images and video generated by *Stable Diffusion*.[9] But is this trend fostering heightened innovation in public relations, or if it is simply building better chatbots? How human creativity and emotion are incorporated into the creation and use of AI synthetic personas and virtual influencers will determine their importance in shaping communication strategies.

The Synthetic Breakdown: Definitions and Forms

Before we delve further into personas and influencers, let's start with *synthetic media*. Synthetic media is an umbrella term that can be defined as video, images, virtual objects, sound, and text generated or assisted by AI.[10] This includes deepfake content, AI-generated art prompted by text, virtual content in *virtual reality* (VR) and *augmented reality* (AR) environments, and other emerging content types.[11] This transformative technology is ushering in revolutionary changes for industries like PR that traditionally rely on text, design, and creativity in their communications. Synthetic media accelerates these areas, fostering rapid prototyping and creative content creation, as well as affording more efficient communication and design capabilities.[12] This marks a defining moment of change in PR workforce dynamics.

Applying this to our discussion, let's clarify how AI synthetic personas and virtual influencers are similar and how they are different. As previously defined, *AI synthetic personas* refer to a digital character crafted through AI technologies, simulating the behaviors and characteristics of an actual human.[13] These AI-generated personas find applications in marketing, virtual conversations, conversational interfaces, search operations, and various other contexts. Companies often deploy them as virtual avatars with specific objectives, such as enhancing customer engagement and gaining insights into their target audience. As the conventional need to hire spokespersons, mascots, or celebrities for brand representation evolves, businesses can now create or "rent" synthetic humans, reshaping the face of brand representation.[14] This area is moving fast as Panda and colleagues advance, "Communication specialists are under pressure to unlearn old manual skills and learn new digital capabilities to survive in the new work environment."[15]

Sophisticated AI technologies like Apple's Siri and Amazon's Alexa showcase how AI entities have already become the face of brands. In the evolving landscape of brand representation, a range of intelligent personalities and forms are in development, extending beyond conventional chatbots to include screens, voices, and physical robots. Companies find themselves in the delicate position of navigating shifts in customer interactions, recognizing each AI engagement as an impression of the brand and its performance. For executives, pivotal decisions arise in the meticulous crafting of consumer-facing brand ambassadors, involving considerations of name, voice, and distinct personality traits.[16]

This trend demonstrates the emerging importance of AI "personality training" as a critical business strategy, whereby companies must not only adapt to technological advancements but also manage the persona of AI systems linked with specific brand identities.[17] This necessitates the recruitment of diverse talents, particularly individuals with backgrounds in creative fields, as the fusion of technology and creativity drives effective brand representation. Looking ahead, the experts see a deeper integration of empathy into AI systems, exemplified by startups like Koko, who have developed ML systems that enable chatbots to respond with more sympathy and depth to users' queries and concerns.[18]

AI-generated virtual influencers are similar but different approaches to using AI to convey messages to key publics. This is a computer-generated character or persona that leverages AI to simulate human-like qualities and behaviors but is specifically designed to interact with users on digital platforms, such as social media, and often serve as brand ambassadors or content creators. Unlike traditional influencers who are real individuals, AI-generated virtual influencers are entirely computer-generated entities, capable of generating content, engaging in conversations, and building relationships with their audience through algorithms and pre-programmed responses[19,20]

For PR professionals, this iteration of brand representation represents a shift in the way brands interact with their audiences. As AI systems increasingly become the faces of brands, PR professionals must navigate the challenges associated with ensuring alignment with desired brand values and managing potential ethical and legal concerns. The need for diverse talents, particularly those with creative backgrounds, suggests a broader skill set requirement within the PR industry.[21] In addition, the anticipated incorporation of empathy into AI systems underscores the growing complexity of the PR professional's role, requiring an understanding not only of traditional communication strategies but also of the changing technological landscape and its impact on brand perception.[22]

The Role of Influencers

Much of what we know today about synthetic personas emerged from the influencer movement of the early 2000s. Influencers, who gained traction alongside the creation of social media platforms like Instagram and Facebook, can be defined as individuals known for their ability to disseminate information and wield influence across microblogging platforms like TikTok, Instagram, Facebook, and X/Twitter.[23] Within industry discussions, influencers are often perceived as dynamic and highly followed social media figures who cultivate a loyal community of fans, with many aiming to affect consumer purchase decisions to maximize paid sponsor relationships.

The industry has many categories of influencers. The first and most notorious are *celebrities* or *megainfluencers* who boast over one million followers.[24] Next come *macroinfluencers* with follower counts ranging between 100,000 and one million, followed by *microinfluencers* with 10,000–100,000 followers.[25] *Opinion leaders* and/or *bloggers* constitute the fourth category, denoting individuals considered experts who are well-informed and educated, catering to niche audiences.[26] A fifth category, *nanoinfluencers*, refers to individuals described as small, niche, and highly engaged social media players with follower counts ranging from 1–10,000.[27] Both microinfluencers and nanoninfluencers are viewed as powerful, as they tend to foster close and emotionally invested relationships within their communities.[28] AI-generated influencers have amassed followings comparable to those of megainfluencers. The global influencer market has experienced substantial financial growth, more than doubling in size since 2019, reaching $21.1 billion in 2023.[29] *Influencer marketing* is a form of social media promotion that incorporates endorsements and product placements from individuals with significant online influence. Brands are increasingly leveraging influencer partnerships to tap into vast potential audiences in the competitive marketing landscape. Advertising spending on influencer marketing is projected to grow at an annual rate of 9.91% per year (estimated from 2024–2029) with a resulting market total of $56 billion by 2029.[30]

Recognizing the ability of internet stars to enhance brand visibility, drive engagement, and influence purchasing decisions for millions of users, the upward trajectory of spending on influencer collaborations is expected to continue. Globally, Instagram stands as the primary platform for influencer marketing, with over 80% of marketers forecast to be implementing campaigns by 2024.[31] TikTok comes in a close second, enjoying popularity among content creators, with 54% of marketers projected to use it by 2024.[32] Companies are looking to maximize revenue, but also to harness the influence these creators wield in shaping public opinions and perceptions. In a media landscape where traditional news outlets no longer hold exclusive sway, organizations increasingly view influencers as effective agents for publicity and validation. Influencers, adept at tapping into popular culture, socio-cultural trends, and political themes, play a newly defined role in shaping public discourse and consumer behavior.[33]

The evolving role of influencers as tastemakers is important, as influencers act not only as marketing agents but also as PR practitioners, navigating the intersection of career aspirations, profit motives, advocacy, message management, and community building. The impact of influencers is particularly pronounced among younger demographics, with 72% of Gen Z and millennials actively following influencers.[34] Driven by inspiration, aspiration, voyeurism, and captivating content, teenagers are particularly inclined to follow multiple influencers. Because of this, the world of influencers – propelled by financial investments and AI integration – will continue to gain in importance in the strategic communication and public relations strategies of organizations.[35,36]

BOX 6.1 SYNTHETIC PERSONAS: CRAFTING AI INFLUENCERS

In this activity, you will create your own synthetic persona. Begin by thinking about the personality and characteristics you want your AI influencer to embody. Consider factors such as tone, style, and values that align with your target audience. Once you have established the persona, dive into the design phase. Visualize the appearance of your AI influencer, from clothing style to facial features. What will appeal most to your target audience? What will they respond most positively to? Leverage generative AI tools such as Midjourney or DALL·E 3.

Next, define the skills and capabilities of your AI influencer. Determine its areas of expertise: fashion, sports, food, beauty, entertainment, or a combination. Tailor these skills to resonate with your intended audience. Craft a unique voice for your AI influencer, ensuring it reflects your envisioned persona. Whether it is witty, informative, or conversational, the voice should align with your brand.

Create scenarios whereby your AI influencer interacts with the audience to enhance engagement. This could involve providing recommendations, answering questions, or engaging in casual conversations. For a more realistic interaction, implement technology like NLP. How would your influencer respond in the comments on Instagram? Think about what their social media profile would look like and which platforms would resonate most with their target audience. For additional insights, refer to Lil Miquela and other virtual influencers discussed in this chapter.

Finally, share your creation with others and seek feedback. Encourage discussions on your AI influencer's potential impact and consider ethical implications in its development. Whether you are a marketing professional or simply intrigued by the intersection of AI and influencer culture, this creative endeavor allows you to explore the limitless possibilities of AI-driven personalities. So, dive in, unleash your creativity, and let your AI influencer come to life!

AI-Generated Influencers

AI-generated influencers are an increasingly powerful force in the transformative digital landscape, even more so than the synthetic AI personas being used as spokespeople for brand engagement. While synthetic personas were new and novel in 2016, the public moved significantly further online during the COVID19 pandemic, leading to increased Zoom and chatbot fatigue.[37] AI-generated influencers represent the next frontier for this corner of AI, as they involve newer systems gaining ground toward capabilities of autonomous thought that could potentially surpass human mental capacities presented in an approachable influencer package. While the creation of a digital "brain" is still distant, recent advancements hint at a new era of digital creation that may reduce human involvement.[38] For example, in 2023, a Spanish advertising agency created Aitana (Figure 6.1), an AI character who earns $10,000 per month from brand contracts, highlighting the growing potential of virtual influencers.[39] Other virtual influencers like @lilmiquela, @noonoouri, and

FIGURE 6.1 The AI influencer Aitana, who was created by a Spanish advertising agency, on Instagram

@shudu have gained substantial followings, with advanced creation tools making them increasingly lifelike.[40]

As technology progresses, virtual influencers, both in static images and videos, are poised to become ubiquitous aspects of online interaction. The emergence of *deepfakes*, whereby celebrity faces are superimposed on real actors, raises security concerns, but fully virtual creations animated from still images offer cheaper, faster, and easier options for brands.[41,42] Platforms are already implementing AI labeling requirements to address this challenge, making it possible for consumers to distinguish between real individuals and AI creations. This shift could pose obstacles for human influencers, potentially reshaping the online economy once driven by content creators as AI-simulated content becomes more the norm.[43,44]

Advantages and Disadvantages of AI-Generated Personas and Influencers

Starting in the mid-2010s, the incorporation of computer-generated models in advertising, fashion, and social media marked a trend toward utilizing synthetic AI spokespeople.[45] A notable instance is Yumi, the digital ambassador representing the Japanese skincare company SK-II. Yumi showcased the capability of artificial intelligence to emulate lifelike human movements. Developed in partnership with Soul Machines and utilizing Google's NLP platform, Yumi stands as an impactful digital brand representative.[46] Beyond aesthetic appeal, the brand claims Yumi extends practical value by providing skincare guidance and global customer care services around the clock, exemplifying the advantages of employing synthetic AI spokespeople in enhancing user engagement and expanding brand outreach.[47] Later in this chapter, we will delve into Yumi more closely.

In a similar development, platforms like D-ID (an AI-generated video creation platform) are working to showcase the capabilities of synthetic media to generate AI spokespeople for marketing purposes. Utilizing a combination of GPT-3 and Stable Diffusion, D-ID's AI platform generates individually rendered spokespersons capable of conveying messages in diverse styles. While increasingly realistic, challenges such as avatar mouths syncing with spoken words create lingering concerns about the synthetic quality of the voice and its application. D-ID addresses brand reservations toward embracing generative AI by building in safety measures including content filtering, copyright issue prevention, text moderation, and digital watermarking.[48] This is the careful balance required in navigating the advantages of scalability and creativity against potential authenticity and ethics concerns.[49]

AI influencers represent the ultimate intersection of influencer culture and disruptive technology, as "AI influencers are the ultimate intersection of influencer culture and disruptive technology."[50] As technology and social interaction continue to advance, the exploration of AI-generated influencers presents both advantages and disadvantages that warrant careful regulation and ethical considerations. On the downside, if not managed closely, AI influencers have the potential to become potent tools for disseminating propaganda or dangerous *disinformation.*[51] The amplified reach and influence of AI-generated entities could inadvertently contribute to the spread of misinformation or biased narratives, highlighting the need for ethical guidelines and regulatory frameworks.[52]

Conversely, on a more optimistic note, the rise of AI influencers could democratize influencer marketing, providing opportunities for brands with limited budgets to engage in impactful digital campaigns. The prospect of brands developing their own AI digital personas to spearhead their social media presence could redefine influencer marketing strategies. This shift might lead to increased accessibility and affordability for businesses aiming to leverage the influence of digital personas without the high costs associated with human influencers. As AI influencers carve out a unique and significant niche in the social media landscape, businesses, marketers, and even traditional influencers must observe and question whether this represents the next major evolution in digital marketing or is just a high-tech passing fad.[53]

As we continue to investigate the intriguing world of synthetic personas, we will examine two prominent illustrations: Yumi (Figure 6.2) and Miquela (Figure 6.3). These digital beings not only demonstrate the potential of AI, but also serve as prime examples of how technology and virtual personalities are increasingly intertwined. Exploring their characteristics and impact provides valuable insights into the dynamic intersection of AI and the creation of compelling online personas.

Meet Yumi, SK-II's autonomous animated digital influencer

FIGURE 6.2 Yumi, the AI synthetic spokesperson introduced by skincare brand SK-II

lilmiquela ⦾   ···

○ ○ ▽   • – •   ⊓

Liked by **hikm** and **others**
lilmiquela I've been hesitant to say it, and very
"anti" this but after a very exciting and
exhilarating morning of exploration, i've... more

View all 105 comments

December 7, 2023

FIGURE 6.3   The AI-generated influencer Miquela, as represented on "her" Insta-gram account

AI Synthetic Persona: Yumi

In 2019, Japanese skincare company SK-II introduced Yumi, one of the first AI-generated spokespeople developed in collaboration with Soul Machines, a New Zealand startup specializing in creating fully animated, digital people.[54] Soul Machines has been engaged in this work for brands such as AutoDesk and Mercedes Benz. Unlike traditional **brand ambassadors**, Yumi represented a departure from the norm by being a singular, dedicated, AI-generated spokes-person exclusively associated with SK-II. Her primary function was to offer personalized skincare advice to the brand's global customer base, targeting twentysomething-year-old Japanese women in particular. This approach sought to streamline customer service by deploying a single, artificially intelligent entity capable of addressing beauty questions at all hours on the company's website.

Yumi's creation combined Google's NLP platform with detailed face scans to generate a lifelike appearance. While Yumi was initially based on a real person, Soul Machines emphasized that she would develop her own personality and movements over time. This unique feature set her apart from other CGI influencers and underscored the technology's potential for nuanced, artificially intelligent movement. According to Greg Cross, chief business officer (CBO) of Soul Machines, the company's focus is on creating authentic reactions and movements that aim to capture the essence of human personality beyond scripted gestures, marking a significant shift in the landscape of AI technology.[55]

The advantages of employing an AI-generated spokesperson like Yumi extended beyond her ability to provide continuous and cost-effective customer service. Yumi was designed to offer more than just scripted responses, with plans to move from NLP to natural language generating engines. This evolution represented a significant step forward in creating digital humans that could generate unique and contextually relevant responses on the fly. Despite the inherent challenges of making Yumi's presence truly lifelike, SK-II was optimistic about her potential to foster more personable interactions, addressing the limitations of traditional text-based chatbots. However, as the industry embraced AI-generated spokespersons, some voiced concerns about the potential loss of the genuine human connection and emotional depth that traditional human ambassadors brought to brand interactions. Furthermore, the risk of technological glitches and unforeseen ethical issues emerged as potential disadvantages, requiring careful consideration in the ongoing development and utilization of such innovative technologies. As Sandeep Seth, SK-II's CEO, noted, Yumi's super intelligence and authenticity reflected the core values of the brand while acknowledging the need for a balanced approach to ensure meaningful and ethical engagement with consumers.[56]

AI Influencer: Miquela

Researchers Block and Lovegrove examined an illuminating case study of Lil Miquela Sousa (@lilmiquela on Instagram), a synthetic – or CGI – megainfluencer with a microinfluencer style.[57] Stunningly realistic, she has amassed a following of over three million on Instagram since her debut in 2016. What is more, she has collaborated with mainstream brands such as Prada and Samsung. Despite achieving considerable success, her creators at Brud, a company self-described as a "transmedia studio that creates digital character-driven story worlds," portray her as an underground character, fostering strong vivid connections with indie, underground, and disaffected Gen Z communities.[58] Miquela engages her 'Miqalien' fans by prompting interactions, such as opinions on her hairstyle or participation in Instagram stories, creating a unique storytelling world across Instagram, TikTok, and YouTube.[59]

Moving further into Block and Lovegrove's study, they explore the authenticity of Miquela and CGI influencers in the context of strategic communication disciplines and their disruption of traditional notions of *authenticity*.[60] Despite being a digital construct, Miquela is considered authentic in her digital context, successfully engaging social media audiences through her storytelling skills. The analysis suggests that Miquela's creators use algorithms to maximize her uncanniness and influence among followers and detractors. Miquela's role as a Generation Z tastemaker and her success in the media industry demonstrate the strategic use of her bespoke character in a crowded media landscape.

Furthermore, the research explores the paradoxical connection between Miquela's persona and her targeting of a Gen Z audience, especially in the context of aspirational luxury fashion brands. Despite the potential disconnect, the study argues that Miquela's promotion of these brands elevates her status, allowing her to discuss social and humanitarian issues while bringing novelty and Gen Z engagement to the partnering brands. The research emphasizes the potential positive impact of CGI influencers for brands, with Miquela serving as a practitioner and a practice in the hands of luxury, mainstream, indie brands, non-profits, and social movements. However, concerns about the potential negative impact on younger audiences call for further research on the social impact, ethical considerations, and legal implications of CGI influencers in the field of strategic communication.[61]

Moving from the exploration of Yumi and Miquela's personas, it is essential to focus on the ethical considerations associated with the use of AI-generated figures. These digital entities, with their ability to captivate audiences and engage with renowned brands, prompt important questions about the ethical implications of utilizing artificial intelligence in shaping realistic personalities. Addressing – or at the very least, acknowledging – these concerns allow us to better understand the ethical boundaries and potential societal impacts in the evolving landscape where technology meets virtual representation.

BOX 6.2   ETHICAL CONSIDERATIONS IN SYNTHETIC PERSONA ENGAGEMENT

As public relations professionals explore the dynamic realm of synthetic personas, three ethical considerations take center stage. First and foremost, the commitment to transparency and disclosure becomes pivotal, ensuring that audiences are informed about the artificial nature of these entities.

Additionally, maintaining authenticity and trustworthiness emerges as a crucial consideration, striking a delicate balance between innovation and the core values of the brand. Finally, privacy and data security demand careful attention, emphasizing the ethical imperative to protect individuals' rights and privacy in the creation and interaction with synthetic personas.

1. Transparency and disclosure: PR professionals must prioritize transparency when utilizing synthetic personas. Clear and explicit disclosure to the audience about the persona's artificial nature is crucial to maintaining trust. Ethical considerations involve ensuring that the audience members are aware that they are interacting with a synthetic entity, fostering transparency in communications and preventing potential deception.
2. Authenticity and trustworthiness: Maintaining the authenticity of the brand message is paramount. PR professionals should carefully consider the potential impact of synthetic personas on the overall credibility and trustworthiness of the brand. Striking a balance between innovation and authenticity is essential to prevent any misalignment with the core values of the organization or the expectations of the audience.
3. Privacy and data security: The creation and management of synthetic personas often involve the use of data and personal information. PR professionals must prioritize the privacy of individuals whose data might be used to inform the persona. Adhering to data protection regulations, obtaining informed consent, and implementing robust security measures are ethical imperatives to safeguard the privacy and rights of individuals involved in the creation or interaction with synthetic personas.

Ethical Concerns

A primary ethical concern for PR professionals when using synthetic AI personas and virtual influencers revolves around transparency. In fact, the Public Relations Society of America (PRSA) Code of Ethics serves as the cornerstone of public relations, guiding professionals with its principles of honesty, transparency, and responsible communication.[62] Transparency is essential to maintain trust between organizations and their audiences. It is encouraged that PR professionals should openly disclose when they employ AI-generated influencers, chatbots, or virtual spokespeople, ensuring that individuals engaging with these entities are aware of their non-human origin.[63,64,65] For example, when using a chatbot for customer service, a clear initial message stating that users are interacting with an AI assistant rather than a human representative helps establish transparency.[66]

Privacy considerations in AI-driven PR involve the responsible handling of user data. PR professionals must ensure that any data collected during interactions with synthetic personas adheres to privacy regulations and ethical standards. For instance, if an AI-generated influencer is designed to provide personalized recommendations, PR teams need to be transparent about the data they collect, obtain user consent, and employ security measures to safeguard sensitive information.[67]

The ethical dilemma of potential manipulation arises when synthetic AI personas are used to sway public opinion or behavior. PR professionals should avoid exploiting the persuasive power of AI to deceive or coerce audiences. This includes using AI-generated influencers to spread misinformation or create artificial trends that manipulate public perceptions.[68,69] Striking a balance between effective communication and ethical AI considerations is paramount in maintaining the integrity and credibility of the public relations industry.

Expanding our ethical exploration, it is crucial to consider the impact of deepfakes – sophisticated manipulations of audio and video content – when assessing the ethical dimensions of AI-generated personas. As technology advances, the potential for deepfakes adds a layer of complexity to the ethical discourse. Understanding the implications of deepfakes is essential for navigating the ethical challenges inherent in AI-generated personas, as these advancements raise concerns about misinformation, trust, and the responsible use of technology in shaping virtual identities.

Deepfakes

It is important to consider deepfakes when evaluating ethical implications of synthetic personas and virtual influencers, as PR practitioners will have to work harder in the coming years to prove fake media is fake and actual media is real. As truth itself comes into question, deepfakes present the most perilous threat to everything from accurate journalism to the human ability to discern AI-generated media. Deepfakes are defined as "a specific kind of synthetic media where[by] a person in an image or video is swapped with another person's likeness."[70] This media employs deep learning algorithms to create hyper-realistic content, often manipulating or replacing existing video or audio footage with fabricated material. Technology enables the generation of content that appears convincingly genuine, making it challenging to distinguish from authentic media. Deepfakes are commonly associated with face-swapping applications, whereby the likeness of one person is seamlessly transposed onto another's face in videos. The term "deepfake" originated in late 2017 when it was coined by a Reddit user named Deepfakes.[71] This person established a dedicated space on the online news and aggregation site, where they shared explicit videos utilizing open-source face-swapping technology. This technology then witnessed its initial widespread application in the form of non-consensual deepfake pornography, primarily directed toward women.[72] The disturbing trend has proliferated significantly since its emergence at the end of 2017.[73]

Over time, the term has evolved to encompass a broader category known as "synthetic media applications."[74] This category includes both pre-existing creations that predate the Reddit platform and newer innovations like StyleGAN, which generate realistic images of individuals that do not exist. Deepfakes remain differentiated from synthetic media, which is the broader term previously discussed encompassing various types of computer-generated content, which includes but is not limited to deepfakes. Synthetic media includes a spectrum of content creation techniques, from basic computer graphics to more advanced applications like deepfakes.[75] While deepfakes specifically focus on leveraging deep learning to create realistic manipulations of existing content, synthetic media encompass a wider range of computer-generated media that may not necessarily aim to mimic or alter existing material in a deceptive manner.[76,77]

It is not easy to identify deepfakes. Experts even have difficulty. However, to identify a deepfake, PR professionals should pay attention to various visual and auditory cues. Observing facial details such as excessive or limited blinking, mismatched eyebrows, misplaced hair, or unnatural skin appearance, including excessive airbrushing or pronounced wrinkles, can raise suspicions. Additionally, discrepancies between a person's voice and their physical appearance, such as a heavyset man with a higher-pitched feminine voice, may indicate manipulation.[78] Considering the reflections in a person's glasses, evaluating lighting is crucial, as deepfakes often struggle to accurately represent natural lighting physics. Despite the potential threats, deepfake content is sometimes labeled as such by creators taking credit for their work.[79]

For PR practitioners, the rise of deepfakes introduces significant challenges, as the use and sophistication of the technology continue to rise alongside the deployment of synthetic personas and virtual influencers. The consequences of crossing these two streams are highly detrimental, with defamation emerging as a major risk. Even if the quality of a deepfake is not impeccable, the potential for recognizable figures to be portrayed negatively can harm reputations. Plausible deniability further compounds the issue, as deepfakes provide a tool not only to create fake content but also to dismiss genuine events as fabricated. PR leaders must look to adopt a proactive approach by identifying vulnerable areas within their infrastructure, such as telecom systems or video conferencing software. Mitigation strategies include using semantic passwords, ensuring voice authentication and biometric security tools are up to date, and educating employees about the increasing threat of deepfake attacks.[80] Collaborative efforts to build a societal immune system involving thorough scrutiny of the sources and authenticity of media, and engendering real transparency are essential to counter the pervasive influence of deepfakes[81,82]

Conclusion

Political commentator and author Nina Schick put it best in interview with *Wired* magazine editor Greg Williams when she said, "Any technological solutions will be useless unless we humans are able to adapt to this new environment where fake media is commonplace."[83] In contemplating the future implications of AI synthetic spokespeople and CGI influencers on the public relations industry, it becomes clear that the disruptive nature of these technologies extends beyond specific sectors to reshape the very foundations of PR practices. The advent of these digital entities challenges traditional notions of authenticity, demanding a re-evaluation of communication strategies. As brands increasingly rely on AI-powered ambassadors, the practice of PR shifts toward more technologically integrated, data-driven storytelling.

The adoption of AI synthetic spokespeople and virtual influencers raises questions about trust and transparency in brand communication. PR professionals will need to navigate the delicate balance between leveraging the innovative capabilities of these technologies and maintaining genuine and meaningful connections with audiences. CGI influencers' ability to engage consumers on a personalized level introduces a new dimension to relationship-building in PR. It necessitates a departure from conventional approaches, encouraging practitioners to explore novel ways of crafting narratives that resonate with the digitally savvy and discerning audiences of the future.

Finally, a positive aspect of integrating AI into the PR landscape is the opening of avenues for real-time analytics and feedback, which provides invaluable insights into audience preferences and behaviors. This data-driven approach not only enhances the effectiveness of PR campaigns but also demands a higher level of adaptability from professionals in interpreting and responding to dynamic market trends. The disruptive influence of AI synthetic spokespeople and CGI influencers foreshadows a constantly updating PR landscape in which innovation, adaptability, and a nuanced understanding of technology will be integral to success.

Reflections

1. How has the integration of artificial intelligence affected traditional public relations practices, and what are the key elements of synthetic personas in this evolving landscape?
2. In what ways do influencers, spokespeople, and AI-generated synthetic personas intersect within the context of PR, and what roles do they play in shaping positive connections between organizations and their audiences?
3. What are the advantages and challenges associated with the utilization of AI-generated synthetic personas in PR, and how do these entities contribute to the dynamic communication strategies of modern organizations?

4. How have Yumi and Miquela, as two prominent synthetic AI-generated influencers, uniquely shaped and contributed to the landscape of influencer culture, and what insights do their personas offer into the evolving dynamics between technology and the influencer industry?
5. Explain how ethical considerations come into play when employing synthetic personas in PR campaigns. What responsible integration strategies can be implemented to address potential concerns?
6. Can you identify specific examples of successful PR endeavors that effectively utilize synthetic personas? How do these instances provide insights into the ever-evolving relationship between technology and public relations?

Notes

1 Mike Elgan. "How 'synthetic media' will transform business forever." *Computer World*. November 1, 2022. www.computerworld.com/article/3678172/how-synthetic-media-will-transform-business-forever.html
2 Mike Elgan. "How 'synthetic media' will transform business forever." *Computer World*. November 1, 2022. www.computerworld.com/article/3678172/how-synthetic-media-will-transform-business-forever.html
3 Jake Traylor. "AI-generated 'synthetic media' is starting to permeate the internet." *NBC News*. March 3, 2023. www.nbcnews.com/tech/tech-news/ai-generated-synthetic-media-future-content-rcna72958
4 E. Block & R. Lovegrove. "Discordant storytelling, 'honest fakery,' identity peddling: How uncanny CGI characters are jamming public relations and influencer practices." *Public Relations Inquiry*. 2021. 10(3): 265–293. https://doi.org/10.1177/2046147X211026936
5 G. Panda, A. K. Upadhyay, & K. Khandelwal. "Artificial intelligence: A strategic disruption in public relations." *Journal of Creative Communications*. 2019. 14(3): 196–213. https://doi.org/10.1177/0973258619866585
6 E. Block & R. Lovegrove. "Discordant storytelling, 'honest fakery,' identity peddling: How uncanny CGI characters are jamming public relations and influencer practices." *Public Relations Inquiry*. 2021. 10(3): 265–293. https://doi.org/10.1177/2046147X211026936
7 Tod Maffin. "Meet your new (Synthetic) brand spokesperson." *LinkedIn*. December 13, 2022. www.linkedin.com/pulse/meet-your-new-synthetic-brand-spokesperson-tod-maffin?trk=pulse-article
8 Laura McQuarrie. "SK-II's 'Yumi' is an AI-powered digital human ambassador." *TrendHunter.com*. June 19, 2019. www.trendhunter.com/trends/brand-spokespersons
9 Nasdaq. "AI transforming but not replacing public relations professionals." *Nasdaq*. November 20, 2023. www.nasdaq.com/articles/ai-transforming-but-not-replacing-public-relations-professionals
10 Mike Elgan. "How 'synthetic media' will transform business forever." *Computer World*. November 1, 2022. www.computerworld.com/article/3678172/how-synthetic-media-will-transform-business-forever.html
11 Mike Elgan. "How 'synthetic media' will transform business forever." *Computer World*. November 1, 2022. www.computerworld.com/article/3678172/how-synthetic-media-will-transform-business-forever.html

12 Mike Elgan. "How 'synthetic media' will transform business forever." *Computer World.* November 1, 2022. www.computerworld.com/article/3678172/how-synthetic-media-will-transform-business-forever.html

13 Swapnil Morandé & Mitra Amini. "Digital persona: Reflection on the power of generative AI for customer profiling in social media marketing." 2023. *Qeios.*; Xinshi Chen, Shuang Li, Hui Li, Shaohua Jiang, Yuan Qi, & Le Song. "Generative adversarial user model for reinforcement learning based recommendation system." In *International Conference on Machine Learning.* 2019. 1052–1061. http://proceedings.mlr.press/v97/chen19f.html

14 Mike Elgan. "How 'synthetic media' will transform business forever." *Computer World.* November 1, 2022. www.computerworld.com/article/3678172/how-synthetic-media-will-transform-business-forever.html

15 G. Panda, A. K. Upadhyay, & K. Khandelwal. "Artificial intelligence: A strategic disruption in public relations." *Journal of Creative Communications.* 2019. 14(3): 196–213. https://doi.org/10.1177/0973258619866585

16 Tuyet-Mai Mguyen & Sara Quach. "The effect of AI quality on customer experience and brand relationship." *Journal of Consumer Behaviour.* 2022. 21(3): 481–493; Shuili Du & Chunyan Xie. "Paradoxes of artificial intelligence in consumer markets: Ethical challenges and opportunities." *Journal of Business Research.* 2021. 129: 961–974. https://doi.org/10.1016/j.jbusres.2020.08.024

17 H. James Wilson, Paul Daugherty, & Nicola Morini Bianzino. "When AI becomes the new face of your brand." *Harvard Business Review.* June 27, 2017. https://hbr.org/2017/06/when-ai-becomes-the-new-face-of-your-brand

18 H. James Wilson, Paul Daugherty, & Nicola Morini Bianzino. "When AI becomes the new face of your brand." *Harvard Business Review.* June 27, 2017. https://hbr.org/2017/06/when-ai-becomes-the-new-face-of-your-brand

19 Sean Sands, Carla Ferraro, Vlad Demsar, & Garreth Chandler. "False idols: Unpacking the opportunities and challenges of falsity in the context of virtual influencers." *Business Horizons.* 2022. https://doi.org/10.1016/j.bushor.2022.08.002

20 Jbid Arsenyan & Agata Mirowska. "Almost human? A comparative case study on the social media presence of virtual influencers." *International Journal of Human-Computer Studies.* 2021. 155: 102694. https://doi.org/10.1016/j.ijhcs.2021.102694

21 Nasdaq. "AI transforming but not replacing public relations professionals." *Nasdaq.* November 20, 2023. www.nasdaq.com/articles/ai-transforming-but-not-replacing-public-relations-professionals

22 Tuyet-Mai Mguyen & Sara Quach. "The effect of AI quality on customer experience and brand relationship." *Journal of Consumer Behaviour.* 2022. 21(3): 481–493.

23 E. Block & R. Lovegrove. "Discordant storytelling, 'honest fakery,' identity peddling: How uncanny CGI characters are jamming public relations and influencer practices." *Public Relations Inquiry.* 2021. 10(3): 265–293. https://doi.org/10.1177/2046147X211026936

24 E. Block & R. Lovegrove. "Discordant storytelling, 'honest fakery,' identity peddling: How uncanny CGI characters are jamming public relations and influencer practices." *Public Relations Inquiry.* 2021. 10(3): 265–293. https://doi.org/10.1177/2046147X211026936

25 E. Block & R. Lovegrove. "Discordant storytelling, 'honest fakery,' identity peddling: How uncanny CGI characters are jamming public relations and influencer practices." *Public Relations Inquiry.* 2021. 10(3): 265–293. https://doi.org/10.1177/2046147X211026936

26 E. Block & R. Lovegrove. "Discordant storytelling, 'honest fakery,' identity peddling: How uncanny CGI characters are jamming public relations and influencer

practices." *Public Relations Inquiry*. 2021. 10(3): 265–293. https://doi.org/10.1177/2046147X211026936

27 E. Block & R. Lovegrove. "Discordant storytelling, 'honest fakery,' identity peddling: How uncanny CGI characters are jamming public relations and influencer practices." *Public Relations Inquiry*. 2021. 10(3): 265–293. https://doi.org/10.1177/2046147X211026936

28 E. Block & R. Lovegrove. "Discordant storytelling, 'honest fakery,' identity peddling: How uncanny CGI characters are jamming public relations and influencer practices." *Public Relations Inquiry*. 2021. 10(3): 265–293. https://doi.org/10.1177/2046147X211026936

29 Valentina Dencheva. "Influencer marketing market size worldwide from 2016 to 2023." *Statista*. September 27, 2023. www.statista.com/statistics/1092819/global-influencer-market-size/

30 *Statista*. April 2024. www.statista.com/outlook/amo/advertising/influencer-advertising/worldwide

31 Ying Lin. "Top influencer marketing platforms in 2024 [Dec 2023 Update]." *Oberlo*. www.oberlo.com/statistics/top-influencer-marketing-platforms

32 Ying Lin. "Top influencer marketing platforms in 2024 [Dec 2023 Update]." *Oberlo*. www.oberlo.com/statistics/top-influencer-marketing-platforms

33 E. Block & R. Lovegrove. "Discordant storytelling, 'honest fakery,' identity peddling: How uncanny CGI characters are jamming public relations and influencer practices." *Public Relations Inquiry*. 2021. 10(3): 265–293. https://doi.org/10.1177/2046147X211026936

34 E. Block & R. Lovegrove. "Discordant storytelling, 'honest fakery,' identity peddling: How uncanny CGI characters are jamming public relations and influencer practices." *Public Relations Inquiry*. 2021. 10(3): 265–293. https://doi.org/10.1177/2046147X211026936

35 E. Block & R. Lovegrove. "Discordant storytelling, 'honest fakery,' identity peddling: How uncanny CGI characters are jamming public relations and influencer practices." *Public Relations Inquiry*. 2021. 10(3): 265–293. https://doi.org/10.1177/2046147X211026936

36 G. Panda, A. K. Upadhyay, & K. Khandelwal. "Artificial intelligence: A strategic disruption in public relations." *Journal of Creative Communications*. 2019. 14(3): 196–213. https://doi.org/10.1177/0973258619866585

37 J. Moss. "The future of well-being is now." *American Journal of Health Promotion*. 2021. 35(8): 1173–1177. https://doi.org/10.1177/08901171211055313

38 Andrew Hutchinson. "The age of virtual influencers is coming, bringing a range of new considerations for brands." *Social Media Today*. December 5, 2023. www.socialmediatoday.com/news/the-age-of-virtual-influencers-coming/701664/

39 Andrew Hutchinson. "The age of virtual influencers is coming, bringing a range of new considerations for brands." *Social Media Today*. December 5, 2023. www.socialmediatoday.com/news/the-age-of-virtual-influencers-coming/701664/

40 Andrew Hutchinson. "The age of virtual influencers is coming, bringing a range of new considerations for brands." *Social Media Today*. December 5, 2023. www.socialmediatoday.com/news/the-age-of-virtual-influencers-coming/701664/

41 Andrew Hutchinson. "The age of virtual influencers is coming, bringing a range of new considerations for brands." *Social Media Today*. December 5, 2023. www.socialmediatoday.com/news/the-age-of-virtual-influencers-coming/701664/

42 Nina Schick. "Deepfakes are jumping from porn to politics: It's time to fight back." *Wired*. December 12, 2020. www.wired.co.uk/article/deepfakes-porn-politics

43 Jbid Arsenyan & Agata Mirowska. "Almost human? A comparative case study on the social media presence of virtual influencers." *International Journal of Human-Computer Studies*. 2021. 155: 102694. https://doi.org/10.1016/j.ijhcs.2021.102694

44 Tuyet-Mai Nguyen, Sara Quach, & Patamaporn Thaichon. "The effect of AI quality on customer experience and brand relationship." *Journal of Consumer Behaviour*. 2022. 21(3): 481–493. https://doi.org/10.1002/cb.1974

45 Laura McQuarrie. "SK-II's 'Yumi' is an AI-powered digital human ambassador." *TrendHunter.com*. June 19, 2019. www.trendhunter.com/trends/brand-spokespersons

46 Laura McQuarrie. "SK-II's 'Yumi' is an AI-powered digital human ambassador." *TrendHunter.com*. June 19, 2019. www.trendhunter.com/trends/brand-spokespersons

47 Laura McQuarrie. "SK-II's 'Yumi' is an AI-powered digital human ambassador." *TrendHunter.com*. June 19, 2019. www.trendhunter.com/trends/brand-spokespersons

48 Tod Maffin. "Meet your new (Synthetic) brand spokesperson." *LinkedIn*. December 13, 2022. www.linkedin.com/pulse/meet-your-new-synthetic-brand-spokesperson-tod-maffin?trk=pulse-article

49 Tod Maffin. "Meet your new (Synthetic) brand spokesperson." *LinkedIn*. December 13, 2022. www.linkedin.com/pulse/meet-your-new-synthetic-brand-spokesperson-tod-maffin?trk=pulse-article

50 Taylor Reily. "AI influencers: The social media personalities that don't exist." *Yahoo! Finance*. September 15, 2023.

51 Jeongwon Yang & Regina Luttrell. "Digital misinformation & disinformation: The global war of words." In *The Emerald Handbook of Computer-Mediated Communication and Social Media*, pp. 511–529. Emerald Publishing Limited, 2022.

52 Taylor Reily. "AI influencers: The social media personalities that don't exist." *Yahoo! Finance*. September 15, 2023.

53 Taylor Reily. "AI influencers: The social media personalities that don't exist." *Yahoo! Finance*. September 15, 2023.

54 Ruth Reader. "Cult beauty brand SK-II's new spokesperson is a total fake." *Fast Company*. June 18, 2019. www.fastcompany.com/90364120/cult-skincare-line-sk-iis-new-spokesperson-yumi-is-so-fake

55 Ruth Reader. "Cult beauty brand SK-II's new spokesperson is a total fake." *Fast Company*. June 18, 2019. www.fastcompany.com/90364120/cult-skincare-line-sk-iis-new-spokesperson-yumi-is-so-fake

56 Ruth Reader. "Cult beauty brand SK-II's new spokesperson is a total fake." *Fast Company*. June 18, 2019. www.fastcompany.com/90364120/cult-skincare-line-sk-iis-new-spokesperson-yumi-is-so-fake

57 E. Block & R. Lovegrove. "Discordant storytelling, 'honest fakery,' identity peddling: How uncanny CGI characters are jamming public relations and influencer practices." *Public Relations Inquiry*. 2021. 10(3): 265–293. https://doi.org/10.1177/2046147X211026936

58 Makena Rasmussen. "Brud, creators of virtual human Lil Miquela, announce a new direction." *Virtual Humans*. September 21, 2021. www.virtualhumans.org/article/brud-creators-of-virtual-human-lil-miquela-announce-a-new-direction

59 E. Block & R. Lovegrove. "Discordant storytelling, 'honest fakery,' identity peddling: How uncanny CGI characters are jamming public relations and influencer practices." *Public Relations Inquiry*. 2021. 10(3): 265–293. https://doi.org/10.1177/2046147X211026936

60 E. Block & R. Lovegrove. "Discordant storytelling, 'honest fakery,' identity peddling: How uncanny CGI characters are jamming public relations and influencer practices." *Public Relations Inquiry*. 2021. 10(3): 265–293. https://doi.org/10.1177/2046147X211026936

61 E. Block & R. Lovegrove. "Discordant storytelling, 'honest fakery,' identity peddling: How uncanny CGI characters are jamming public relations and influencer practices." *Public Relations Inquiry*. 2021. 10(3): 265–293. https://doi.org/10.1177/2046147X211026936

62 *PRSA code of Ethics*. PRSA. (n.d.). www.prsa.org/about/prsa-code-of-ethics
63 G. Panda, A. K. Upadhyay, & K. Khandelwal. "Artificial intelligence: A strategic disruption in public relations." *Journal of Creative Communications*. 2019. 14(3): 196–213. https://doi.org/10.1177/0973258619866585
64 Laura McQuarrie. "SK-II's 'Yumi' is an AI-powered digital human ambassador." *TrendHunter.com*. June 19, 2019. www.trendhunter.com/trends/brand-spokespersons
65 Michele Ewing. "Navigating ethical implications for AI-driven PR practice." *www.prsa.org*. September 2023. www.prsa.org/article/navigating-ethical-implications-for-ai-driven-pr-practice
66 Michele Ewing. "Navigating ethical implications for AI-driven PR practice." *www.prsa.org*. September 2023. www.prsa.org/article/navigating-ethical-implications-for-ai-driven-pr-practice
67 Michele Ewing. "Navigating ethical implications for AI-driven PR practice." *www.prsa.org*. September 2023. www.prsa.org/article/navigating-ethical-implications-for-ai-driven-pr-practice
68 Nina Schick. "Deepfakes are jumping from porn to politics: It's time to fight back." *Wired*. December 12, 2020. www.wired.co.uk/article/deepfakes-porn-politics
69 Mike Elgan. "How 'synthetic media' will transform business forever." *Computer World*. November 1, 2022. www.computerworld.com/article/3678172/how-synthetic-media-will-transform-business-forever.html
70 Meredith Somers. "Deepfakes, explained." *MIT Sloan*. July 21, 2020. https://mitsloan.mit.edu/ideas-made-to-matter/deepfakes-explained
71 Meredith Somers. "Deepfakes, explained." *MIT Sloan*. July 21, 2020. https://mitsloan.mit.edu/ideas-made-to-matter/deepfakes-explained
72 Nina Schick. "Deepfakes are jumping from porn to politics: It's time to fight back." *Wired*. December 12, 2020. www.wired.co.uk/article/deepfakes-porn-politics
73 Nina Schick. "Deepfakes are jumping from porn to politics: It's time to fight back." *Wired*. December 12, 2020. www.wired.co.uk/article/deepfakes-porn-politics
74 Meredith Somers. "Deepfakes, explained." *MIT Sloan*. July 21, 2020. https://mit-sloan.mit.edu/ideas-made-to-matter/deepfakes-explained
75 Meredith Somers. "Deepfakes, explained." *MIT Sloan*. July 21, 2020. https://mit-sloan.mit.edu/ideas-made-to-matter/deepfakes-explained
76 Mike Elgan. "How 'synthetic media' will transform business forever." *Computer World*. November 1, 2022. www.computerworld.com/article/3678172/how-synthetic-media-will-transform-business-forever.html
77 Meredith Somers. "Deepfakes, explained." *MIT Sloan*. July 21, 2020. https://mit-sloan.mit.edu/ideas-made-to-matter/deepfakes-explained
78 Jeongwon Yang & Regina Luttrell. "Digital misinformation & disinformation: The global war of words." In *The Emerald Handbook of Computer-Mediated Communication and Social Media*, pp. 511–529. Emerald Publishing Limited, 2022.
79 Meredith Somers. "Deepfakes, explained." *MIT Sloan*. July 21, 2020. https://mitsloan.mit.edu/ideas-made-to-matter/deepfakes-explained
80 Meredith Somers. "Deepfakes, explained." *MIT Sloan*. July 21, 2020. https://mitsloan.mit.edu/ideas-made-to-matter/deepfakes-explained
81 Meredith Somers. "Deepfakes, explained." *MIT Sloan*. July 21, 2020. https://mitsloan.mit.edu/ideas-made-to-matter/deepfakes-explained
82 Kyle Heim & Stephanie Craft. "Transparency in journalism." In *The Routledge Handbook of Mass Media Ethics* (2nd ed.), edited by L. Wilkins and C. G. Christians. Routledge, 2020. https://doi-org.libezproxy2.syr.edu/10.4324/9781315545929
83 Nina Schick. "Deepfakes are jumping from porn to politics: It's time to fight back." *Wired*. December 12, 2020. www.wired.co.uk/article/deepfakes-porn-politics

7

AI-POWERED ENHANCEMENTS IN MEDIA RELATIONS

Exploring Potential and Ethical Considerations in Public Relations

Hollin Nies and Liang Zhao

Learning Objectives

1. Explore the impact of AI on media relations and understand the broader applications of AI technology on the communications field, including how AI tools can assist in providing real-time media research, targeted outreach, and sentiment analysis, as well as daily tasks such as drafting emails, generating campaign ideas, and maintaining relationships with journalists to streamline workflow and improve efficiency.
2. Examine the ethical implications and risks associated with leveraging AI in media and public relations regarding bias, plagiarism, and authenticity, as well as what strategies may be necessary to mitigate these risks in professional practice.
3. Consider the future implications of AI use in media relations and conjunction with the potential advancements in AI technology, its evolving role in shaping communication strategies, relationship management, and content creation in the media landscape.
4. Discover and apply practical techniques for integrating AI tools into media relations practices, including conducting effective media research, leveraging sentiment analysis for targeted outreach, and navigating ethical considerations to ensure responsible and effective use of AI in professional contexts.

Introduction

Many technological advancements in recent decades have transformed *media relations*, from the telephone to the internet to social media. Most recently, the efficiency and accessible nature of *artificial intelligence* (AI) is making the

DOI: 10.4324/9781032671482-10

technology unavoidable for media professionals, as much of our work is about personalized communication.

AI has been around for several decades, with its formal foundation attributed to a conference at Dartmouth College in 1956. Over the past 20 or so years, we truly started to see the maturation of the technology and the possibilities that lie within it. Artificial intelligence is set to affect nearly 40% of all jobs, according to a recent analysis by the International Monetary Fund (IMF),[1] although we can assume that this percentage will continue to grow quite rapidly.

The following represents a brief timeline of notable developments shaping AI.

- Late 1990s and early 2000s: The rise of the internet made data more available and AI training more effective. There have always been numerous academics, professionals, and technologists who have touted the power of AI.
- 2000s and 2010s: The machine and deep learning advancement boosted interest and investment in AI technologies, coupled with more advanced computing power.
- 2015–2020: Tech companies developed more user-friendly AI tools. Sam Altman, Greg Brockman, Reid Hoffman, Jessica Livingston, Peter Thiel, Elon Musk, Amazon Web Services (AWS), Infosys, and YC Research announced the formation of OpenAI in December of 2015.[2]
- 2020s: With more easily accessible AI application programming interfaces (APIs), companies and consumers can access AI for various use cases.

OpenAI's launch of ChatGPT in 2020 was a watershed moment for the AI community, businesses, and consumers, as it was quickly recognized as one of the most advanced and accessible language models to date. ChatGPT and other similar tools have quickly become co-pilots for many professionals across various industries, and it is no different in the field of *public relations* (PR). As of November 2023, ChatGPT hit 100 million weekly users and over two million developers were using the company's API, including the majority of Fortune 500 companies.[3] With Microsoft, OpenAI, Google, and other technology companies rolling out AI products, PR professionals who acknowledge AI and utilize it to its full potential across media relations, crisis management, and *strategic communications* will have an advantage over laggards. According to Harvard Business School Professor Karim Lakhani, a certified expert in workplace technology and AI, "AI won't replace humans – but humans with AI will replace humans without AI."[4]

AI and Media Relations

AI has fundamentally shifted how media relations are conducted in less than two years. Before AI, tasks like media monitoring required tedious scanning of media outlets for the right reporter. Processes like maintaining and updating media databases involved consistent tracking of reporter details, tasks that have only increased in their time consumption and manual nature, given the rapid evolution of the *communications landscape* in recent years. AI can be used to help research, ideate, and generate new content ideas. PR professionals equipped with AI tools are poised to outperform those who have yet to embrace this new and exciting technological copilot.

Media Strategy and Ideation

Creating a media or campaign strategy requires creativity and deep knowledge of the media landscape. AI can help facilitate this creative process and remove possible roadblocks that stem from parsing through the wealth of content from social media, news outlets, online discussions, and company websites to iden-tify emerging trends and popular and existing themes in public coverage. In instances when there is a large amount of information, the ability to *analyze data* and segment audience demographics and interests allows PR professionals to be more intentional with their media strategy. With carefully curated feedback, AI can be trained to guide the creative process and act as a thought partner in testing out approaches and story angles.

Messaging and Media Training

AI is a significant asset in enhancing storytelling and messaging. Tools like Chat-GPT and other language learning models excel in conducting media-specific research and coverage analysis to produce insights that help prep spokespeople more holistically, inclusive of generating possible questions a journalist might ask. Another great way to use AI tools is to help craft Q&As, especially in an-ticipating and preparing for challenging questions, and to assist PR professionals and spokespeople in speech analytics. While these tools will never be able to replace experienced media trainers who can advise on media styles and nuances, tools like the AI feedback partner Poised can offer a low-risk environment for spokespeople to practice their speeches and presentations and garner real-time feedback on speech delivery, such as pace, tone, and clarity.

Media Monitoring

Media monitoring has historically been a labor-intensive task usually managed by junior staff members starting off their day with reading news about their cli-ents, a rite of passage but also a learning experience. The ability to filter through large volumes of news articles and become familiar with an outlet, its respective reporters, and their coverage are learned skills that every PR professional needs to do in order to understand the news cycle and relate it back to their clients and organizations. AI tools like CisionOne and Meltwater can quickly pull coverage and distill sentiment analytics around public opinion and media trends, helping PR professionals make more informed decisions in shaping media strategies and responding to trending narratives.

Media Research

Building and updating media contact lists – another rite of passage – requires extensive research and attention to detail. PR professionals have to continuously track journalist movements, information that is gathered through social media sites like Twitter and LinkedIn as well as newsletters like *TalkingBizNews*. With AI, PR teams can identify relevant journalists and media outlets for their *outreach efforts*. AI-driven analytics of past journalist coverage can help indicate interest and publication themes and help PR professionals customize their pitches and releases accordingly.

Pitching

According to PR management company Propel, journalists respond, on average, to 3.25% of pitches they receive.[5] That means, for every 100 pitches that a PR professional sends, they will likely receive three responses from reporters, and rarely will all three responses be a "yes," making it an inefficient use of both the PR professional's and the reporter's time. Building a great pitch that distills the content to its essential elements while simultaneously highlighting a new, unique, and intriguing issue is a laborious task. Having a platform like PRophet can help surface relevant journalists in real time, while Propel can enable PR professionals to pitch, monitor, and measure pitching impact, easing the activity of media pitching.

Crisis Communications

AI does not sleep or eat, and it does not have the normal and routine bodily functions that would typically disrupt or pause a professional's workday flow. This is especially valuable in PR, where time is of the essence when a crisis occurs. Because of its 24/7 nature, AI can assist PR professionals in identifying emerging issues from a broader spectrum of sources during a crisis.

Sentiment Analysis and Reporting

Analyzing large amounts of data is where AI really shines, as it can efficiently support *sentiment analysis and reporting* by distilling data from sources such as social media, news articles, blogs, and customer feedback. While putting together a share of voice or media coverage reports could take hours, AI can shave off time from such analytical and time-intensive tasks. As AI captures more content and increases its discernment capabilities, it will be able to pick up sentiment (positive, negative, or neutral), as well as language nuances such as idioms, sarcasm, and emotions with more accuracy.

Building Relationships Using AI

There is a common saying in the industry that PR is "all about who you know." While this adage is not completely true anymore, as communication tools have democratized access to journalists, there is still no denying that PR success often hinges on the ability to connect with the right members of the media and build and *manage relationships* quickly, which includes journalists, influencers, clients, and industry partners.

A robust network of industry professionals and journalists can lead to more media coverage and collaboration opportunities. Having relationships with key members of the media or knowing how to get to them quickly can help a story get picked up. As such, a strong network of clients and industry friendlies can lead to a more well-rounded story and partnership opportunities.

AI can help PR professionals build connections, from identifying relevant media contacts to personalizing communications. It can also streamline one's workflow by copiloting brainstorming sessions, timely communication in moments of crisis, and mapping out media and digital landscapes.

Identifying Relevant Media Contacts

Landing a story with the right journalist at the right time or getting a pitch accepted by an editor can be as thrilling as hitting a home run in the bottom of the ninth inning in a tied baseball game. This moment in baseball is a symphony of precision, skill, and great timing – much like successful media relations. AI can be the coach who can help identify the pitch best suited for the winning swing, it can help PR professionals zero in on members of the media who are most likely to resonate with the pitch. In media relations, platforms like PRophet can short-list reporters, rate the pitches, and make match recommendations.

Personalized Communications

Reporters get hundreds of pitches each day, and when a PR professional does not have the home-field advantage of knowing the reporter, the next best approach is to stand out. AI can play a role in this process by understanding the "field," analyzing a journalist's past articles, coverage, and potential topics of interest with speed and accuracy. PR professionals are then able to leverage this data and personalize communication that is bespoke to each reporter or editor.

Tracking and Managing Relationships

Media lists that are housed in Google Sheets or Excel are part of just about every PR professional's deliverables. AI is now able to streamline this time-consuming task by automating contact management, from updating databases with journalist contacts to tracking beat or affiliation changes. Another way that AI can help enhance the relationship is by tracking and logging communications such as emails, calls, and meetings. Often times, tracking the strengths of relationships and last outreach can be a manual task. For large teams or agencies, quickly accessing insight into journalists–PR relationships is greatly helpful in optimizing relationships and pitches.

Connectivity Analysis

A clear understanding of communication response rate, response time, tone, and sentiment can be helpful for PR professionals to understand journalists' communication preferences, style, and whether or not a follow-up is on future to-do lists. Whether a PR professional is a freelancer, a part of an agency, or at a more established company, a deeper understanding of reporter connectivity can help individuals and teams optimize pitches and follow-ups.

Automating Alerts and Follow-Ups

With a busy schedule and numerous balls up in the air, having a copilot who can send reminders and automate repetitive tasks can sometimes be a game changer. Successful relationships are built on a foundation of consistency, follow-through, and authentic communication. Leveraging technology tools to help remember birthdays, special events, and anniversaries can set a PR professional apart.

Building and nurturing relationships is at the heart of the job for a PR professional, and AI has emerged as a copilot to help deepen connections effectively. Its predictive capabilities can indicate the best time to pitch, the moment to follow up, and possible topics of interest. One can think of AI as the assistant who always knows who to talk to, what to say, and when to say it.

AI-Assisted Content

PR professionals often juggle multiple tasks and are responsible for maintaining consistent brand guidelines, creating compelling narratives, and tailoring messaging for specific channels, different audiences, and various purposes.

On any given day, we write newsletters, press releases, speeches, articles, social media content, interview Q&As, and any additional content about an organization or topic for external or internal distribution. While we should not ask ChatGPT and similar tools to write a press release or blog article and consider the task complete, ChatGPT can help PR professionals start the creative process, find synonyms, test drive content flow, and generally inspire more creativity.

Ideas and Inspiration

Whether it is brainstorming a topic for press releases, finding an intriguing angle for a blog post, reworking social media content to include emojis, or jump-starting a meaningful email to internal team members, AI can be a thought partner throughout the process and inject creativity into the process during these early stages of content creation.

Content Creation

When it comes to longer-form content like blogs, bylines, and op-eds, the ability to adapt to various styles and formats can provide the versatility that the content needs for various outlets and audiences. AI can learn writing styles and brand guidelines to help content creators to adapt to different styles and formats.

Optimizing Content for Various Platforms

Because LinkedIn, TikTok, and Twitter audiences and content formats are varied, posts should all be uniquely tailored for each respective platform. While understanding that each platform has tone, length, and style differences, AI can optimize content accordingly.

Maintaining Consistency

Effective communication and well-crafted content are integral to a brand's success in amplifying its story. Brand guidelines and content are usually painstakingly curated, down to the comma, as it exemplifies a brand's personality and audience. Therefore, consistency in communication is key. AI tools can ensure that content stays true to a brand's voice and guidelines, and it can help maintain consistency across various communication lengths and formats.

Human- vs. AI-Generated Content

Human- and AI-generated content can have very nuanced differentiators. The very fact that AI learns from human-generated content makes this a uniquely complicated question when it comes to distinguishing the two forms of writing, although some aspects stand out more than most: creativity and emotional complexity, rhetorical variation, data origination, and the varied use of contextual interpretation and conversational tone. For instance, look at the following example.

Human-generated prompt: "Draft an email from a PR professional to a journalist pitching a story around a hypothetical startup and its recent funding round."

AI-Drafted Answer, ChatGPT[6]

Subject: Exclusive: [Startup Name] Secures $25M in Seed Funding for Groundbreaking [Tech Innovation]

Dear [Journalist's Name],

I hope this message finds you in great spirits. My name is [your name], representing [startup name], an exciting tech venture that's poised to revolutionize [specific industry].

Key Points:

Seed funding breakthrough: [Startup name] has successfully secured an impressive $25M in seed funding.

Innovative tech: Discover how our groundbreaking [tech innovation] is set to reshape [industry].

Executive insights: Hear from [executive name], the visionary leader behind [startup name's] success.

Exclusive coverage: We invite you to exclusively cover the exciting developments at [startup name]. This could include an interview with [executive name], insights into our tech, or a behind-the-scenes look at our journey.

Next steps: If this piques your interest, we'd love to discuss how we can tailor the story to align with your readership. Please let us know your availability for a brief call or meeting. Thank you for considering [startup name] for this exciting coverage opportunity. We look forward to the possibility of sharing our success story with your esteemed readers.

Best,
[Your full name]
[Your position]
[Your contact information]
[Startup name]

Human-Drafted Answer

Hi X,

I hope your Friday is going well! I saw your piece this morning on the recent drop in female-led tech investments and thought this might be of interest. I recently started working with *company*, a technology platform, and wanted to let you know about the seed round they secured last month – over $25M from over 80% female investors! A huge win for the sector, with hopefully more to come.

If you're thinking about writing a follow-up story on this morning's piece, I'd be happy to connect you with our founder and CEO to discuss the fundraising, the current state of the tech investment landscape, and what the future looks like for the industry as a whole. Any interest? Happy to provide further details if you'd like; just let me know.

Enjoy the weekend!

Best,
X

Creativity and Originality

Referring to the preceding example, it is easy to note the difference in style, tone, and emotion. While AI can imitate many of these aspects, the context of when and how to be formal vs. informal is harder to define under limited parameters– and AI language models have significant limitations in that respect. Delving into the nature of human language can help to highlight other notable differentiators, but it is important to note that (at the time of writing), the majority of AI writing software packages will have many familiar tools available to the average user, and the AI-generated content will have similar tone and formatting across various platforms. There is a big reason for this: 95% of these AI writing tools use the same large language models (LLMs)[7] as their reference point – this means that essentially, they are speaking the same language.

This is especially helpful when it comes to distinguishing between origins, because while AI can *generate content* that is new and innovative in its arrangement, its creativity is surprisingly derivative – and over time, the pattern becomes increasingly evident to its human-centric audience. It is clear that AI struggles with truly novel concepts that fall outside of its training data.

Contextual Understanding and Nuance

Another notable differentiator may seem more obvious: cultural and contextual inferences. Alternative intelligence is hard-pressed to develop a deep or accurate understanding of the subtleties which humans have developed in their linguistic practice. This is not to say that it is incapable, by any means, but it often lacks the capacity to immediately pick up certain nuances in tone, like sarcasm, humor, or culturally specific language or references.

Adaptability in Learning and Data Origination

Humans can learn from a wide variety of source material, adapting to new information quickly and efficiently, while making the necessary intuitive leaps with which machine learning still tends to struggle. Figuring out how and when to apply this learned knowledge is an obstacle that many language models grapple with on the regular: AI systems typically learn from specific datasets and develop algorithms that improve over time; however, by design, its adaptability is confined to the scope of its programming and the nature of the data itself.

Personality and Empathy

Perhaps the most consistent distinguishing element when it comes to human- vs. AI-generated content is the aspect of empathy and personalization – and the lack thereof. As you can see in the preceding example, human-generated content often reflects a more emotionally intelligent manner, intentionally informal to immediately establish a connection to the reader or make it more relatable to its audience. AI, as it stands today, lacks genuine empathy and thus cannot truly relate to human emotions, as its attempts are based on patterns learned from data rather than sincere or meaningful intuition.

BOX 7.1   ACTIVE LEARNING EXERCISE 1: ANNOUNCEMENT ANALYSIS

Objective: To analyze the use of artificial intelligence (AI) in the public relations (PR) industry through real-world examples of recent company announcements.

Instructions

1. Divide the class into small groups, assigning each group a recent news announcement from a publicly traded company.
2. Have each group evaluate the announcement across various public media (company-generated press releases, social media, blog content, etc.).

3. Provide the groups with guiding questions to analyze their assigned announcement, focusing on the following aspects:

   a. What aspect of the announcement was possibly AI generated? Elaborate on why you believe this is the case, focusing on language style, tone, similarity of content, etc.

   b. Are there any areas where they could have utilized AI? Include examples such as the implementation of AI-powered media monitoring tools, AI-driven content generation platforms, AI-based crisis communication strategies, and more.

   c. How, if at all, could the potential use of AI be detrimental to this announcement?

   d. Do we think that this was a responsible use of AI?

4. Allow the groups time to discuss and analyze their announcement, encouraging them to identify key insights and lessons learned.

5. Reconvene as a class and have each group present its findings.

List of Contemporary AI-Powered Tools That Media Relations Professionals Can Use

a *ChatGPT*: The flagship OpenAI chatbot based on an LLM that enables users to refine and steer a conversation toward a desired length, format, style, level of detail, and language.

b *Cision Communications Cloud (CisionOne)*: A comprehensive platform for media monitoring, influencer (media) research, and analytics. It helps in identifying key journalists and tracking media coverage.

c *Propel*: Propel is the only end-to-end solution for PR management, monitoring, measurement and artificial media intelligence (AMI).

d *PRophet*: PRophet uses AI to locate journalist targets in real time.

e *PRNewswire's Press Release Builder*: A tool that generates simple and professional press releases using only a brief description of an announcement and company.

f *Canva*: An easy-to-use AI-powered design platform that allows you to create a variety of graphics for your business, anything from social media images and web banners to marketing brochures, flyers, business cards, presentations, and more.

g *Otter AI*: An AI meeting assistant that records audio, writes notes, captures action items, and generates summaries.

h *Meltwater*: Offers media monitoring and social listening tools. It uses AI to analyze media coverage and social media conversations to provide insights into public sentiment.

i *Brandwatch*: An AI-powered tool for digital consumer intelligence, helping PR professionals understand consumer sentiments, trends, and online discussions about their brand or relevant topics.

j *Hootsuite Insights*: Utilizes AI for social media monitoring and analytics, helping teams to understand social trends and audience sentiments.

k *BuzzSumo*: Provides insights into content performance across the web and social media. It is useful for researching content trends, monitoring competitors, and finding key influencers.

l *Poised:* An AI feedback partner that helps professionals prepare for presentations, customer calls, interviews and more with private real-time feedback and personalized suggestions, helping individuals speak confidently.

m *Crayon*: An AI tool for competitive intelligence. It tracks competitors' digital footprints to provide insights into their strategies.

n *Grammarly*: An AI-powered writing assistant that enhances the quality of written communication, ensuring clarity, correctness, and effectiveness in content.

o *Talkwalker*: This AI-enabled tool offers social listening and analytics, helping brands monitor reputation and gain insights from social conversations.

p *Zoho Social*: Provides AI-driven predictions on the best times to post on social media, enhancing the engagement of campaigns.

q *Prowly*: An AI-driven PR software that helps in finding relevant journalists, creating visual press releases, and managing media relations.

r *MarketMuse*: Uses AI to assist with content research and strategy, helping professionals create content that resonates with their target audience.

s *Audiense*: Offers audience segmentation and insights. It uses AI to analyze audience behaviors and preferences.

Ethical Implications of AI in Media and Public Relations

From voice-activated virtual assistants to personalized content recommendations, AI's presence is ubiquitous across both the personal and professional landscapes, and as it has become increasingly integral to our daily lives, it also demands an increased level of responsibility in its use – particularly in fields that build on human connection and strategic communication, like that of media and public relations.

AI is no longer a speculative concept, but an entrenched reality in the wide-ranging field of communications. It acts as a "strategic disruptor,"[8] streamlining repetitive tasks, interpreting online conversations, and even predicting crises. The symbiotic relationships among AI, media, and PR raises the curtain on a new era, prompting us to explore the ethical dimensions of this alliance.

As we embrace AI's transformative power in these industries, a crucial discourse emerges, centered on ethical considerations and accountability. This section delves into the *ethical implications* of leveraging AI in media and public relations activities, exploring the delicate balance between technological advancement and responsible *professional practice.*

The Ethical Landscape: AI and Trust in PR

AI, when utilizing its most humanoid cognitive abilities in PR activities, offers a dramatic paradigm shift in the field. It automates tasks, interprets online conversations, designs data-driven campaigns, and predicts crises – and its myriad advancements continually redefine the landscape, presenting both opportunities and challenges for the PR industry from the simplest tasks to the most comprehensive and strategically planned initiatives.

And yet while AI augments efficiency, concerns loom about the potential erosion of human-centric qualities vital to PR – trust and storytelling.[9] One of the reasons why the ethical use of AI is important for this profession is because PR professionals are – by the very nature of their profession – the gatekeepers of truth. The information we provide our public audience has been and should always be accepted as truth, and thus be disseminated into the public domain as fact. With the rapid development of AI systems and our overall reliance on their massive potential, this brings along an ethical conundrum when it comes to media and communications efforts, and the avenues where they intersect.

The PR industry, deeply rooted in intuition and human touch, relies on qualities currently beyond AI's grasp – although this may not be the case for long. While *innovation* in the field continues to advance at a breakneck pace, this stands as a pivotal moment for those in the PR sector, as our work must be deeply cognizant of any potential *bias*, accuracy, legitimacy, and accountability when contributing to the space. This cognizance clearly extends to the increased use of AI in the industry, as PR practitioners emphasize the irreplaceability of human creativity, empathy, and meaningful relationships – and as such, we must ensure that AI's broad applications do not threaten these fundamental aspects of our work.

AI in Media: A Double-Edged Sword

As AI integrates into media relations, as with all new and emerging technology, its impact must be weighed against both its impressive advancements and the sincere ethical dilemmas it raises.

Plagiarism and Copyright

One of the most concerning aspects of ethical AI use in contemporary practice is the propensity for *plagiarism* and copyright infringement. The recent dispute over the ownership legitimacy of Kashtanova's *"Zarya of the Dawn"*[10] and *The New York Times*' lawsuit against OpenAI[11] currently making its way through Manhattan courts only further highlight the contentiousness of the complex copyright issue. As AI-generated content becomes more and more prevalent, distinguishing between original and machine-generated work becomes quite challenging– increasingly so, as the line between human and AI authorship only continues to blur. Striking a balance that respects intellectual property while leveraging AI's creative potential is an imperative ethical consideration.

Bias and Accuracy Concerns

Addressing the responsibility and potential biases embedded within AI algorithms is crucial to avoid perpetuating inequalities or discrimination, as human behavior and prejudice are easily transferred to machines. AI-generated content may inadvertently harbor biases or inaccuracies based on the beliefs reflected in the human-generated content it learns from, such as the egregious controversy over Black people being mislabeled as gorillas by Google's early image analysis software in 2015,[12] emphasizing the necessity of further oversight and validation. PR practitioners therefore must bear the responsibility of mitigating unintended consequences and ensuring the integrity of information disseminated to the public.

Legitimacy Concerns and Deepfake Influence

There is a notable rise in deepfakes and synthetic content that poses a sincere threat to the legitimacy in media relations. In the fall of 2023, in one week alone, pop star Taylor Swift, actor Tom Hanks, journalist Gayle King, and YouTube personality MrBeast all reported that AI versions of themselves had been used for cookware marketing, deceptive dental plan promotions, iPhone giveaway offers, and other ads, without their express permission.[13] These incidents are becoming a part of a frequent pattern of blatant AI misuse in publicity and marketing campaigns.

Only recently, OpenAI announced that it is taking steps to prevent the tool's exploitative potential in the 2024 U.S. elections, already a deeply divisive media circus.[14] The use of a synthetic version of a celebrity's voice or AI-manipulated footage challenges the *authenticity* of media content, which means media professionals must constantly grapple with the ethical implications of navigating a landscape where fabricated information can deeply influence public perception.

Transparency and Fairness

And yet, transparent disclosure of AI's involvement in media relations – especially in the coming months as the world adjusts to the rapid technological and regulatory advancement in the AI space – becomes a cornerstone for maintaining trust and ensuring fairness in coverage. PR professionals must navigate the fine line between leveraging AI's capabilities and maintaining openness with stakeholders.[15]

Looking Ahead

As AI cements its presence in PR and media relations, coexistence becomes a key imperative – aiming to shift the narrative from fearmongering and restriction to a careful yet enthusiastic harnessing of potential, with industry professionals braced to adapt to these rapid changes as the market reshapes itself around AI's broad range of benefits.

BOX 7.2   ACTIVE LEARNING EXERCISE 2: ETHICS IN AI APPLICATIONS

Objective: To analyze the ethical implications of using AI in public relations campaigns through a hypothetical scenario and engage in critical discussion.

1. Imagine a PR firm representing a pharmaceutical company launching a new drug targeting a widespread health issue. The firm decides to leverage AI to analyze social media conversations, news articles, and online forums to identify potential influencers and shape public opinion positively about the drug. The AI algorithm identifies individuals who have expressed concerns about the health issue or have shared personal stories related to it. The PR firm then crafts personalized messages, leveraging emotional appeals and tailored content, to engage with these individuals and encourage them to advocate for the drug.

2. Divide the students into small groups and assign each group a role: PR firm representatives, members of vulnerable populations, regulatory authorities, and ethical advisers.

3. Encourage each group to discuss the ethical implications of the scenario from their assigned perspective. Prompt questions could include:

   a. What are the potential benefits and risks of this type of AI-powered PR campaign?

   b. How might the campaign affect vulnerable populations targeted by an algorithm?

   c. What ethical principles should guide the actions of the PR firm in this situation?

d. What role, if any, should regulatory authorities play in overseeing AI use in PR campaigns?

e. How can ethical advisers help a PR firm navigate this dilemma and uphold ethical standards?

4. Have each group present their analysis of the ethical dilemma, outlining potential courses of action and discussing the implications of different decisions from the various perspectives.

5. Facilitate a class-wide discussion, encouraging students to compare and contrast the ethical dilemmas presented in each scenario and explore overarching themes related to ethics in AI applications.

While AI brings forth an unprecedented level of efficiency in any industry, communications professionals – especially those in media and public relations – must safeguard its human-centric values, ensuring the responsible and ethical integration of technology into the space. Education, proactive industry adaptation, and a commitment to ethical practice will guide the PR industry toward a future when AI augments human capabilities without compromising its most important aspect: its integrity.

Anticipating Technological Growth and Challenges

Looking toward the future, we are already seeing shockingly fast technological growth in AI, but as with all forays into new and emerging tech, this is coupled with serious potential pitfalls. As the United States reaches a presidential election year, the rise of misinformation and disinformation – only further accelerated by the rapid advancement of AI tools – has become a growing concern. However, it is easy to see an opportunity for PR professionals to drive positive change by educating across professions and preparing for the challenges posed by AI-driven information landscapes.

Already, we are seeing a response to this exponential growth as industry standards work to embrace AI use with the care and caution it demands. The recent development of the AI ethics guidance by the Public Relations Society of America (PRSA)[16] reflects a strategic response to the industry's biggest concerns. The guidance, an extension of PRSA's existing Code of Ethics, was meticulously crafted by the PRSA AI Workgroup.

The evolving AI landscape brings forth crucial considerations for communicators, particularly in the realm of media and PR professionals. Those of us in this industry must balance the great potential of AI alongside the dangers of copyright infringement, the caustic spread of disinformation, and the cultural biases that are emerging in powerful AI models that we are already seeing in the market. The PRSA guidance, and other efforts to standardize AI development, are at the very least an attempt to emphasize the need for practitioners to recognize that content generated by AI models reflects certain prejudices present in its training data, and until those issues are resolved, we have a professional responsibility to verify and oversee its work, whether it is through fact-checking, proper content sourcing, or avoiding the misappropriation of credit for AI-generated content.

Amidst the current phase in AI's tech development cycle, education is a cornerstone for practitioners and organizations. PR professionals are urged to find their voice, speaking up against unethical practices and assuming the role of the "ethical conscience" throughout AI's development and use.[17] This educational imperative extends beyond individual practitioners to encompass organizations, fostering a collective responsibility for ethical AI use in media and public relations. In exploring AI's potential in transforming media relations, the PR industry stands at a pivotal juncture, balancing the promise of innovation with the imperative of ethical stewardship.

What it boils down to, essentially, is this: embrace the disruption, but do so responsibly – for the journey with AI in media has just begun.

Reflections

1. Consider the broader implications of AI adoption in the media industry and society as a whole. What are some of the potential socioeconomic impacts, changes in job roles, and shifts in power dynamics that may arise from the widespread integration of AI technologies in media relations and beyond?
2. In what ways do you see AI shaping the future of media relations and public relations practices? Think about the potential benefits and challenges associated with integrating AI tools into communication strategies, and consider how organizations can leverage these technologies to enhance their relationships with journalists and other stakeholders.
3. The chapter highlights the ethical implications and risks associated with leveraging AI in media and public relations. Reflect on the concerns raised, such as bias, plagiarism, and authenticity, and consider how organizations can address these issues while harnessing the potential of AI technologies.
4. How might AI-driven content generation affect the overall quality of communication efforts in media relations? Consider the balance between efficiency and authenticity when using AI to generate press releases, social media content, or other materials, and reflect on the importance of maintaining transparency and credibility in communication practices.
5. How has your understanding of the role of AI in media relations evolved while reading this chapter? Do you think these technologies will affect the way organizations interact with the media?

Notes

1 Liang, Annabelle. "Ai to Hit 40% of Jobs and Worsen Inequality, IMF Says." BBC News, January 15, 2024. www.bbc.com/news/business-67977967.
2 Raval, Raval. "OpenAI – Redefining Artificial General Intelligence." LinkedIn, January 11, 2023. www.linkedin.com/pulse/openai-redefining-artificial-general-intelligence-khushbu-raval/?trk=public_post.
3 Porter, Jon. "CHATGPT Continues to Be One of the Fastest-Growing Services Ever." The Verge, November 6, 2023. www.theverge.com/2023/11/6/23948386/chatgpt-active-user-count-openai-developer-conference.
4 Lakhani, Karim. "Ai Won't Replace Humans – But Humans with AI Will Replace Humans without AI." Harvard Business Review, August 4, 2023. https://hbr.org/2023/08/ai-wont-replace-humans-but-humans-with-ai-will-replace-humans-without-ai.
5 "The Propel Media Barometer – Q3 2022." Propel PRM. Accessed February 1, 2024. www.propelmypr.com/research/the-propel-media-barometer-q3-2022.
6 OpenAI. "ChatGPT (Feb 29 Version) [Large Language Model]." 2023. https://chat.openai.com
7 Guinness, Harry. "The Best AI Writing Generators in 2023." Zapier, September 5, 2023. https://zapier.com/blog/best-ai-writing-generator/.
8 Panda, G., A.K. Upadhyay, and K. Khandelwal. "Artificial Intelligence: A Strategic Disruption in Public Relations." Journal of Creative Communications, 2019, 14, 196–213. https://doi.org/10.1177/0973258619866585.
9 Toomey, Sarah. "A PR Professional's Guide: Promoting Education Technology in the Age of Ai." PR Daily, January 4, 2024. www.prdaily.com/pr-professionals-guide-ed-tech-age-ai/.
10 Oelsner, Ben. "How to Navigate the Legal Issues of Using Generative AI to Create Content." KO, March 20, 2023. https://kofirm.com/how-to-navigate-the-legal-issues-of-using-generative-ai-to-create-content.
11 Grynbaum, Michael. "The Times Sues OpenAI and Microsoft over A.I. Use of Copyrighted Work." The New York Times, December 27, 2023. www.nytimes.com/2023/12/27/business/media/new-york-times-open-ai-microsoft-lawsuit.html.
12 Grant, Nico, and Kashmir Hill. "Google's Photo App Still Can't Find Gorillas and Neither Can Apple's." The New York Times, May 22, 2023. www.nytimes.com/2023/05/22/technology/ai-photo-labels-google-apple.html.
13 Hsu, Tiffany, and Yiwen Lu. "No, That's Not Taylor Swift Peddling Le Creuset Cookware." The New York Times, January 9, 2024. www.nytimes.com/2024/01/09/technology/taylor-swift-le-creuset-ai-deepfake.html.
14 Carter, Allison. "AI for Communicators: What's New and Notable." PR Daily, January 17, 2024. www.prdaily.com/ai-for-communicators-whats-new-and-notable-2/.
15 Karsten, Jack, Darrell M. West, Makada Henry-Nickie, Daniel Araya Sunil Johal, Matt Perault J. Scott Babwah Brennen, Kristian Lum Aylin Caliskan, and Jack Malamud Nicol Turner Lee. "How Artificial Intelligence Is Transforming the World." Brookings, June 27, 2023. www.brookings.edu/articles/how-artificial-intelligence-is-transforming-the-world/.
16 PRSA. "Ethical Principles for PR Students & Professionals: PRSSA." PRSA Code of Ethics, Updated Guidelines. Accessed February 1, 2024. www.prsa.org/prssa/about-prssa/ethical-principles.
17 Niell, Marlene S. "PR Professionals as Organizational Conscience." ResearchGate, Baylor University, 2012. www.researchgate.net/publication/270612628_PR_Professionals_as_Organizational_Conscience.

8

DIGITAL DILEMMAS

AI's Influence on Ethical Crisis Communication

Erika J. Schneider and Courtney D. Boman

Learning Objectives

1. Understand the role of generative artificial intelligence (AI) in crisis management, including its benefits and limitations.
2. Evaluate the ethical considerations surrounding the use of generative AI in crisis communication during sensitive situations, specifically perceptions of authenticity and appropriateness.
3. Analyze the emergence of new crisis types, like a scansis (i.e., a scandalized crisis that evokes moral outrage) within the Situational Crisis Communication Theory, to understand stakeholder reactions to AI use in crisis communication.
4. Examine stakeholder reactions, such as moral outrage, and expectations for crisis communication, such as a human-centered approach.

Introduction

In the evolving landscape of crisis management, the integration of generative artificial intelligence (AI), involving systems that can create new content, has become a subject of considerable interest for public relations (PR) professionals. The advent of generative AI introduces new possibilities for crisis management, from simulating crisis scenarios for training purposes to analyzing data for issue tracking. While the precrisis phase seems amenable to the use of AI for prepared messaging, its application in actual crisis communication raises complex questions about authenticity and appropriateness. This case study delves into the aftermath of a university's response to a tragic event, when the disclosure of AI

DOI: 10.4324/9781032671482-11

assistance in crafting crisis communication sparked widespread controversy and moral outrage.

Examining stakeholder perspectives, this study explores the ethical considerations surrounding AI in crisis management, shedding light on the desire for a human-centered approach and the implications of disclosing AI use in sensitive contexts. The nuanced findings contribute to ongoing discussions about the responsible integration of AI in crisis communication, emphasizing the need for transparency, empathy, and a careful balance between technological innovation and human connection. The overarching goal of the case study is to expand and generalize theory applied in the context of how stakeholders perceive an organization's utilization of generative AI in crisis communication and express moral outrage. More specifically, how students reacted in student media in response to a university's utilization of ChatGPT in crisis communication. The chapter will conclude with considerations for utilizing generative AI within crisis management.

Key Concepts

Crisis Management

A *crisis*, which is generally an unexpected event that violates stakeholder expectations and generates negative outcomes, can take many forms, depending on how they emerge.[1] Prior research has identified the concept of a paracrisis (i.e., an issue emerging online that comes into public view),[2] a sticky crisis (i.e., a complex situation that is difficult to navigate),[3] and a scansis (i.e., a scandalized crisis that evokes moral outrage).[4] The use of generative artificial intelligence in crisis management may be particularly useful to public relations professionals. Rooted in public relations literature,[5] *crisis management* is the process of preparing for and responding to adverse events that negatively affect stakeholders. This may involve producing a crisis management plan that addresses risks, develops messages, and assembles a team to act on when a crisis occurs. Within this process, the use of generative AI may be beneficial for a professional to utilize in developing ideas and drafting materials. For instance, the software may help simulate crisis scenarios for workshops and training sessions or analyze data to track issues. While the use of AI in crisis communication may be suitable in the *precrisis phase*, which is the stage before a crisis occurs, less is understood about the implications of utilizing AI within *crisis communication*, or the strategic messaging that serves protect the organization and its publics. This communication must be disseminated quickly in order to contain the situation or reach stakeholders with critical information. As this response requires speed, one might question if the use of AI in creating or assisting with the messaging may help support timeliness. While it may help expedite crisis communication, using AI for specific crisis messaging and disclosing the use of it could be viewed as inappropriate. In February 2023, an institution of higher education utilized AI to assist in creating crisis communication with its students. As stakeholders expressed dissatisfaction with the crisis response, specifically because of the disclosed use of AI, this situation was analyzed as a *scansis*, which is the intersection of a crisis and scandal that occurs when an organization engages in offensive behavior[6] Previous research within scandals have also found organizational crises emerge as scandals when an inappropriate crisis response is utilized.[7]

Artificial Intelligence Scanses

The Situational Crisis Communication Theory is a framework for understanding perceptions of crisis responsibility to identify crisis types and relevant response strategies to utilize in a given crisis.[8,9] As a prescriptive theory, it supports public relations professionals in matching an appropriate crisis response strategy quickly. The theory has been applied in many contexts and new forms of crises, such as a scansis, which was developed to understand how crises developed as socially constructed scandals evoke moral outrage in stakeholders.[10] Coombs and Tachkova found that since scanses involve a violation of norms and moral codes, the use of correction with moral recognition was more effective than an organization using corrective action alone; specifically, it resulted in stronger perceptions of empathy and less moral outrage. Jang and Lee analyzed how discrepancies at different levels of co-orientation, or agreement on understanding stances, can generate moral outrage that leads to a scandalized crisis situation (i.e., scansis).[11]

The authors' Co-oriented Scansis model explained how scansis research adds to understanding injustice within crisis and can emerge from discrepancies between an organization and its publics' perceptions of a situation. Applying the concept of a scansis within the use of AI in crisis communications may help explain stakeholders' reactions.

To further explore the application of scansis to AI-based crises, this study examined a controversial incident at Vanderbilt University following a mass shooting at Michigan State University in 2023. In response to the incident, Vanderbilt's Office of Equity, Diversity and Inclusion used AI through ChatGPT to draft an email addressing the tragedy, leading to a nationwide backlash and discussion about the use of the technology. In an effort to better understand stakeholder perceptions of the university officials' inclusion of a note that acknowledges AI assistance in crisis communication, this analysis is guided by the following overarching research question:

RQ1: How did stakeholders perceive the university's utilization of ChatGPT in crisis communication?

BOX 8.1   ETHICS IN AI APPLICATION: EXPECTATIONS AND MORAL VIOLATIONS

Think about the expectations you have for an organization communicating a crisis response. What follows are a series of ethical dilemmas related to AI applications in public relations. Think about your standards for how an organization should produce communication and instances when an organization goes against social norms. Share your reflections on the ethical implications and potential consequences of using AI in public relations.

Dilemma #1: Deciding between using AI to expedite crisis communication, which is faster and more efficient, and maintaining authenticity of a human author.

Dilemma #2: Assessing the appropriateness of AI for creating crisis communication in response to high-severity crises involving loss of life or sensitive situations vs. low-severity crises, such as those that create minor inconveniences.

Dilemma #3: Addressing biases in AI-generated content that may inadvertently perpetuate stereotypes or favor certain narratives over others.

Dilemma #4: Weighing the extent of AI assistance in developing crisis management plans.

These ethical dilemmas highlight the complex nature of public perceptions and expectations of organizations and their decision-making processes. They also include challenges that a public relations professional may experience when incorporating AI into crisis communication strategies while balancing technological innovation with ethical responsibilities.

Case Study Methodology

This research endeavor aimed to analyze stakeholder responses to the allegations that Vanderbilt used ChatGPT to formulate an email in response to a crisis situation. To do so, a qualitative case study was used, as it provides an in-depth examination of a real scenario while advancing theory related to the case with conceptual generalizations regarding the use of a scansis-based crisis caused by AI use.[12] Using systematic procedures, the intent of this case study was to provide insights into stakeholder's responses to the scansis, with the intent of providing practical recommendations.

Case Description

On February 13, 2023, a mass shooting occurred at Michigan State University in East Lansing, Michigan, USA. In the aftermath, several universities provided their own responses to support their communities. On February 16, 2023, the Peabody Office of Equity, Diversity and Inclusion at Vanderbilt University, a private university in Nashville, Tennessee, USA, sent an email its student body, which was approximately 13,710 students during the 2022–2023 academic year,[13] that reflected on the Michigan shooting that occurred three days prior. The email encouraged reflection on the event to ensure a safe and inclusive environment to honor victims of the tragedy and, at the end of the message above the signature, the following sentence was written in smaller font: "(Paraphrase from OpenAI's ChatGPT AI language model, personal communication, February 15, 2023)."[14]

The inclusion of this footnote, which indicated that generative artificial intelligence was used to assist in the message, created backlash not only among students but across the nation as news outlets such as *Bloomberg*,[15] *USA TODAY*,[16] and *The Washington Post*[17] reported on the situation. The controversy surrounding the use of generative artificial intelligence quickly escalated, creating discussions on the ethical implications of relying on AI in crisis communication, which often involves sensitive information. Vanderbilt's student newspaper, *The Vanderbilt Hustler*, published a series of articles that conveyed a range of student perspectives, much of which raised concerns about a lack of authenticity and appropriateness of using generative AI in crisis communication. In the days that followed, the university and its leaders issued an apology and two deans in the office stepped back from their roles but were reinstated months later.

Analysis Approach

The communication analyzed stemming from this situation included five articles published by *The Vanderbilt Hustler*, the student newspaper, from February 17 to March 25, 2023. In addition to the articles, the public comment section was also analyzed to garner insights into stakeholders' perceptions of the scansis. The five articles include "Peabody EDI Office Responds to MSU Shooting with Email Written Using ChatGPT" (published February 17),[18] "Peabody EDI Deans to Temporarily Step Back Following ChatGPT-Crafted Message about MSU Shooting" (published February 19),[19] "Chancellor Diermeier Calls ChatGPT-Crafted Response to MSU Shooting "Unfortunate," Discusses AI in the Classroom" (published February 25),[20] "FELLAS: Vanderbilt's ChatGPT Email Is Automated Hypocrisy" (published Feb 26),[21] and "HARRIS: In Defense of Dean Nicole Joseph" (published March 25),[22] and 29 total comments posted in each of the articles' public comment section on the online newspaper's webpage. The identified articles selected were articles relevant to the crisis published within the timeline. As the student newspaper, it shared perspectives of a key stakeholder group, as students were closely involved and affected by the crisis, and provided a nuanced understanding of how the student body experienced it within the greater academic environment. Prior research has analyzed university crisis responses in the context of organizational communication, such as its effects on perceptions of the severity of the crisis.[23] The initial email sent by officials and some institutional responses were not provided publicly but directly to the campus community, making the articles in the student newspaper the most direct accounts. Although this communication does not capture the direct perceptions of various stakeholder groups, it may reveal conceptual generalizations and themes to inform scansis research.

Using guidance from similar studies with AI crisis research[24] and inductive thematic analyses,[25] two researchers read the communication separately to identify initial themes. Once completed, the researchers assessed discrepancies in interpretations and clarified consistency of themes to ensure construct validity. Based on these discussions, the researchers wrote brief descriptions of the recurring themes and identified exemplars from the articles and comments to best represent the analysis.

Analysis and Discussion of Themes

The guiding research question asked how stakeholders perceived Vanderbilt's utilization of ChatGPT in response to the shooting that occurred at Michigan State. Three themes emerged from the case study. The first theme addresses the moral outrage stakeholders experienced toward the use of AI in this situation, which leads to the second theme in addressing what expectations stakeholders have toward communication efforts. Based on the articles and comment section, it emerged that crisis communication must prioritize a human-centered approach that embraces a genuine and authentic approach. Finally, the need to address the use of AI in crisis management as a whole appeared, setting the stage for future conversations on how the power of this complex technology can be harnessed within our field. All themes, along with exemplars of evidence, are discussed next.

Reactions Toward the Use of AI in a University Response

A central theme that emerged from the communication is the moral outrage students expressed while criticizing the appropriateness of using ChatGPT in crafting the crisis communique. The Michigan State University shooting was perceived to be a serious incident that requires human empathy. Indicators of moral outrage included labeling the communication as "disgusting," "disrespectful," and as a demonstration of "poor judgment," which was linked to expressions of insincere empathy when AI was used to communicate about the tragic event. Another stated, "There is a sick and twisted irony to making a computer write your message about community and togetherness because you can't be bothered to reflect on it yourself."

The outrage was directed not only at the office for utilizing the tool but also at the irony of utilizing it within a university system with harsh penalties for plagiarism policy violations. The context became salient, and the disconnect between the use of AI and the professed values fueled a sense of moral outrage, with students questioning the sincerity of the institution's values and stated commitments. Expressions of moral outrage indicated that there were violations of moral codes and societal norms that the students expected from the university. More specifically, there was specific dissatisfaction with how the organization responded to the crisis, which was publicly exposed by the media. This aligns with scansis research, which shares the socially constructed nature and moral outrage in response to a message perceived as inappropriate.[26] As students had expectations of human authorship but AI assistance was utilized, perceptions of unfairness were enhanced. The incident not only sparked a dialogue about the responsible use of technology in crisis communication but also led to reflections on the university's communication practices, ethical considerations, and the societal implications of leveraging AI in sensitive contexts.

Prioritizing a Human-Centered Approach to Crisis Communications

The students' reactions to the office's response illustrated the desired qualities of crisis communication, such as emotional depth and authenticity. It became evident that the use of AI in this context is inappropriate, as crises – especially those that are high severity and involve fatalities – require human authorship. One student stated, "It's hard to take a message seriously when I know that the sender did not even take the time to put their genuine thoughts and feelings into words. In times of tragedies such as this, we need more, not less, humanity." The reactions underscored a distinct preference for a human-centered approach in crisis communication, and perspectives reinforced the notion that the use of ChatGPT or similar AI tools in crafting crisis communications is seen as incompatible with the sincerity and human connection essential during high-severity crises.

Not only are emotional depth and authenticity important for initial announcements or responses to a crisis, such as Vanderbilt's email, but there may be instances when a genuine dialogue or conversation between an organization and its public is needed in response to a crisis. Unlike an announcement, dialogue is a "tool for mutual understanding . . . but dialogue cannot be enacted in situations that treat dialogue as a strategic communication tool to persuade others, so pre-determined goals can be achieved."[27] If an organization is striving to initiate a genuine dialogue with its community to aid in crisis relief or counseling, key principles (e.g., addressing risk, trust, positive regard, mutuality, propinquity, empathy, commitment, authenticity, and psychological readiness) must be present. In the case of Vanderbilt's response, these principles were not upheld when receivers of the message were looking for conversational support. One student highlighted that the use of ChatGPT fell short of this dialogical expectation by stating, "The idea that this email was part of an attempt to engage in 'conversations' suggests a bleak irony if one side of the conversation is actually an AI bot."

The desire for more humanity in communication regarding scansis reflects a broader concern about the potential dehumanization and detachment associated with relying on AI in a context when emotional or personal engagement is paramount. This collective perspective underscores the need for genuine, human-driven responses in crisis communication to effectively convey empathy, understanding, and authenticity.

BOX 8.2   THE IMPACT OF AI ON CRISIS MESSAGING

Let us explore the effectiveness and perception of AI integrations in crisis communications firsthand. First, get into small groups, with each group faced with the following hypothetical scenario: You are serving as a PR professional for your university, which experiences a crisis when severe weather prevents the community's ability to travel to campus. Half of the groups are asked to develop a crisis response strategy that expresses concern for the community and empathy for those facing negative effects of the severe weather. The other groups are assigned the same guidelines, but to only utilize generative AI, such as ChatGPT, to develop the crisis communication. After all groups have a response, the groups that used traditional methods will be asked to present their responses, followed by the groups that solely utilized generative AI tools. After presentations, have a discussion about the perceived appropriateness, authenticity, ethics, and potential advantages or disadvantages of AI assistance in crisis communication. The following questions may be useful in guiding the discussion: How do you feel about the way AI communicated concern and empathy for the community, and how does it compare to the message produced by traditional methods? Was there a notable difference in the "human touch" that made one more effective at responding to the situation? Based on the outcomes of the conversation, collectively create a list of 3–5 best practices for using AI in crisis communication.

Ethical Considerations of AI in Crisis Management

In addition to expressions of moral outrage, indicating moral violations, and a desire for human-centered approaches in crisis communication, this scansis unveiled clarity in how stakeholders felt about the unethical use of AI in crisis management. A student noted that university leaders made remarks about appropriate uses of AI within the university setting, but there was little support for the two women faculty members who stepped back from their positions within the office because of this scansis. They shared skepticism about the authenticity of emails from administrators, adding, "But, any argument specifically aimed against the ethicality of an administrator sharing words not written entirely by themself should have long ago challenged dozens of mass emails received by the student body with parallel intensities." Another student expressed discontent by stating, "I consider this more of a mask-off moment than any sort of revelation about the disingenuous nature of academic bureaucracy."

Although it was noted that AI cannot replace emotion, they stated, "As a student receiving consoling email after email about tragedy, I believe it has long been evident that scripts, templates, and formulas probably have been the voices behind our university leaders." The nuanced perspective emerging from this scrutiny suggests a careful evaluation of the ethical implications associated with the use of AI in crisis management, urging for re-evaluating institutional practices surrounding the integration of artificial intelligence in sensitive contexts. It also emphasizes the need to reassess how actors are positioned to be responsible for the crisis and how historically marginalized populations may be disproportionately framed as parties responsible, such as the Black women leaders involved in the Vanderbilt scenario.

Notedly, students recognized that scripts and templates may be a part of the crisis management process, which shows an extent of perceived appropriateness and acceptance of crisis management plans. Artificial intelligence within these spaces may be beneficial to expedite message dissemination, but it is clear that there remains a desire for the human hand in responses in order to convey genuine emotion and authenticity. The study revealed how feelings and perceptions of the AI disclosure led to greater coverage of the scansis. This is not to say that AI assistance should not be disclosed when used, but instead to consider appropriate versus inappropriate uses of AI within crisis management. The desire for personal and empathetic communication during tragic events was evident. A student noted that even when it was not disclosed, it was evident that prewritten protocols and frameworks are used within the writing process. This detection reflects a need for leaders, spokespeople, and public relations professionals to ensure crisis management plans are used appropriately. The sentiment was anchored in the belief that genuine emotion and authenticity are best conveyed through human touch, and discontent was expressed toward those not fully disclosing the assistance of AI in crafting messages, which reveals a broader concern about trust and accountability.

In the precrisis phase of the crisis lifecycle, professionals may identify risks and create prepared messaging in anticipation of a crisis; however, the reliance on artificial intelligence tools, such as ChatGPT, raises concerns about the ability of pre-scripted content to capture the dynamic and sensitive nature of real-time crises adequately. AI in crisis management can empower PR professionals through strategic integration of advanced analytics, monitoring, and rapid response systems to allow for more informed decision-making and timely actions to mitigate the consequences of a crisis. At the same time, it is important to reserve expressions of emotion and empathy to human authors in order to foster trust among stakeholders.

Among other issues that generative AI may pose, research has shared other controversial stories, including a science fiction magazine overwhelmed with AI-generated story submissions, many of which are suspected to be low-quality machine-generated; academic integrity with the use of ChatGPT on campuses; and how ChatGPT can provide outputs that describe how to facilitate not only unethical behavior but illegal behavior.[28] As these platforms could both be the reason a crisis occurs and the reason a crisis response is deemed ineffective, future research might consider other ethical considerations of generative AI and its uses in public relations. Still, there remains an opportunity for platforms to be developed responsibly to help maximize benefits.

Future research may help clarify circumstances that delineate appropriate and inappropriate situations for using crisis communications. Additionally, Coombs and Tachkova found that the use of corrective action and moral recognition during a scansis may reduce moral outrage and increased empathy.[29] This may be investigated to assess the outcome of an organization publicly providing a scansis response that includes details on how they are correcting the situation, such as reviewing guidelines for AI assistance in crisis messaging and recognizing and acknowledging the moral violation committed. In the present case, Vanderbilt's chancellor shared how they felt the response was a wake-up call on how ChatGPT will affect our lives. Moreover, as AI becomes more popular and accepted in society, it may be of interest to continue exploring the effects of disclosing AI assistance in crisis communication, and long-term impacts on organizational reputation and stakeholder trust.

Conclusion

The intersection of generative AI and crisis management has provided valuable insights into the ethical considerations and stakeholder reactions associated with the use of AI in crafting crisis communication. The case study, centered around a university's response to a tragic event, highlighted the complex dynamics that emerge when AI is disclosed in sensitive contexts. The moral outrage expressed by stakeholders, particularly students, emphasized a deep-seated desire for authenticity and a human-centered approach in crisis communication, especially during high-severity events.

The findings underscored the potential disconnect between the perceived appropriateness of AI use in the precrisis phase, where it may aid in prepared messaging, and the challenges of maintaining authenticity in real-time crisis communication. The scansis crisis type, informed by the Situational Crisis Communication Theory, proved to be essential to understanding stakeholders' reactions and potential strategies for responding to those reactions. It is important to note that AI assistance should always be disclosed if utilized in communication to remain transparent, but key insights direct professionals to focus on the extent AI is used in crisis management and the need for re-evaluation of institutional practices. As technology continues to evolve, it will remain essential for PR students, professionals, educators, and scholars to understand the balance between technological innovation and human connection. Future research is encouraged to delve deeper into delineating circumstances for the ethical use of AI in crisis communication.

Reflections

1. In what ways did stakeholders perceive the use of AI in crisis communication as a violation of moral codes and societal norms, and how does your perspective align with it?
2. What recommendations can be made for PR professionals and scholars regarding the responsible integration of AI in crisis communication?
3. Reflect on the challenges associated with balancing technological innovation and human connection in the context of crisis communication. How can organizations navigate this balance to ensure effective crisis communication that aligns with stakeholder expectations?
4. If you were a PR professional identifying risks and drafting potential crisis response strategies in the precrisis phase, to what extent would you use generative AI, and how would you use the tools judiciously to respect the need for human-centered authenticity?

Notes

1 Coombs, W. Timothy. "Protecting Organization Reputations during a Crisis: The Development and Application of Situational Crisis Communication Theory." *Corporate Reputation Review* 10 (2007): 163–176.
2 Coombs, W. Timothy, and J. Sherry Holladay. "The Paracrisis: The Challenges Created by Publicly Managing Crisis Prevention." *Public Relations Review* 38, no. 3 (2012): 408–415.

3 Coombs, W. Timothy, Sherry J. Holladay, and Rick White. "Corporate Crises: Sticky Crises and Corporations." In *Advancing Crisis Communication Effectiveness*, pp. 35–51. Routledge, 2020.

4 Coombs, W. Timothy, and Elina R. Tachkova. "Scansis as a Unique Crisis Type: Theoretical and Practical Implications." *Journal of Communication Management* 23, no. 1 (2019): 72–88.

5 Diers-Lawson, Audra. *Crisis Communication: Managing Stakeholder Relationships*. Routledge, 2019.

6 De Maria, William. "After the Scandal – Recovery Options for Damaged Organizations." *Journal of Management & Organization* 16, no. 1 (2010): 66–82.

7 Diers-Lawson, Audra. *Crisis Communication: Managing Stakeholder Relationships*. Routledge, 2019.

8 Coombs, W. Timothy. "Choosing the Right Words: The Development of Guidelines for the Selection of the "Appropriate" Crisis-Response Strategies." *Management Communication Quarterly* 8, no. 4 (1995): 447–476.

9 Coombs, W. Timothy. "Protecting Organization Reputations during a Crisis: The Development and Application of Situational Crisis Communication Theory." *Corporate Reputation Review* 10 (2007): 163–176.

10 Coombs, W. Timothy, and Elina R. Tachkova. "Scansis as a Unique Crisis Type: Theoretical and Practical Implications." *Journal of Communication Management* 23, no. 1 (2019): 72–88.

11 Jang, Heesoo, and Suman Lee. "Introducing the Co-Oriented Scansis (CoS) Model: A Case of Chatbot, Lee-Luda." *Public Relations Review* 49, no. 4 (2023): 102360.

12 Yin, Robert K. *Case Study Research: Design and Methods*. Vol. 5. Sage, 2009.

13 U.S. News & World Report *Review of Vanderbilt University Student Life. U.S. News & World Report*, n.d., www.usnews.com/best-colleges/vanderbilt-3535/student-life.

14 Peabody Office of Equity, Diversity and Inclusion. "Email: Webview: Reflecting on Gun Violence and Inclusive Environments." Received by Perrotta Rachael, 16 Feb. 2023. https://t.e2ma.net/message/ul182h/m74zooz.

15 Van Natta, Virginia. "ChatGPT's Use in Condolence Email after Shooting Angers Students." *Bloomberg.com*, 18 Feb. 2023, www.bloomberg.com/news/articles/2023-02-18/chatgpt-s-use-in-condolence-email-after-shooting-angers-students. Accessed 5 Feb. 2024.

16 Mendoza, Jordan. "Vanderbilt University Apologizes for Using ChatGPT for 'Disgusting' Email on Michigan State Shooting." *USA Today*, 21 Feb. 2023, www.usatoday.com/story/news/education/2023/02/21/vanderbilt-apologizes-chatgpt-email-msu-shooting/11314144002/.

17 Wu, Daniel. "Vanderbilt Apologizes for Using ChatGPT to Write Message on MSU Shooting." *The Washington Post*, 21 Feb. 2023, www.washingtonpost.com/nation/2023/02/21/vanderbilt-chatgpt-michigan-shooting/.

18 Perrotta, Rachael. "Peabody EDI Office Responds to MSU Shooting with Email Written Using ChatGPT." *The Vanderbilt Hustler*, 17 Feb. 2023, vanderbilthustler.com/2023/02/17/peabody-edi-office-responds-to-msu-shooting-with-email-written-using-chatgpt/.

19 Lele, Aaditi. "Peabody EDI Deans to Temporarily Step Back Following ChatGPT-Crafted Message about MSU Shooting." *The Vanderbilt Hustler*, 19 Feb. 2023, vanderbilthustler.com/2023/02/19/peabody-edi-deans-to-temporarily-step-back-following-chatgpt-crafted-message-about-msu-shooting/.

20 Perrotta, Rachael. "Chancellor Diermeier Calls ChatGPT-Crafted Response to MSU Shooting 'Unfortunate', Discusses AI in the Classroom." *The Vanderbilt Hustler*, 25 Feb. 2023, vanderbilthustler.com/2023/02/25/chancellor-diermeier-calls-chatgpt-crafted-response-to-msu-shooting-unfortunate-discusses-ai-in-the-classroom/.

21 Fellas, Nora. "FELLAS: Vanderbilt's ChatGPT Email Is Automated Hypocrisy." *The Vanderbilt Hustler*, 26 Feb. 2023, vanderbilthustler.com/2023/02/26/fellas-vanderbilts-chatgpt-email-is-automated-hypocrisy/.
22 Harris, Elise. "HARRIS: In Defense of Dean Nicole Joseph." *The Vanderbilt Hustler*, 25 Mar. 2023, vanderbilthustler.com/2023/03/25/harris-in-defense-of-dean-nicole-joseph/.
23 Hong, Seoyeon, and Bokyung Kim. "Exploring Social Media Use in University Crisis Communication: An Experiment to Measure Impact on Perceived Crisis Severity and Attitudes of Key Publics." *Journal of Contingencies and Crisis Management* 27, no. 1 (2019): 61–71.
24 Jang, Heesoo, and Suman Lee. "Introducing the Co-Oriented Scansis (CoS) Model: A Case of Chatbot, Lee-Luda." *Public Relations Review* 49, no. 4 (2023): 102360.
25 Theaker, Alison, and Heather Yaxley. *The Public Relations Strategic Toolkit: An Essential Guide to Successful Public Relations Practice*. Routledge, 2017.
26 Coombs, W. Timothy, and Elina R. Tachkova. "Scansis as a Unique Crisis Type: Theoretical and Practical Implications." *Journal of Communication Management* 23, no. 1 (2019): 72–88.
27 Kent, Michael L., and Anne Lane. "Two-Way Communication, Symmetry, Negative Spaces, and Dialogue." *Public Relations Review* 47, no. 2 (1 Jun. 2021): 102014. https://doi.org/10.1016/j.pubrev.2021.102014.
28 Ray, Partha Pratim. "ChatGPT: A Comprehensive Review on Background, Applications, Key Challenges, Bias, Ethics, Limitations and Future Scope." *Internet of Things and Cyber-Physical Systems* 3 (2023): 121–154.
29 Coombs, W. Timothy, and Elina R. Tachkova. "Scansis as a Unique Crisis Type: Theoretical and Practical Implications." *Journal of Communication Management* 23, no. 1 (2019): 72–88.

PART IV

Data Analytics

9

A DUAL PERSPECTIVE

A Review of Recent Research on Artificial Intelligence in Public Relations

Christopher J. McCollough

Learning Objectives

1. To establish a baseline knowledge of what industry and academic research has to offer on the nature of artificial intelligence (AI) disruption of the practice of public relations (PR).
2. To understand the influence of AI on teaching and learning, and how educators in public relations are now adapting to its presence in professional practice.
3. To compare the benefits of the integration of AI in the classroom and in practice against the body of concerns associated with its use.

Introduction

The emerging body of literature about Artificial Intelligence (AI) in public relations (PR) and in the broader context of mass communication illustrates a duality in perspective on the impact of the emergent technology on the discipline. Many scholars point to the rapid integration of AI in practice and its merits in helping make work in the discipline more efficient and useful, and they call for the need to adapt teaching and learning to help prepare students to work effectively with AI in the discipline. At the same time, other scholars point out the risks of adopting AI in practice without a responsible, critical consideration of its integration in practice. This chapter offers a brief look at the emerging body of literature in its two strongest areas of examination: impact on practice and its integration into the classroom. In the process, the duality in perspective will become clear in both areas of examination.

DOI: 10.4324/9781032671482-13

Answering the Call for Scholarship to Understand the Impact of Artificial Intelligence

AI prevalence in public relations is both transformative in practice and a source of concern among scholars, educators, and industry professionals. Early commentary from practitioners and scholars have already identified its capacity to predict trends of publics and monitor social media conversations,[1] to detect fake news stories[2,3] and to facilitate speech recognition, decision-making, visual enhancements, and historical data.[4] Nevertheless, the discipline is calling for a deeper exploration of the impact of AI in practice.[5] The following is a brief discussion of some of the strongest areas of focus in the field on AI's impact on practice in public relations.

Macro Influence and Industry Disruption

Scholarship on AI's emergence focuses on both the practice of public relations and strategic communication, and on the net impact of its integration on daily tasks, ethics, and principles of best practices. Like other technologies, AI offers several advantages in incorporation: flexibility, change, innovation, and creativity, and the ability to facilitate new successful solutions for the marketplace.[6] Predictably, there is a reported growth in adoption of *generative AI* in industry use by chief executive officers (CEOs) and chief experience officers (CXOs). A survey of 1,684 leaders examining the current state of AI use in organizations demonstrates a steady adoption of the technology in practice; 55% reported that their organizations have adopted AI, while 40% indicated intent to increase investment in AI because of the advance in generative AI.[7]

This does not, however, reflect the perspective of leaders responsible for strategic communication. A recent body of interviews among communication leaders suggests more skepticism and discomfort with over-reliance on AI in the workplace, with some offering limited support for responsible experimentation with AI, largely from communication executives in technology-driven companies.[8] That said, other recent contributions in academic and trade literature offer some additional general observations from executives in public relations on the value and role of public relations in the discipline. A recent report from the Institute for Public Relations notes that communication leaders are generally comfortable with using generative AI, while noting the need for continuous learning among practitioners and that its use requires effective implementation of guidelines or "guardrails" to support appropriate use.[9] Perceived value and need for training are themes present in specific areas of trade research, as well.

Impact on Best Practices and Technician Work

Much of the literature on generative AI in public relations is exploring its impact on specific tasks in the discipline. Specifically, considerations regarding how AI will affect the division of labor in organizations, productivity, and how we think about normative areas of practice drive much of the conversation and research focus. The following subsections cover the most common themes present in recent literature on the impact of AI on practice.

Augmentation of Technician's Work

Reports on the perceptions of the value of generative AI suggest an appreciation from leaders in strategic communication of the value of the technology in enhancing technician's work, particularly "lower-value" communication tasks. One executive stated that they use it behind the scenes for support in generating new ideas, story angles, and content development.[10] Ragan and the Conference Board conducted a survey of 174 marketing specialists in the fall of 2023 and identified the use of generative AI as an initial step to inspire thinking for better than half of those responding (53%), followed by use to support writing press releases/articles (40%), conduct of research (40%), and to generate social media content (33%).[11]

BOX 9.1   GENERATIVE AI AND THE 21ST-CENTURY PRESS RELEASE

As it becomes clear the generative AI tools are an asset to be used ethically to many practitioners, it is important to remember that the tools are only as effective as their users. The following activity is intended to help public relations students and practitioners looking to upskill to get comfortable with what effective use of a generative AI platform to augment writing should look like.

1. Sit down at your computer and access ChatGPT at https://chat.openai.com/.
2. Type in the prompt "Write me a press release."
3. Once it finishes compiling the body of text, take some time to read over its work and answer the following questions:
   a. Is the document properly formatted as a press release?
   b. Does it observe Associated Press rules of writing?
   c. What is missing from the press release to be effective in meeting your needs?

4. Now, once you note what is incorrect and missing in the document produced, go back to the prompt, and give it more specific instructions based on what you previously identified.

5. Repeat this process until the document compiled closely reflects what you might produce independent of the platform.
6. Now, consider the following questions from the perspective of an educator and a practitioner:

   a. How much time and effort does it require to produce a professional-grade press release from a generative AI platform?
   b. How did this make my work more efficient when compared to my traditional process?
   c. Even though the platform produced the text, did the process involve any less of your cognition, critical analysis, or careful revision to become a polished document?

Executives note that AI does not yet have a major role in influencing the overall strategy. Those interviewed note that AI has had impact on production, delivery, and workflow, but that it is tactical and subordinate to larger strategies, apart from cases when AI can serve in predictive capacities to identify potential future outcomes.[12] Senior communicators and executives in research indicated a guarded approach to adoption. Qualitative interviews with 28 senior-level communicators indicated a sense of concern related to the remaining shortcomings of AI tools and *algorithms*, particularly a broader misperception of AI as "a magical solution to everything," when it still requires human thought to derive accurate meaning and value from what AI generates. Additionally, those interviewed cited inherent biases in AI that contribute to problems with its application in research and content generation.[13]

Research and Strategy

Addressing research in public relations, scholars have recently pointed out the capacity of AI to increase efficiency and to better understand individuals and strategic publics in terms of preferences, buying patterns, and habits of consumers to shape content.[14] Scholars have also identified practitioners using AI tools for data analysis, including detailed public profiles of key audiences that include psychographic and demographic breakdowns.[15]

AI can also support research that informs practitioner perspectives on current news coverage, information accuracy, current campaigns, and current trends.[16,17,18] Research also descibes how social media listening and analytics,[19,20] and A/B message testing,[21,22] are being used to inform content creation and strategic narratives. This perceived efficiency extends to performance in data analysis.[23]

Researchers are also establishing that AI can inform strategic planning, and the evaluation that monitors campaign effectiveness.[24,25] Other scholars have noted the value of AI in strategic selection of *influencers* and media platform selection for tactical development of strategies.[26,27,28] Predictive analytics have also emerged as a resource that can anticipate outcomes, such as trends, crises, and sales that help optimize organizational decision making.[29]

Strategic Communication Functions

Drawing on *Excellence Theory*,[30,31] researchers are beginning to identify how practitioners can leverage data and AI to reinforce the position of public relations in organizations. Insights gleaned from data can help public relations become a more strategic function and demonstrate its value to organizations.[32,33,34] Authors caution that practitioners are largely unprepared in data knowledge and skills.[35,36,37] The 2020–2021 "North American Communication Monitor" surveyed 1,046 communicators, and two-thirds reported a "great need" to develop their data competencies to help organizations remain nimble.[38] The gap between respondents perceived importance of data competency and the assessment of their own competency was the most pronounced among competencies considered, at 15.7%.[39]

Strategic application of AI is also clearly related to strategic consideration of specific public relations tactics. In support of media relations work, network analyses generated through AI can identify and amplify influencers and journalist outreach.[40,41,42] Reflecting data from the trade surveys noted earlier, scholars and practitioners are noting the value of AI platforms like ChatGPT in their content development work.[43] Speaking to employee relations and training, AI can build and monitor *chatbots* and *gamification* to assist in training and motivation of employees,[44] and to help organizations with consumer relations.[45] There is also a growing body of research demonstrating the value of AI in enhancing traditional consumer relations tasks.[46,47]

In parallel with the prevalent use of data to facilitate stronger environmental scanning an issues management[48,49] a growing area of application of artificial intelligence is its application in analysis to facilitate more efficient listening that can enhance practitioners' responsiveness on matters related to issues and crisis management. AI tools are capturing sentiment in social and earned media, enabling practitioners to response more quickly to emerging crises.[50,51,52]

Competency and Ethical Considerations

The 2020–2021 "North American Communication Monitor" indicated that by self-report, 39.7% of PR practitioners say they lack data competency, 39.1% self-reported deficiencies with technology, and more than three-quarters of respondents indicated organizations should provide training for their profes-sional communicators,[53] reinforcing a growing body of research indicating that while practitioners see the value of data insights and AI, they lack the appropriate skill to make best use of the information.[54,55] In response to these concerns, the Arthur W. Page Society developed an approach called "CommTech" which is in-tended to help chief commercial officers (CCOs) better apply data and analytics to create campaigns that leverage *hypertargeting* to drive business outcomes.[56]

Scholars have articulated ethical considerations about the use of AI in practice in public relations that merit consideration,[57] including subfields in the mass communication discipline like strategic health communication,[58] advertising,[59] public relations, journalism, and public diplomacy work.[60,61] Concerns about fake news, deepfakes, and other abuses and failures in use of AI[62] leading to con-troversies[63] prompt consideration of students incorporating ethical frame works like *utilitarianism*, *deontology*, and *virtue ethics* to build skills in effectively evaluating the ethics of specific AI applications, as well as updating industry codes of ethics to account for the emergent forms of technology AI presents.[64]

The Impact of Artificial Intelligence on Pedagogy

The focus of scholarship and discussion on AI in the curriculum parallels schol-arship on practice in weighing the abundant benefits against the risks and chal-lenges associated with errors in use and malicious applications of AI. A recent report discussing the impact of generative AI in higher education discussed the implications of different forms of the technology on comprehensive institutional policy.[65] The report points out the need for institutions to establish some uni-form, baseline policies and practices, while highlighting the potential benefits of generative AI in helping overcome matters of inequity among different institu-tions and helping improve skilled labor gaps globally.[66]

Others evaluating the impact of AI platforms have identified concerning trends in the impact on the mindset and skillset of graduates. Survey analysis of students' perceptions about chatbot use indicates a deep dependance on the platform in completing coursework, leading the authors to call for a deeper ex-amination of student use to determine how deep the dependence goes, likening it to an addiction.[67] These findings reflect prior pedagogical research identifying potential triggers for this behavior, including emotional states, like loneliness or anxiety, and environmental cues, such as academic pressures or the sheer ubiquity of digital devices. For a student feeling overwhelmed, the immediate assistance of a chatbot can be enticing, leading to repeated and excessive use.[68,69]

Pedagogical literature emerging in parallel with the use of AI in mass com-munication subfields has called for its examination and responsible integration over the past few years. Scholars have established that AI is a key component of digital marketing and public relations strategies for recognizable brands in a variety of industries.[70] Graduates with an established proficiency in digital platforms, including AI, perform better on the job market than do those who are without such skills.[71,72] Authors have also called for students in the media and communication fields to be educated as responsible, ethical consumers and producers on digital platforms and AI,[73] and the need for an understanding of the contemporary effects theory in an evolving field.[74]

Journalism and mass communication scholars and educators note the need for scholarship and adaptation of pedagogy in practice to better situate the discipline to integrate generative AI that enhances skill and prepares graduates for mass communication fields, including public relations. Authors have advocated for actively integrating AI into classrooms at large and small programs equitably to encourage professional proficiency, ethical application, and a strong grounding in media literacy, regardless of where a student attends school.[75]

To make an emphatic point, one mass communication educator co-authored an essay with ChatGPT to illustrate the abilities and limitations of ChatGPT in journalism and mass communication, using an interview style approach of posing questions and permitting ChatGPT to respond to the queries.[76] The result is a piece showing the platform has tremendous potential to grow and also could potentially pose some threats to those working in the industry, and that both indicate a deeper need for study of generative AI platforms like ChatGPT and DALL·E to establish their relevance to journalism and mass communication education.[77]

Research on Public Relations Pedagogy

Taking cues from organizations like the Commission on Public Relations Education (CPRE), scholars and educators in public relations are studying what skills are essential for young professionals, and a growing call from CPRE is for a clear understanding of the necessary integration of training in technology, including AI, to help close the gap between the classroom and industry.[78] Public relations pedagogical literature presents arguments addressing both the benefits and potential challenges that the integration of AI poses to the discipline, aspiring professionals, and practitioners in the field. We will begin with scholarship that establishes the demand for and growth of technologies like AI in the public relations classroom.

AI Integration in the Public Relations Classroom

Seemingly in response to the call of the CPRE to integrate more closely with professional practice, studies show a prevalence of courses, certificates, and degree programs geared toward production and management of digital platforms in support of public relations and strategic communication.[79] The authors also note an emphasis on an integrated mindset, that the writer-technician skill sets dominate most institutions' curricula, that *data analytics* and *data visualization* are growing forms of PR instruction among the programs analyzed, that branding was a critical consideration in this new area of practice, and that forms of high-impact learning and a philosophical focus on professional development drive the programs analyzed.[80]

Curriculum shifts spurred by the rapid growth in AI use also prompted scholarship analyzing the need for a careful attention to how public relations students are taught. Content analysis of job descriptions show a strong presence of desired skillsets in AI and digital platforms for entry-level practitioners.[81] Scholars also answer the call of the CPRE to better integrate industry practice in the classroom through research on integration, including technologies like AI.[82,83,84] Other have examined how they better meet industry needs in the discipline, while tending to the holistic education of graduates and managing their own professional expectations.[85] Striking that balance speaks to a fundamental change in thinking about how educators in public relations and strategic communication approach engaging in high-impact learning practices.

Concerns About AI in the Public Relations Classroom

Concerns about the integration of AI in the industry and classroom focus on erosion in personal development and potential pressure to eschew traditional standards of ethical best practices.[86] Other concerns about students using generative AI platforms are leading some scholars in the discipline to the conclusion that an erosion in writing and production skills and an over-reliance on the platforms will lead future practitioners toward a more business-oriented thinking absent of liberal arts foundation.[87] There is also a more direct call for the need to critique integration of AI in the public relations classroom, and to scale back an effusive tendency toward optimism and futurity, characterizing it as cheerleading in the PR educator's community.[88] These criticisms are grounded in a deeper concern that AI presents a clear potential to enable organizations driven by a profit to deem AI platforms as viable replacements for practitioners.

Critical scholars couch their concerns in terms of larger trends that serve to erode the personal and professional development of practitioners.[89] They argue that a growing *neoliberalism* in higher education prioritizes instrumental skills, like AI use, over a value-laden education – specifically, that the growth in experiential learning that prioritizes companies training their own workforces is part of a larger corporate agenda in higher education. While they are careful not to condemn the use of AI in practice, they point to the need to remember the broader body of knowledge and skills aspiring practitioners need to build in their college educations. Others who present a cautionary perspective on the matter also point to the need to be vigilant about broader holistic education, and point to the need for a strong commitment to ethics in integrated courses, due to the potential risks that poor use and abuse of the platforms and their potential to undermine best practices in the discipline, in addition to potential concern related to rising incidence of the use of misinformation and disinformation in political, commercial, and public contexts.[90,91]

BOX 9.2 ETHICS EXERCISE: DRAWING DISTINCTIONS ON AI USE IN PRACTICE

Within this chapter, you have read about the duality around AI's integration into public relations in both the classroom and industry. Included in the conversation has been a dialogue that is balancing its benefits against a body of concern about what the discipline may be sacrificing in its integrations, both in pragmatic and critical terms. For some, concerns center around academic and professional integrity. Others focus on the fear of erosion in professional acumen.

Through an earlier activity, you were invited to examine how to effectively make use of one platform, ChatGPT, in composing professional copy that incorporates a full professional perspective. Generative AI has progressed well past textual production. DALL·E offers the means to enable users to create images through the use of prompts. LANDR and Podcastle are AI-supported audio editing platforms that permit users to edit and even replace words using existing recordings to make audio editing more efficient.

In February of 2024, filmmaker Tyler Perry recently canceled an $800 million studio expansion in Atlanta, Georgia following his review of OpenAI's Sora capacity to produce realistic video footage, drawing his concerns about the value of investing in production space and expanding personnel. Professional concerns about AI's capacity to replace human professionals aside, the idea of powerful, convincing tools producing professional-grade content takes on greater concerns in an era when information ethics are being challenges on digital and social channels daily.

For this activity, you should sit down with a colleague or classmate, take a look at these platforms, and think on the following ethics prompt.

1. Given the level of quality thought that has to go into effectively using generative AI platforms, what are the factors that an ethical practitioner should take into account when making use of the platforms to produce quality work?

2. Consider the growing body of generative AI tools and list some ways bad actors could use these platforms to attack individuals and organizations.
3. Knowing potential ways bad actors can make use of any of these platforms and make your organization or client the focus of a reputational attack, what ethical approaches can we use as practitioners to protect our organizations and ourselves?
4. Now consider the possibility of an employer or client to as us to make use of these platforms in questionable ways to help advance their organization by damaging other individuals or organizations. What are the tools ethics has taught us to use to combat these approaches in our work?

Conclusion

Artificial intelligence (AI) is a growing part of professional practice in public relations, and its benefits to daily practice ensure that it will grow in its application and value. With that said, research to date is a work in progress and has far to go to help professionals and educators fully understand AI's impact on the discipline. Practitioners and scholars demonstrate how AI can inform research and strategy, and make daily tasks more efficient, while pointing out the need for study of it to better understand the impact of its rapid integration into practice. Concerns about a lack of adequate knowledge and training, potential for unethical application, and organizations' perceptions about its cost-effectiveness eroding stability of the profession balance literature expressing optimism.

From the pedagogical perspective, the growth of AI in industry prompts discussion about how its growth with reshape institutional policies, as well as how we teach and learn in the discipline. Scholars and educators point to the need for thorough technical training and a commitment to ethics education as viable means to mitigate the concerns posed by scholars studying the discipline and practitioners expressing concerns experienced daily. The body of work ahead has much to offer the discipline and educators in considering how we responsibly integrate AI into professional practice to leverage the benefits it offers.

Reflections

1. A commonly expressed perspective among educators and practitioners in public relations is the need to be lifelong learners. How does the implementation of AI in practice reinforce this principle for educators and practitioners?
2. Scholars express concerns that profit-driven organizations will take the integration of AI in public relations work as an opportunity to reduce staffing for

strategic communication work. Understanding the limits of AI, why is this less likely to take place under current conditions?

3. Scholars and educators both emphasize the need for ethics education as we continue to implement AI. How does a healthy grounding in ethics help enhance the use of AI in public relations work?

4. Consider the fact that we clearly have optimistic and pessimistic views of AI's presence in public relations work. Considering what you have read, do you view its integration optimistically or pessimistically?

Notes

1 Luttrell, R., and A. Wallace. "Why and how PR pros should embrace artificial intelligence." *PR Daily* (2019).

2 Waugh, R. "How artificial intelligence has the ability to detect fake news." *The Telegraph* (2019).

3 Ozbay, Feyza Altunbey, and Bilal Alatas. "Fake news detection within online social media using supervised artificial intelligence algorithms." *Physica A: Statistical Mechanics and Its Applications* 540 (2020): 123174.

4 Chemouil, Prosper, Pan Hui, Wolfgang Kellerer, Yong Li, Rolf Stadler, Dacheng Tao, Yonggang Wen, and Ying Zhang. "Special issue on artificial intelligence and machine learning for networking and communications." *IEEE Journal on Selected Areas in Communications* 37, no. 6 (2019): 1185–1191.

5 Luttrell, Regina, Adrienne A. Wallace, Christopher J. McCollough, and Jiyoung Lee. "The digital divide: Addressing artificial intelligence in communication education." *Journalism & Mass Communication Educator* 75, no. 4 (2020): 470–482.

6 Türksoy, Nilüfer. "The future of public relations, advertising and journalism: How artificial intelligence may transform the communication profession and why society should care?" *Türkiye İletişim Araştırmaları Dergisi* 40 (2022): 394–410.

7 Chui, Michael, Lareina Yee, Bryce Hall, and Alex Singla. "The state of AI in 2023: Generative AI's breakout year." *McKinsey*. 2023. Retrieved from: https://www.mckinsey.com/capabilities/quantumblack/our-insights/the-state-of-ai-in-2023-generative-ais-breakout-year.

8 McCorkindale, T. "Generative AI in organizations: Insights and strategies from communication leaders." *Institute for Public Relations*. Retrieved February 20, 2024: 2024.

9 McCorkindale. "Generative AI in organizations."

10 McCorkindale. "Generative AI in organizations."

11 Churchville, Sara. "Marketing & communications center: AI makes human expertise and creativity." *The Conference Board*, 2023.

12 McCorkindale. "Generative AI in organizations."

13 O'Neil, Julie, Emily S. Kinsky, and Michele E. Ewing. "Insights from senior communicators: Navigating obstacles, leveraging opportunities, and leading teams to capitalize on data and analytics." *Public Relations Review* 49, no. 4 (2023): 102362.

14 Panda, Geetanjali, Ashwani Kumar Upadhyay, and Komal Khandelwal. "Artificial intelligence: A strategic disruption in public relations." *Journal of Creative Communications* 14, no. 3 (2019): 196–213.

15 Wiencierz, Christian, and Ulrike Röttger. "Big data in public relations: A conceptual framework." *Public Relations Journal* 12, no. 3 (2019): 1–15.

16 Clark, C. "How can you apply AI for more effective public relations? Agility." *PR*. March 23, 2021. Retrieved February 15, 2024: 2021.

17 Kaput, M. "Ways AI could transform PR and communications." *Marketing Artificial Intelle-Gence Institute*. www.marketingaiinstitute.com/blog/how-ai-could-transform-pr-and-com munications (20).

18 Panda, et al. "Artificial intelligence", 196–213.

19 Coursaris, Constantinos K., Wietske Van Osch, and Brigitte A. Balogh. "Informing brand messaging strategies via social media analytics." *Online Information Review* 40, no. 1 (2016): 6–24.

20 Mohamed, Kareem, and Ümmü Altan Bayraktar. "Artificial intelligence in public relations and association rule mining as a decision support tool." *SSRG International Journal of Humanities and Social Science* 9, no. 3 (2022): 23–32.

21 Weiner, M., M. DiStaso, P. Draper-Watts, C. Ehrhart, A. Fitzsimmons, J. Gilfeather, M. Hamid et al. "The communicator's guide to research, analysis, and evaluation." *Institute for Public Relations*. Retrieved March 14, 2021: 2021.

22 Wiencierz and Röttger. "Big data in public relations", 1–15.

23 Rogers, C. "How artificial intelligence and big data will affect the future of PR." *Institute for Public Relations*. Retrieved November 11, 2019: 2021.

24 Fitzpatrick, Kathy R., and Paula L. Weissman. "Public relations in the age of data: Corporate perspectives on social media analytics (SMA)." *Journal of Communication Management* 25, no. 4 (2021): 401–416.

25 Weiner, et al. "The communicator's guide to research, analysis, and evaluation", 2021.

26 Clark. "How can you apply AI for more effective public relations?", 2021.

27 Kaput. "Ways AI could transform PR and communications."

28 Panda, et al. "Artificial intelligence", 196–213.

29 Clark. "How can you apply AI for more effective public relations?", 2021.

30 Dozier, David M., Larissa A. Grunig, and James E. Grunig. *Manager's guide to excellence in public relations and communication management*. Routledge, 2013.

31 Grunig, James E. "Furnishing the edifice: Ongoing research on public relations as a strategic management function." In *Public relations and communication management*, pp. 1–26. Routledge, 2013.

32 Fitzpatrick and Weissman. "Public relations in the age of data: Corporate perspectives on social media analytics (SMA)", 401–416.

33 Weiner, Mark, and Sarab Kochhar. "Irreversible: The public relations big data revolution." *Institute for Public Relations* (2016): 1–31.

34 O'Neil, et al. "Insights from senior communicators", 102362.

35 Meng, J., B.H. Reber, B.K. Berger, K.K. Gower, and A. Zerfass. "North American Communication Monitor 2020–2021: The impact of COVID-19 pandemic, ethical challenges, gender issues, cyber security, and competence gaps in strategic communication." Tuscaloosa, AL: The Plank Center for Leadership in Public Relations, 2021.

36 Virmani, Swati, and Anne Gregory. *AI and big data readiness report-assessing the public relations profession's preparedness for an AI future*. CIPR, 2021.

37 Zerfass, Ansgar, Jens Hagelstein, and Ralph Tench. "Artificial intelligence in communication management: A cross-national study on adoption and knowledge, impact, challenges and risks." *Journal of Communication Management* 24, no. 4 (2020): 377–389.

38 Meng, et al. "North American Communication Monitor 2020–2021", 105.

39 Meng, et al. "North American Communication Monitor 2020–2021", 109.

40 Galloway, Chris, and Lukasz Swiatek. "Public relations and artificial intelligence: It's not (just) about robots." *Public Relations Review* 44, no. 5 (2018): 734–740.

41 Panda, et al. "Artificial intelligence." *Journal of Creative Communications*, 196–213.

42 Wiencierz, Christian, and Ulrike Röttger. "Big data in public relations", 1–15.

43 Cloosterman, M. "ChatGPT is a gift for brand leaders." 2023. Retrieved February 20, 2024 from: https://page.org/blog/chatgpt-is-a-gift-for-brand-leaders.

44 O'Neil, Julie, Michele E. Ewing, Stacey Smith, and Sean Williams. "Measuring and evaluating internal communication." *Current Trends and Issues in Internal Communication: Theory and Practice* (2021): 201–222.

45 Men, Linjuan Rita, Alvin Zhou, and Wan-Hsiu Sunny Tsai. "Harnessing the power of chatbot social conversation for organizational listening: The impact on perceived transparency and organization-public relationships." *Journal of Public Relations Research* 34, no. 1–2 (2022): 20–44.

46 Ledro, Cristina, Anna Nosella, and Andrea Vinelli. "Artificial intelligence in customer relationship management: literature review and future research directions." *Journal of Business & Industrial Marketing* 37, no. 13 (2022): 48–63.

47 Arief, N. Nurlaela, and Aurik Gustomo. "Analyzing the impact of big data and artificial intelligence on the communications profession: A case study on Public Relations (PR) practitioners in Indonesia." *International Journal on Advanced Science, Engineering and Information Technology* 10, no. 3 (2020): 1066–1071.

48 Kent, Michael L., and Adam J. Saffer. "A Delphi study of the future of new technology research in public relations." *Public Relations Review* 40, no. 3 (2014): 568–576.

49 Triantafillidou, Amalia, and Prodromos Yannas. "How public relations agencies in Greece respond to digital trends." *Public Relations Review* 40, no. 5 (2014): 815–817.

50 Kaput. "Ways AI could transform PR and communications."

51 Lynch, Chris. "How PR pros should prepare for artificial intelligence." *Ragan's PR Daily* (2018).

52 Panda, et al. "Artificial intelligence", 196–213.

53 Meng, et al. "North American Communication Monitor 2020–2021", 105.

54 Virmani, and Gregory. *AI and big data readiness report-assessing the public relations profession's preparedness for an AI future.*

55 Zerfass, Ansgar, Jens Hagelstein, and Ralph Tench. "Artificial intelligence in communication management", 377–389.

56 "CommTech quickstart guide." *Arthur W. Page Society*. 2020. Retrieved from: https://knowledge.page.org/report/commtech-quickstart-guide/

57 Gouda, Nikhil Kumar, Santosh Kumar Biswal, and Binish Parveen. "Application of artificial intelligence in advertising & public relations and emerging ethical issues in the ecosystem." *International Journal of Advanced Science and Technology* 29, no. 6 (2020): 7561–7570.

58 Ward, Jamie, and Alisa Agozzino. "Is it broken or just bruised? Evaluating AI and its ethical implications within the PR and health care industries." In *The emerald handbook of computer-mediated communication and social media*, pp. 639–652. Emerald Publishing Limited, 2022.

59 Rubin, Victoria L. "Manipulation in marketing, advertising, propaganda, and public relations." In *Misinformation and disinformation: Detecting fakes with the eye and AI*, pp. 157–205. Cham: Springer International Publishing, 2022.

60 Crawford, Kate. *The atlas of AI: Power, politics, and the planetary costs of artificial intelligence.* Yale University Press, 2021.

61 Yang, Jeongwon, and Regina Luttrell. "Digital misinformation & disinformation: The global war of words." In *The emerald handbook of computer-mediated communication and social media*, pp. 511–529. Emerald Publishing Limited, 2022.

62 Luckin, Rosemary. *Machine learning and human intelligence: The future of education for the 21st century.* London: UCL IOE Press. UCL Institute of Education, University of London, 20 Bedford Way, WC1H 0AL, 2018.

63 Hermann, Erik. "Leveraging artificial intelligence in marketing for social good – an ethical perspective." *Journal of Business Ethics* 179, no. 1 (2022): 43–61.

64 McCollough, Christopher J., Adrienne A. Wallace, and Regina Luttrell. "Artificial intelligence: The dark side, ethics, and implications." In *The emerald handbook of computer-mediated communication and social media*, pp. 671–684. Emerald Publishing Limited, 2022.

65 Hancock, Roland, Middle East, Szabolcs Mezei, Maren Bryne Aas, and Brecht Gijsbertsen. "Reconsidering Education policy in the era of Generative AI." *G20 Policy*. 2023.

66 Hancock, et al. "Reconsidering Education policy in the era of Generative AI", 3.

67 Salah, Mohammed, Fadi Abdelfattah, Hussam Alhalbusi, and Muna Al Mukhaini. "Me and my AI bot: Exploring the 'AI holic' phenomenon and university students' dependency on generative AI chatbots-is this the new academic addiction?" 2023. Retrieved from: https://www.researchsquare.com/article/rs-3508563/v2

68 Brubaker, Rogers. *Hyperconnectivity and its discontents*. John Wiley & Sons, 2022.

69 Sarfi, Tahere, Shaghayegh Nosrati, and Maryam Sabzali. "Trust, information, and COVID-19 conspiracy theories: Cross-cultural implications for crisis management and public health." *Migration Letters* 20, no. S4 (2023): 522–536.

70 Mitić, Vladimir. "Benefits of artificial intelligence and machine learning in marketing." In *Sinteza 2019-International scientific conference on information technology and data related research*, pp. 472–477. Singidunum University, 2019.

71 Chawinga, Winner Dominic. "Taking social media to a university classroom: Teaching and learning using Twitter and blogs." *International Journal of Educational Technology in Higher Education* 14, no. 1 (2017): 1–19.

72 Prasad, Priyanka, and Pooja Saigal. "Social media marketing: Tools and techniques." In *Application of gaming in new media marketing*, pp. 202–214. IGI Global, 2019.

73 Galloway, Chris, and Lukasz Swiatek. "Public relations and artificial intelligence: It's not (just) about robots." *Public Relations Review* 44, no. 5 (2018): 734–740.

74 Bourne, Clea. "AI cheerleaders: Public relations, neoliberalism and artificial intelligence." *Public Relations Inquiry* 8, no. 2 (2019): 109–125.

75 Luttrell, Regina, Adrienne A. Wallace, Christopher J. McCollough, and Jiyoung Lee. "The digital divide: Addressing artificial intelligence in communication education." *Journalism & Mass Communication Educator* 75, no. 4 (2020): 470–482.

76 Pavlik, John V. "Collaborating with ChatGPT: Considering the implications of generative artificial intelligence for journalism and media education." *Journalism & Mass Communication Educator* 78, no. 1 (2023): 84–93.

77 Pavlik. "Collaborating with ChatGPT", 92.

78 McCollough, Christopher J., Adrienne A. Wallace, and Regina M. Luttrell. "Connecting pedagogy to industry: Social and digital media in public relations courses." *Teaching Journalism & Mass Communication* 11, no. 1 (2021): 36–48.

79 McCollough, et al. "Connecting pedagogy to industry", 36–48.

80 McCollough, et al. "Connecting pedagogy to industry", 41–42.

81 Brunner, Brigitta R., Kim Zarkin, and Bradford L. Yates. "What do employers want? What should faculty teach? A content analysis of entry-level employment ads in public relations." *Journal of Public Relations Education* 4, no. 2 (2018): 21–50.

82 DiStaso, M. W. "Undergraduate public relations in the United States: The 2017 commission on public relations education report." *Journal of Public Relations Education* 5, no. 3 (2019): 3–22.

83 Luttrell, Regina M., and Luke W. Capizzo. *Public relations campaigns: An integrated approach*. SAGE Publications, Incorporated, 2020.

84 Krishna, Arunima, Donald K. Wright, and Raymond L. Kotcher. "Curriculum rebuilding in public relations: Understanding what early career, mid-career, and senior PR/communications professionals expect from PR graduates." *Journal of Public Relations Education* 6, no. 1 (2020): 33–57.

85 Beaupre, Jean, Adrienne A. Wallace, and Hannah Walters. "The future of experiential learning: The role of client-based projects in developing career-ready competencies." *2022 Annual Spring Conference*, p. 68, 2022.

86 Swiatek, Lukasz, and Chris Galloway. "Artificial intelligence and public relations." *The Routledge Companion to Public Relations* (2022).

87 Vujnovic, Marina, Lukasz Swiatek, Dean Kruckeberg, and Chris Galloway. "What is AI teaching us about public relations education?" In *Artificial intelligence in public relations and communications: Cases, reflections, and predictions*, p. 137. Quadriga University of Applied Sciences, 2023.

88 Bourne. "AI cheerleaders", 109–125.

89 Vujnovic, Marina, and Dean Kruckeberg. "Running against the tide: Educating future public relations and communications professionals in the age of neoliberalism." *ESSACHESS – Journal for Communication Studies* 14, no. 1 (27) (2021): 161–179.

90 Luttrell, et al. "The digital divide", 470–482.

91 Luttrell, Regina, Lu Xiao, and Jon Glass, eds. *Democracy in the disinformation age: Influence and activism in American politics*. Routledge, 2021.

10
LISTENING AND AI

Travis Loof

Learning Objectives

1. Readers will understand the ethical issues related to the use of artificial intelligence (AI) in sentiment analysis, including privacy concerns, transparency, and the need for human oversight.
2. Readers will be able to explain how AI-enhanced sentiment analysis is applied in public relations (PR) to monitor and strategize communication efforts.
3. Readers will identify potential biases in AI sentiment analysis models and discuss how these biases can impact the accuracy, reliability, and fairness of analyses.
4. Readers will analyze how the quality and composition of training data affect the performance and reliability of AI models in sentiment analysis.
5. Readers will trace the development of sentiment analysis from manual methods to AI-enabled techniques, recognizing key technological advancements that have enhanced its capabilities.

Introduction

Communication theorist and political scientist Harold Lasswell famously articulated the communication process as, "Who, says what, in which channel, to whom, with what effect" (p. 37).[1] Indeed, the meaning of this famous quote is debated in classrooms across the world, both for its ability to succinctly capture the communication process but also to provide a basis for understanding each part of the communication process. In this chapter, we will be using this quote to frame our investigation of social listening as a powerful tool for those in public relations (PR).

DOI: 10.4324/9781032671482-14

Lasswell's contribution to communication theory has been discussed in other venues,[2] but for our purposes, Lasswell provides two great starting points for understanding how concepts of *social listening* can be super charged with the application of artificial intelligence (AI). First, Laswell, following in the tradition of Berelson, utilized and expanded the expanded the *content analysis* methodology. Content analysis is simply a way of counting the *manifest* – that is, the literal – content of a media message. In this way, early content analysis focused on the "what" of Laswell's quote. In other words, content analysis provided a way to rigorously research actual words or content of messages. With technological and methodological advancement, researchers and practitioners begin to expand the subject of their study to analyze the *what effect* or the meaning and opinion of those messages. This is called the *latent content* within a message. This change from the literal to the implied or latent content was more formalized as sentiment analysis, though sometimes it is referred to as social listening or opinion mining.

Latent content is the content of a message that provides *sentiments*, opinions, attitudes, or emotions that underlie the explicit or manifest content of a message. Let's look at an example, "Just another day at the office. Everything is going as expected." The manifest content of this message is that the day is normal in every sense of the word. However, the latent content of this message could be much more nuanced. For example, this message could be conveying dissatisfaction, boredom, or sarcasm. If this statement was found in an employee satisfaction survey along with several other instances of outright or implied dissatisfaction, we might surmise that employee morale is low. This, in its most basic form, is a *sentiment analysis*. Sentiment analysis is the active method of extracting and analyzing opinions from – traditionally – text, but now with technological advances also in video, images, and audio files. In our example, we have determined the sentiment of the fictitious employees by aggregating the latent content of messages to conduct a proverbial temperature check. In the following chapter, we will examine how sentiment analysis has been used to gauge public opinion in a variety of contexts, the biases, and limitations of using sentiment analysis, the intersection of AI within sentiment analysis, and overall, how AI can be used as a tool for evaluating the impact of communication strategies.

BOX 10.1   PR INDUSTRY AND AI

This exercise is designed to help students understand and apply basic principles of content analysis within the context of public relations and AI-enhanced sentiment analysis tools. The activity will allow students to engage directly with real-world data, analyze sentiment and emotion in public discourse about a brand, and reflect on the implications of AI tools in PR.

Activity Description

- Group setup: Students will work in groups of 2–5.
- Content selection: Each group (or the instructor) selects a brand, product, or service, and each group chooses one media property for analysis (e.g., a social media platform page [owned, user created, or search] or product reviews).
- Content analysis: Students sort the chosen content by recency and each member identifies two pieces of content. They evaluate each post or review on the following three dimensions:

  - Valence: Positive, negative, or neutral.
  - Excitement/energy level: High vs. low.
  - Emotional type: Anger, disgust, fear, anxiety, sadness, happiness, relaxation, desire.

- Group discussion (pair and share): In their groups, students discuss the following:

  - From their analysis, what are the common themes currently being discussed about the brand?
  - How could AI and sentiment analysis enhance this process?
  - Any content that might be confusing for AI to analyze due to ambiguity or complexity.
  - Strategic recommendations for the client based on the content analysis.
  - Groups then share their findings with the class.

What Is the Need?

Sentiment analysis is pivotal in a variety of industries because of its capacity to interpret thoughts, feelings, and emotions via text. As more of our everyday life is carried out with the help of digital communication, that communication can provide valuable signals about the internal workings of large groups of people and the psychology of individuals. Sentiment analysis, emerging from the rich history of content analysis, has become crucial in understanding public opinion. It goes beyond merely analyzing text, interpreting the context and emotional tone behind words to leverage AI and *machine learning* (ML) for in-depth insights. This analytical process categorizes the emotions expressed in text as positive, negative, or neutral, extending traditional content analysis by focusing on the emotional undertones of communication.

Sentiment analysis provides many different benefits. For example, sentiment analysis can provide an in-depth understanding of customer needs, preferences, and pain points. By evaluating the emotional tone behind feedback and reviews, businesses can tailor their products, services, and marketing strategies more effectively to meet customer expectations. In this way, sentiment analysis can be used as a powerful customer service tool. As a customer service tool, it can highlight prevalent customer issues and help predict potential future complaints. By listening to social conversations and analyzing sentiments, businesses can proactively address concerns, improving customer satisfaction and loyalty. The opportunities that sentiment analysis opens for business and marketing extend beyond customer support to being able to communicate with stakeholders more effectively. With the aid of sentiment analysis, marketers and message creators can develop messaging that will resonate with the audience. In this way, sentiment analysis enables communicators to better understand their audience and thus communicate more effectively.

Sentiment analysis also can play an important role in crisis communication and reputation management. With continuous monitoring, public relations practitioners can more quickly identify and address potential crises or threats to their organization's reputation. In the viral content world, quickly and effectively countering inaccurate or damaging content is predicated on both the response and response time.

Finally, for those who effectively use it, sentiment analysis provides a competitive advantage in the form of up-to-date business intelligence. This occurs in two ways: first in listening to your customer's conversation (as discussed previously), and second because it also allows for more strategic planning by comparing your brand sentiment against those of your competitors. This can allow for more informed decisions about market position and customer perceptions. For example, by analyzing both your own customer sentiment and that of your competitors, you may be able to spot underserved customers or needs. Each of these benefits plays a crucial role in how businesses interpret and react to public opinion, shaping their strategies for better alignment with customer expectations and market trends.

From Manual to Machine: The Evolution of Sentiment Analysis

In this section, we will trace the path of sentiment analysis from the laborious methods involved in manual sentiment analysis to more modern and technologically sophisticated methods with AI-enabled sentiment analysis. In the early days of sentiment analysis, the analysis and collection of message content were primarily completed by humans. This stage in the evolution of sentiment analysis could be considered manual sentiment analysis. This type of analysis is still commonly used, but technological solutions are paving the way for a more efficient and effective use of this analysis technique. In manual analysis, researchers and analysts must pay meticulous attention to their data, such as customer feedback or surveys, and categorize that sentiment into specific groups or topical themes. This type of sentiment analysis is thus more subjective and time-intensive, is potentially more error prone, and is even limited by the volume of data that can be managed by an individual or by a team. In this most basic form, sentiment analysis starts to isolate the latent content of messages, but is still limited by the scope of what is humanly possible. Some may argue that manual sentiment analysis is more of an art than a science. In response, this author would argue that manual sentiment analysis is a science when it is well executed and provides the necessary materials for reproducibility. This notion of reproducibility – the ability to use one set of rules in one situation and get the same result while using those same rules in a different situation – was greatly aided in the second by the second evolution of sentiment analysis which is automated analysis.

Sentiment analysis is useful for understanding the polarity of emotions within a given human text. With the dawn of the internet and computer age, society saw a dramatic increase in the amount of information sources. To conduct a sentiment analysis in an information-rich environment, like the one we live in today, automated computer processing was incorporated into sentiment analysis. In this type of sentiment analysis, researchers and analysts were no longer confined by the limitations of human capacity to evaluate large datasets. Instead, automated systems emerged that used software to help parse the vast amounts of data that were being created and subsequently collected for analysis. In this software-enabled sentiment analysis, humans no longer had to count or group emotionally charged content; rather, humans would need to tell the software what information to process and how that information would be composed by using *dictionaries* (or lexicons). Much like the dictionary with which you are probably familiar, sentiment analysis dictionaries are also a set or list of words and phrases. The function of these software dictionaries is for humans to instruct the software on interpreting and classifying the target text. Additionally, automated sentiment analyses also make use of *rule-based algorithms*, the instructions or steps that are to be automatically carried out.

Let's look at a tasty example, making a sandwich, to better understand what rule-based algorithms are. If we were to program an algorithm to make a sandwich, we would need to specify the ingredients, the order of operations (which ingredient do we start with), and instructions to build a sandwich. Now let us combine both the use of dictionaries and rule-based algorithms within an automated sentiment analysis. In sentiment analysis, we could process the phrase "Today was a good day" by classifying each word according to a dictionary which would categorize the words based on predefined features such as tone (positive or negative), pronoun use, discreet emotion, and various other human created categories. Each of these categorizations would occur because the rule-based algorithms would compare the target content against the relevant dictionaries to produce our analysis.

One of the most prominent types of automated sentiment analysis tools is Linguistic Inquiry and Word Count (LIWC).[3] LIWC has been rigorously tested and used across multiple disciplines and fields.[4] The most current iteration, at the time of this writing, is LIWC-22. LIWC-22 has over 100 built in dictionaries, with the ability to create user-defined or context-specific dictionaries. The predefined dictionaries are continually put to the test by research both in terms of analysis but also by correlation with other measurements outside of textual analysis. The effective combination of a user-friendly interface and easy-to-manage dictionaries in programs like LIWC make for an effective method of analyzing text. However, even as these systems allowed for new opportunities to process text at an unprecedented scale, these methods still struggled with the nuances of language – the irony, the context, the shades of meaning that elude rule-based logic. This limitation, compiled with a still ever-growing amount of data, would be addressed by another technological advancement: AI-enabled sentiment analysis.

Before we begin to better understand how social listening is used within AI, it is important that we first have a firm understanding of what AI is. AI has many different definitions, but broadly speaking, it is programming that functions in ways that emulate cognitive processing analogous to the way humans think.[5] This definition is intentionally broad but can be refined when we start to understand that different AI architectures are used for different needs. The adage "Use the right tool for the right job" rings true for the world of AI, which has several different types of tools for many jobs. To socially listen — that is, read (and now even watch or listen) – to the variety of text created on the internet, a specific type of AI is needed; this type of AI is called *natural language processing* (NLP). As the name suggests, this architecture is meant to understand or process natural language. NLP is helpful because much of the data or conversations that PR practitioners want to listen to – like social media – are in an *unstructured data* format. Most available data is unstructured, such as digital conversations and posts, videos, images, audio files, and various information stored in formats like those used by Microsoft Word and portable document files (PDFs). Structured data is information that is harnessed in tables and relational databases with meaningful predetermined formats. Computers (and many data scientists) love working with structured data because it is direct and to the point. However, the world in which we live and communicate is often the fuzziness of natural language. To exemplify this difference, let's return to the example we discussed in the introduction: "Just another day at the office. Everything is going as expected." From a structured data perspective, we could count the number of words, we could count the types of words (verbs, adjectives, etc.) but when we start getting into the meaning of the words and the relationship between the words and even between the sentences, we begin to see the powerful potential of NLP. Using NLP allows for the understanding and meaningful structure of huge volumes of human, meaning-rich, language. Getting even more specific, we can use NLP to understand the sentiment of messaging online.

The most current form of sentiment analysis, AI-enabled sentiment analysis, offers the ability to understand context and more nuanced emotional expressions such as sarcasm. This transition was ushered in through the development of AI technology, particularly within the realms of ML and NLP. These technologies allowed for the processing of even larger datasets, the ability to recognize patterns that human analysts may miss, and – most importantly – the ability to apply a contextual understanding to the material. Two important technological advancements facilitated this shift from automated to AI-integrated sentiment analysis. First, advancements in computational power allowed machine learning to become more commercially available and thus a more realistic endeavor for those outside of computer science and AI. Second, as more information was in digital form, this meant that computer scientists could capture larger datasets to *(pre)train* and *fine-tune* existing models.

With these two improvements, AI-enabled sentiment analysis was able to not just read words, but to understand the words in a context that would be familiar to a human. Contextual understanding means that the program accounts for the surrounding text and situations in which the words are used to arrive at an interpretation of the intended meaning of the message. For example, the words *cool*, *hot, and cold* could refer to temperature in one context or to a personal evaluation of one's demeanor in another context. AI can help distinguish between these uses based on the surrounding words and overall theme of the text. Indeed, AI models using advanced NLP techniques can even correctly analyze idioms. Idioms or idiomatic expressions are phrases that cannot be deduced from the literal meaning of the words. For example, the idiomatic expression "The elephant in the room" is understood to mean an obvious but undiscussed issue. An automated sentiment analysis that does not include various idiomatic expression dictionaries could incorrectly interpret the statement to be about the logistics of pachyderms and interior design, rather than how we understand it – quite impressive for software. Beyond being able to correctly interpret idiomatic language and figures of speech, AI-integrated sentiment analysis is also much better at picking up on the subtleties in language like sarcasm, humor, and irony (all of which are a consistent challenge for rule-based dictionary systems). In complex and large datasets, whereby opinions and sentiment might be ambiguous, this type of analysis is crucial at teasing out the intention of a message by understanding the content. However, as we will see as this chapter progresses, AI-integrated sentiment analysis is far from perfect! Though it can recognize *some* sarcasm and *some* humor, it is not a perfect science – and misinterpretation by AI is still present. As such, a best practice is to apply a *human-in-the-loop* decision framework to any instance whenever AI is incorporated into a workflow.

Levels of Sentiment Analysis

All sentiment analyses are not the same, and the scope or focus of the analysis can further distinguish them. Sentiment analysis can use distinct levels, with each level being tailored for specific textual analysis needs and subsequently giving unique insights. The primary levels include the document level, the phrase or sentence level, and the aspect level. It is important to know how semantic information is analyzed to understand the application of each level of analysis. We will discuss these starting from the least used and most broad application, document-level analysis, and moving to the most often used level, aspect-level analysis, which provides a more granular view of sentiment.

Document-Level Analysis

This level assesses the overall sentiment of a complete text such as a report, book chapter, or several pages of a text. The goal of this type of analysis is to extract sentiment across the entire text, which is often filled with *noise* and patterns inherent in the text. From a technical point of view, this type of analysis is the most challenging due to the need to interpret the context and the interrelation of words and phrases across an entire text. However, document-level analysis still offers the benefit of understanding the overarching tone of lengthy texts.

Sentence/Phrase-Level Analysis

This level, sometimes discussed as being separate levels, involves dissecting larger text into individual sentences to identify their sentiment. It's particularly effective for understanding specific reactions or feelings expressed in shorter text segments, providing insights into the varied sentiments within a document. Each sentence is analyzed independently, making it useful for texts with a broad range of sentiments. Much like sentence-level analysis, phrase-level analysis is well equipped to evaluate sentiments, however, the focus is often on opinion words at the phrase level. This approach is particularly relevant in areas like multi-line product reviews or texts in which phrases express sentiments about single or multiple aspects of a product. Both sentence and phrase analysis are commonly used within social media listening. This is because social media content is often short-form text that can convey distinct sentiment. As such, practitioners can analyze sentiments, tone, opinions, and emotions in aggregate to develop actionable insights. Compared to a document-level analysis, this level offers a more nuanced understanding of sentiment within a target text because it accounts for the subjectivity associated with individual words within phrases and sentences.

Aspect-Level Analysis

The most detailed form of sentiment analysis is the aspect-level analysis. This level concentrates on specific elements or features about a product, service, or topic. It identifies sentiments about both broad topics and specific aspects of investigation, such as a product's price or quality. For example, in a product review, the sentence-level analysis would give an overall sentiment of the review, but aspect-level analysis would identify sentiments about specific features of the product like its design, durability, price, etc. Aspect-level analysis provides detailed insights that help businesses make targeted improvements, tailor marketing strategies, and better meet customer needs and preferences. It can focus on the subject of interest rather than on the overarching impression as found in sentence/phrase-level analysis.

Each level of sentiment analysis has its unique purpose and offers different insights. Document-level analysis is ideal for overarching sentiment assessments in large texts. Phrase-level analysis provides intermediate insights, bridging the gap between sentence and document levels. Sentence-level analysis is suitable for brief, straightforward texts. Aspect-level analysis, the most detailed, is critical for comprehensive product reviews or in-depth feedback analysis.

AI-Integrated Sentiment Analysis Across Industries

Sentiment analysis plays a pivotal role in shaping business strategies. It allows for an alignment of strategy with customer expectations and market trends, thereby facilitating more informed decision-making. In the following subsections, we will look at ways that various industries use sentiment analysis to uncover insights that can lead to strategic advantage in the marketplace.

Customer Service

Customer service is improved with the use of sentiment analysis because businesses can evaluate interactions between the business and the consumer across time and over many different outlets. For example, sentiment analysis is used to evaluate qualitative responses to customer feedback and satisfaction survey data. In doing so, businesses can uncover aggregate concerns and sentiments which they may have not known about before. Businesses can analyze sentiment expressing in product reviews to uncover a number of insights related to product quality and insights into customer preferences, and even to find areas that are in need of improvement.[6]

Healthcare

Picture a hospital receiving the feedback, "Efficient staff but long wait times." Here, sentiment analysis dissects this feedback, revealing underlying patient experiences (if evaluated at the aspect level). Healthcare providers analyze patient feedback and social media discussions for sentiment trends related to specific treatments, hospital services, and overall care experiences. This analysis identifies patient concerns and areas needing improvement, leading to strategic decisions in patient care policies, facility improvements, and service quality enhancement. Thus, sentiment analysis can be used to improve patient outcomes and satisfaction. In our example, the feedback is not just about efficient staff but also about understanding and addressing the issue of wait times. In aggregate, this could lead to operational changes that enhance overall patient satisfaction and streamline hospital services.

Finance and Banking

Consider a customer review for a mobile banking application, "Love the mobile app, but loan processing is slow." In this context, sentiment analysis separates positive feedback from critical concerns. A bank could use this dual-edged comment to refine their digital platform while streamlining loan processes, ensuring improvement in customer service and product offerings. Financial institutions use sentiment analysis to understand customers' perspectives on their services and those of competitors. Insights gained help in developing better products, refining customer service approaches, and strategically positioning their services against competitors, leading to enhanced customer retention and acquisition.

National Security and Law Enforcement

In national security, sentiment analysis is applied to monitor online discussions for potential threats and public safety concerns. Indeed, open-source intelligence (OSINT) often uses AI-integrated sentiment analysis to monitor public opinion in conflict areas.[7] This involves analyzing social media sentiments and trends across varying contexts, languages, and cultures. The strategic use of insights gathered from sentiment analysis can aid in effective crisis management and public safety. Sentiment analysis in this sphere goes beyond mere words, capturing the undercurrent of public sentiment toward safety and security issues. This can also help law enforcement better understand the communities where they serve.

Retail

Retailers apply sentiment analysis to customer reviews and feedback to understand consumer preferences and trends. This informs decisions on merchandise expansion, marketing strategies, and product improvements. Analyzing sentiments expressed in product reviews provides insights into customer preferences and areas needing improvement, guiding retailers in tailoring their offerings to meet market demand. Take a retail brand analyzing reviews like "Great designs, but sizes run small." Retailers use sentiment analysis to capture mixed feedback, informing design adjustments and accurate sizing information in their product descriptions, aligning more closely with consumer expectations and demands. In retail, aspect-level sentiment analysis is particularly valuable, as each aspect can be seen as a potential opportunity for expansion.

Education

Educational institutions can employ sentiment analysis to assess several important metrics such as feedback on courses, instructors, and facilities, and to help in student recruiting campaigns. For example, analyzing student and prospective student sentiment can help in tailoring educational offerings, improving teaching methods, and enhancing the overall educational experience. This strategic application of sentiment analysis aids in attracting more students and improving educational outcomes. In education, sentiment analysis might reveal student feedback like "Course is informative, but lacks interactive elements." This insight guides educational institutions in modifying their curriculum, perhaps by incorporating more interactive elements, thereby enhancing the learning experience and attracting more students.

Insurance

Insurance companies use sentiment analysis to evaluate customer feedback on policies and claim processes. Insights from this analysis inform improvements in customer service and policy adjustments. Analyzing customer sentiments guides the development of new insurance products and services, leading to better customer satisfaction and competitive positioning in the market. Analyzing customer feedback like "Claim process is smooth, but customer support needs improvement" is invaluable for an insurance company. This helps streamline their claim process while also enhancing their customer support, thus improving overall customer satisfaction and policyholder retention. In industries, like insurance, where decisions can have life-changing impacts, it is important to maintain a human-in-the-loop framework, even for AI-enabled sentiment analysis.

In this sample of industries, sentiment analysis serves as a critical tool, unearthing layers of consumer and public sentiment, guiding strategic decisions, and leading to improved outcomes and customer experiences.

BOX 10.2   ERROR NOT FOUND: ETHICAL DILEMMA DISCUSSION

This exercise is designed to engage students in critical thinking about the ethical implications of using AI-driven sentiment analysis tools in sensitive decision-making processes such as college admissions and employment.

Learning Objectives

- Identify ethical concerns: Students will identify and discuss the ethical issues associated with using AI sentiment analysis in college admissions and employee hiring.
- Debate the use of public data: Students will explore the implications of utilizing publicly available data (including social media) for making decisions that have significant impact on the lives of individuals.

Activity Description

- Group setup: Divide the class into small groups of 3–5 students.
- Scenario presentation: Present a scenario whereby an AI sentiment analysis tool capable of detecting very subtle public sentiments is proposed to be used by a university's admissions board and a company's human resources (HR) department. This tool analyzes publicly available information, including social media profiles, to assess the suitability of candidates for admission or employment.

Role Assignment

- Assign roles within each group:

    - Supporters: Argue in favor of using AI sentiment analysis, focusing on benefits such as increased efficiency and potential for uncovering deep insights about candidates.
    - Opponents: Argue against the use of AI sentiment analysis, focusing on ethical concerns like privacy invasion, potential biases, and the impact of misinterpretations.
    - Moderators: Facilitate discussion, ensuring that all voices are heard and guiding the debate toward constructive conclusions.

Debate

- Each group conducts a structured debate on the ethical considerations of using such technology. Discussions should cover:
  - The fairness of using publicly available data in decision-making.
  - Potential biases in AI analysis and their implications.
  - Privacy concerns and the impact of AI decisions on individuals' futures.

Guideline Development

Following the debate, each group develops a set of ethical guidelines that could be implemented to govern the use of AI in these decision-making processes.

Groups present their findings and proposed guidelines to the class. A collective discussion can be held to refine these guidelines, drawing on insights from all groups to develop a comprehensive ethical framework.

This exercise allows students to directly engage with real-world ethical dilemmas, encouraging them to think deeply about the role of technology in society and the moral responsibilities of those who deploy such technologies.

The PR Perspective: AI's Role in Public Relations

For public relations professionals, AI-enabled sentiment analysis can be a game-changer for evaluating the effectiveness of communication strategies. In this section, we will look at some practical use case scenarios for AI-enabled sentiment analysis.

Competition Analysis

AI-enabled sentiment analysis can be used to analyze a competitor's communication strategy. By gaining this business intelligence, organizations can garner insights into what works (or does not work) within their industry or sector. It can also highlight areas of a target market that are being underserved, providing a valuable opportunity to expand and grow.

Message Optimization

Sentiment analysis can also identify the types of content that are most effective with different audiences in different circumstances. These complex patterns are much deeper than a human practitioner's surface-level analysis alone. Message optimization can thus be used to tailor tone and style of communication to align with the audience preferences. AI and sentiment analysis can assist in message optimization because the sender of a message can now know more about the receiver of a message than ever before. Indeed, with AI's aid, those communication patterns can be matched for mathematically optimal reception.

Crisis Management

Ongoing social listening is imperative for crisis management. AI can help monitor and flag negative sentiment trends or controversial topics, allowing PR professionals to develop and execute crisis management programs at the onset of an issue rather than waiting for an issue to reach viral critical mass and spill over into public discussion. AI and sentiment analysis allow PR teams to be proactive in managing their stakeholder expectations, especially before they might otherwise escalate.

Campaign Impact Assessment

As discussed in this chapter, AI and sentiment analysis are particularly good at quantifying qualitative data. As such, they provide an excellent resource for PR professionals to analyze the reach and impact of campaigns and ongoing conversations across digital spaces and forms of media. AI can incorporate engagement metrics within a sentiment analysis to parse out the effectiveness of messages and campaigns. This is because AI can provide insight into how effectively a campaign resonated with a given audience.

Target Audience Analysis

Sentiment analysis can also provide PR practitioners with insights into the nature of their actual audience as compared to what is assumed to be their audience. In other words, AI can evaluate social media and online content to understand the preferences and interests of a target audience to better understand the psychographic makeup of a given audience. This could confirm what is already known about the target audience, highlight inconsistencies between the suggested target audience and the target audience's reality, or even suggest further segmenting of an audience to tailor specific strategies accordingly.

As AI continues to evolve, its integration into sentiment analysis offers profound possibilities for PR professionals. While it is crucial to be aware of the limitations and ethical considerations, AI provides powerful tools for understanding and measuring the impacts of communication strategies. PR practitioners who effectively harness these tools can gain a significant edge in crafting strategies that resonate with their audiences and achieve desired outcomes.

Confronting the Challenges of AI-Integrated Sentiment Analysis

Now that we have a firm understanding of the evolution, application, and level of analyses in sentiment analysis, let us turn to the potential biases and limitations that are inherent in the technology. Understanding these challenges is crucial for practitioners to ensure that the application of sentiment analysis is accurate, ethical, and appropriate for a given context.

While powerful, sentiment analysis is not infallible. Biases creep in from initial data collection to the final interpretation of the results. The foundation of any sentiment analysis is the data or messages that it processes. AI models learn from the data they are fed. If the training data contains inherent biases, the AI model is likely to replicate these biases in its analysis. Let us look at how data can create biases or limitation with sentiment analysis. First, much automated data collection relies on dictionaries to translate meaning; AI integrations require training data to understand how to classify data. The training data of any AI is an important consideration for any user of AI because the internal logic and patterns of the training data are used to create the rules for understanding the context. What does this mean? It means that the training data may have a set assumptions or biases that will also then be present in any subsequent analysis with a model that uses that training data. For example, consider the prompt "*Las Vegas is a cool place*" – if an AI model was trained on a corpus of weather forecasts, it would be more likely to interpret text as being related to a meteorological or temperature prediction rather than an evaluation of the entertainment value of the city. In this way, we can see that the assumptions of the training data would influence later analysis. Additionally, if the training model or the data under investigation is of poor quality, the results are likely to mirror the lackluster data.

Beyond bias being related to what is contained within the training data, bias is also introduced by what is excluded from datasets. If a sentiment analysis AI model is trained predominantly on online product reviews from a specific demographic, its ability to accurately interpret sentiments from different demographics may be compromised. For example, sentiment expression varies significantly across cultures and languages. A model trained on English language data exclusively might misinterpret or fail to accurately capture sentiments expressed in other languages, across cultural contexts, or in text from a place where English is a secondary language. Recent work has begun to ensure that localized texts are predicting the same outcomes across contexts.[8]

Bias can also be intentionally introduced into analysis in what is called data poisoning. Data poisoning occurs when biases and errors are – sometimes intentionally – introduced into data and training sets to essentially trick the AI into incorrect or faulty interpretations and assumptions. Data poisoning is often nefarious; however, some have used a form of data poisoning to protect intellectual property. This is the case with a program called Nightshade.[9] Nightshade injects specific computer code into images that are not perceived by the human eye. When these images with the embedded code are incorporated into training data, it will cause the AI model to incorrectly identify and categorize images, which will influence image generative AI. Inadvertent data poisoning can also lead to a phenomenon known as *concept drift*.

Concept drift occurs when a text's subsequent interpretations start moving from the original meaning, iteratively and linguistically, to a meaning based on mathematical probabilities rather than current human meaning. Concept drift is a critical limitation within sentiment analysis because language changes over time. If the meaning of a word changes, the interpretation must also change. For example, the term *"sick"* traditionally meant someone was ill; however, a modern slang interpretation would mean something may be cool or amazing (or so I am told). This means that AI models need to be continuously updated and fine-tuned to ensure the interpretation's accuracy matches the human understanding.

AI models can also suffer from overfitting or underfitting of the training data to new, unseen data. For example, overfit AI models will perform well on training data but perform poorly on any new data because it is too different from the training set. Likewise, underfitting occurs when a model is too simple to capture complexities of a more nuanced dataset, leading to inaccurate sentiment interpretations and predictions. If a sentiment analysis model is trained exclusively on product reviews, its ability to classify political rhetoric may be greatly reduced. As such, the quality of the data is as important as the fit between the training set and the real-world use of the model.

A final limitation of AI-integrated sentiment analysis is a common limitation of AI: the lack transparency and interpretability of a given model. That is, the ability of humans to interpret and understand the interworking of a model. AI models, especially deep learning models, are often described as *black boxes* because humans cannot "see into" the model to understand how an AI came to a conclusion. In reality, the inability to understand these types of AI is due to their complex and non-linear nature. In other words, the complexity of the operations required to make such predictions is often beyond humans' capacity to fully grasp in terms of either content and/or scale. This lack of transparency can be a significant challenge, especially when trying to understand the rationale behind a particular sentiment analysis outcome. Another way to think about this limitation is that in some AI-integrated sentiment analyses, humans can understand the result and it may even match what they know to be true, but they are not exactly sure how the model reached that conclusion. This uncertainty raises serious ethical questions when sentiment analysis is used to make consequential decisions across a variety of disciplines. Responses to this limitation include keeping humans in the loop and increased use of *explainable AI* (XAI). XAI is a great complement with sentiment analysis because users understand how insights are gathered and can explain the results of the analysis from start to finish.

While sentiment analysis – particularly AI-integrated sentiment analysis – offers valuable insights into human emotions and opinions, it is crucial to approach its application with an understanding of its potential biases and limitations. Practitioners must ensure diverse and representative datasets, be mindful of cultural and linguistic nuances, and strive for transparency and accountability in AI models to harness the full potential of sentiment analysis responsibly.

Reflections

1. How do AI and machine learning technologies differ from traditional data analysis methods in sentiment analysis?
2. Consider a scenario in which NLP might misinterpret the sentiment of a text. How can such errors be mitigated?
3. Explain the concept of a human-in-the-loop framework for a sentiment analysis.
4. What are some of the ethical considerations when using AI for sentiment analysis?
5. How can data poisoning and concept drift affect the accuracy of AI models? What strategies can be employed to combat these issues?

Notes

1 Lasswell, Harold D. "The Structure and Function of Communication in Society." In *The Communication of Ideas: A Series of Addresses*, edited by Lyman Bryson, 37–51. New York, NY: Institute for Religious and Social Studies, 1948.
2 Sapienza, Zachary S., Narayanan Iyer, and Aaron S. Veenstra. "Reading Lasswell's Model of Communication Backward: Three Scholarly Misconceptions." In *Advances in Foundational Mass Communication Theories*, 38–61. Routledge, 2018.
3 Pennebaker, James W., Martha E. Francis, and Roger J. Booth. "Linguistic Inquiry and Word Count: LIWC 2001." *Mahway: Lawrence Erlbaum Associates* 71, no. 2001 (2001): 2001.
4 Koutsoumpis, Antonis, Janneke K. Oostrom, Djurre Holtrop, Ward Van Breda, Sina Ghassemi, and Reinout E. de Vries. "The Kernel of Truth in Text-Based Personality Assessment: A Meta-Analysis of the Relations between the Big Five and the Linguistic Inquiry and Word Count (LIWC)." *Psychological Bulletin* 148, no. 11–12 (2022): 843.
5 Cambria, Erik, Rui Mao, Melvin Chen, Zhaoxia Wang, and Seng-Beng Ho. "Seven Pillars for the Future of Artificial Intelligence." *IEEE Intelligent Systems* 38, no. 6 (2023): 62–69.
6 Huang, Huang, Adeleh Asemi Zavareh, and Mumtaz Begum Mustafa. "Sentiment Analysis in E-Commerce Platforms: A Review of Current Techniques and Future Directions." *IEEE Access*, published August 29, 2023. DOI: 10.1109/ACCESS.2023.307308.
7 Williams, Heather J., and Ilana Blum. *Defining Second Generation Open Source Intelligence (OSINT) for the Defense Enterprise*. Santa Monica: Rand Corporation, 2018.

8 Jackson, Samantha, Barend Beekhuizen, Zhao Zhao, and Yi Cheng Zhao. "LLMs and Linguistic Competency: An Exploration of GPT-4 and a Non-Hegemonic English Variety." *Newhouse Impact Journal* 1, no. 1 (2024): 8.
9 Shan, Shawn, Wenxin Ding, Josephine Passananti, Haitao Zheng, and Ben Y. Zhao. "Prompt-Specific Poisoning Attacks on Text-to-Image Generative Models." arXiv preprint arXiv:2310.13828 (2023).

11
LEVERAGING ARTIFICIAL INTELLIGENCE IN SEO AND SEM FOR PUBLIC RELATIONS

Adrienne A. Wallace

Learning Objectives

1. Describe the role of artificial intelligence (AI) in enhancing search engine optimization (SEO) and search engine marketing (SEM) strategies within the field of public relations (PR).
2. Demonstrate how AI tools can be utilized to optimize paid media strategies, such as pay-per-click (PPC) campaigns, by automating bid management and targeting specific audience segments in PR campaigns.
3. Examine the ethical considerations involved in using AI-driven SEO and SEM tools, focusing on data privacy, user consent, and the mitigation of algorithmic biases.
4. Assess the impact of integrating the PESO Model© with AI on the effectiveness of PR strategies, particularly in terms of improving the visibility, engagement, and overall impact of media campaigns across paid, earned, shared, and owned media channels.

Introduction

Artificial intelligence (AI), search engine optimization (SEO), and search engine marketing (SEM) are increasingly influential in the field of public relations (PR). Each of these technologies offers unique advantages that can enhance PR strategies, from data analysis and audience targeting to visibility and engagement. By leveraging AI across the well-known and highly adopted PESO Model© as an integrated communications tool, public relations practitioners can create more data-driven, efficient, and impactful SEO and SEM strategies,

DOI: 10.4324/9781032671482-15

ultimately leading to a more robust online presence and better engagement with their target audiences.

The PESO Model©, developed by Gini Dietrich, stands for paid, earned, shared, and owned media.[1] This integrated communications model helps public relations practitioners create cohesive and strategic campaigns. When combined with AI, the effectiveness of the PESO Model© in SEO and SEM is significantly amplified (Figure 11.1).

Paid media: AI optimizes SEM strategies, such as pay-per-click (PPC) campaigns, by automating bid management, targeting specific audience segments, and personalizing ad content. This ensures higher engagement and better return on investment (ROI).

Earned media: AI tools analyze large datasets to identify trends and influencers, enabling PR professionals to craft pitches that resonate more effectively with journalists and bloggers. This boosts the chances of earning valuable backlinks and media coverage, enhancing SEO.

Shared media: AI enhances the reach and impact of shared content by predicting which types of content are most likely to be shared and by whom. This drives organic traffic and engagement, indirectly benefiting SEO.

Owned media: AI aids in content creation and optimization, ensuring that website and blog content is not only relevant and engaging but also optimized for search engines. This improves organic search rankings and overall visibility.

Using AI to include the PESO Model© in SEO and SEM strategies, PR professionals can provide a robust framework for PR practices. AI enhances decision-making through data-driven insights, SEO ensures long-term visibility and credibility, and SEM offers immediate reach and engagement. By integrating these technologies, PR professionals can create more dynamic, responsive, and effective campaigns, ultimately enhancing their ability to manage public perception and achieve strategic objectives.

The modern PR professional's need for SEO and SEM in the digital age cannot be overstated. They are fundamental to navigating the complex landscape of online information and ensuring that PR efforts achieve their strategic objectives.

Artificial intelligence (AI) in PR involves using machine learning (ML) algorithms and data analytics to automate tasks, generate insights, and optimize campaigns. AI can analyze vast amounts of data to identify trends, sentiments, and emerging issues, enabling PR professionals to craft more effective and timely responses. For instance, AI-powered tools can monitor social media platforms and news outlets to gauge public sentiment, providing real-time feedback on public reactions to PR initiatives.[3] This capability

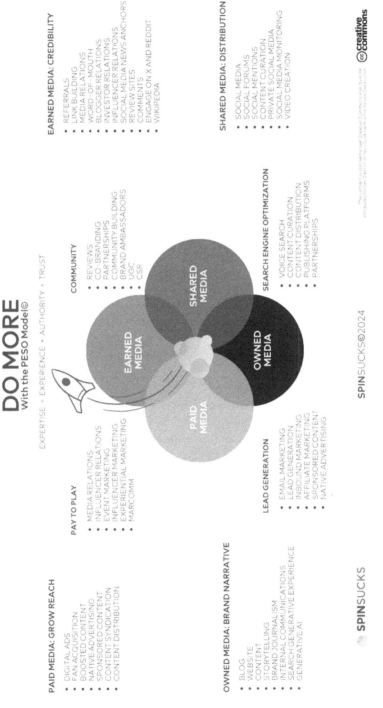

DO MORE
With the PESO Model©

EXPERTISE + EXPERIENCE + AUTHORITY + TRUST

PAID MEDIA: GROW REACH
- DIGITAL ADS
- FAN ACQUISITION
- BOOSTED CONTENT
- NATIVE ADVERTISING
- SPONSORED CONTENT
- CONTENT SYNDICATION
- CONTENT DISTRIBUTION

OWNED MEDIA: BRAND NARRATIVE
- BLOG
- WEBSITE
- CONTENT
- STORYTELLING
- BRAND JOURNALISM
- INTERNAL COMMUNICATIONS
- SEARCH GENERATIVE EXPERIENCE
- GENERATIVE AI

PAY TO PLAY
- MEDIA RELATIONS
- INFLUENCER RELATIONS
- EVENT MARKETING
- INFLUENCER MARKETING
- EXPERIENTIAL MARKETING
- MARCOMM

COMMUNITY
- REVIEWS
- CO-BRANDING
- PARTNERSHIPS
- COMMUNITY BUILDING
- BRAND AMBASSADORS
- UGC
- CSR

LEAD GENERATION
- EMAIL MARKETING
- LEAD GENERATION
- INBOUND MARKETING
- AFFILIATE MARKETING
- SPONSORED CONTENT
- NATIVE ADVERTISING

SEARCH ENGINE OPTIMIZATION
- VOICE SEARCH
- CONTENT CURATION
- CONTENT DISTRIBUTION
- PUBLISHING PLATFORMS
- PARTNERSHIPS

EARNED MEDIA: CREDIBILITY
- REFERRALS
- LINK BUILDING
- MEDIA RELATIONS
- WORD-OF-MOUTH
- BLOGGER RELATIONS
- INVESTOR RELATIONS
- INFLUENCER RELATIONS
- SOCIAL MEDIA NEWS ANCHORS
- REVIEW SITES
- COMMENTS
- ENGAGE ON X AND REDDIT
- WIKIPEDIA

SHARED MEDIA: DISTRIBUTION
- SOCIAL MEDIA
- SOCIAL FORUMS
- SOCIAL MENTIONS
- CONTENT CURATION
- PRIVATE SOCIAL MEDIA
- SOCIAL MEDIA MONITORING
- VIDEO CREATION

PAID MEDIA
EARNED MEDIA
SHARED MEDIA
OWNED MEDIA

SPINSUCKS©2024

SPINSUCKS

FIGURE 11.1   Artificial intelligence emerges as a robust collaborator across the PESO Model©, enhancing efficiency, generating insights, and amplifying overall impact[2]

allows for proactive adjustments to strategies, enhancing the effectiveness of PR campaigns.

Search engine optimization (SEO) is the practice of optimizing online content to improve its ranking on search engine results pages (SERPs). In the context of PR, SEO ensures that press releases, blog posts, and other digital content are easily discoverable by search engines like Google. Effective SEO involves keyword research, quality content creation, and technical optimization. By incorporating SEO strategies, PR professionals can increase the visibility of their messages, ensuring that the target audience finds relevant content when searching for related topics. This organic visibility is crucial for building credibility and authority in the digital space.[4]

Search engine marketing (SEM), which includes paid advertising strategies like PPC ads, complements SEO by providing immediate visibility on search engines.[5] In PR, SEM can be used to amplify messages and reach broader audiences quickly.[6,7] For example, promoting a press release or a corporate announcement through paid search ads can ensure that the message reaches the top of search results, enhancing its reach and impact. SEM campaigns can be precisely targeted based on demographics, interests, and behaviors, allowing for more effective audience engagement.[8]

This chapter aims to cover the essentials of AI's role in SEO and SEM in relation to public relations, providing a balanced mix of theoretical insights, practical advice, and forward-looking perspectives.

Foundational Concepts of AI in SEO and SEM

AI and Machine Learning

AI embodies the replication of human intelligence processes by machines, especially computer systems.[9] These processes include learning (the acquisition of information and rules for using the information), reasoning (using the rules to reach approximate or definite conclusions), and self-correction. ML, a subset of AI, empowers systems to learn from data patterns and make decisions with minimal human intervention.[10] The dynamic nature of ML algorithms allows them to adapt to new data independently, making them invaluable in processing and analyzing the colossal datasets generated by online activities.[11]

In the context of search engines, AI and ML algorithms sift through and analyze vast amounts of data to understand user behavior, improve search result relevancy, and personalize user experiences. This capability is important for SEO and SEM, as it enables marketers to fine-tune their strategies based on predictive analytics and real-time insights.[12]

AI and ML are transformative technologies that significantly enhance the functionality and efficiency of search engines. In the context of search engines,

AI and ML are instrumental in delivering accurate, relevant, and personalized search results. These technologies enable search engines to understand and process natural language queries, enhancing their ability to interpret user intent beyond mere keyword matching. For instance, Google's RankBrain and BERT (bidirectional encoder representations from transformers), are ML-based components of its search algorithm, which helps process and understand complex and ambiguous queries by learning from past search data.[13] As confirmed by Google on October 26, 2015, RankBrain utilizes ML to process and interpret the billions of searches that Google handles every day.[14]

AI and ML are pivotal in improving the overall user experience (UX). They enable search engines to personalize search results based on individual user behavior and preferences, thereby increasing the relevance of the information presented. Additionally, these technologies help in identifying and filtering out spam and low-quality content, ensuring that users receive credible and valuable information. Consequently, AI and ML are integral to the evolution of search engines, driving advancements in accuracy, personalization, and overall search quality.[15]

Evolution of Search Engines

The evolution of search engines has been significantly influenced by advancements in AI technologies, leading to enhanced accuracy, relevance, and UX. Initially, search engines relied primarily on basic keyword matching and rudimentary algorithms to rank web pages.[16] However, the integration of AI has transformed these systems into sophisticated tools capable of understanding complex queries and delivering highly relevant results. The journey of search engines from rudimentary information retrieval tools to sophisticated AI-driven entities underscores the transformative impact of AI. Early search engines ranked websites based on basic metrics like keyword density and the quantity of backlinks.[17] However, these criteria often led to manipulative practices that degraded the quality of search results.

The advent of AI and ML in search technologies marked a paradigm shift toward prioritizing content quality, user intent, and overall UX. Google's introduction of RankBrain, the ML algorithm previously discussed, was a significant milestone.[18] RankBrain interprets the nuances of search queries and user intent, refining search results to better match user needs. This evolution reflects a broader trend toward semantic search, where the focus is on understanding the contextual meaning behind queries rather than relying solely on exact keyword matches.[19]

AI technologies, particularly ML and natural language processing (NLP), have been pivotal in this evolution. For instance, Google's introduction of Rank-Brain marked a significant advancement.[20] RankBrain enables the search engine to process and understand ambiguous and previously unseen queries by learning from vast amounts of search data. This capability allows for a more nuanced understanding of user intent beyond simple keyword matching.[21]

Additionally, AI has facilitated the development of personalized search results. By analyzing user behavior, preferences, and historical data, search engines can tailor results to individual users, enhancing relevance and user satisfaction. AI also plays a crucial role in combating spam and low-quality content, ensuring that search results are trustworthy and valuable.[22]

Overall, the integration of AI technologies has revolutionized search engines, making them more intelligent, responsive, and user-centric. These advancements have not only improved search accuracy but also significantly enhanced the overall UX, setting a new standard for information retrieval in the digital age.

Principles of SEO and SEM: The AI Influence

The integration of AI and ML into digital marketing strategies, especially SEO and SEM, represents a pivotal shift in how brands interact with their audiences online.[23] SEO and SEM are critical components of digital marketing strategies, playing a pivotal role in PR.[24] SEO involves optimizing online content to improve its visibility and ranking on SERPs through organic means. SEM, on the other hand, encompasses paid advertising strategies, such as PPC campaigns, to achieve immediate visibility on search engines.[25]

AI's integration into SEO and SEM has revolutionized the way PR professionals approach these strategies.[26] AI technologies, particularly ML and NLP, enhance the effectiveness of SEO by enabling more precise and relevant keyword optimization, content creation, and technical adjustments. For example, AI-driven tools can analyze vast datasets to identify trending keywords, predict user intent, and suggest content improvements that align with search engine algorithms. This capability ensures that PR content is not only discoverable but also resonates with the target audience.[27]

Other viable uses of AI in public relations provides numerous advantages for professionals related to SEO and SEM, including the following:

Real-time media monitoring: AI-powered media monitoring allows tracking of brand mentions, monitoring of industry trends, and staying ahead of competitor activities across various digital channels. This enables prompt responses to emerging issues and strategic shaping of PR campaigns.

Personalized communication: According to Accenture, 91% of consumers prefer brands that offer personalized recommendations.[28] ML algorithms can analyze extensive datasets to better understand audience preferences, behaviors, and sentiments, enabling more personalized communication.

Efficient and strategic press release distribution: AI facilitates precise targeting of journalists and influencers, ensuring that press releases reach the right people at the right time.

AI-powered reporting and analysis: AI-driven reporting and analysis tools provide detailed insights in real-time, simplifying the process of tracking and measuring ROI. Deloitte's findings indicate that organizations using automation see significant time and cost savings, boosting efficiency.[29]

Advanced content creation and optimization: NLP enables quick generation of high-quality press releases, blog posts, and social media content. AI-driven content optimization tools further refine messaging based on audience behavior and preferences.

Brainstorming and idea generation: AI-powered tools are invaluable for generating ideas. They analyze current trends and historical data to suggest new perspectives and angles for your brainstorming sessions, providing a wealth of fresh and creative concepts for your PR campaigns.

In SEM, AI facilitates more efficient and targeted advertising campaigns. SEMrush's *Think Big With AI* report[30] revealed that in 2023, 67% of businesses leveraged AI for content marketing and SEO.[31] Generative AI enables advertisers to produce copy and design in seconds rather than hours. This efficiency benefits both publishers and advertisers. AI has already become an integral part of our daily lives. AI algorithms can analyze user behavior, preferences, and demographic data to create highly personalized ad campaigns. These campaigns can be dynamically adjusted in real time based on performance metrics, ensuring optimal reach and engagement.[32] This level of precision in targeting enhances the effectiveness of PR tactics and initiatives by ensuring that messages reach the most relevant audiences.

Additionally, AI helps PR professionals monitor and measure the impact of their SEO and SEM efforts. Advanced analytics powered by AI can track user interactions, measure engagement, and provide insights into campaign performance. This data-driven approach enables continuous optimization and refinement of PR strategies, leading to more successful outcomes. The integration of AI into SEO and SEM has provided PR professionals with powerful tools to enhance the visibility, relevance, and impact of their messages. By leveraging AI, PR strategies can be more targeted, efficient, and adaptive, ultimately improving their effectiveness in each campaign.[33]

SEO and SEM are cornerstone strategies in digital marketing designed to enhance online visibility and engage targeted audiences. SEO focuses on optimizing websites to rank higher in organic search results.[34] In contrast, SEM involves paid advertising tactics to increase visibility quickly. AI's role in redefining these strategies is profound, leveraging data-driven insights to optimize campaigns for maximum effectiveness.

Other PR tactics in SEO/SEM utilizing AI are the following.

- **AI-driven keyword research and content optimization:** Traditional keyword research, reliant on manual analysis, has evolved into a sophisticated AI-driven process. AI tools now predict keyword effectiveness by analyzing search trends, competition, and correlating user intent with content relevance. This predictive capability enables marketers to craft content strategies that resonate with target audiences and align with search engine algorithms.[35]
- **Enhancing UX with AI:** AI technologies offer unprecedented insights into user behavior, preferences, and engagement patterns. By analyzing this data, AI applications recommend structural, content, and navigational improvements to websites, ensuring that they meet the highest UX standards.[36] Improved UX not only satisfies users but also signals to search engines that a website is a valuable resource, thereby boosting its SEO ranking.
- **AI in link-building strategies:** Building a robust backlink profile is a critical SEO strategy. AI tools streamline this process by identifying potential link-building opportunities, assessing the quality of linking domains, and suggesting outreach strategies.[37] This automation saves time and resources, allowing marketers to focus on building meaningful partnerships and high-quality content.
- **Ad optimization and personalization in SEM:** In the realm of SEM, AI's impact is particularly noticeable in the optimization of PPC campaigns. AI algorithms automate bid management, ensuring ads are placed at the optimal cost per click.[38] Furthermore, AI-driven personalization tailors ad content to individual users based on their previous online behavior, search history, and preferences. This level of customization enhances ad relevancy, improving click-through rates and conversion rates.
- **Predictive analytics for strategic decision-making:** AI's predictive analytics capabilities allow marketers to forecast trends, user behavior, and campaign performance.[39] This foresight enables proactive adjustments to SEO and SEM strategies, optimizing them for anticipated changes in the digital landscape.

By integrating AI into SEO and SEM, PR professionals can achieve more targeted, efficient, and effective campaigns. This technological synergy enhances the visibility of websites and ads and fosters a more engaging and personalized UX for internal and external stakeholders.

AI Technologies in SEO and SEM In PR: Exploring SEO Tools Tailored to Your Needs

Begin by uncovering valuable keywords using tools such as Ahrefs and SEMrush. Ahrefs suggests keywords based on search intent, while SEMrush identifies trending topics and related ideas. Next, effortlessly optimize your content with Surfer

BOX 11.1   PR AND AI STRATEGY WORKSHOP

Title: AI-Enhanced PR Campaign Design

Objective: To apply AI tools and strategies in designing a comprehensive PR campaign that leverages SEO and SEM for improved engagement and visibility.

Instructions

1. **Preparation**

   a. Provide students with an overview of various AI tools and their applications in SEO and SEM (e.g., Ahrefs, SEMrush, Surfer SEO, SpyFu, Moz Pro).

   b. Divide students into small groups and assign each group a fictitious company or a PR scenario (e.g., launching a new product, crisis management, brand repositioning).

2. **Activity**

   a. **Campaign design (30 minutes):** Each group designs a PR campaign for their assigned scenario, incorporating AI tools for SEO and SEM. They should:

      - Identify target keywords using AI-driven keyword research tools.
      - Plan content creation and optimization strategies using AI content tools.
      - Develop a paid media strategy using AI for ad optimization and personalization.
      - Outline how they will measure and analyze the campaign's performance using AI analytics tools.

   b. **Presentation (20 minutes):** Each group presents their PR campaign to the class, explaining how they used AI tools in their strategy and how they expect these tools to enhance their campaign's effectiveness.

3. **Feedback and discussion (20 minutes)**

   a. After each presentation, the class provides feedback on the proposed campaigns. Discuss the strengths and potential areas for improvement, focusing on the innovative use of AI tools and their anticipated impact.

   b. Facilitate a discussion on the practical challenges of implementing AI in PR campaigns and potential solutions.

4. **Reflection (10 minutes)**

a. Ask students to write a brief reflection on how AI can transform PR practices and the key takeaways from designing an AI-enhanced PR campaign. Discuss these reflections in a concluding session.

SEO, focusing on structure, readability, and linking. Stay ahead of the curve with SpyFu and Moz Pro. These advanced tools analyze competitors' websites using sophisticated algorithms. SpyFu provides comprehensive competitor data, while Moz Pro identifies backlinks and recommends strategies. For an all-in-one solution, consider Post Cheetah. It covers everything from keyword research to content optimization, offering real-time data and competitor insights, and aids in writing and SEO. Remember to choose tools wisely based on your specific needs and budget. Experiment to find the perfect fit for your project. See the end of the chapter for a list of free, freemium, and premium tools useful in exploring SEO-related objectives.

AI-Powered Research for Maximum Impact

Navigating SEO keyword research in PR can be complex, but AI simplifies the process of uncovering high-value keywords. AI dives deep into search data to pinpoint popular keywords and identifies less competitive options. This approach allows you to target niche areas effectively. For example, instead of targeting broad terms like "running shoes," AI might suggest more specific phrases like "best running shoes for women with wide feet," capturing users with strong purchasing intent. AI understands search intent by analyzing user behavior, ensuring your keyword strategy aligns with what users are seeking.[40]

AI-Driven Optimization for Enhanced User Engagement

AI-powered content optimization tools leverage data analysis to implement effective SEO strategies. These tools examine top-ranking content to identify successful elements such as structure, readability, and engaging titles. By optimizing your content accordingly, you enhance UX and improve search engine rankings. They also enhance readability by recommending improvements like concise sentences and bullet points for better engagement. Additionally, they ensure professional standards by checking grammar and detecting plagiarism. The evolution of IBM's Watson[41] is a great case study to examine related to AI-powered intelligent document understanding. Empowered by data insights, ML helps you create content that not only meets SEO criteria but also resonates with your audience, driving conversions on your website.

AI-Enhanced SEO Competitor Analysis

Looking to surpass your competitors in PR through SEO? AI can offer valuable assistance. AI-powered tools analyze competitor websites, dissecting their keywords, backlinks, and content strategies. This analysis reveals their strengths and weaknesses, providing you with a competitive edge. Moreover, AI identifies untapped keywords and topics your competitors may have overlooked.[42] This insight can help you develop a unique content strategy that attracts new audiences and fills content gaps.

AI-SEO and the PESO Model©

The PESO Model©[43] provides a strategic framework for integrating paid, earned, shared, and owned media. Pairing AI-SEO tools with the PESO Model© can elevate your content strategy to new heights. For paid media, AI algorithms craft compelling ad copy and analyze performance metrics for optimal ROI. In earned media, AI monitors brand mentions and evaluates media coverage effectiveness. For shared media, AI suggests content topics and tones that resonate with your audience, fostering engagement and community building. Finally, in owned media, AI generates and optimizes content to enhance discoverability and engagement across your owned channels. Artificial intelligence serves as a powerful ally across the PESO Model©, enhancing efficiency, insights, and overall effectiveness.

Enhancing User Experience Through AI-SEO

UX is paramount in SEO, and AI can assist in achieving a user-centric approach. AI-powered SEO applications optimize website loading speeds and ensure mobile-friendliness, important factors as mobile searches dominate modern online life.[44] A well-organized structure and clear navigation enhance user engagement and signal value to search engines, improving your site's ranking.

Personalizing Content for Individual Users

AI can improve website personalization by leveraging user data to deliver tailored content and recommendations. Imagine a website that remembers user preferences and customizes results based on their interests and behaviors. This personalized approach increases user satisfaction and encourages repeat visits and conversions.

AI Writing Assistants for Compelling Content

AI writing assistants streamline content creation by analyzing trends and user behavior to suggest relevant topics and ideas.[45] These tools go beyond brainstorming to outline content, suggest supporting data, and ensure logical flow and accuracy. They help overcome writer's block and expedite the research process while maintaining a personal touch in your writing style.

The Role of Human Expertise in AI-SEO

I have said this once, and I will say it again: the robots will not take your job; however, someone adept at using AI to expedite and automate tasks with robots might. While AI automates many SEO tasks, human expertise remains indispensable. AI assists in keyword discovery, content optimization, and competitor analysis, providing valuable insights. However, human interpretation and strategic decision-making based on AI data are essential for crafting effective SEO strategies by PR professionals.[46] Public relations practitioners use AI insights to inform strategic goals, interpret data trends, improve empathy, and ensure ethical SEO practices that prioritize quality content and UX – this remains unchanged, even today.[47]

Challenges and Ethical Considerations

The integration of AI in SE and SEM has changed how businesses approach digital marketing. These AI-driven tools analyze vast amounts of data to deliver personalized and efficient marketing strategies. However, the increasing reliance on AI raises significant concerns about data privacy and user consent, which are particularly pertinent to the field of PR.

Implications for Data Privacy

The use of AI in SEO and SEM relies heavily on collecting and analyzing personal data. This includes browsing history, search queries, location data, and even demographic information. While this data helps marketers create more effective campaigns, it also raises significant privacy concerns.[48]

1. **Data collection and consent:** One of the primary concerns is whether users are adequately informed about the extent of data collection.[49] Many users are unaware of the breadth of data being collected and how it is being used. This lack of transparency can lead to breaches of trust between consumers and companies.
2. **Regulatory compliance:** Governments worldwide are implementing stricter data privacy regulations. The General Data Protection Regulation (GDPR) in the European Union (EU) and the California Consumer Privacy Act (CCPA) are two prominent examples. These regulations require businesses to obtain explicit consent from users before collecting their data and to provide options for users to opt out of data collection.[50] Non-compliance can result in substantial fines and legal repercussions.

3. **Data security:** Ensuring the security of collected data is another critical aspect. AI systems must be designed with robust security measures to prevent data breaches and unauthorized access.[51,52] Companies must invest in advanced encryption and security protocols to protect user information.[53] The White House even has an opinion on how this should be upheld in a report by the National Science and Technology Council.[54]

User Consent and Ethical Considerations

User consent is at the heart of data privacy. For AI-driven SEO and SEM tools to operate ethically, they must prioritize transparent data practices and obtain informed consent from users.[55] This involves clear communication about what data is being collected, how it will be used, and who will have access to it.[56,57]

1. **Transparency and communication:** PR professionals play a vital role in communicating data practices to the public. Clear and honest communication about data collection practices can build trust and mitigate privacy concerns.[58] Companies should provide easily accessible privacy policies and consent forms that are straightforward and understandable.[59,60]
2. **Building trust:** Trust is a cornerstone of effective public relations. By prioritizing user privacy and consent, businesses can foster trust and loyalty among their audience.[61] This involves not only complying with legal requirements but also adhering to ethical standards that respect user privacy.[62]
3. **Balancing personalization and privacy:** AI-driven personalization can enhance UX, but it must be balanced with privacy considerations.[63] PR professionals must advocate for strategies that respect user preferences and boundaries, ensuring that personalization efforts do not infringe on privacy rights.[64]

Ensuring Accuracy in AI

Accuracy in AI-driven SEO and SEM tools is a necessity for effective marketing. These tools rely on algorithms that analyze vast amounts of data to make predictions and decisions. The accuracy of these systems depends on the quality of data on which they are trained and the robustness of the algorithms themselves.

1. **Data quality:** High-quality data is essential for accurate AI predictions. Inaccurate or incomplete data can lead to erroneous conclusions, affecting the effectiveness of SEO and SEM campaigns. PR professionals must advocate

for rigorous data collection and validation processes to ensure the integrity of the data used in AI systems.

2. **Algorithmic robustness:** AI algorithms must be designed to handle diverse datasets and adapt to new information. Continuous monitoring and updating of algorithms are necessary to maintain their accuracy.[65] This requires collaboration between data scientists, internal and agency PR research departments, and PR professionals to ensure that the AI systems align with marketing goals and ethical standards.

3. **Transparency and explainability:** Ensuring that AI systems are transparent and their decisions are explainable is crucial for maintaining trust. PR professionals should push for AI models that can provide clear explanations for their recommendations, enabling better understanding and accountability.[66,67,68]

Mitigating Bias in AI

Bias in AI systems can arise from various sources, including biased training data, algorithmic design, and unintended consequences of model deployment. Mitigating these biases is essential to ensure fair and ethical marketing practices.

1. **Biased training data:** AI systems learn from historical data, which may contain biases reflecting societal prejudices.[69] For example, if an AI system is trained on data that underrepresents certain demographics, it may produce biased outcomes.[70] PR professionals must work with data scientists and researchers to identify and correct biases in training data.

2. **Algorithmic bias:** Even with unbiased data, algorithms can introduce biases through design choices.[71] These biases can affect SEO and SEM practices, leading to unfair targeting and exclusion of certain groups. Regular audits and fairness checks are necessary to identify and mitigate algorithmic biases. As the saying goes: bias in, bias out.[72]

3. **Ethical AI design:** Designing AI systems with ethical considerations in mind is imperative.[73] This includes implementing fairness constraints, ensuring diversity in training data, and involving diverse teams in the development process. PR professionals can advocate for ethical AI practices by promoting inclusivity and fairness in marketing strategies.[74]

Implications for Public Relations

PR professionals play an influential role in addressing the challenges of accuracy and bias in AI-driven SEO and SEM. Their responsibilities include advocating for ethical AI practices, ensuring transparent communication, and maintaining

BOX 11.2   PR AND ETHICS WITH AI IN SEO/SEM

Title: Ethics Debate and Case Study Analysis on AI in SEO/SEM
Objective: To understand and critically evaluate the ethical implications of using AI in SEO and SEM within public relations, focusing on data privacy, bias, transparency, and user consent.

Instructions

1. **Preparation**

   a. Divide students into small groups.
   b. Review the November 2023 Public Relations Society of America (PRSA) report *Promise & Pitfalls: The Ethical Use of AI for Public Relations Practitioners.*[75]
   c. Assign each group a case study that highlights ethical issues in AI-driven SEO and SEM. Examples could include cases involving data breaches, algorithmic bias, lack of transparency in data use, etc.

2. **Activity**

   a. **Case Study Analysis (20 minutes):** Each group analyzes their assigned case study, identifying the ethical issues presented. They should consider the following questions:

      • What are the main ethical concerns in this case?
      • How does the use of AI in SEO/SEM contribute to these concerns?
      • What could have been done differently to address these issues?

   b. **Group Presentation (15 minutes):** Each group presents their case study analysis to the class, highlighting the ethical issues and their proposed solutions.
   c. **Ethics Debate (25 minutes):** After the presentations, conduct a class-wide debate on the broader ethical implications of using AI in SEO/SEM. Divide the class into two sides: one advocating for the benefits of AI in SEO/SEM despite ethical concerns, and the other emphasizing the need for stricter ethical guidelines and regulations.

3. **Reflection (10 minutes)**

   a. Conclude the activity with a reflective discussion. Ask students to consider how they, as future PR professionals, can balance the use of AI in SEO/SEM with ethical responsibilities. Have them write a brief reflection on what they learned from the activity.

public trust.[76,77] Indeed, this is such an important part of the evolution of PR that PRSA wrote a report that instills practitioners with best practices, fair use, and advice on issues common to the modern PR professional.[78] Implications for PR include, but are not limited to, the following.

1. **Ethical advocacy:** PR professionals must champion ethical AI practices within their organizations. This involves advocating for unbiased data collection, transparent algorithms, and regular audits to identify and mitigate biases. The PRSA issued a special report related to AI and PR to thoughtfully and ethically guide PR professionals related to the trials and tribulations of AI-generated content of all kinds.[79]
2. **Transparent communication:** Clear and honest communication about the use of AI in marketing is essential for building trust. PR professionals should ensure that consumers are informed about how AI systems work, what data is collected, and how it is used.[80] Transparency can alleviate concerns about bias and inaccuracies.
3. **Building and maintaining trust:** Trust is a cornerstone of effective public relations.[81] By addressing the challenges of AI accuracy and bias, PR professionals can build and maintain trust with their audiences. This involves not only adhering to ethical standards, but also actively engaging with consumers to address their concerns and feedback.
4. **Educational initiatives:** PR teams should lead initiatives to educate both internal stakeholders and the public about AI's capabilities and limitations. By fostering a deeper understanding of AI, they can promote informed decision-making and ethical practices.[82]

The Role of Public Relations

Public relations professionals are crucial in navigating the intersection of AI, SEO, SEM, and data privacy, as outlined previously. They must advocate for ethical data practices and work to align marketing strategies with privacy regulations and user expectations. PR strategies should emphasize transparency, user education, and trust-building to ensure that AI-driven marketing efforts are both effective and respectful of user privacy.[83]

While AI has transformed SEO and SEM, enhancing precision and efficiency, it also poses significant data privacy challenges. As discussed earlier, ensuring transparent data practices, obtaining informed user consent, and prioritizing data security are essential steps in addressing these challenges and will remain hallmarks of the PR professional. Public relations professionals play a pivotal role in fostering ethical data practices, building trust, and ensuring that AI-driven marketing respects user privacy.[84]

Emerging Trends: The Impact of AI on SEO and SEM in Public Relations

The future of AI in SEO promises advancements in NLP and voice search optimization. AI's ability to understand search queries and user intent will evolve, shaping content creation strategies focused on meeting user needs rather than keyword matching. Ethical AI use remains crucial, emphasizing quality content creation and responsible SEO practices that benefit users and align with search engine guidelines.

As AI continues to evolve, specialists will focus on strategic planning, leveraging AI insights to create impactful, user-centric content that drives engagement and conversions, staying ahead by embracing AI-driven SEO tools to discover optimal keywords, refining content effectively, and gaining a competitive edge. AI's transformative impact on SEO for PR professionals offers unparalleled benefits, from data gathering and time-saving capabilities to ensuring that your content stands out in a competitive landscape. Adapting to the evolving world of SEO with AI-powered tools that empower your digital PR strategy and keep your website ahead of the curve, ensuring accuracy, and mitigating bias in AI-driven SEO and SEM are critical challenges that require ongoing attention from practitioners. Public relations professionals are uniquely positioned to address these challenges by advocating for ethical AI practices, ensuring transparent communication, and maintaining trust. By collaborating with data scientists and marketers, PR professionals can help create AI systems that are both effective and fair, ultimately benefiting both businesses and consumers.[85]

As AI continues to evolve, its implications for SEO and SEM in PR are profound and multifaceted. Emerging trends in AI are poised to reshape the landscape of digital marketing, offering new tools and methodologies that enhance the efficiency, accuracy, and effectiveness of PR campaigns. The final part of this chapter discusses several key AI-driven trends that are likely to affect SEO and SEM in the context of public relations in the upcoming years.

Natural Language Processing and Understanding

One of the most significant trends in AI is the advancement of NLP and natural language understanding (NLU). These technologies enable AI systems to comprehend and generate human language with increasing accuracy. In the realm of SEO, NLP and NLU allow for a more nuanced analysis of search queries, enabling search engines to better understand user intent and deliver more relevant results. For SEM, these advancements facilitate the creation of more targeted and contextually appropriate advertisements. PR professionals can leverage NLP to craft more compelling and personalized content, enhancing audience engagement and improving the overall effectiveness of communication strategies.[86]

Voice Search Optimization

The proliferation of voice-activated devices, such as smart speakers and virtual assistants, is driving the need for voice search optimization. AI processes and interprets voice commands, which often differ significantly from text-based queries in structure and language. As voice search becomes increasingly prevalent, PR practitioners must adapt their SEO strategies to account for the conversational nature of voice queries.[87] This involves optimizing content for long-tail keywords (keywords that are more specific and detail that hone your search faster) and natural language phrases, ensuring that information is easily accessible through voice search. Effective voice search optimization can enhance visibility and reach, providing a competitive edge in the digital marketplace.[88]

AI-Powered Content Creation and Curation

AI-driven content creation tools are revolutionizing the way content is produced and curated. NLP and NLU tools can generate high-quality articles, social media posts, and other forms of content based on predefined parameters and data inputs. For SEO and SEM, AI-generated content can be optimized for specific keywords and tailored to target audiences with precision. Additionally, AI-powered content curation systems can analyze vast amounts of data to identify trending topics, perform sentiment analysis and hone in on the most relevant content, allowing PR professionals to stay ahead of industry trends and maintain a dynamic online presence. The ability to rapidly produce and distribute optimized content enhances both the efficiency and impact of PR campaigns.[89]

Predictive Analytics and Personalization

Predictive analytics, driven by AI, is transforming the ability to forecast trends and behaviors in SEO and SEM and is a strength of NLP technologies. By analyzing historical data and identifying patterns, AI systems can predict future search trends, consumer preferences, and market developments. This enables PR professionals to anticipate changes and adapt their strategies proactively. Furthermore, AI's capacity for personalization allows for the creation of highly tailored marketing messages that resonate with individual users. Through NLP and NLU, AI creates personalized content and advertisements that significantly improve engagement and conversion rates, making PR efforts more effective and measurable.[90]

Ethical Considerations and Transparency

As AI becomes more integrated into SEO and SEM, ethical considerations surrounding data privacy, bias, and transparency gain prominence, especially as these language tools are implemented in campaigns. AI systems must be designed and implemented in ways that respect user privacy and mitigate biases in data analysis and decision-making. PR professionals have a critical role in advocating for ethical AI practices, ensuring that marketing strategies are transparent and equitable.[91] PR folks are bound by the PRSA Code of Ethics[92] and the aforementioned AI addendum.[93] This includes clearly communicating data collection practices, obtaining informed consent, and promoting fair representation in AI-driven content.

Preparing for Change: How PR Professionals Can Navigate AI, SEO, and SEM

To thrive in the rapidly evolving arena of AI, SEO, and SEM, PR professionals must adopt a proactive and strategic approach to stay ahead. They need to not only prepare for the changes AI brings to the industry but also proactively learn and advance toward the next innovation. The following subsections describe several key recommendations for PR professionals to navigate and leverage these advancements.

Continuous Learning and Skill Development

The dynamic nature of AI, SEO, and SEM necessitates continuous learning and skill development. PR professionals should invest in ongoing education through workshops, webinars, and certifications related to AI technologies and digital marketing strategies. Staying updated with the latest trends and best practices in AI, SEO, and SEM will enable PR practitioners to implement cutting-edge techniques and maintain a competitive edge. Additionally, fostering a culture of learning within PR teams can encourage knowledge sharing and collective growth.

Leveraging Advanced Analytics and Insights

By utilizing predictive analytics, PR practitioners can anticipate changes in consumer behavior and adjust their campaigns proactively. AI-powered analytics tools offer profound insights into audience behavior, search patterns, and market trends. PR professionals should leverage these tools to gain a deeper understanding of their target audience and tailor their strategies accordingly. Advanced analytics also facilitate more accurate measurement of campaign effectiveness, allowing for data-driven decision-making and continuous optimization.

Embracing AI-Powered Content Creation

AI-driven content creation tools can enhance the efficiency and quality of PR outputs. These tools can generate relevant and optimized content at scale, freeing up time for PR professionals to focus on strategic planning and creative tasks. Integrating AI into content creation processes allows for the production of personalized and engaging content that resonates with specific audience segments. PR professionals should explore and adopt AI tools that align with their content strategy and objectives, ensuring a balance between automation and human creativity.

Focusing on Ethical AI Practices

As AI technologies become more prevalent, ethical considerations surrounding data privacy, bias, and transparency are increasingly important. PR professionals must advocate for ethical AI practices within their organizations, ensuring that AI applications respect user privacy and mitigate biases. Transparent communication about data collection and use practices is essential to build trust with audiences. PR practitioners should also be involved in the development and implementation of AI systems to ensure they align with ethical standards and promote fairness and inclusivity.

NLP and NLU Considerations

The rise of NLP and NLU in voice-activated devices and conversational AI has transformed how users interact with search engines. PR professionals should optimize their SEO strategies for voice search, focusing on natural language queries and long-tail keywords. Understanding the nuances of conversational search can enhance the visibility and reach of PR content. Additionally, PR practitioners should explore opportunities to engage with audiences through conversational AI platforms, such as chatbots and virtual assistants, to provide real-time interactions and support.

Collaborating With AI Experts

Integrating AI into PR strategies effectively requires collaboration with AI experts, PR researchers, and data scientists. PR professionals should seek partnerships with AI specialists to develop and implement advanced AI solutions tailored to their needs. Collaborating with AI experts can provide valuable insights into the capabilities and limitations of AI technologies, ensuring that PR strategies are both innovative and feasible. This interdisciplinary approach can lead to the development of more robust and effective PR campaigns.

Conclusion

The rapidly evolving landscape of AI, SEO, and SEM presents both challenges and opportunities for PR professionals. By committing to continuous learning, leveraging advanced analytics, embracing AI-powered content creation, focusing on ethical practices, optimizing for voice search, and collaborating with AI experts, PR practitioners can navigate this complex landscape effectively. These strategies will enable PR professionals to enhance their campaigns, build stronger relationships with their audiences, and maintain a competitive advantage in the digital age.

Reflections

1. How can AI technologies, such as NLP and ML, enhance the effectiveness of SEO and SEM strategies in public relations? Provide specific examples from current industry practices.
2. Discuss the ethical considerations that PR professionals must address when integrating AI into their SEO and SEM strategies. How can transparency and user consent be effectively managed in AI-driven marketing campaigns?
3. Evaluate the impact of the PESO Model© when combined with AI on creating cohesive and strategic PR campaigns. How does this integration improve the efficiency and effectiveness of paid, earned, shared, and owned media strategies?
4. Reflect on the role of continuous learning and skill development for PR professionals in the context of AI, SEO, and SEM. What steps can practitioners take to stay updated with the latest advancements and maintain a competitive edge in the digital marketing landscape?

Free, Freemium, and Premium Tools

Ahrefs: All-in-one SEO toolset (https://ahrefs.com/).

Answer the Public: Discover what people are asking questions about online (https://answerthepublic.com/).

Free Keyword Research Tool (Ryan Robinson): For a simple tool (www.ry-rob.com/keyword-tool/).

Google Keyword Planner: For researching paid keywords (https://ads.google.com/home/tools/keyword-planner/).

Google Trends: Explore what people are searching for in real time (https://trends.google.com/trends/).

Keyworddit: The Reddit keyword research tool (www.highervisibility.com/seo/tools/keyworddit/).

Majestic: Develop backlink strategies (https://majestic.com/).

MOZ Link Explorer: Free backlink checker to get insights for link building (https://moz.com/link-explorer).

MOZ Keyword Explorer: The best all-around free SEO keyword research tool (https://moz.com/explorer).

Portent Idea Generator: Combines topics with catchy "click bait" like blog titles (www.portent.com/tools/title-maker/).

Post Cheetah: Comprehensive SEO tools leveraging AI (https://postcheetah.com/).

SEMRush: For advanced SEO professionals (www.semrush.com/).

SpyFU: Download competitors' most profitable keywords and ads for both paid and organic content (www.spyfu.com/).

SurferSEO: Optimize existing content to improve rank and visibility (https://surferseo.com/).

Notes

1 Dietrich, Gini. "A 2024 PESO Model© Primer for Communicators." *Spin Sucks* (blog). Entry posted 2024. Accessed March 29, 2024. https://spinsucks.com/communication/pr-pros-must-embrace-the-peso-model/.

2 Dietrich, Gini. "A 2024 PESO Model© Primer for Communicators." *Spin Sucks* (blog). Entry posted 2024. Accessed March 29, 2024. https://spinsucks.com/communication/pr-pros-must-embrace-the-peso-model/.

3 James, Michael. "The Ethical and Legal Implications of Using Big Data and Artificial Intelligence for Public Relations Campaigns in the United States." *International Journal of Communication and Public Relations* 9, no. 1 (2024): 38–52.

4 Chaffey, Dave, and Fiona Ellis-Chadwick. *Digital Marketing*. 7th ed. Harlow, England: Pearson, 2019.

5 Google. "Search Engine Optimization (SEO) Starter Guide." *Google Search Central* (blog). Accessed May 20, 2024. https://developers.google.com/search/docs/fundamentals/seo-starter-guide.

6 Wilson, Lee. *Tactical SEO: The Theory and Practice of Search Marketing*. Kogan Page Publishers, 2016.

7 Odden, Lee. *Optimize: How to Attract and Engage More Customers by Integrating SEO, Social Media, and Content Marketing*. John Wiley & Sons, 2012.

8 Lewis, Kent. "SEM PR – When Search Engine Marketing Meets Public Relations Part 1 of 2." *Anvil Media Inc.* (blog). Accessed April 15, 2024. www.anvilmediainc.com/marketing-resources/articles/sem-pr-1/.

9 IBM. "What is Artificial Intelligence (AI)?" *IBM*. Last modified n.d. Accessed April 20, 2024. www.ibm.com/topics/artificial-intelligence.

10 IBM. "What is Artificial Intelligence (AI)?" *IBM*. Last modified n.d. Accessed April 20, 2024. www.ibm.com/topics/artificial-intelligence.

11 SAS. "Machine Learning: What It is and Why It Matters." *SAS Insights* (blog). Entry posted 2024. Accessed June 20, 2024. www.sas.com/en_us/insights/analytics/machine-learning.html.

12 SEMRush Team. "A Beginner's Guide to AI SEO." *SEMRush Blog*. Entry posted December 12, 2023. Accessed May 20, 2024. www.semrush.com/blog/ai-seo/.

13 Nayak, Pandu. "Understanding Searches Better Than Ever Before." *The Keyword* (blog). https://blog.google/products/search/search-language-understanding-bert/.

14 MOZ. "Google RankBrain." *MOZ Blog*. Last modified October 26, 2015. Accessed June 24, 2024. https://moz.com/learn/seo/google-rankbrain.

15 Nayak, Pandu. "Understanding Searches Better Than Ever Before." *The Keyword* (blog). https://blog.google/products/search/search-language-understanding-bert/.

16 MOZ. "How Search Engines Work: Crawling, Indexing, and Ranking the Beginner's Guide to SEO." *MOZ Blog*. Entry posted 2024. Accessed April 20, 2024. https://moz.com/beginners-guide-to-seo/how-search-engines-operate.

17 MOZ. "How Search Engines Work: Crawling, Indexing, and Ranking the Beginner's Guide to SEO." *MOZ Blog*. Entry posted 2024. Accessed April 20, 2024. https://moz.com/beginners-guide-to-seo/how-search-engines-operate.

18 MOZ. "Google RankBrain." *MOZ Blog*. Last modified October 26, 2015. Accessed June 24, 2024. https://moz.com/learn/seo/google-rankbrain.

19 Marketbrew.AI. "How Google's AI Overviews Work." *MarketBrew.AI* (blog). Entry posted n.d. Accessed May 20, 2024. https://marketbrew.ai/a/google-ai-overviews.

20 MOZ. "Google RankBrain." *MOZ Blog*. Last modified October 26, 2015. Accessed June 24, 2024. https://moz.com/learn/seo/google-rankbrain.

21 SEMRush. "Google RankBrain and SEO: Everything You Need to Know." *SEMRush Blog*. Entry posted December 12, 2023. www.semrush.com/blog/google-rankbrain/.

22 Tucker, Elizabeth. "New Ways We're Tackling Spammy, Low-Quality Content on Search." *The Keyword* (blog). Entry posted March 5, 2024. Accessed March 6, 2024. https://blog.google/products/search/google-search-update-march-2024/.

23 Dwivedi, Yogesh K., Elvira Ismagilova, D. Laurie Hughes, Jamie Carlson, Raffaele Filieri, Jenna Jacobson, Varsha Jain et al. "Setting the Future of Digital and Social Media Marketing Research: Perspectives and Research Propositions." *International Journal of Information Management* 59 (2021): 102168.

24 Das, Subhankar. *Search Engine Optimization and Marketing: A Recipe for Success in Digital Marketing*. Chapman and Hall/CRC, 2021.

25 Google. "Search Engine Optimization (SEO) Starter Guide." *Google Search Central* (blog). Entry posted 2024. Accessed July 2, 2024. https://developers.google.com/search/docs/fundamentals/seo-starter-guide.

26 Deterding, Whitney. "How to Use AI In Public Relations to Amplify Your Strategy." *Spinsucks* (blog). https://spinsucks.com/communication/ai-public-relations-strategy/.

27 Deterding, Whitney. "How to Use AI In Public Relations to Amplify Your Strategy." *Spinsucks* (blog). https://spinsucks.com/communication/ai-public-relations-strategy/.

28 Accenture. "Personalized Marketing Services & Solutions." *Accenture*. Last modified n.d. Accessed June 21, 2024. www.accenture.com/us-en/services/interactive/propelling-growth-personalization.

29 Deloitte Insights. *Automation with Intelligence Reimagining the Organisation in the 'Age of With'*, 2019. Accessed July 21, 2024. www2.deloitte.com/content/dam/Deloitte/tw/Documents/strategy/tw-Automation-with-intelligence.pdf.

30 Semrush. *Think Big with AI: Transforming Small Business Content Marketing*, 2024. Accessed June 21, 2024. www.semrush.com/goodcontent/api/ai-content-marketing-report/download/Think_Big_with_AI_Small_Business_Content_Marketing_in_2024.pdf.

31 Kelly, Brenna. "Embracing AI in Advertising: A Game Plan and Tools to Get Started." *Semrush Blog*. Entry posted March 11, 2024. Accessed June 25, 2024. www.semrush.com/blog/ai-advertising/.

32 Kelly, Brenna. "Embracing AI in Advertising: A Game Plan and Tools to Get Started." *Semrush Blog*. Entry posted March 11, 2024. Accessed June 25, 2024. www.semrush.com/blog/ai-advertising/.

33 Deterding, Whitney. "How to Use AI In Public Relations to Amplify Your Strategy." *Spinsucks* (blog). https://spinsucks.com/communication/ai-public-relations-strategy/.

34 SEMRush Team. "A Beginner's Guide to AI SEO." *SEMRush Blog*. Entry posted December 12, 2023. Accessed May 20, 2024. www.semrush.com/blog/ai-seo/.

35 MOZ. "How Search Engines Work: Crawling, Indexing, and Ranking The Beginner's Guide to SEO." *MOZ Blog*. Entry posted 2024. Accessed April 20, 2024. https://moz. com/beginners-guide-to-seo/how-search-engines-operate.

36 Hotjar. "8 Ways to Improve UX Design with AI (and Which Tools to Use)." *Hotjar by Contentsquare* (blog). Entry posted December 14, 2023. Accessed June 26, 2024. www.hotjar.com/blog/impact-ai-ux-design/.

37 Ellis, Mirian. "SEO Learning Center: Backlinks." *MOZ* (blog). Entry posted November 20, 2023. Accessed July 7, 2024. https://moz.com/learn/seo/backlinks.

38 Kelly, Brenna. "Embracing AI in Advertising: A Game Plan and Tools to Get Started." *Semrush Blog*. Entry posted March 11, 2024. Accessed June 25, 2024. www.semrush. com/blog/ai-advertising/.

39 Haleem, Abid, Mohd Javaid, Mohd Asim Qadri, Ravi Pratap Singh, and Rajiv Suman. "Artificial Intelligence (AI) Applications for Marketing: A Literature-based Study." *International Journal of Intelligent Networks* 3 (2022): 119–132.

40 Marketbrew.AI. "Search Intent 101: Understanding And Optimizing For User Intent." *Marketbrew.AI* (blog). Entry posted n.d. Accessed June 28, 2024. https://marketbrew. ai/a/user-search-intent-seo.

41 IBM. "IBM Watson Discovery." *IBM*. Last modified n.d. Accessed June 25, 2024. www.ibm.com/products/watson-discovery.

42 BlogFox. "AI-Driven Competitor Content Gap Analysis: Find Untapped Opportunities." *BlogFox*. Entry posted June 23, 2024. Accessed June 28, 2024. https://blogfox. ai/post/ai-driven-competitor-content-gap-analysis-find-untapped-opportunities.

43 Dietrich, Gini. "A 2024 PESO Model© Primer for Communicators." *Spin Sucks* (blog). Entry posted 2024. Accessed March 29, 2024. https://spinsucks.com/communication/pr-pros-must-embrace-the-peso-model/.

44 Johnsen, Maria. *The Search Engine Revolution: From Past to Present and Beyond*. Maria Johnsen, 2024.

45 Prakash, Gourav, and Dhruv Sabharwal. "AI Revolution in Online Media: Transforming Content Creation, Distribution, and Consumption." *Media and AI: Navigating*: 179.

46 Regan Communications Group. "Using AI to Revolutionize Public Relations." *Regan Communications Group* (blog). Entry posted October 13, 2023. Accessed May 28, 2024. https://regancomm.com/using-ai-to-revolutionize-public-relations/.

47 PR Daily Staff. "5 Ways PR Pros Want to Use AI in the Future." *PR Daily* (blog). Entry posted February 9, 2024. Accessed May 3, 2024. www.prdaily.com/5-ways-pr-pros-want-to-use-ai-in-the-future/.

48 Tyson, Alec, and Emma Kickuchi. "Growing Public Concern about the Role of Artificial Intelligence in Daily Life." *Pew Research Center* (blog). Entry posted August 28, 2023. Accessed June 8, 2024. www.pewresearch.org/short-reads/2023/08/28/ growing-public-concern-about-the-role-of-artificial-intelligence-in-daily-life/.

49 Faverio, Michelle. "Key Findings about Americans and Data Privacy." *Pew Research Center* (blog). Entry posted October 18, 2023. Accessed June 9, 2024. www.pewre-search.org/short-reads/2023/10/18/key-findings-about-americans-and-data-privacy/.

50 Wallace, Adrienne A., and Jason Dodge. "What GDPR Means for You (Yes, You) and Your Business." *BlackTruck Media & Marketing* (blog). Entry posted April 26, 2018. Accessed April 5, 2024. https://blacktruckmedia.com/blog/gdpr-business-data-privacy/.

51 Oseni, Ayodeji, Nour Moustafa, Helge Janicke, Peng Liu, Zahir Tari, and Athanasios Vasilakos. "Security and Privacy for Artificial Intelligence: Opportunities and Challenges." *arXiv preprint arXiv:2102.04661* (2021).

52 Elliott, David, and Eldon Soifer. "AI Technologies, Privacy, and Security." *Frontiers in Artificial Intelligence* 5 (2022): 826737.

53 Dilmaghani, Saharnaz, Matthias R. Brust, Grégoire Danoy, Natalia Cassagnes, Johnatan Pecero, and Pascal Bouvry. "Privacy and Security of Big Data in AI Systems:

A Research and Standards Perspective." In *2019 IEEE International Conference on Big Data (Big Data)*, pp. 5737–5743. IEEE, 2019.

54 Fast-Track Action Committee on Advancing Privacy-Preserving Data Sharing and Analytics Networking and Information Technology Research and Development Subcommittee of the National Science and Technology Council. *National Strategy to Advance Privacy-Preserving Data Sharing and Analytics*. By National Science and Technology Council, March 2023. Accessed June 3, 2024. www.whitehouse.gov/wp-content/uploads/2023/03/National-Strategy-to-Advance-Privacy-Preserving-Data-Sharing-and-Analytics.pdf.

55 Hallahan, Kirk. "Responsible Online Communication." *Ethics in Public Relations: Responsible Advocacy* (2006): 107–131.

56 Yanisky-Ravid, Shlomit, and Sean Hallisey. " 'Equality and Privacy by Design': Ensuring Artificial Intelligence (AI) Is Properly Trained & Fed: A New Model of AI Data Transparency & Certification As Safe Harbor Procedures." *Available at SSRN 3278490* (2018).

57 Larsson, Stefan, and Fredrik Heintz. "Transparency in Artificial Intelligence." *Internet Policy Review* 9, no. 2 (2020).

58 Larsson, Stefan, and Fredrik Heintz. "Transparency in aAtificial Intelligence." *Internet Policy Review* 9, no. 2 (2020).

59 Baiada, Federica. "AI in SEO: How to Navigate Legal Challenges and Ensure Compliance." *Search Engine Land* (blog). Entry posted September 26, 2023. Accessed June 12, 2024. https://searchengineland.com/ai-seo-legal-challenges-compliance-432396.

60 Fast-Track Action Committee on Advancing Privacy-Preserving Data Sharing and Analytics Networking and Information Technology Research and Development Subcommittee of the National Science and Technology Council. *National Strategy to Advance Privacy-Preserving Data Sharing and Analytics*. By National Science and Technology Council, March 2023. Accessed June 3, 2024. www.whitehouse.gov/wp-content/uploads/2023/03/National-Strategy-to-Advance-Privacy-Preserving-Data-Sharing-and-Analytics.pdf.

61 White, Candace L., and Brandon Boatwright. "Social Media Ethics in the Data Economy: Issues of Social Responsibility for Using Facebook for Public Relations." *Public Relations Review* 46, no. 5 (2020): 101980.

62 Public Relations Society of America (PRSA). *PROMISE & PITFALLS: The Ethical Use of AI For Public Relations Practitioners Guidance from the PRSA Board of Ethics and Professional Standards (BEPS)*, November 20, 2023. Accessed June 2, 2024. www.prsa.org/docs/default-source/about/ethics/ethicaluseofai.pdf.

63 Aula, Ville, and Tero Erkkilä. "AI and Transparency." In *Handbook on Public Policy and Artificial Intelligence*, pp. 170–180. Edward Elgar Publishing, 2024.

64 Public Relations Society of America (PRSA). *PROMISE & PITFALLS: The Ethical Use of AI For Public Relations Practitioners Guidance from the PRSA Board of Ethics and Professional Standards (BEPS)*, November 20, 2023. Accessed June 2, 2024. www.prsa.org/docs/default-source/about/ethics/ethicaluseofai.pdf.

65 Janssen, Marijn, Paul Brous, Elsa Estevez, Luis S. Barbosa, and Tomasz Janowski. "Data Governance: Organizing Data for Trustworthy Artificial Intelligence." *Government Information Quarterly* 37, no. 3 (2020): 101493.

66 Felzmann, Heike, Eduard Fosch-Villaronga, Christoph Lutz, and Aurelia Tamò-Larrieux. "Towards Transparency by Design for Artificial Intelligence." *Science and Engineering Ethics* 26, no. 6 (2020): 3333–3361.

67 Shneiderman, Ben. "Bridging the Gap between Ethics and Practice: Guidelines for Reliable, Safe, and Trustworthy Human-Centered AI Systems." *ACM Transactions on Interactive Intelligent Systems (TiiS)* 10, no. 4 (2020): 1–31.

68 Bélisle-Pipon, Jean-Christophe, Erica Monteferrante, Marie-Christine Roy, and Vincent Couture. "Artificial Intelligence Ethics Has a Black Box Problem." *AI & Society* (2023): 1–16.
69 Ntoutsi, Eirini, Pavlos Fafalios, Ujwal Gadiraju, Vasileios Iosifidis, Wolfgang Nejdl, Maria-Esther Vidal, Salvatore Ruggieri et al. "Bias in Data-Driven Artificial Intelligence Systems – An Introductory Survey." *Wiley Interdisciplinary Reviews: Data Mining and Knowledge Discovery* 10, no. 3 (2020): e1356.
70 Olteanu, Alexandra, Carlos Castillo, Fernando Diaz, and Emre Kıcıman. "Social Data: Biases, Methodological Pitfalls, and Ethical Boundaries." *Frontiers in Big Data* 2 (2019): 13.
71 Mayson, Sandra G. "Bias in, Bias Out." *YAle lJ* 128 (2018): 2218.
72 Mayson, Sandra G. "Bias in, Bias Out." *YAle lJ* 128 (2018): 2218.
73 Long, Duri, and Brian Magerko. "What is AI Literacy? Competencies and Design Considerations." In *Proceedings of the 2020 CHI Conference on Human Factors in Computing Systems*, pp. 1–16. 2020.
74 Public Relations Society of America (PRSA). *PROMISE & PITFALLS: The Ethical Use of AI For Public Relations Practitioners Guidance from the PRSA Board of Ethics and Professional Standards (BEPS)*, November 20, 2023. Accessed June 2, 2024. www.prsa.org/docs/default-source/about/ethics/ethicaluseofai.pdf.
75 Public Relations Society of America (PRSA). *PROMISE & PITFALLS: The Ethical Use of AI For Public Relations Practitioners Guidance from the PRSA Board of Ethics and Professional Standards (BEPS)*, November 20, 2023. Accessed June 2, 2024. www.prsa.org/docs/default-source/about/ethics/ethicaluseofai.pdf.
76 Buhmann, Alexander, and Candace L. White. "Artificial Intelligence in Public Relations: Role and Implications." In *The Emerald Handbook of Computer-Mediated Communication and Social Media*, pp. 625–638. Emerald Publishing Limited, 2022.
77 James, Michael. "The Ethical and Legal Implications of Using Big Data and Artificial Intelligence for Public Relations Campaigns in the United States." *International Journal of Communication and Public Relation* 9, no. 1 (2024): 38–52.
78 Public Relations Society of America (PRSA). *PROMISE & PITFALLS: The Ethical Use of AI For Public Relations Practitioners Guidance from the PRSA Board of Ethics and Professional Standards (BEPS)*, November 20, 2023. Accessed June 2, 2024. www.prsa.org/docs/default-source/about/ethics/ethicaluseofai.pdf.
79 Public Relations Society of America (PRSA). *PROMISE & PITFALLS: The Ethical Use of AI For Public Relations Practitioners Guidance from the PRSA Board of Ethics and Professional Standards (BEPS)*, November 20, 2023. Accessed June 2, 2024. www.prsa.org/docs/default-source/about/ethics/ethicaluseofai.pdf.
80 Hermann, Erik. "Leveraging Artificial Intelligence in Marketing for Social Good – An Ethical Perspective." *Journal of Business Ethics* 179, no. 1 (2022): 43–61.
81 Stacks, Don W. *Primer of Public Relations Research*. Guilford Publications, 2016.
82 McCollough, Christopher J., Adrienne A. Wallace, and Regina Luttrell. "Artificial Intelligence: The Dark Side, Ethics, and Implications." In *The Emerald Handbook of Computer-Mediated Communication and Social Media*, pp. 671–684. Emerald Publishing Limited, 2022.
83 Public Relations Society of America (PRSA). *PROMISE & PITFALLS: The Ethical Use of AI For Public Relations Practitioners Guidance from the PRSA Board of Ethics and Professional Standards (BEPS)*, November 20, 2023. Accessed June 2, 2024. www.prsa.org/docs/default-source/about/ethics/ethicaluseofai.pdf.
84 Ewing, Michele E. "Navigating Ethical Implications for AI-Driven PR Practice." *PRSA Strategies & Tactics* (blog). Entry posted September 2023. Accessed May 28, 2024. www.prsa.org/article/navigating-ethical-implications-for-ai-driven-pr-practice.

85 Ewing, Michele E. "Navigating Ethical Implications for AI-Driven PR Practice." *PRSA Strategies & Tactics* (blog). Entry posted September 2023. Accessed May 28, 2024. www.prsa.org/article/navigating-ethical-implications-for-ai-driven-pr-practice.

86 Deterding, Whitney. "How to Use AI In Public Relations to Amplify Your Strategy." *Spinsucks* (blog). https://spinsucks.com/communication/ai-public-relations-strategy/.

87 Dodge, Jason. Episode 14. "Who's Leading Voice Search, Optimizing for Leads Over Rankings, and Does Navigation Influence SEO?" September 1, 2017. In *The Redirect*. Podcast, audio, 25:08. Accessed May 3, 2024. https://blacktruckmedia.com/podcast/redirect-podcast-episode-14/.

88 Dodge, Jason. Episode 14. "Who's Leading Voice Search, Optimizing for Leads Over Rankings, and Does Navigation Influence SEO?" September 1, 2017. In *The Redirect*. Podcast, audio, 25:08. Accessed May 3, 2024. https://blacktruckmedia.com/podcast/redirect-podcast-episode-14/.

89 Hootsuite. "Create Engaging and Effective Social Media Content." *Hootsuite Blog.* Entry posted June 26, 2024. Accessed May 7, 2024. https://help.hootsuite.com/hc/en-us/articles/4403597090459-Create-engaging-and-effective-social-media-content.

90 Abbas, Qaisar. "The Impact of Personalization Strategies on Consumer Engagement and Conversion Rates in Digital Marketing," January 10, 2024. https://www.multiresearchjournal.com/admin/uploads/archives/archive-1705742232.pdf.

91 Public Relations Society of America (PRSA). *PROMISE & PITFALLS: The Ethical Use of AI For Public Relations Practitioners Guidance from the PRSA Board of Ethics and Professional Standards (BEPS)*, November 20, 2023. Accessed June 2, 2024. www.prsa.org/docs/default-source/about/ethics/ethicaluseofai.pdf.

92 PRSA. "PRSA Code of Ethics." *Public Relations Society of America.* Last modified 2000. Accessed May 25, 2024. www.prsa.org/about/prsa-code-of-ethics.

93 Public Relations Society of America (PRSA). *PROMISE & PITFALLS: The Ethical Use of AI For Public Relations Practitioners Guidance from the PRSA Board of Ethics and Professional Standards (BEPS)*, November 20, 2023. Accessed June 2, 2024. www.prsa.org/docs/default-source/about/ethics/ethicaluseofai.pdf.

PART V

Mis/DisInformation and AI + PR

12

GENERATING AI PASTS AND FUTURES, DOING PUBLIC RELATIONS IN THE PRESENT

David Gurney and Michelle Maresh-Fuehrer

Learning Objectives

1. Identify the ways that strategic communicators can effectively and ethically integrate AI tools into their practice.
2. Apply the PRSA Code of Ethics to the use of generative AI for PR practice.
3. Discuss the risks strategic communicators face as a result of emerging AI technologies.
4. Describe the ways that generative AI reflects participatory and remix culture.

Introduction

Amidst the predictable choruses of expressions of grief, gun control advocacy, and offerings of thoughts and prayers in the aftermath of the 2023 shootings at Michigan State University, one response stood out not so much for what it contained but rather in how that response was composed. In some ways, the email sent out within Vanderbilt University to the students, faculty, and staff of its Peabody College of Education and Human Development was much the same as any other.

> In the wake of the Michigan shootings, let us come together as a community to reaffirm our commitment to caring for one another and promoting a culture of inclusivity on our campus. By doing so, we can honor the victims of this tragedy and work towards a safer, more compassionate future for all.[1]

The statement is evenly balanced, showing both sensitivity and hopefulness, all while not "taking sides" on the political debates typically launched in

DOI: 10.4324/9781032671482-17

response to mass shootings. However, a closing line was included, an honest reference, identifying the origin of the message as a "Paraphrase from OpenAI's ChatGPT AI language model." With a signature line below this reference further identifying the Peabody Office of Equity, Diversity, and Inclusion and the members of its leadership team as being responsible for it, the message creates some cognitive dissonance, at least in the year 2023. Evidencing this dissonance is a follow-up email credited to Associate Dean Nicole Joseph sent the following day and quoted in *The Vanderbilt Hustler* student newspaper shortly thereafter:

> While we believe in the message of inclusivity expressed in the email, using ChatGPT to generate communications on behalf of our community in a time of sorrow and in response to a tragedy contradicts the values that characterize Peabody College . . . . As with all new technologies that affect higher education, this moment gives us all an opportunity to reflect on what we know and what we still must learn about AI.[2]

There is a tone of contrition present in this passage, though it is careful about positioning ChatGPT not as an unacceptable tool in and of itself, but rather this particular use of it as an instance of misjudging the event-defined context in which to use it – prefacing that admission with a verification that the Peabody Office believes in the message underscores that the issue is more the context of the message than its content. The latter half of the quoted passage clarifies that ChatGPT is a technology among other new technologies that will ultimately be a presence in the longer term, even if our current moment is one of experimentation, trepidation, and uncertainty.

Artificial intelligence (AI) and the cadre of technologies that it describes – ones striving to replicate the work of human cognition on some level – is becoming a more widespread and accessible category of tools at our disposal in so many fields, not the least being strategic communication. In fact, 61% of surveyed public relations (PR) professionals currently use or are interested in using AI in their workflow, with typical applications including writing press releases and social media copy, conducting research, and crafting pitches.[3] Despite any apprehension surrounding the use of generative AI, PR practitioners largely recognize its usefulness for enhancing the profession. However, communication leaders stress the importance of using AI as a tool rather than a core strategy.[4] This is because – as illustrated in the Vanderbilt example – AI lacks the emotional intelligence and human understanding needed for effectively building and maintaining relationships with stakeholders.

However much it may still have felt like a shallow excuse to the Peabody community at Vanderbilt, Joseph's note is accurate about us being in a period of adapting to and reflecting upon these new communication tools. In light of a tragedy, a note of reassurance and resilience being drafted automatically from a large language model may feel like a definitively hollow gesture in 2023, but will it always feel that way? Even if it appears nakedly inauthentic to us now, how different is its algorithmic automation of human expression based upon the study of thousands – if not millions – of such statements that had been made before then the way in which we always build our current and future communication on what has come prior? After all, AI is an automation of what we already do in human cognition.

While the ontological underpinnings of AI content generation will continue to be contested and hammered out in the coming years, we – as communicators of the present moment – must come to some understanding of how these technologies should be used now. As such, this chapter will look at a few small cases of such content circulating in 2023, a year that will always be remembered as a watershed for the proliferation of AI content generation, and consider what they can tell us about the role AI should and should not play in our work as strategic communicators. In addition to the Vanderbilt incident already roughly chronicled, we will look at two instances of AI-generated images being used in political messaging, in one case, a candidate's camp propagating falsified images of a political rival, and in another, a political party using such images in a more elaborate video production to undercut its opposing party's likely candidate for the U.S. presidency. The result will offer some perspective on the dangers present for strategic communicators in the tools of emerging AI technologies and the potential pathways forward as we attempt to integrate these tools both effectively and ethically.

Ethics and Synthesis in Communication

As with all new technological innovations, strategic communicators must be prepared to adapt their uses to existing ethical frameworks. The Public Relations Society of America (PRSA) Code of Ethics guides the practice of many U.S.-based public relations practitioners. This code consists of six provisions of conduct, and according to the PRSA Board of Ethics and Professional Standards, at least five of them relate to the use of generative AI.[5] In this section, we explore the three most closely aligned with the aims of this chapter.

The "Free Flow of Information" code provision exists to protect and advance the free flow of accurate and truthful information. AI can be used to gather data and create meaningful insights, but it also creates the potential to spread *misinformation*, or false information that is disseminated without harmful intent.[6] For example, both PR campaigns and the crisis communication planning process emphasize the importance of using research to guide communication strategies. A practitioner may choose to use AI tools to summarize scientific results concerning the potential impacts of a public health risk, such as COVID19, or to generate a report about a company's financial earnings to share with stakeholders. While this may seem relatively straightforward, large language models like ChatGPT cannot separate fact from fiction, so the tool may be ultimately learning and generating misinformation.

Dubbed by researchers as an *AI hallucination*, large language models may perceive "patterns or objects that are nonexistent or imperceptible to human observers, creating outputs that are nonsensical or altogether inaccurate."[7] ChatGPT frequently generates fictional answers when asked to create a list of sources. One study in the healthcare industry found that as much as 30% of the sources generated by the chatbot were either fake or unverifiable.[8] AI hallucinations are not limited to text, either. AI can quickly generate images that appear plausible but deviate from reality or, as with deepfakes, depict events that never happened. An ethical problem then arises when practitioners use this content without first checking for accuracy and validating the sources of information. While AI can be a useful starting point for identifying information and resources, practitioners must be equipped to scrutinize media for signs of manipulation and cross-reference information and sources to verify accuracy.

Next, the "Disclosure of Information" provision focuses on building trust with the public by revealing all information needed to make responsible decisions. According to the code, this includes being honest and accurate in communications, correcting misunderstandings or erroneous information, investigating the truthfulness and accuracy of information, and avoiding deceptive practices. In strategic communication, the use of AI in and of itself may appear deceptive to some key stakeholders – especially if practitioners are not upfront about using such tools. For example, when considering the case that opens this chapter, practitioners may argue that the use of ChatGPT to generate a crisis response statement does not differ much from the typical process of scripting response templates based on what typically "works" in similar situations. As such, it may seem unnecessary to disclose the use of AI to stakeholders when using it in such a manner. However, managing relationships with stakeholders requires honesty and transparency – even if it is ultimately met with criticism. Although the reference to ChatGPT may have been inadvertently left tacked on to Peabody's crisis response statement, it adheres to the ethical code of being honest about using AI to construct the message. However, effective public relations also requires understanding stakeholders' expectations and taking a contingency approach based on many factors, including the context in which the communication occurs. In this sense, it is no surprise that the public may view the use of AI during crisis response as lacking authenticity and genuine concern.

Finally, the code provision concerning "Enhancing the Profession" refers to the need for public relations professionals to strengthen the public's trust in the profession. AI poses several reputational risks to the PR profession, especially concerning the potential for disinformation, or false information that is deliberately created and shared with harmful intent, to be spread about a client or organization.[9] In a series of experiments, one researcher found that ChatGPT could shift its tone to tailor messages to different mediated platforms, making it capable of promoting propaganda by customizing narratives for specific communities.[10] Deepfakes may also be used to spread fake but realistic videos and images to cause harm to a brand's reputation or financial status. This occurred to some extent in May 2023 when fake images depicting an explosion at the Pentagon went viral on Twitter, causing a brief dip in the stock market.[11] These examples illustrate the need for practitioners to educate the public on the existence of disinformation tactics and guide clients and organizations in efforts to recognize reputational threats and craft crisis communication plans for situations where AI has been used to create malicious content.

Though the information presented in this chapter may sound alarming, the goal is not to shy away from using AI – these tools present many opportunities for enhancing the PR profession. Rather, the idea is that we must continuously adapt our practice as new technologies emerge. One set of executives at global PR firm Edelman argue that the continued evolution of AI requires practitioners to take on the role of "orchestrators" by "understanding context, making ethical choices, and building stakeholder relationships that a machine cannot fully grasp."[12]

In the Introduction section of this chapter, we allude to how AI is not really an instance of new practice but rather one of new process. While generative AI feels radically new, all communication and culture is based on being able to enter pre-existing structures and work with their affordances. While those affordances are not immutable, that does not mean that any message can successfully be

---

BOX 12.1   HOW WELL DOES GENERATIVE AI FUNCTION AS A PR TOOL

Enter the following prompts into ChatGPT and make note of how the suggested PR tactics change based on the information provided in the prompt.

- Identify strategies for recruiting students to a university's PR program.
- Identify strategies for recruiting students to a PR program at a research university.
- Identify strategies for recruiting Latino/a/x students to a PR program at a research university.

Based on your analysis, discuss the strengths and limitations of using AI as a tool for brainstorming potential PR strategies and tactics.

constructed in a manner completely separate from the messages that have preceded it. There is always synthesis – the combinations of pre-existing parts – at play in our communication. In other words, our notions of authenticity and originality are matters of degree and determination rather than ontological difference. This is apparent when one considers AI-generated content in light of much of what has been described and studied as "participatory culture," particularly meme culture in the early part of the 21st century.

Henry Jenkins is the scholar whose work has been most prominent in describing and popularizing participatory culture in communication and media studies. His book *Convergence Culture: Where Old and New Media Collide* helped to put a spotlight on how then-emerging media platforms – such as chat rooms, video games, and video sharing platforms – were allowing many who had seemingly been part of the passive audience for mass media texts in the 20th century to exercise newly visible forms of agency in using elements of the texts to generate new content that could extend, complicate, and/or react to the texts.[13] This itself was an extension of research in fan studies that Jenkins and others had been doing since before the widespread adoption of networked digital media, whereby they had looked at the various products of fan culture, including fan fiction, fan (or filk) music, and fan films and videos done using analog media and shared through informal but physical distribution networks such as mailing lists and fan conventions.[14]

What shifted most in the early 21st century was not audience participation resulting in synthesized communication itself, though the digital media tools and ecosystem did indeed allow for more fan content to be made, but rather the scale at which such communication could be shared. Furthermore, while much fan culture tended to be born of deep engagement with some specific entertainment property, often based in the genres of science fiction or fantasy, the affordances of digital media also allowed for more casual engagement with cultural texts to become the basis for creation, leading many scholars to consider how a more evident "remix culture" was pointing to the inherently messy ways that all cultural expression is built on expression that precedes it.[15] While the ramifications for how we conceive of and police intellectual property are still in flux, there is no doubt that internet culture has generally come to be dominated by the recirculation and recombination of content in the forms of social media posts, viral videos, and all that falls under the general heading of "meme" culture.[16] In this context, one can readily see the work of generative AI as an extension of what has come before in terms of culture being inherently participatory and a product of remix or synthesis. Critical cultural theory is just beginning to contend with this to help us understand the ontology of AI doing these human activities at our behest.[17] In a more popular sense, we are all contending with it now as communicators when deciding how to use various tools to construct the messages for our intended audiences.

Imagining the Future

One way that generative AI was used for political messaging in 2023 was imagining future outcomes. Political speech has long been a space in which candidates and their proxies will prognosticate about the negative impacts of a rival winning an election as a way of warning potential voters into voting accordingly. In 1964, during Lyndon Baines Johnson's bid to retain the U.S. Presidency, his campaign aired (only once) what is the most discussed – even if not the most impactful – political television advertisement in history. *Daisy* depicts a young girl in a field, counting as she pulls petals from a daisy. After she makes some mistakes in her count, she pauses at nine and looks up as a man's voice over a loudspeaker begins counting down from ten as though there will be a missile launch. Indeed, the image locks in a freeze frame and after zooming into the child's right eye, the count completes and the ad cuts to a nuclear mushroom cloud, over which Johnson's voice intones, "These are the stakes! To make a world in which all of God's children can live, or to go into the dark. We must either love each other, or we must die."[18] While the ad does not show Johnson's Republican opponent, Barry Goldwater, pushing a launch button or in some other way directly causing this cataclysm, the implication is clear; a vote for Goldwater – or a vote not for Johnson – means that the future could hold devastation and destruction.

It is easy to imagine how generative AI can potentially add to the verisimilitude of such a speculative ploy, and at least one instance in which this was put into practice is present an advertisement titled *Beat Biden,* released via the official YouTube channel for the U.S. Republican National Committee (RNC) on April 25, 2023.[19] The ad uses layered messaging with onscreen text initially pondering, "What if the weakest president we've ever had were re-elected," as the voice of an unidentified female reporter intones, "This just in: we can now call the 2024 presidential race for Joe Biden," before segueing into Biden's voice beginning a presumed victory speech with "My fellow Americans . . . ." While all of this linguistic expression could be put together without AI, the images accompanying it are a series of still images depicting Biden and Vice President Kamala Harris surrounded by supporters as they celebrate this prospective event, things much harder to fabricate without generative AI, at least in as much uncanny detail as is present in the ad. However, even these images are only an extension/enhancement of the synthesized images that have long been circulating as part of the participatory culture of the internet.

As the ad continues, more anonymous reporters' voices describe a series of negative events – China invading Taiwan, a financial crash, unprecedented numbers of aspiring migrants crossing into the United States from Mexico, San Francisco being "closed" in light of criminal activity – that presumably follow sometime after the simulated 2024 victory of Biden and Harris. Each AI-generated image of explosions underscore each of these, uniformed military personnel with weapons drawn in city streets, emptied out bank buildings, etc., that help to make these prospects feel all the more real and tangible. Already more overt in its negative attack by naming its target rather than intimating it as *Daisy* had, *Beat Biden* also fans the speculative fear by providing the accompanying images.

Like the Peabody Office's email message, this ad – both onscreen in faded text in the upper left corner and in its YouTube description box – does clearly indicate AI-generated content is present, and the RNC having done so seems even more truly intended than Peabody's in that there was no backtracking once the ad was released. In this sense, it meets the PRSA's ethics provision for "Disclosure of Information." Nonetheless, the public reaction was one of some concern and consternation. Initially, many news outlets were relatively reserved in their reporting, marking the noteworthiness of this first political ad released by an established political party or candidate to utilize AI-generated imagery and its "dystopian" and "unsettling" qualities.[20] Some pointed to a recurring problem with such imagery in its tendency to include more and/or strangely formed teeth and fingers than an actual photograph would.[21] Sam Cornale, the executive director of the Democratic National Committee (DNC), pointed to it as a desperate maneuver, tweeting, "When your operative class has been decimated, and you're following MAGA Republicans [for "Make America Great Again," a Trump slogan] off a cliff, I suppose you have no choice but to ask AI to help."[22]

Some users on YouTube were more pointed in their commentary. Resorting to using AI-generated imagery was called out to indicate the lack of objective evidence that the RNC could use to attack Biden: "Because when facts dont [sic] fit your story there [sic] always AI."[23] Others noted that the quality of the images, while perhaps convincing enough at a glance, also bore the degraded marks of AI forgery, as with the commenter who posted, "Thank god AI can't make good commercials yet. I still have a job for now."[24] At least one comment gets right to the point in classifying the sort of information being conveyed:

> So lies and misinformation? That's all the GOP [Grand Old Party, meaning the Republican Party] has as an argument? It's not even like you made an ad criticizing his record, which you'd have PLENTY to criticize him for. [sic] No, instead you just make up some scary hypothetical outcomes without any valid reasoning or beneficial policy alternatives.[25]

Calling the ad out as "misinformation" gets to a core issue of such imagery being used to create that speculative peek into a future that cannot indeed be visualized. But does this truly rise to the level of misinformation or, in terms of the PRSA Code of Ethics, does it hinder the "Free Flow of Information"?

In looking back at Daisy and, by extension, many of the negative political ads that have followed it, generative AI cannot itself be wholly blamed for this sort of message. After all, speculating about a future state of affairs to sway others to behave a certain way in the present or near future is what deliberative rhetorical

---

BOX 12.2   A CEO'S DIGITAL DEFENSE

Reflect upon whether the use of AI is ethical in the following scenario.

The CEO of a large corporation is publicly scrutinized when allegations about their treatment of past employees surfaces and results in claims of discrimination. Knowing that they have what is viewed as an "unfriendly" face, the CEO uses an app to create a deepfake avatar of themselves presenting a statement in response to the crisis.

---

appeals have done for multiple millennia. The Johnson campaign may not have used AI, instead staging the scenario of Daisy utilizing an actor and pre-existing audio and visual footage, but it nonetheless created an effective bit of deliberative rhetoric that could cause worry and persuade potential voters to not pursue a future – presumably under a Goldwater presidency – that is (and now will always remain) purely speculative. How can we achieve accuracy and truthfulness when imagining such potential future outcomes? The real answer here is leaning more heavily toward predictive analytics and scientific modeling based upon existing empirical evidence of similar events from the past, and there are limitations stemming from this that public relations professionals need to accept. However, it is also true that public relations professionals must accept that such deliberative rhetorical strategies will be a part of the communication landscape in which they operate.

The most novel troubling aspect of *Beat Biden* introduced by AI is not so much the rhetorical strategy at play but rather the potentially confusing photo-realistic character of the images, putting Biden and Harris in a then-plausible but fabricated situation that later would become entirely implausible with Biden dropping out of the 2024 race in July of 2024. The ad also offers striking visions of migrant hordes at the U.S.–Mexico border and martial law in the streets of a major U.S. city, among others, that add up to a sort of dystopian apocalyptic nightmare. Being a deliberative missive, it is hard to classify as true disinformation, and, especially with disclaimers of its AI origins, it is also not actual misinformation. However, while it can be seen as potentially making the message more effective in attaining its goal of producing anxiety in voters, it does not fully adhere to the provision of "Enhancing the Profession" because, at least in our current moment, it has a strong likelihood of damaging trust.

Reimagining the Past

Another instance of political messaging infused with AI-generated imagery – in this case, issued by a candidate's rapid response team – came just a few weeks after the *Beat Biden* video's release. This other video was posted via Twitter, the platform now known as X, by the DeSantis War Room, the rapid response team of Florida Gov. Ron DeSantis, in his attempt to gain the Republican nomination for the U.S. Presidency in 2024.[26] Rather than being composed entirely of AI-generated images like *Beat Biden*, this untitled video contains primarily genuine footage of DeSantis's rival for the nomination, former President Donald Trump, from the past. The key argument forwarded by the video is that Trump showed weakness and was wrong to have not fired Dr. Anthony Fauci, the acting director of the National Institute of Allergy and Infectious Disease, during the first year of the COVID19 pandemic while Trump was in the final year of his presidential term. While sentiments may have been mixed across the political spectrum during the actual time of Trump and Fauci's working relationship, it has since become exceedingly clear that a majority of Republican voters do not approve of how Fauci steered precautionary health measures in the U.S. during the pandemic, making the Trump/Fauci connection one that could potentially be a political liability for Trump.[27]

The video includes many genuine images of both men, several in which they are pictured together in the context of press conferences or briefings during the pandemic. Still, it includes a few key images generated by AI that make the relationship between Trump and Fauci appear even closer and friendlier than the actual images do. While those real photographic images all show the men in close proximity appearing collegial and even happy, the three AI-generated images each show Trump and Fauci embracing, with Trump pushing his face against Fauci's in a manner suggesting that he may even be kissing his then-adviser. The effect is one that potentially amplifies and augments the case that Trump was not just weak regarding Fauci but also fond of Fauci, especially given the inclusion of another genuine piece of video in the spot in which Trump dismisses a claim that he would be firing Fauci and describes Fauci as a "wonderful man."

DeSantis's bid to take the Republican presidential nomination over Trump ultimately crumbled after DeSantis's loss to Trump in the 2024 Iowa Caucus in January 2024.[28] Even if this video issued by his rapid response team helped to dampen the support for Trump among Republicans, that was clearly not enough to produce the ultimate result that DeSantis's team was seeking. As such, the video is more noteworthy as an early instance of using AI-generated images to reframe or reimagine something from the past, to alter history. Going beyond the questionable deliberative rhetoric of the *Beat Biden* images, the DeSantis War Room clip causes deeper concern about how generative AI may be used going forward to muddy the waters and confuse the public in the realm of politics and beyond. Unlike the ad from the RNC or the email from the Peabody Office, there were no clear markings indicating how AI had been used either within the clip or surrounding its release, violating the expectations of the "Disclosure of Information" provision, and the vast majority of the images and soundbites included were genuine. It was only the work of journalists and internet sleuths that brought the fabricated AI images to light. The mixing of both real and forged content is one that is more concerning, as digital forensics expert Hany Farid explained, "It was particularly sneaky to intermix the real and the fake images, as if the presence of the real image would give more credibility to the other images."[29] This damages the "Free Flow of Information," causing confusion over what is truthful and accurate. The greater trickery at play here makes this case the starkest of the examples we are considering, the one that challenges our conception of ethical communication the most. In other words, it is most clearly an example of misinformation – though likely disinformation – being shared.

Yet, even this instance is an extension of the manner in which humans can retrospectively read more into past events, using such tactics to make a point that may have a basis in a sort of truth (i.e., that Trump and Fauci did have a working relationship that Trump did not publicly seek to end) but take that truth into a direction of exaggeration and editorializing. This fits the practice of truthiness that satirist Stephen Colbert helped introduce into the American English lexicon in 2005, a concept now commonly understood as describing "a truthful or seemingly truthful quality that is claimed for something not because of supporting facts or evidence but because of a feeling that it is true or a desire for it to be true."[30] This is not a practice that many want to defend. Still, it is one that precedes AI and thus is only being enhanced by the technology, allowing for the creation of compelling false "evidence" that can help make truthiness feel more truthful. Trump himself was culpable in spreading similar work with AI just a few weeks prior to this clip when he shared a chaotic video with AI-generated audio masquerading as the voices of Elon Musk, George Soros, Dick Cheney, Adolf Hitler, and even "The Devil," as a parody of DeSantis's actual chaotic – but not nearly as well attended – campaign launch on Twitter.[31] While the apparent absurdity of that audio, including a dead dictator and a religion-based personification of evil, makes the fakeness of the clip more apparent, it still has the possibility of helping shape opinion. This all underscores just how complicated the use of generative AI tools is. Even if public relations professionals can readily avoid mixing AI generated content into their messaging in misleading ways, they will have to come to terms with how others are deploying and find ways to stick with the best practices that truly will result in "Enhancing the Profession."

Public Relations in the Present

Returning to the email from the Peabody Office of Equity, Diversity, and Inclusion after having considered the more extreme political messaging examples of using generative AI makes the email sent by that office seem rather mild. After all, the email contained the statement disclosing its ChatGPT origins, and nothing in the statement was inaccurate or misleading. It nicely meets the PRSA Code of Ethics in some compelling ways. Of course, based on Joseph's follow-up response, we already know this was not enough. The ontology, or nature, of AI-generated content is such that much of the public is not ready for its deployment. As one then–senior-level student commented to *The Vanderbilt Hustler*, "Deans, provosts, and the chancellor: Do more. Do anything. And lead us into a better future with genuine, human empathy, not a robot . . . . [Administrators] only care about perception and their institutional politics of saving face."[32] This critique is telling in how it conflates the mechanics of AI – "a robot" – with the perception that the message's intention is merely "saving face." The reality of such situations when an organization may have some stake – any school shooting is an attack on the sanctity of the educational space – but not so much that they can actually affect policy or outcomes is one that constrains organizations into offering messages of solidarity and support more than action and change. This would be the case whether ChatGPT was used or not.

However, this student reaction highlights how the status of generative AI in public relations of the present is precarious. While the promise of AI for public relations is very real, the ontological hurdle is one that cannot be overlooked. In that regard, generative AI will likely have to remain an auxiliary piece of the public relations professional's toolkit to use in planning and brainstorming until more stakeholders are ready for more robust deployment. It may never – and probably should not ever – extend to incorporating images or sounds of a re-imagined (or uncaptured) past, as with the Trump/Fauci images, or even the more defensible speculative images of deliberative rhetoric. Still, both of those uses – along with many others that we can only begin to imagine – will continue to be part of the terrain in which we operate. The best that we can do is to hold strong in our ethical use and, in doing so, push back against the confusion and manipulation of public opinion whenever it affects our stakeholders.

Reflections

1. In the chapter, several tactics are discussed that meet the PRSA Code of Ethics yet result in public scrutiny or outrage. What can PR practitioners do to ensure that they are meeting stakeholder expectations regarding their campaigns?
2. What factors might influence the public's perceptions of using AI in strategic communication?
3. What are some arguments in favor of and against the idea that PR practitioners have a responsibility to educate the public about manipulative AI tactics, such as deepfakes?
4. In what ways does AI pose reputational risks to organizations?
5. How might PR practitioners combat misinformation that AI has caused?

Notes

1 Peabody Office of Equity, Diversity and Inclusion, February 16, 2023, https://t.e2ma. net/message/ul182h/m74zooz.

2 Quoted in Rachael Perrotta, "Peabody EDI Office Responds to MSU Shooting with Email Written Using ChatGPT," *The Vanderbilt Hustler*, February 17, 2023, sec. Campus Safety, https://vanderbilthustler.com/2023/02/17/peabody-edi-office-responds-to-msu-shooting-with-email-written-using-chatgpt/.

3 Muck Rack, "The State of AI in PR 2023," May 4, 2023, http://muckrack.com/blog/2023/05/04/state-of-ai-in-pr.

4 Tina McCorkindale, "Generative AI in Organizations: Insights and Strategies from Communication Leaders," (Institute for Public Relations, February 7, 2024), https://instituteforpr.org/ipr-generative-ai-organizations-2024/.

5 Linda Staley et al., "Promises & Pitfalls: The Ethical Use of AI for Public Relations Practicioners," (Public Relations Society of America, November 20, 2023), www.prsa.org/professional-development/ai-insights.

6 Claire Wardle and Hossein Derakhshan, "Information Disorder: Toward an Interdisciplinary Framework for Research and Policy Making," (Council of Europe, September 27, 2017), https://edoc.coe.int/en/media/7495-information-disorder-toward-an-interdisciplinary-framework-for-research-and-policy-making.html.

7 IBM, "What Are AI Hallucinations?," accessed February 22, 2024, www.ibm.com/topics/ai-hallucinations.

8 Charles Bankhead, "Hallucination, Fake References: Cautionary Tale about AI-Generated Abstracts," *Medpage Today*, July 28, 2023, www.medpagetoday.com/ophthalmology/generalophthalmology/105672.

9 Wardle and Derakhshan, "Information Disorder."

10 Machine Learning Center at Georgia Tech, "Understanding AI-Generated Misinformation and Evaluating Algorithmic and Human Solutions," *AIhub*, April 21, 2023, https://aihub.org/2023/04/21/understanding-ai-generated-misinformation-and-evaluating-algorithmic-and-human-solutions/.

11 Shannon Bond, "Fake Viral Images of an Explosion at the Pentagon Were Probably Created by AI," *NPR*, May 22, 2023, sec. Untangling Disinformation, www.npr.org/2023/05/22/1177590231/fake-viral-images-of-an-explosion-at-the-pentagon-were-probably-created-by-ai.

12 Matthew Harrington and Gary Grossman, "The Symbiosis of AI and Communications: Augmenting Creativity and Strategy for the Future," (USC Annenberg, November 2023), https://issuu.com/uscannenberg/docs/cpr_relreport24-final-digsnglpgs?fr=sZT FiZjY3OTgxOTM.

13 Henry Jenkins, *Convergence Culture: Where Old and New Media Collide* (NYU Press, 2006).

14 Camille Bacon-Smith, *Enterprising Women: Television Fandom and the Creation of Popular Myth* (University of Pennsylvania Press, 1992); Matt Hills, *Fan Cultures* (Psychology Press, 2002); Henry Jenkins, *Textual Poachers: Television Fans & Participatory Culture* (Routledge, 1992).

15 Lawrence Lessig, *Remix: Making Art and Commerce Thrive in the Hybrid Economy* (Penguin, 2008); Jonathan Lethem, "The Ecstasy of Influence: A Plagiarism," *Harper's Magazine*, February 2007, https://harpers.org/archive/2007/02/the-ecstasy-of-influence/; Eduardo Navas, *Remix Theory: The Aesthetics of Sampling* (Birkhäuser, 2014).

16 David Gurney, "Recombinant Comedy, Transmedial Mobility, and Viral Video," *The Velvet Light Trap* 68 (2011): 3–13, https://doi.org/10.1353/vlt.2011.0018; Limor Shifman, *Memes in Digital Culture* (MIT Press, 2013).

17 Eduardo Navas, *The Rise of Metacreativity: AI Aesthetics After Remix* (Taylor & Francis, 2022).

18 "Daisy," September 7, 1964, https://en.wikipedia.org/wiki/File:Daisy_(1964).webm.

19 *Beat Biden*, 2023, www.youtube.com/watch?v=kLMMxgtxQ1Y.

20 Zeeshan Aleem, "Why the RNC's AI Attack Ad against Joe Biden Is Unsettling," *MSNBC*, April 25, 2023, www.msnbc.com/opinion/msnbc-opinion/biden-republican-ai-attack-ad-rcna81370; Olivia Land and O'Neill, "Republican National Committee Slams Biden Re-Election Bid in AI Ad," *New York Post*, April 25, 2023, https://nypost.com/2023/04/25/republican-national-committee-slams-biden-re-election-bid-in-ai-ad/; Alex Thompson, "Republicans Slam Biden Re-Election Bid in AI-GeneratedAd,"*Axios*,April25,2023,www.axios.com/2023/04/25/rnc-slams-biden-re-election-bid-ai-generated-ad.

21 Kris Holt, "Republicans Attack Biden with a Fully AI-Generated Ad," *Engadget*, April25,2023,www.engadget.com/republicans-attack-biden-with-a-fully-ai-generated-ad-184055192.html.

22 Sam Cornale, "When Your Operative Class Has Been Decimated, and You're Following MAGA Republicans off a Cliff, I Suppose You Have No Choice but to Ask AI to Help," Tweet, *Twitter*, April 25, 2023, https://twitter.com/samcornale/status/1650820257882202112.

23 @jwhowl8431, "Comment on Beat Biden," comment, April 25, 2023, www.youtube.com/watch?v=kLMMxgtxQ1Y.

24 @brenito20879, "Comment on Beat Biden," comment, April 25, 2023, www.youtube.com/watch?v=kLMMxgtxQ1Y.

25 @GrumpDog, "Comment on Beat Biden," comment, April 25, 2023, www.youtube.com/watch?v=kLMMxgtxQ1Y.

26 @DeSantisWarRoom, "Donald Trump Became a Household Name by FIRING Countless People *on Television* But When It Came to Fauci . . .," Tweet, *Twitter*, June 5, 2023, https://twitter.com/DeSantisWarRoom/status/1665799058303188992.

27 StephanieMurray,"FauciIstheVillaininNewGOPCampaignAds,"*Politico*,February4, 2022, www.politico.com/news/2022/02/04/fauci-villain-new-gop-campaign-ads-0 0005430; Sheryl Gay Stolberg, "Republicans, Wooing Trump Voters, Make Fauci Their Boogeyman," *The New York Times*, February 7, 2022, sec. U.S., www.nytimes.com/2022/02/07/us/politics/fauci-republicans-trump.html.

28 Nicholas Nehamas et al., "Ron DeSantis Ends Campaign for President," *The New York Times*, January 21, 2024, sec. U.S., www.nytimes.com/2024/01/21/us/politics/desantis-drops-out.html.

29 Quoted in Shannon Bond, "DeSantis Campaign Shares Apparent AI-Generated Fake Images of Trump and Fauci," *NPR*, June 8, 2023, sec. Untangling Disinformation, www.npr.org/2023/06/08/1181097435/desantis-campaign-shares-apparent-ai-generated-fake-images-of-trump-and-fauci.

30 Merriam-Webster, Inc, "Truthiness Definition & Meaning," *Merriam-Webster Dictionary*, accessed February 21, 2024, www.merriam-webster.com/dictionary/truthiness.

31 MackDeGeurin,"TrumpTrollsDeSantisandMuskWithaHitlerDeepfake,"*Gizmodo*, May 25, 2023, https://gizmodo.com/desantis-trump-musk-twitter-hitler-deepfake-campaign-1850475254.

32 Quoted in Perrotta, "Peabody EDI Office Responds to MSU Shooting with Email Written Using ChatGPT."

13

GENERATIVE AI, ALGORITHMS, AND ETHICS

A Case for Critical Digital Literacy in PR

Laurence José

Learning Objectives

1. Understanding the integration of generative artificial intelligence (AI) systems in the digital landscape.
2. Analyzing and identifying questions to consider for an ethical use of AI in public relations (PR).
3. Examining the meaning of digital literacy for PR professionals.

Introduction

Saying that the work of public relations (PR) professionals is affected by the fast-changing media landscape has almost become a hackneyed phrase today. Media consumption habits continue to change, catalyzed by *algorithms* and social media platforms that shape, control, and – as some might – manipulate consumers' habits. Yet, artificial intelligence (AI), with the release of new and more powerful tools, has recently raised pressing questions for the PR industry and the communications field in general. "Pivotal shift" and other hyperbolic statements are frequently employed to describe the impact of AI on the PR industry.[1] Though AI is not new, the rapid deployment of *generative AI*, catalyzed by OpenAI and the release of ChatGPT in November 2022,[2] makes it impossible today to ignore and not address the effects and very tangible consequences of this technology for communications professionals. In a November 2023 article, *The Washington Post*[3] described the impact of generative AI as "a business game-changer" that transforms "a wide range of processes, including customer service, content creation, and software coding." If gauging its exact long-term

DOI: 10.4324/9781032671482-18

impact on the PR field remains an open question, there is little doubt or controversy in stating that generative AI has become a buzzword in educational and professional settings.

Beyond the initial hype that followed OpenAI's release of its generative chatbot to the public, the fast-evolving possibilities and tools that these AI systems provide keep changing the PR game and the very definition of what it means to be a PR professional today. For instance, just between November 2022 and the time of this writing, the discussion surrounding the use of generative AI has shifted from having access to generative AI through a website like OpenAI to generative AI becoming embedded in our experiences working with many – if not most – digital tools, whether they are word-based, visual-based, or even video-based. Consequently, the question for professionals is not so much anymore, "Should I use or not use generative AI?" but rather, "How can I best integrate generative AI into my work" and "What does it mean to use generative AI and what are the consequences for my work and what I stand for?" Drawing from these critical questions, the present chapter provides insights on how to think about generative AI in terms of adding value and, perhaps most importantly, on how to preserve agency so that any use of generative AI remains consistent with one's ethical values.

Ultimately, this chapter contends that the explosion of generative AI, with its possibilities and the challenges it raises, offers an opportune moment for advocating for *critical digital literacy* at a time when it may be both difficult to resist the hype and easy to forget our ethical responsibilities, given the larger impact of this technology and what it entails. In this way, this chapter also answers the call for a "public relations scholarship [that] takes the technologies surrounding AI seriously while simultaneously critiquing them."[4]

Generative AI in the Current Digital Landscape

When asked how companies should think about AI and its consequences for professionals, business professor and workplace technology expert Karim Lakhani said, "AI won't replace humans – but humans with AI will replace humans without AI."[5] This is a statement that most, if not all, communication professionals and educators have heard over the past few months. And this is not different for the PR field. The question is not anymore about whether to use generative AI but rather to learn how to best use it. Indeed, since the initial release of ChatGPT and its subsequent versions, many conversations – if not most of them – have focused not so much on whether PR professionals should adopt these tools but rather on how they can adopt them to maximize their use and remain competitive at a time when technology provides us with tools that can "take on the role of collaborator, seamlessly transforming our scattered ideas and outlines into cohesive and compelling narratives, press releases, or pitches."[6] Increased efficiency and productivity seems to be the promise from the tech industry. And what PR professional wouldn't want this?

The Democratization of AI

After its release, ChatGPT quickly became a global phenomenon, democratizing generative AI with the possibility to create content in a few clicks, readily available at anyone's fingertips. In his February 2023 *New York Times* article, Kevin Roose described the decision by OpenAI to release ChatGPT, an AI-powered chatbot, as resulting in an "AI arms race" in the tech industry.[7] It is true that one would be hard-pressed today to find any tech news without a mention of AI. With the AI race in the tech industry, generative AI tools have become rapidly integrated and layered into different existing software programs. They also gained sophistication and power, with the possibility for all users (i.e., not just beta users) to create multimodal content with a simple text-based prompt. Notable examples include OpenAI's release to the general public of DALL·E, its text-to-image model, and Adobe's introduction in March 2023 of Firefly,[8] a model focused on image and text-effect generation, set to be integrated into its Creative Cloud applications. All of this contributed to making generative AI pretty much unavoidable and part of work everywhere, including in many of the mainstream software ecosystems used by communications professionals. For instance, in February 2023, Microsoft launched Copilot, an generative AI companion promoted for its seamless integration into the Office 365 apps and described as able to complete tasks such as "writing or editing content, summarizing meetings from live conservations, or creating presentations," among others.[9] Similarly, in March 2023, Google announced that it was adding generative AI features to its work apps, allowing users to be supported by AI collaborators.10 At the time of this writing, AI-generated summaries are now listed at the top of a Google search, further amplifying the ubiquity of AI in digital tools in our professional and civic spheres (cf., Microsoft launched a version of its search engine Bing with GPT-4 built-in in February 2023, though its use required then getting on a waiting list). This integration also concerns visual design software. For example, Adobe Illustrator, Adobe Photoshop, and Canva, to name a few, today offer integrated generative AI features enabling users to create or edit work by simply entering a text-based prompt.

Impact on Required Skills

Besides making opting out of using it quasi-impossible, the integration and democratization of generative AI into the digital landscape also means that AI literacy may soon become a fundamental expectation for many jobs, including for PR professionals. Though the fear of being replaced or losing the human

BOX 13.1 ACTIVITY #1: TESTING THE INTEGRATION OF GENERATIVE AI IN A PR CREATIVE WORKFLOW

Imagine you are a PR professional tasked with developing a visual campaign for a client. The client seeks customized imagery. You already know that you will have limited time and means to design your own visuals from scratch. After drafting a preliminary campaign plan with a theme for the imagery, you are at the stage of developing drafts for the different visuals. You determined that the visuals would include a mix of realistic images (3–4) and icon-type images (5–8) to be used across different platforms. To produce the visuals, use the following two approaches.

- Approach 1

  Develop a series of descriptive keywords corresponding to the types of visuals you are looking for. Do a search with these keywords on a few open-source image websites (photography-based and icon-based websites). Save the images that you consider to be the best candidates for your project. Note: if an image is a good candidate pending minor editing, save it and take notes of the editing requirements (deleting the background around an object, adjusting the opacity or vibrance, etc.). Make sure to check the licensing of each image and attribution requirements, and include them as meta-information in your files.

- Approach 2

  Instead of keywords, develop a series of text-based prompts for generating the visuals you are looking for. Input each prompt into an AI image generator platform of your choice. Note: many software programs offer integrated AI-generator tools capable of generating different types of visuals, from images to graphic and videos. For the purpose of this activity, you may use AI image-generator platforms or an integrated AI tool. Use each prompt at least twice on the same platform to compare the outputs. Save the images that you consider to be the best outputs for your project, along with the prompts.

After comparing the image results for each keyword/prompt, write a 2–3-page memo describing the pros and cons of each approach. Consider the following questions to develop your memo.

- How would you characterize your overall experience with each approach? Which approach is more effective for streamlining your workflow? How so? Consider factors such as efficiency, precision, control, and time.

- What are you losing vs. gaining with each approach?
- What is the role of language to uncover potential imagery in both approaches? Think particularly about elements you would not consider when using one approach over the other (for example, keywords as means to discover existing images that may correspond more or less to what you are seeking vs. detailed descriptive prompts to generate an image based on what you think you are looking for).
- How much editing does each approach require? Consider both the level of editing of the outputs (i.e. images) and the refinement of the inputs used to generate or search each image (i.e. adjustment of the prompts and keywords).
- How do the two approaches compare and differ with regard to the kinds of visual design competencies a PR professional should possess?
- What are the implications of each approach regarding copyrights and image licensing? How would this information be included in the campaign and the communication with your client? Make sure to check the latest court rulings regarding claiming copyrights for unedited AI-generated images.[11]

Close your memo with 3–5 recommendations for PR professionals seeking to use generative AI tools to create visual-based content.

touch cannot be ignored – making AI the basis for a PR strategy may be an attractive option for many companies – it is also difficult not to get excited and amazed by what these new AI-powered systems can do and how easily they can increase productivity. Need to write a media pitch? A press release? Generative AI now allows you to create or edit our drafts in just a few seconds. In such a context, AI literacy seems easily reducible to learning how to leverage AI tools best. Just think about the possibilities AI offers for analyzing large datasets to enable us to anticipate public opinions. And yet, this is not all it should be.

While knowing how to use generative AI to increase productivity is an important skill for any PR professional today, it is not enough. Or, better said, it should not be enough. That is, using generative AI systems should not just be about learning how to increase work outputs, or how to make work processes more efficient. It should also come with careful consideration about what these systems are, how they are built, and what their use implies for the very function of communication and the mission of PR. Given the explosion of generative AI tools, knowing how to pick the right tool for the right task is a mandatory skill, as is curiosity and a willingness to test tools. It is worth noting that it is very easy to lower our ethical guard when faced with incessant breaking stories of yet another AI application in PR. If the "AI is not replacing as much as it is becoming a companion for PR professionals" stance seems to be widely accepted, it is not enough to gauge the deeper significance of these tools and what is at play when we use them.

Challenging the Black Box of AI Technology

Understanding how generative AI functions requires technical expertise. Yet, it is also fair to say that today, we – professionals and citizens – have all heard about the capabilities of generative AI and its basic functioning. *Large language models* (LLMs) and *machine learning* (ML), albeit technical, are terms that most of us have encountered, if only in news reports about the latest generative AI innovation. Though this chapter is not arguing that a PR professional seeking to use generative AI must be a computer scientist, it does contend that having a basic knowledge of how these systems work is fundamental for making informed and ethical choices. In many ways, this echoes Hannah Freedman's call in her piece on "The Future of Media Relations: Navigating AI's Impact on PR" and the necessity for PR professionals to "be curious."[12] But more than demonstrating curiosity for testing different generative AI tools based on one's specific needs and the promises made by the tech companies for increased efficiency and power, this chapter advocates for the kind of intellectual curiosity that compels us to broaden our gaze and to interrogate these systems by looking behind the screen and challenging the black box of technology.

Understanding the Basics

Going back to LLMs, one important idea is to understand that they "are the algorithmic basis for chatbots like OpenAI's ChatGPT and Google's Bard."[13] What does this mean? Well, basically that any generative chatbot needs "a computer algorithm that processes natural language inputs and predicts the next word based on what it's already seen. Then it predicts the next word, and the next word, and so on until its answer is complete."[14] Without possessing computer scientist–level expertise, understanding this fundamental element regarding data inputs as building blocks for a generative AI system to work becomes a way to ask key questions regarding the outputs, the labor involved in these systems, and the origin of the data.

Data Output, Quality, and (Invisible) Labor

The amount of and quality of the data used to train these models has consequences on the output. Not only does the data source affects the system's likelihood to reproduce biases and stereotypes,[15] but the training itself has a cost. One of the recent controversies concerns the hidden and underpaid labor behind these generative AI systems, which has been compared to modern slavery. In her May 2024

Wired article, Caroline Haskins notes that "97 African workers who do AI training work or online content moderation for companies like Meta and OpenAI published an open letter to President Biden, demanding that US tech companies stop systemically abusing and exploiting African workers."[16] The human cost behind generative AI and the reality of "data labelers" was signaled and denounced as early as January 2023, just a few weeks after the release of ChatGPT.[17] So before using an AI system and embracing it uncritically as the latest technological innovation, it may be worthwhile to research how it is designed and understand that using it may mean participating in the exploitation of workers and violating one's own ethical standards. Pleading ignorance and invoking the black box dimension of these technologies cannot be an excuse anymore.

Data Origin

The question surrounding the origin of the data used to train these systems and its implications on copyrights is another highly controversial element. Since the initial release of ChatGPT to the public, more voices have come forward to point out the intellectual propriety issue, including for AI image generators.[18] This, too, is part of opening the black box of technology to understand and challenge what AI actually is. Generative AI is not magic. It is fed with data (i.e., content) produced by people and organizations who may not have agreed to have their work used in such a way. Though the question is not settled – is generative AI violating copyrights or is it acting more like a reader, using existing data to become itself 'smarter' so that it can generate its own content? – it is clear today that an responsible approach warrants that one, at the very least, seeks to understand how a specific system is trained and how it treats content produced by others. The recent decision by the European Union (EU) requiring that companies deploying generative AI disclose the use of copyrighted material by "publishing summaries of copyrighted data used for training"[19] speaks to the urgency of this question and the legal/ethical ramifications surrounding AI. At the very least, this is an argument for any professional to stay curious and up to date.

Controlling the Data

In addition to interrogating and seeking to understand the basic mechanisms underlying the technology, PR professionals must ask questions regarding the protection of the data they input and the integrity of the data generated.

Privacy and Information Integrity

Examples of good questions to ask are: How are the data or prompts fed into an AI system to generate or edit work protected? What are the guardrails? Recent examples such as the OpenAI ChatGPT's conversation histories leak[20] are a clear invitation to remain cautious and informed, especially when one inputs copyrighted data from a client. This is important not just because the data may be leaked, but also because any inputted content may become training data for the AI system itself. Differently put, professionals should think twice before entering client copyrighted data for, let's say, creating a press release or generating a business report. This is yet another reminder that understanding the basics of these digital tools, as their integration in the PR workflow may become more seamless, is a fundamental requirement for professionals today, including for protecting the integrity of its clients' information (cf., the 2023 PR council guidelines on generative AI).[21]

Transparency and Accuracy

The question regarding transparency is as much about understanding the origin of the training data (as discussed previously in this chapter) and checking for accuracy – yes, generative AI systems can *hallucinate* – as it is about disclosing when and how AI is used in the PR workflow. Besides the ethical ramifications of presenting AI-generated work as one's own, submitting work that was entirely or partially created by an AI system to a client without disclosing it can also quickly result in copyright challenges. Work that is entirely produced with AI may not be copyrightable and may even infringe copyright laws (ex., using an image generator to create a visual for a campaign).[22] Therefore, developing the reflex of documenting any use of generative AI in a project workflow seems like a reasonable guideline. This idea of 'documenting' is closely connected to flagging the use of generative AI for users and not being misleading. What makes generative AI tools so powerful is also what makes them challenging, if not dangerous. Generative AI produces content that becomes increasingly difficult to identify as AI-generated. Controversies faced by tech companies regarding the catalyzing effect of AI in the propagation of fake news are good examples of the kinds of challenges communications professionals face today. For instance, Meta announced in February 2024 that it would start flagging AI-generated images on its platforms Facebook, Instagram, and Threads.[23] This initiative by Meta exemplifies the pressure and ethical challenges companies are facing today regarding their roles in the publication of potentially misleading AI-generated content. Meta is not the first to do this. In September 2023, TikTok started offering tools to label AI-generated content to creators.[24] Similarly, Google announced that it "would label AI-generated videos that look real" on its video platform YouTube.[25] It is safe to say that with the increasing focus on AI's impact on society, the development of deepfake technologies, and the questions it raises about information literacy and our ability to distinguish AI-generated from non–AI-generated content, any company that uses AI to create communication artifacts and/or hosts AI outputs to interface with audiences may soon have to include this kind of metadata to be more transparent.

Understanding Responsibility: When the Chatbot Gets It Wrong, Who Is Responsible?

Accuracy and transparency also raise questions about responsibility when mistakes happen due to an AI system like a chatbot used to interface with clients. In a recent lawsuit, Air Canada argued that it was not responsible for the wrong information its chatbot gave passenger Jack Moffat in 2022 regarding its bereavement policy. When trying to purchase a next-day ticket to attend his grandmother's funeral, Jack Moffat was led to believe that he would be entitled to a retroactive discount if he filed a claim under the company's bereavement policy. When the company later refused to give him a partial refund, stating that the information provided by the chatbot was inaccurate and that the policy was readily available on the website, Moffat filed a claim with the Civil Resolution Tribunal (CRT) that ultimately ruled in his favor and ordered Air Canada to pay "$812 (CAD) in damages and tribunal court fees."[26] Besides being a good cautionary tale, this example is good reminder of why keeping a 'human touch' in communication matters. Yes, using AI warrants that PR professionals define clear guidelines regarding authenticity and transparency, but it also requires a careful examination of who is controlling the communication and, ultimately, what it means to be a PR professional.

Conclusion: Toward Critical Digital Literacy

Even a cursory look into the black box of generative AI gives us important insights regarding the kind of digital literacy PR professionals should possess today.

Moving Beyond Technical Competencies

In a context whereby opting out of AI may not be possible anymore and whereby each passing day seems to come with yet another news story out regarding the latest identified risks of generative AI – at the time of this writing, Google just published research stating that "that most image-based disinformation is now AI-generated"[32] – a critical perspective seems to be a necessary component of digital literacy skills for PR professionals. That is, in light of what generative AI is and can do, a responsible use of the technology requires one to actively interrogate and challenge the opacity of these systems. This means both learning about their basic technical functions and how they can eventually be integrated into a PR workflow, as well as learning what the technology is, how it works,

BOX 13.2 ACTIVITY 2: DEVELOPING ETHICAL STANDARDS

You work for a PR agency. Your boss asked you to prepare a short presentation on the implications and best practices for ethically integrating generative AI tools into the agency's workflow. Like most of the industry, your boss has been bombarded with news and briefs regarding the latest tech advances and the promises of generative AI for streamlining workflow processes, boosting creativity, and delivering more customized content. Amidst all the good news, discussions surrounding issues such as hallucinations, unregulated data harvesting, copyright violations, and lack of transparency have also come to your boss' attention. The goal of your presentation is not only to help the agency make informed decisions regarding the use of generative AI but also to serve as a preliminary outline for revising the agency's policies and ethical guidelines based on the latest technological developments.

Follow the following steps to prepare the presentation.

1. Identifying relevant examples
   Select 3–4 generative AI tools that are popular in the PR industry – try to select tools from different categories (ex: text generators, visual and video generators, sound generators).
2. Explaining the basics
   For each tool, provide a short summary of:

   a. How it can enhance a PR work.
   b. What it requires to be effective; this includes elements such as required skills (such as writing skills for producing and editing prompts to make them effective, technical skills to edit AI-generated videos or photos, information literacy skills to evaluate the content produced by an AI system), as well as cost considerations (cf., subscription-based vs. free models, tools integrated in existing software).

3. Asking the critical questions for an ethical use
   Drawing from specific relevant examples of generative AI mishaps and recent controversies (include and be ready to speak about these examples), establish a list of critical questions for a PR agency to consider before incorporating such an AI generative tool into its workflow. Examples of recent debates surrounding generative AI include unethical data harvesting practices[27] and the impact on content creators opposing the use of their work as training data for generative AI models,[28] misinformation[29] and harms created by systems being trained on biased data,[30]

sustainability and the environmental cost of generative AI systems,[31] and privacy and safety of the data inputted in these systems.

4. Testing and assessing

Apply the questions developed under step 3 to test and assess each generative AI system that you selected in step 1. Note: this requires that you research the policies and information provided by the different companies regarding the design of these systems.

5. Creating a decision tree

Design a flowchart visualizing a roadmap for how to decide whether to adopt a specific generative AI tool.

6. Revising and getting feedback

End the presentation with a list of best practices to ensure that the roadmap accounts for the fast evolution of AI tools and includes a mechanism for including the voices of employees' and customers' concerns.

and what it requires. Increased efficiency, creativity, power, and precision matter. However, so does respecting the work of others and making sure that one does not participate in exploitive labor practices or in the destruction of the environment (the environmental cost of generative AI is quickly becoming an important topic of discussion).[33] While many digital literacy frameworks already acknowledge that digital literacy goes beyond technical skills – see for instance, the Joint Information Systems Committee (Jisc) framework,[34] the Bryn Mawr digital competencies framework,[35] or the EU's digital competence framework[36] – the current debates surrounding the impact of generative AI in our professional and civic lives offer an opportune moment to (re)assert the importance for developing digital literacy skills that combine technical competencies and a critical understanding of the technology. Doing so also requires that PR professionals understand their role in the deployment of generative AI.

Reclaiming Agency

More than being users who adopt innovative digital tools for enhancing work processes and outputs, professionals also have the power to develop ethical standards to guide their use of generative AI. Such standards can then become ways to develop critical questions that help all users to gain a deeper understanding of what these technologies are and do. In this way, ethical guidelines are a means to empower and regain agency. Admittingly, as previously mentioned, the integration of AI into every aspect of the digital landscape makes it harder to push back. At the same time, the ubiquity of AI tools is precisely the reason why looking behind the screen and challenging the opacity of these systems is more important than ever. Such a stance is as much about preserving one's own ethical standards at it is about reclaiming agency over the technology as professionals and citizens. For example, simply understanding that a computer is not a brain and that LLMs are built on statistics and "work by looking for patterns in huge troves of text and then using those patterns to guess what the next word in a string of words should be"[37] can be enough to remember that AI-generated content is not magical and is entirely dependent on the quality of the data it was trained on.

Developing Inclusive Listening Practices

An effective way to develop critical digital literacy is to listen not only to the voices of those who promote AI systems, but also to those who caution and educate us about the pitfalls of this technology. The March 2021 article "On the Dangers of Stochastic Parrots: Can Language Models Be Too Big?"[38] co-authored by Emily Bender, Angelica McMillan, Timnit Gebru, and Margaret Mitchell (pseudonym, Shmargaret Shmitchell) offers one of the most famous and striking examples of a piece designed to educate us about the realities and limits of LLMs. The article highlights how LLMs do not understand but merely repeat words like "parrots" based on guesswork (which is the meaning of "stochastic"), encode biases, are too large to allow for an analysis of what exactly is in the training data, and require a tremendous amount of energy. Besides demystifying and providing an accessible perspective on a highly technical system, this article also serves as a reminder of what is at play for dissonant voices. Not only did the article go viral, it also resulted in the (forced) departure from Google of two of the co-authors, both co-lead of the ethical AI team at Google: Timnit Gebru in December 2020[39] and Margaret Mitchell in February 2021.[40]

In a competitive professional landscape whereby the hype surrounding generative AI is (still) loud and difficult to resist, many people – mostly women of color – have been working relentlessly to demystify and open the black box of technology to expose the cost of AI. Given this chapter's argument, extending an invitation at this point to read the August 2023 *Rolling Stone* article "These Women Tried to Warn Us about AI"[41] seems like a fitting conclusion. While the voices of Timnit Gebru, Joy Buolamwini, Safiya Noble, Rumman Chowdhury, Seeta Peña Gangadharan, and Meredith Broussard, to name a few, may not always be the ones that are foregrounded in the industry when seeking information about the latest AI tool and what it can do, the reality of these technologies and their role in the PR industry make it an injunction for professionals to seek out, listen to, and learn from these voices. The possibilities and challenges surrounding generative AI are, in this way, also a reminder of our collective responsibilities as communications professionals who have agency and decide what technology to use or not.

Reflections

1. What are the main challenges for PR professionals today when it comes to generative AI? What are some of the key questions PR professionals should ask themselves before choosing a specific generative AI system? What is an ethical vs. an unethical use of generative AI in the PR field?
2. What are some best practices to choose the AI tool that is right for you? What are some elements that would make you choose vs. not choose a specific AI tool?
3. What are productive vs. non-productive definitions of AI literacy for PR professionals?
4. What are the prerequisites for a PR professional to develop critical digital literacy skills? What does it entail, given the fast evolution of technology?
5. How can the PR industry lead or influence the ethical development of generative AI?

Notes

1 Artzi, Ohad Ben. "Council Post: Four Ways Ai Is Changing the Public Relations Industry." *Forbes*, December 1, 2023. www.forbes.com/sites/forbesbusinesscouncil/2023/11/30/four-ways-ai-is-changing-the-public-relations-industry/.
2 Roose, Kevin. "How CHATGPT Kicked off an A.I. Arms Race." *The New York Times*, February 3, 2023. www.nytimes.com/2023/02/03/technology/chatgpt-openai-artificial-intelligence.html.
3 "Generative AI is a Business Game-Changer, but Only If It's Built on Solid Foundations." *The Washington Post*, November 23, 2023. www.washingtonpost.com/creativegroup/aws/generative-ai-is-a-business-game-changer-but-only-if-its-built-on-solid-foundations/.
4 Swiatek, Lukasz, Chris Galloway, Marina Vujnovic, and Dean Kruckeberg. "Humanoid Artificial Intelligence, Media Conferences and Natural Responses to Journalists' Questions: The End of (Human-to-Human) Public Relations?" *Public Relations Inquiry* 13, no. 1 (December 15, 2023): 113–121. https://doi.org/10.1177/2046147x231221828.
5 Ignatius, Adi. "AI Won't Replace Humans – But Humans With AI Will Replace Humans Without AI." *The Harvard Review*, August 3, 2023. https://hbr.org/2023/08/ai-wont-replace-humans-but-humans-with-ai-will-replace-humans-without-ai/.
6 Freedman, Hannah. "The Future of Media Relations: Navigating AI's Impact on PR." *Ragan PR Daily*, October 27, 2023. www.prdaily.com/the-future-of-media-relations-navigating-ais-impact-on-pr/.
7 Roose, Kevin. "How CHATGPT Kicked off an A.I. Arms Race." www.nytimes.com/2023/02/03/technology/chatgpt-openai-artificial-intelligence.html.
8 Adobe News – "Adobe Unveils Firefly, a Family of New Creative Generative ai." March 21, 2023.https://news.adobe.com/news/news-details/2023/Adobe-Unveils-Firefly-a-Family-of-new-Creative-Generative-AI/default.aspx.
9 Microsoft News Center. "Introducing Microsoft 365 Copilot: Your Copilot for Work." March 16, 2023. https://news.microsoft.com/2023/03/16/introducing-microsoft-365-copilot-your-copilot-for-work/.
10 Abril, Danielle. "Google Is Adding AI To Its Work Apps: Here Is What That Means." *The Washington Post*, March 14, 2023. www.washingtonpost.com/technology/2023/03/14/google-workspace-ai/.

11 Davis, Wes. "AI-Generated Art Cannot Be Copyrighted, Rules a US Federal Judge." *The Verge*, August 19, 2023. www.theverge.com/2023/8/19/23838458/ai-generated-art-no-copyright-district-court.

12 Freedman, Hannah. "The Future of Media Relations: Navigating AI's Impact on PR." https://www.prdaily.com/the-future-of-media-relations-navigating-ais-impact-on-pr/.

13 Mearian, Lucas. "What Are LLMS, and How Are They Used in Generative AI?" *Computerworld*, February 7, 2024. www.computerworld.com/article/1627101/what-are-large-language-models-and-how-are-they-used-in-generative-ai.html.

14 Mearian, Lucas. "What Are LLMS, and How Are They Used in Generative AI?" *Computerworld*. https://www.computerworld.com/article/1627101/what-are-large-language-models-and-how-are-they-used-in-generative-ai.html.

15 Nicoletti, Leonardo, and Dina Bass. "Humans Are Biased: Generative AI Is Even Worse." *Bloomberg.com*, June 9, 2023. www.bloomberg.com/graphics/2023-generative-ai-bias/.

16 Haskins, Caroline. "The Low-Paid Humans behind AI's Smarts Ask Biden to Free Them from 'Modern Day Slavery'." *Wired*, May 22, 2024. www.wired.com/story/low-paid-humans-ai-biden-modern-day-slavery/.

17 Perrigo, Billy. "OpenAI Used Kenyan Workers on Less than $2 per Hour: Exclusive." *Time*, January 18, 2023. https://time.com/6247678/openai-chatgpt-kenya-workers/.

18 Associated Press. "Visual Artists Fight Back against AI Companies for Repurposing Their Work." *NBCNews.com*, August 31, 2023. www.nbcnews.com/tech/tech-news/visual-artists-fight-back-ai-companies-repurposing-work-rcna102760.

19 EU AI Act: First Regulation on Artificial Intelligence | News, December 19, 2023. www.europarl.europa.eu/pdfs/news/expert/2023/6/story/20230601STO93804/20230601STO93804_en.pdf.

20 Kan, Michael. "OpenAI Confirms Leak of CHATGPT Conversation Histories." *PCMAG*, March 22, 2023. www.pcmag.com/news/openai-confirms-leak-of-chatgpt-conversation-histories.

21 PR Council. "PR Council Guidelines on Generative AI", April 26, 2023. https://pr-council.net/wp-content/uploads/2023/04/PR-Council-Guidelines-on-Generative-AI-042423.pdf.

22 PR Council. "PR Council guidelines on Generative AI."

23 Bond, Shannon. "Meta Will Start Labeling AI-Generated Images on Instagram and Facebook." *NPR*, February 6, 2024. www.npr.org/2024/02/06/1229317971/meta-labeling-ai-generated-images-instagram-facebook-artificial-intelligence.

24 Perez, Sarah. "TikTok Debuts New Tools and Technology to Label Ai Content." *TechCrunch*, September 19, 2023. https://techcrunch.com/2023/09/19/tiktok-debuts-new-tools-and-technology-to-label-ai-content/.

25 Bond, Shannon. "YouTube Will Label AI-Generated Videos That Look Real." *NPR*, November 14, 2023. www.npr.org/2023/11/14/1212986395/youtube-will-label-ai-generated-videos-that-look-real.

26 "Air Canada Chatbot Costs Airline Discount It Wrongly Offered Customer." *CBS News*, February 19, 2024. www.cbsnews.com/news/aircanada-chatbot-discount-customer/.

27 Metz, Cade, Cecilia Kang, Sheera Frenkel, Stuart A. Thompson, and Nico Grant. "How Tech Giants Cut Corners to Harvest Data for A.I." *The New York Times*, April 6, 2024. www.nytimes.com/2024/04/06/technology/tech-giants-harvest-data-artificial-intelligence.html.

28 Hunter, Tatum. "Artists Are Fleeing Instagram to Keep Their Work Out of Meta's AI." *Washington Post*, June 6, 2024. www.washingtonpost.com/technology/2024/06/06/instagram-meta-ai-training-cara/.

29 "Air Canada Chatbot Costs Airline Discount It Wrongly Offered Customer." *CBS News*.

30 Buolamwini, Joy. "Unmasking the Bias in Facial Recognition Algorithms | MIT Sloan." *MIT Sloan*, December 13, 2023. https://mitsloan.mit.edu/ideas-made-to-matter/unmasking-bias-facial-recognition-algorithms.

31 Hao, Karen. "Ai Is Taking Water from the Desert." *The Atlantic*, March 4, 2024. www.theatlantic.com/technology/archive/2024/03/ai-water-climate-microsoft/677602/.

32 Maiberg, Emanuel. "Google Researchers Say AI Now Leading Disinformation Vector (and Are Severely Undercounting the Problem)." *404 Media*, May 28, 2024. www.404media.co/google-says-ai-now-leading-disinformation-vector-and-is-severely-undercounting-the-problem/.

33 Crawford, Kate. "Generative AI's Environmental Costs Are Soaring – and Mostly Secret." *Nature News*, February 20, 2024. www.nature.com/articles/d41586-024-00478-x.

34 Jisc. "Individual Digital Capabilities." n.d. https://digitalcapability.jisc.ac.uk/what-is-digital-capability/individual-digital-capabilities/.

35 Bryn Mawr College. "What Are Digital Competencies?" n.d. www.brynmawr.edu/inside/offices-services/digital-competencies/what-they-are.

36 Misheva, Galina. "The Digital Competence Framework (DigComp)." *Digital Skills and Jobs Platform*, April 21, 2021. https://digital-skills-jobs.europa.eu/en/actions/european-initiatives/digital-competence-framework-digcomp.

37 Weil, Elizabeth. "ChatGPT Is Nothing Like a Human, Says Linguist Emily Bender." *Intelligencer*, March 1, 2023. https://nymag.com/intelligencer/article/ai-artificial-intelligence-chatbots-emily-m-bender.html.

38 Bender, Emily M., Timnit Gebru, Angelina McMillan-Major, and Shmargaret Shmitchell. "On the Dangers of Stochastic Parrots." *Proceedings of the 2021 ACM Conference on Fairness, Accountability, and Transparency (FAccT '21)*, March 1, 2021. https://doi.org/10.1145/3442188.3445922.

39 Hao, Karen. "We Read the Paper That Forced Timnit Gebru Out of Google. Here's What It Says." *MIT Technology Review*, January 10, 2022. www.technologyreview.com/2020/12/04/1013294/google-ai-ethics-research-paper-forced-out-timnit-gebru/.

40 Schiffer, Zoë. "Google Fires Second AI Ethics Researcher Following Internal Investigation." *The Verge*, February 19, 2021. www.theverge.com/2021/2/19/22292011/google-second-ethical-ai-researcher-fired.

41 Lorena O'Neil, "Women Sounded the Alarm on AI's Dangers Long Before ChatGPT. Why Didn't We Listen?" *Rolling Stone*, August 12, 2023. https://www.rollingstone.com/culture/culture-features/women-warnings-ai-danger-risk-before-chatgpt-1234804367/.

14

DISINFORMATION IN THE ERA OF GENERATIVE AI

Challenges, Detection Strategies, and Countermeasures

Jason Davis

Learning Objectives

1. Analyze digital content into its basic component types (text, images, audio, and video) to understand and detect patterns and inconsistencies that serve as key indicators for misinformation.
2. Recognize the strengths and weaknesses of each media type in conveying information and influencing audiences. Explain how misinformation and disinformation campaigns exploit the differences between media types by combining multiple formats strategically to achieve malicious goals.
3. Identify the key elements of misinformation and disinformation campaigns, including emotional appeal, sensationalism, and audience targeting through social engineering.
4. Explain the importance of evidence-based debunking in communication theory, including the provision of credible evidence, thorough research, and simple, strategically framed messaging to refute inaccuracies.
5. Analyze the importance of shifting from reactive to proactive PR strategies in addressing misinformation threats and identify key components of a proactive strategy, including scenario modeling, real-time monitoring, staged rapid response materials, and sustained proactive measures.

Introduction

Left unchecked, the risks associated with misinformation and disinformation in today's digital landscape can cause irreparable damage to a brand's reputation and bottom line. To mitigate these risks, it is crucial for communications professionals to have robust detection and response strategies in place. This chapter dives into

DOI: 10.4324/9781032671482-19

the tactics and tools used to identify false information, from leveraging artificial intelligence (AI)-powered monitoring platforms to tapping into the expert methods of seasoned investigators. By incorporating these approaches, PR professionals can quickly identify potential threats and take proactive measures to protect their organizations' reputations and maintain transparency with their stakeholders. This chapter is divided into three sections, described in the following subsections.

Unmasking the Shadows: The Art of Detection

In this section, we examine the methods and tools employed in the detection of misinformation and disinformation. From advanced technological solutions to the human intuition of seasoned investigators, we explore how public relations professionals can proactively identify misinformation and disinformation circulating in the digital realm. Strategies for real-time monitoring, data analysis, and pattern recognition are described, providing a comprehensive guide to staying one step ahead in the battle against falsehoods.

Deconstructing Deceit: The Power of Debunking

Once misinformation is identified, the next crucial step is to debunk it effectively. This section dissects the anatomy of deceptive narratives, unveiling the psychological and communicative tactics employed to mislead audiences. With a focus on evidence-based debunking, we explore the art of crafting compelling counter-narratives and strategies to effectively communicate the truth. Case studies and real-world examples illustrate the power of debunking in restoring accuracy and credibility.

Strategies for Combat: Navigating the Misinformation Battlefield

The final section is a strategic guide to combating misinformation and disinformation in the realm of public relations. Drawing on insights from various disciplines, we examine proactive measures to prevent the spread of false information, including media literacy campaigns, ethical content creation, and engagement with stakeholders. Through a comprehensive approach that combines detection, debunking, and strategic communication, public relations professionals can not only mitigate the impact of misinformation but actively contribute to a more resilient and informed public discourse.

Unmasking the Shadows: The Art of Detection

The concept and threats associated with digital misinformation and disinformation are not new and have represented a growing challenge in the field of communications for decades.[1] Over the last five years, however, the evolution of digital and social media platforms combined with some truly stunning advances in *generative artificial intelligence* have amplified the speed and scale of these threats significantly.[2] Navigating this challenging landscape has become even more convoluted with the addition of generative AI and the concepts of fully and partially synthetic media added to the mix.

The terms misinformation and disinformation are generally well established, with *misinformation* referring to the spread or dissemination of inaccurate or misleading information, often unintentionally shared without malicious intent.[3] On the other hand, *disinformation* involves the deliberate creation and distribution of false or misleading content with the intent to deceive or manipulate public opinion.[4] The concept of synthetic media produced using generative AI, however, is a more fluid one requiring further refinement, particularly when set against the complexity of an algorithm-driven digital information landscape.

One critical clarification involves the tendency to refer to content created using generative AI models such as stable diffusion generators or large language models (LLMs) as "fake." However, in the same way that important distinctions are made by communication scholars between misinformation and disinformation, it is important to clarify the distinction between synthetic media and human-generated content. *Synthetic media* refers to media content, including images, videos, audio, or text, that is generated using artificial intelligence (AI) and machine learning (ML) algorithms versus content created by human authors. In both cases, the digital media created (synthetic or human) can be factual and accurate information – or completely fabricated content with either malicious or benign intent. For this reason, it is important to separate the method in which content is generated from its likelihood to contain malicious disinformation.[5]

Analysis of the Data

As human analysts, to detect misinformation and disinformation effectively, we must first understand the nature of the different formats through which it is delivered. For this purpose, digital content can be divided into four basic component types: text, images, audio, and video. Initial parsing of content through this lens provides a critical first step in understanding and analyzing a piece of media for potential misinformation and disinformation. Rendering a piece of content into its base components offers an opportunity to analyze and detect the patterns and inconsistencies that serve as key indicators for misinformation more effectively. Both generative AI models and their corresponding digital detection algorithms are typically designed to function within one of these four basic media types. When pressed to perform beyond their core domain, the performance of both generators and detectors rapidly degrades to the point of futility. These limitations are important to consider, particularly when considering detection analytics and their ability to perform assessments on a piece of content and determine if it is authentic, manipulated or synthetically generated.

Each media type brings its own strengths and weaknesses to the effectiveness of a piece of content. Misinformation campaigns often exploit these differences by combining multiple media types in strategic ways, carefully balancing factors like intent, cost, impact, technical capabilities, and target audience vulnerabilities. Understanding the distinct characteristics of each medium can better illuminate how they are leveraged for both positive and malicious purposes. Examining this dynamic with two fundamental media types – text and images – demonstrates their specific advantages and limitations in conveying information and influencing audiences.[6]

Text

- High instructional clarity (the ability to tell people exactly what you want them to think or do).
- Low barrier to create, disseminate, and consume at scale.
- Low information density.
- High cognitive load on the audience makes short content most impactful (headline, caption, call to action statement).
- High reliance on source credibility also requires source misattribution as a key part of attacks.

Images

- High content medium allowing for rapid, information-rich delivery.
- The visual nature of the medium reinforces validity and reduces the need for source credibility.
- High audience impact factor (emotional, memorable, believable).
- Low barrier to create, disseminate, and consume at scale.
- Subject to interpretation without directed context.

The most impactful misinformation and disinformation campaigns use combinations of these two modalities to leverage the validity and high impact created by photorealistic images and the messaging clarity of short text components.[7] The low level of sophistication required to create this type of content, combined with the ease of rapid distribution on social media channels, makes this approach ideal for large-scale disinformation campaigns. In these instances, malicious actors often rely on simple high volume/low conversion approaches (flooding) to create damaging narratives rather than developing more advanced socially engineered or tailored attacks on a target audience.[8] One of the most common examples of this approach is recontextualization, whereby unrelated images are used out of

Le Matin du Monde
@dumonde

Catholics of France please join us this
morning in a moment of prayer asking
our father for peace across Europe.

05:06 AM · Sep 27, 2023 · Twitter for iPhone

745   12.3K   23.7K   127.6K

FIGURE 14.1   Disclaimer: The images in this figure were generated in our research lab using an open-source stable diffusion generator model; the social media post example was created using a fake tweet generator (https://codebeautify.org/fake-tweet-generator#) and all information in it is completely fabricated and was not distributed on any platform

context to reinforce simple narratives involving classic propaganda techniques such as discrediting of an entity or a call to action. However, the rise of generative AI has amplified this tactic by allowing for the creation of virtually any images an attacker may desire in support of a specific disinformation narrative. Figure 14.1 demonstrates the increased impact created when these two modalities are combined to drive home – in this case – a relatively benign call to action narrative.

Audio

- Leverages voice recognition to create inherent credibility.
- Creates a strongly targeted impact on an individual's brand through direct narrative misattribution.
- Temporally flexible and can be used to convey past or real-time narratives (simulating fake "hot mic" examples or previously recorded covert conversations).
- Significantly higher level of sophistication and effort required to create this type of content

Video

- High information density.
- High level of inherent credibility associated with this media type.

- Requires the highest level of time, effort, and sophistication to create or manipulate this type of content with realism.

Deepfakes are a type of synthetic media that uses artificial intelligence (AI) and ML algorithms to create realistic, manipulated, or fabricated audio, video, or image content that appears authentic. This type of manipulated content is typically created by swapping faces, voices, or other elements between different media sources.[9] Deepfakes offer another example demonstrating how separate media types are most effective when created or manipulated and combined into the now ubiquitous concept of *deepfakes*.[10] While this technique is not new, the barriers to creating compelling content of this type are rapidly falling with the injection of generative AI capabilities into the process. What was once deemed the most sophisticated type of disinformation, requiring nation-state or production studio–level capabilities, has now become widely accessible to the public. Through AI-enabled applications, even basic content creation skill sets are now sufficient to produce surprisingly convincing content, and analysts must look carefully at the seams between modalities for human-detectable inconsistencies. For example, pairing audio with lip movements is still challenging to achieve over longer sequences, along with speaker cadence, pitch, and emotion. While this type of high-quality fake content is becoming more common, knowing where to look for inconsistencies still offers human analysts some line of defense (Table 14.1).

The rates, channels, and patterns associated with the dissemination of misinformation and disinformation can also offer some valuable insights and enable the early identification of malicious disinformation networks and influential actors.[11] The sheer numerical complexity of digital media propagation networks

TABLE 14.1 Misinformation Content Strengths and Weaknesses by Media Type

Characteristics	Text	Images	Audio	Video
Information density	Low	High	Low	High
Technical skill	Low	Low	High	High
Credibility	Low	High	High	High
Strengths	High instructional clarity	High impact, emotional, memorable	Voice attribution, temporally flexible	High impact, emotional, memorable
Weaknesses	High cognitive processing load requires short content	Contextually subjective	Moderately resource-intensive	Time- and resource-intensive

requires significant computational methods and capabilities, combined with a deep understanding of the data science associated with real-time data streams.[12] The nature of this inherent complexity often places it more within the fields of computer and data science than the domain of public relations professionals. It is helpful, however, to touch on some of the key underlying drivers that provide the fundamental impetus behind the propagation of disinformation and fake news.

Perhaps unsurprisingly, widespread dissemination of misinformation and disinformation is underpinned by a reward system driven by behavioral advertising models with valuation premiums directly tied to volumes of attention.[13] This underlying digital monetization structure represents the fulcrum that sets up a heavily skewed balance favoring the creation of immediate sensationalized content designed to capture eyeballs and clicks over accurate and verifiable content. The balance between these two value propositions is in continual tension throughout the digital media landscape. Though economically driven at their root, it places potentially unbalanced decisions and their consequences squarely in the domain of public relations professionals charged with proactively protecting the value of a brand or trying to mitigate the damage of disinformation attacks or internal missteps.

Human Analysis in Misinformation Detection: Unraveling the Source Tapestry

While the breathtaking evolution of generative AI has created the potential for significant new challenges, human capabilities still play a crucial role in the detection of misinformation and disinformation through a combination of methods that leverage their cognitive abilities, contextual understanding, and semantic investigation skills. One fundamental approach that leverages many of these human-centered capabilities is source verification. The underpinning of this critical validation process involves extended scrutiny beyond the content itself to look at the credibility and reputation of the entities disseminating information.[14] This method is foundational to the analyst's toolkit, providing a reliable compass to navigate the tumultuous sea of digital information.

Source Verification

To verify the authenticity of information, understanding its origin and providence is critical. Tracing information back to its source, particularly through a maze of social media propagation channels, can be challenging, but this determination is a vital first step in assessing an information source's authenticity and credibility. At the core of source verification is the evaluation of the trustworthiness of information and its origins, and low source transparency can be a strong indicator that information authenticity has been compromised.[15] However, even information appearing to come directly from its source should be assessed for credibility by examining its record, historical accuracy, longevity, and adherence to journalistic standards.

Source verification can be a time-consuming and even overwhelming concept to think about when stacked against the sheer volume of digital content the average user must parse every day. One approach to make this process more manageable is the curation of a stable list of reliable sources that cover key elements of an organization's information ecosystem. Once this curated list of trusted sources is established, it can be used to confirm the validity of information more quickly. The value of these validated and trusted sources will continue to rise as public access to generative AI tools continues to lower the barriers to both malicious and benign digital content creation. Organizations and individuals that establish a highly transparent set of sharable standards for how and where they get the information they provide will be well positioned in this rapidly evolving landscape whereby premiums on digital trust continue to rise.

Cross-Referencing Information

To bolster the verification process, analysts cross-reference information across multiple sources. Consistency among various reputable sources lends greater credibility to the information, while discrepancies raise flags for closer scrutiny. The following bulleted items are common approaches to cross-referencing.

* *Identifying biases and agendas:* When analyzing content, it is important to identify potential bias in the source, as well as internal biases. Understanding the motivations behind information dissemination aids in gauging the reliability of the provided content. The presence of biases or hidden agendas can significantly compromise the impartiality of a source, while internal biases can create heightened vulnerability to bias aligned misinformation narratives. When cross-referencing and fact-checking, it is important to take a disciplined approach that seeks information rather than affirmation. This can be achieved by deliberately structuring cross-referencing channels that span polarizing segments such as political, economic, or social agendas.
* *Audience analysis:* Consideration is given to the intended target audience of a source. Understanding who the information caters to can provide insights into potential biases, helping to assess a source's objectivity and content consistency more accurately. This can also offer valuable insights later when designing message framing for counter-narratives.

Fact-Checking

Fact-checking involves systematically verifying claims and statements against established facts.[16] Analysts consult reputable fact-checking organizations or databases to validate or debunk information; however, the time lag between the appearance of disinformation and the availability of fact-checking information can limit its utility for time-sensitive information such as breaking news.[17] As the importance of fact-checking continues to rise, a number of AI-driven automated fact-checking systems have been developed. These systems can be generally divided into explainable and non-explainable approach types, with explainable approaches using more reference-based systems that focus on verifying input claims based on trusted sources and databases. Non-explainable approaches rely on more complex models that apply content analysis or propagation data patterns to make assessments. Both automated approaches offer assistance to human fact-checkers, but the effectives is often limited by the complexity of context surrounding many claims. For example, these systems are well suited to fact-checking explicit claims such as "a 7% increase in murder rates from 2017–2020 in a specific city" but lack the capabilities to address more general claims like "offshore wind turbines are causing whales to beach themselves." Although several real-world systems have been developed, the ambiguous nature of many of the claims commonly used in disinformation campaigns still require human-in-the-loop decision-making and verification.[18]

Metadata Examination

Metadata – including information about the creation and modification of files – offers valuable insights into the origin and authenticity of digital media. Inspection of metadata for discrepancies in timestamps, digital watermarks, exchangeable image file format (EXIF) data, geolocations, or other software and device information can quickly reveal potential manipulations. Genuine content typically bears consistent and unaltered metadata. Unfortunately, the fundamental mechanisms used to move content into and across social media platforms can modify or launder out many types of metadata and digital watermarks. This can significantly compromise the metadata associated with a piece of content, depending on the platform and the number of times it has been uploaded, downloaded, zipped, attached, imported into editing software, or reposted using common content-sharing methods such as screen capture or derivative images. Despite these caveats, the availability of metadata can be a powerful tool for detecting disinformation, and many highly effective digital detection tools utilize this approach.[19] However, in the absence of high-fidelity metadata, these same tools quickly become ineffective, and it is important to understand at a basic level how and when a detection tool operates in this capacity before relying on it fully.

In the evolving and expanding landscape of digital misinformation, human analysis can still combine technical expertise with a critical eye to uncover signs of deception. By routinely employing healthy skepticism and these fundamental best practices, it is still possible to play an active role in safeguarding the integrity of information authenticity over deception.

Help Is on the Way: Digital Approaches to Detecting Misinformation and Disinformation

In the same way that generative AI tools are typically limited to functionality within one of the four media types, so too are the digital detection tools being developed. Thus, any robust approach to digital detection requires not one super analytic but rather a suite of digital tools that cover each of the different media types as needed. The rate at which this technology landscape continues to evolve is still too fragmented to identify clear winners and losers reliably. However, a variety of successful detection approaches have begun to emerge for each media type, along with improvements in reliability and algorithmic robustness.

Text Detection

Text detectors employ various strategies to identify anomalies in the language, coherence, and meaning that characterize artificially generated or manipulated content. It is important to note that these types of detectors are not designed to be fact-checking solutions but rather typically operate based on one of three discrete approaches: detections, attribution, or characterization (DAC). At the simplest level, detection-focused digital tools attempt to provide binary decision information based on the analytics training data (i.e. if this text is synthetically generated or not). Digital tools designed for the attribution level typically attempt to provide source-related information (i.e., if it is coming from the author or organization it is purporting to be from, or not), or in the case of synthetic text, attribution analytics may be able to determine if a specific LLM was used to create the text, or not. Both the detection and attribution approaches may also leverage metadata analysis to examine timestamps, authorship, and publication platform information to help make determinations, as synthetic or manipulated text can lack historical context or exhibit unusual metadata patterns. Additionally, pattern recognition algorithms may discern repetitive structures or recurring features indicative of automated text generation. Finally, characterization tasks represent the most challenging AI/ML approach, and attempts to address the nature of the content patterns within a piece of text to make determinations based on an algorithm's specific training data. This type of analysis generally requires massive pretrained models that can leverage extremely large quantities of training data such as those used by OpenAI's GPT4 or Google Bard. These models can analyze text and make reliable characterization assessments related to the presence of a variety of content features, such as common propaganda techniques or maliciously directed attack language.

Generally, detection and attribution analytics attempt to make their determinations by analyzing patterns and identifying deviations from natural language.[20] This type of statistical analysis involves scrutinizing word frequency, sentence structure, and syntactic patterns, looking for disparities from typical statistical norms. More contextual understanding considers anomalies in relevance, inconsistencies, or logical flow, revealing signs of synthetic text or the presence/absence of specific styles or tactics. As a result, these analytics are very sensitive to the length of text provided for analysis and considerable performance degradation has been observed with text below 2,000 characters (~300 words) in length.[21] Combinations of DAC approaches can help enhance the accuracy and robustness of digital text detection tools, but it is very early in the development cycle for these technologies and it is important to recognize current limitations, both in terms of capability and reliability.

Image Detection

Similar to text detection tools, synthetic and manipulated image detectors employ a variety of approaches to determine if an image has been synthetically generated or modified using common image manipulation techniques such as paste slice, inpainting, faceswaps, or aging filters.[22] While some of these techniques can be visually confirmed by human analysts, most operate by looking for artifacts and deviations requiring pixel-level analysis. By scrutinizing images at the pixel level, analytics seek out the irregularities or repetitive noise patterns that can present in synthetic images and serve as digital fingerprints invisible to the human eye.[23] Deviations in metadata structures such as timestamps, geolocation, and camera information are also commonly integrated into image analytics, with discrepancies or inconsistencies signaling potential synthetic or manipulated content. More recently, advanced deep learning models have been developed that leverage training on extensive datasets encompassing both real and synthetic images.[24] Through sheer volumes of training data, these models leverage learned features to distinguish between the visual patterns associated with authentic and synthetic content. Often referred to as *black box models*, these models are often so complex that the mechanisms by which they perform their detections are unknown even to the model developers.[25]

Turning to more human-readable approaches, visual features such as texture, edge, and lighting inconsistencies represent high-value detection targets, as synthetic images can struggle to replicate realistic variations of these features. Detectors and human analysts can both scrutinize these aspects, identifying deviations from the natural nuances found in genuine photographs. While certain image features remain particularly challenging for synthetic image generators to reliably produce, these visual tells are rapidly diminishing with each new model training cycle. However, certain recurring inconsistencies remain such as text-based elements (signs, name tags, or Tshirt logos) and complex fine detail elements such as human hands and fingers. Similarly, complex scenes with groups of people in them often contain visual artifacts in the faces of background individuals that can be readily identified with a close visual inspection and provide additional human readable evidence that an image is synthetically generated.

Synthetic Audio Detection

Recent advances in the production of synthetic audio using generative AI models have resulted in a significant increase in both the quantity and quality of disinformation attacks incorporating this modality. Previously, the domain of technically sophisticated cybercriminals and nation-states, the ability to create nearly flawless voice clones of an individual with an audio sample of 30 seconds or less has catapulted this form of disinformation into a mainstream threat vector. Fortunately, highly effective synthetic audio detection tools capable of combating this emerging threat have also been developed using a variety of analytic approaches.[26] The primary technique involves the use of spectral analysis, which examines the frequency content of the audio signal. The synthetic audio contains distinctive spectral patterns created during the generation process which can be identified by detectors and used to differentiate synthetic audio samples from authentic voice recordings. In a similar but distinct approach, waveform analysis can be used to examine the shape and structure of the audio signal and compare it to those of genuine audio samples. This type of analytic is particularly effective at identifying and localizing artifacts introduced during the generation of synthetic audio and has proven to be effective as a general method for detection, while for particularly high-value targets or persons of interest (POIs), specific voice biometric models can be trained to detect characteristic anomalies unique to an individual speaker's voice.

Video Detection

Although the ability to create fully synthetic video using generative AI is not yet as advanced as the other modalities, it is progressing rapidly. Recently, applications allowing for the direct conversion of an individual's still images into fully animated video clips demonstrate just how quickly the technology is approaching mainstream access and adoption. While detecting manipulated videos, particularly deepfakes, now demands more careful scrutiny, several important tactics can still aid in assessing the authenticity of a video.[27] The most common and reliable approach targets the presence of inconsistencies in facial expressions and synchronization of lip movements with audio. Identifying unnatural movements in facial features that do not align with spoken words remains one of the most common and detectable artifacts associated with deepfake manipulations.[28] Other common indicators include unnatural eye movements and the absence of realistic gaze changes often caused by a deepfake algorithm's inability to replicate complex natural eye behavior. As discussed earlier in this section, analyzing discrepancies between modalities (in this case audio and visual elements), such as mismatches in lip movements and spoken words, also provides crucial cues for potential manipulation. The scene surrounding the speaker is often overlooked but also contains valuable information that can help determine a video's authenticity. Many deepfake algorithms encounter challenges in replicating realistic backgrounds, leading to inconsistencies or blurriness. In fact, the most common style of deepfake video remains the basic "talking head" type of video containing a single speaker and a static background. Lighting and shadow inconsistencies on the subject's face can also indicate manipulation, particularly during head motion. Beyond visual analysis, reverse video searching to verify the source and context of the video is a fundamental step, with authentic videos more likely to originate from reputable sources. In addition to reverse video searching, performing a reverse image search on individual frames of a video is another effective strategy, helping identify instances when the content has been previously flagged or labeled as manipulated content.[29] Reverse searching strategies can be particularly effective with deepfake content, as this type of disinformation often leverages existing images or videos, making them more readily traceable through reverse search methods.

Deconstructing Deceit: The Power of Debunking

Evidence-based *debunking* in communication theory involves strategically dispelling misinformation or false beliefs by presenting credible evidence and factual information. In the face of misinformation, public relations professionals utilizing evidence-based debunking deploy verifiable data to refute inaccuracies and set the record straight in service to the brand. This method hinges on the timely provision of robust evidence, thorough research, and simple, strategically framed messaging. Before an effective debunking strategy can be developed, however, it is important to first understand the nature of the beast.

Identification of misinformation often requires the conscious deconstruction of its formulaic but highly effective elements. Emotional appeal and a sense of urgency are an almost universal element in any disinformation campaign. Whether designed to strategically tug at heartstrings or create a sense of fear and vulnerability, content designed to evoke strong emotional responses is one of the first markers of potential misinformation. This type of emotionally charged content supports two highly desirable outcomes for any disinformation campaign. It is highly memorable and highly shareable, contributing to both its stickiness at the individual level and its rapid dissemination across digital platforms. Sensationalism, characterized by exaggerated or attention-grabbing narratives, is another cornerstone of misinformation and is designed to ensure maximal capture of audience attention. This formulaic sensationalism emerges quantifiably when researchers perform analysis across large datasets and find that statistically fake news contains longer titles, fewer technical terms and significantly high numbers of adjectives and adverbs.[30] Audience targeting through social engineering may also be used to align with individuals' confirmation bias by reinforcing pre-existing beliefs or biases. This well-established tactic leverages human cognitive behaviors making it more likely for individuals to accept and propagate content that resonates with their worldview.[31]

Structurally, the design and nature of social media platforms also amplifies the impact of misinformation, providing fertile ground for its rapid spread through likes, shares, and reposts. Simultaneously, the inherently low priority these platforms place on source verification creates additional burden on human analysis methods such as fact-checking and source verification. This additional burden can further delay detection and the development of effective counter-narratives while allowing the continued dissemination of inaccurate content. The multi-modal nature of these platforms also allows for combinations of the highest impact content to be delivered readily, ranging from synthetic and manipulated text and images to persuasive audio and video feeds. Regardless of delivery platform, awareness and identification of these recurring elements represents a critical first step in navigating the complex landscape of misinformation and allows practitioners to transition mindsets more effectively from prey to hunter.

Crafting Effective Counter-Narratives Using Evidence-Based Debunking

After identifying misinformation, the next critical step is to refute it convincingly. To achieve this requires an examination of the inner workings of deceptive narratives and an understanding of the psychological manipulation techniques and communication strategies used to deceive audiences. With a focus on systemic vulnerabilities and evidence-based debunking, it becomes possible to explore the development of compelling counter-narratives and strategies to effectively communicate and defend the truth. Case studies and real-world examples illustrate effective debunking strategies in restoring accuracy and credibility.

Mind the Gap

Speed of response is a critical component to creating effective counter-narratives, particularly when uncertainty or ambiguous situations emerge in the absence of factual and readily accessible information. During these informational gaps, consumers tend to share rumors more readily in an attempt to fill this gap and create stability and control over uncertain situations.[32] Left unaddressed, this informational gap can initiate a powerful misinformation cascade, as repeated exposure can enhance a message's potency through familiarity effects.[33] This concept of misinformation stickiness has been well documented in many studies and can continue to exert secondary influences on behaviors even after effective debunking efforts.[34] This continued influence effect (CIE) operates under the concept that misinformation is not replaced by factual corrections but instead goes into competition with these new sources of information.[35] This approach is also consistent with the concept that retraction of misinformation is insufficient on its own, as the CIE effect suggests that the creation of this informational gap does not create the required competitive narrative. This theory instead suggests that to achieve effective debunking results, at a minimum, tactics such as repetitive exposure and the provision of multiple evidence-based counter-narratives are required.[36] The content of the rebuttal is also critical to effectively crafting counter-narratives to misinformation. However, the decision on how best to approach the substance of rebuttal messaging can be nonlinear and should consider multiple factors in addition to the speed of the response. As with simple removal of misinformation, generic flagging of misinformation as false does little in and of itself to reduce believability.[37] To maximize debunking efficacy, further tuning and refinement of two additional factors should be considered when crafting a counter-narrative: message framing and messaging form.

Research by Nyhan and Reifler suggests that narratives framed in ways that are inconsistent with an audience's world viewpoint can elicit backfire responses and lead to entrenchment behaviors and even stronger connections to misinformation.[38] To avoid this outcome, when audience segmentation information is available, it may be advantageous to tune critical language to align with an audience demographic worldview. This message tuning can avoid confirmation bias–driven reductions in messaging impact. Where alignment may not be possible, minimizing counter-view language may still reduce messaging rejection and entrenchment among certain audiences.

In some cases, it may be more efficient to utilize alternate approaches rather than focusing on countering a piece of misinformation. In such cases when countering misinformation offers diminishing returns, more direct behavioral interventions that focus on designing choice architectures that favor desired outcomes can be more productive. This tactic is described by behavioral economists as "nudging," and it allows consumers to make certain choices without eliminating their ability to make a free choice.[39] These behavioral intervention approaches have the advantage of creating a forced choice that automatically reaches any person making the decision in question on a decidedly tilted playing field. For example, the decision to accept website cookies just prior to accessing desired content might be considered a more productive approach than attempting to counter deeply entrenched misinformation narratives around data and information privacy. Other examples, such as modifying registration strategies from an opt-in decision to an opt-out decision, can be a far more effective approach with segments that have been casually exposed to misinformation but are not deeply and ideologically opposed to a behavioral outcome. In another example, Johnson & Goldstein looked at organ donation rates in countries that required an opt-in strategy and found their willingness to donate was in the range of 15–20%, while in countries where people must opt out, rates were typically over 90%.[40]

BOX 14.1 CRAFTING EFFECTIVE COUNTER-NARRATIVES

Messaging style can span the range from quantitative information to emotional storytelling, and crafting an effective counter-narrative may require developing multiple versions that fall along this spectrum. However, to be effective these versions should contain several consistent elements delivered in a debunking sandwich.[41]

Evidence: Simple and clearly stated core facts using headlines and graphic captions where possible. Avoid complex or technical language.
Visualization: Use visualizations such as graphics, fonts, and colors to reinforce and emphasize core evidence.
Damage control: When referencing misinformation is required, provide a clear warning messaging prior to presenting the misinformation followed by an alternative rational or motivation for why the misinformation is inaccurate and why misinformers may be incentivized to promote this false narrative. Using neutral language rather than strongly negative emotional language may also help minimize any emotional connections to the misinformation in the audience.
Restate and reinforce: Restate and reinforce the core facts as the final piece of information processed.

Work with a partner to define a potential misinformation narrative threat that could be highly damaging to an organizational brand of your choosing. Using this narrative, create a debunking sandwich and discuss effective rapid deployment strategies using various communication channels and any modifications that would be required across different channels.

New Tools, Same Old Humans

The integration of AI into debunking processes is still evolving as an emerging field of research. As digital detection capabilities continue to improve, the opportunity to leverage valuable efficiencies associated with AI appears promising. Two of the most important value propositions associated with AI systems are the ability to deliver speed and capacity.[42] As was discussed previously, the timely response to misinformation narratives is one of the critical components to mitigating its spread and stickiness. Automated real-time detection systems offer the opportunity to continuously monitor data streams and filter, flag, and elevate content of concern. As volumes of misinformation continue to rise, the development and integration of these tools will become a critical part of the debunking process. Despite the incredible speed at which these technologies are advancing (both in terms of misinformation creation and detection), the cognitive behavior of the humans that consume it remains more static. It is important to apply the same evidence-based debunking principles to any automated solutions an organization may be considering.

For example, automated removal and generic flagging of information as false remain relatively ineffective as a debunking strategy, regardless of whether it is done by human operators or AI systems.[43] The ability to incorporate additional evidence-based functionality remains a critical component, and the concept of explainable AI has become an area of intense research.[44] As this area of research continues to evolve, it deserves careful monitoring – as well as careful scrutiny, despite the allure of a single elegant technical solution.

Strategies for Combat: Navigating the Misinformation Battlefield

Pivoting from reactive techniques designed to counter damaging misinformation represents an important shift in mindset and strategy. The growing pervasiveness of misinformation presents a substantial and ever-present risk that can and should be planned for. Creating a more proactive PR strategy requires a combination of scenario modeling, real-time monitoring, staged rapid response materials, and sustained proactive measures designed to help inoculate key audiences using media literacy campaigns, tailored prebunking tactics, and a stable of external social media supporters.

When developing an organizational strategy with finite resources, it is important to focus on the largest threat vectors first. In 2021, over 800 million tweets were being posted per day, and over 10 billion TikTok videos were being watched per hour.[45] When it comes to speed and scale, the largest threat vector for misinformation lies squarely in the algorithm-driven landscape of social media platforms. While the underlying algorithms that drive propagation rates across these platforms lie under a heavy veil of proprietary protections and competitive advantage, dissemination at scale can be achieved through a combination of three basic factors: account number, quantity of content, and engagement levels with a piece of content.[46]

If we consider these underlying factors and their alignment with the growing capabilities of generative AI, the potential for a synthetic wave of misinformation becomes significantly elevated. Already, these capabilities can be used to create thousands of tailored synthetic personas and profiles in a matter of hours with simple gaming-level computational capabilities feeding the *number of accounts*. The same capabilities allow for the creation of massive amounts of unique content that can provide a consistent narrative and create the illusion of consensus while satisfying *quantity of content* criteria.[47] Finally, combinations and versioning of tailored content designed to align with an audience's world views[48] and create the strong emotional responses most likely to drive engagement[49] optimize the final key metric of *user engagement* (comments, likes, shares, views etc.). As with content flagging and retraction policies, direct access to these algorithmic levers is typically out of an organization's control (beyond the platforms themselves). Despite this, leveraging an understanding of these fundamental mechanisms can be critical in developing effective monitoring, response, and deployment strategies, given the potential impact of AI-driven content creation.

Locked and Loaded

If social media channels can be identified as the most significant threat vector for damaging organizational misinformation, then prioritizing tactics directed toward this communication landscape remains practical. In this way, many of the strategies associated with social media crisis communication (SMCC) theory[50] remain relevant but may require some adaptation in light of the injection of generative AI into the misinformation landscape.[51]

The SMCC model, which examines information adoption and flow between connected media, audiences, and organizations, can be applied to disinformation attacks using the same general emphasis on crisis, type, origin, organizational infrastructure, message form, and strategy.[52] To effectively execute this approach, organizations must create, maintain, and resource misinformation response infrastructure armed with rapidly tunable and deployable counter-narratives. Achieving this readiness state requires a commitment to threat scenario planning, real-time detection and monitoring efforts, corrective content creation, deployment of prebunking and general media literacy inoculation initiatives, and the development of a stable of credible third-party supporters/influencers ready to amplify an organization's messaging.[53]

Anticipate the Calm Before the News Cycle Storm

Generative AI has enabled a new misinformation threat type by creating the ability to easily insert realistic visual misinformation into highly anticipated public knowledge gaps. Examples of this type of narrative capture have emerged, with numerous prominent examples reaching mainstream awareness following the viral propagation of the synthetically generated Donald Trump arrest images in New York or the synthetically generated images of Russian President Vladimir Putin kneeling and kissing the ring of President Xi just prior to the much-anticipated Chinese president's visit to Moscow in March 2023. This type of "precontextualization" can be directed at any highly anticipated upcoming event from corporate earnings calendars to election cycle events to visits by world leaders or high-profile entertainers. Prior to the mainstream arrival of generative AI capabilities, similar attacks could be constructed using recontextualized images or carefully photoshopped manipulations, but these labor-intensive approaches often lacked the real-time and specific situational details that synthetically generated images can produce in seconds.

While both generative AI and social media platforms have attempted to limit these types of high-profile targets and viral events, their initial success has been limited at best. The recent viral propagation of unsanctioned synthetically generated explicit images of Taylor Swift on X in January of 2024 demonstrates how even clearly damaging synthetically generated content of high-profile POIs can still be created (despite attempts at ethical generator guardrails) and social media platform attempts to detect and limit such content. What is yet unclear is the damage these types of attacks may cause to not only the brands of the targeted individual or organization but also to the software developers and social media platforms associated with an attack. While vulnerabilities through software and platforms remain generally high, they can be further amplified by additional public attention in anticipation of upcoming events. Maintaining a calendar of strategic events tracking these potentially high-threat windows of increased vulnerability may be a valuable addition to an organization's threat playbook.

Human–Machine Collaborative Monitoring

As the sheer volume of misinformation enabled by generative AI content continues to rise, the ability of humans to manage information stream monitoring manually becomes impractical. To address this rising tide, ML algorithms designed to monitor and moderate content have been developed with varying degrees of success.[54] While automated algorithmic detection, attribution, and characterization methods continue to advance at various rates for each of the media types, reliable detection systems have currently yet to be developed. The challenges associated with development of automated solutions is further exacerbated by the continued advances in AI generation capabilities resulting in a technology arms race that leaves detection solutions continually playing catch-up. To enhance monitoring effectiveness, a combination of automated and human review that leverages the relative strengths of each may represent the most viable strategy. In this integrated dynamic, researchers have explored human–AI collaboration and proposed leveraging models to delegate decision-making based on prediction certainty.[55] This approach allows models to address the massive volumes of content, filter and flag potentially harmful content, and handle straightforward cases while involving humans in more complex situations, along with recommendations accompanied by the provision of explainable evidence.

Corrective Flagging, Retraction, and Debunking

Flagging with a disclaimer allows users to view content, but significant unresolved controversy still exists in the literature surrounding the ethics, efficacy, and approach to systems for flagging and removal.[56] Given that mandates to regulate these processes typically lie exclusively within the authority of global governments and platform policymakers, most organizations are limited in understanding the most effective way to navigate and initiate requests for timely content flagging and removal. Instead, efforts associated with rapid corrective communication through evidence-based debunking are more directly in an organization's control and may offer a more productive opportunity to intercept and minimize damaging misinformation narratives.[57] Having these counter-narratives ready and tailored for ease of distribution across different platform channels allows for third-party influencers to boost an organization's debunking efforts.[58]

Inoculation Through Prebunking and Media Literacy

Combined with more general media literacy efforts, *prebunking* specific narratives has demonstrated effectiveness even against well-established misinformation narratives and worldview contradictions.[59] Recent research suggests that applying general warnings about the misinformation forms and tactics people may encounter can provide an initial layer of inoculation protection, followed by a second element of tailored material containing more topic-specific prebunking messages. For example, research by van der Linden and Leiserowitz demonstrated that inoculation against an established climate disinformation campaign could be achieved by providing people with a simple warning message.[60] In this case, politically motivated groups use misleading tactics to try to convince the public that there is significant disagreement among scientists or a second, more detailed communication containing the general warning accompanied by traditional evidence-based prebunking messaging.

In both cases, meaningful levels of resistance to the disinformation were generated in the audiences, with the full messaging providing greater protection. More encouragingly, these protective efficacy patterns were conserved regardless of the person's prior attitude toward the topic (climate change) being measured as negative, positive, or neutral. This demonstrates the value of deploying effective inoculation strategies even when the topic is well established in the mainstream media, highly politicized, and polarizing.[61] This research suggests that even general inoculation warning messaging can be an effective strategy that can be deployed prior to the emergence of a fully materialized disinformation campaign. This approach can be combined with an organization's use of threat modeling and scenario planning to move significantly upstream in the misinformation communication flow proactively.

Amplify Through Online Presence and Relevant Influencers

With a focus on social media channels as the dominant AI-driven threat vector for misinformation, a comprehensive response plan should include leveraging similar social media amplification mechanisms in threat response. In addition to traditional disinformation management, establishing the support of influential non-malicious creators provides value in two important ways: their support increases the credibility of an organization's response and provides additional messaging amplification mechanisms.[62] The competition for influential non-malicious voices can be pivotal in influencing how information is perceived and disseminated. Developing and strengthening engagement with influencers that align with organizational content can effectively create additional trusted sources across diverse platforms. To support this diverse stable of third-party content creators, an organization must develop readily sharable, platform-specific content with strong engagement components. This basic formula facilitates a win-win scenario by feeding the common underlying algorithmic drivers of social media platforms and creating value for the influencers while stimulating the propagation mechanisms that amplify the organizational messaging.

For example, create simple, visually engaging content of the appropriate media type (i.e., effective content design will differ for text-driven platforms such as Reddit, audio-driven podcasts, or more image and video-centered platforms like Instagram and TikTok). Additionally, employ common platform-relevant engagement strategies (i.e., directed questions or request for opinion to drive comment engagement coupled with language designed to drive likes, shares, and views). Once established, empowering this network of third-party influencers with additional digital literacy and inoculation content can also help strengthen and validate this important external reinforcement mechanism.[63]

The injection of AI into the misinformation landscape has dramatically amplified the threat of speed and scale, while simultaneously complicating detection efforts through the addition of both malicious and benign synthetic content. The current technical arms race between generative AI's ability to both create and detect flawless content continues to advance with no resolution in sight. As the complexity of these capabilities improves, the ability to create synthetic content that is indistinguishable from human-generated content seems inevitable. For communication practitioners, this may mean that digital tools capable of identifying and addressing damaging misinformation through simple detection and retraction are not realistic. Instead, a more integrated approach is required whereby rapid detection remains an important part of digital tool development to combat misinformation and disinformation but is insufficient in and of itself.[64] Instead, a more comprehensive approach is required that includes detection (is it synthetic or human generated?), attribution (is it coming from the source it says it is coming from?) and characterization (is it malicious or benign, what is the intent, and who is the target audience?). These two additional layers represent progressively more challenging tasks for AI/ML-driven tools, so it is not surprising that simple binary detection strategies that focus primarily on leveraging statistical differences in non-human readable metadata, pixel-level artifacts, or token prediction remain the current focus of many emerging tools.

These limitations set the stage for integrated solutions that require collaborative interaction between digital systems and human communication professionals. The complexity of this task grows even higher when considering the need for a human-in-the-loop decisions requiring interpretable evidence capable of supporting effective countermeasures regardless of whether they originate from AI/ML-driven recommendations or human decision-makers. These limitations set the stage for integrated solutions that require collaborative interaction between digital systems and human communication professionals. If this is the case, short of the global throttling of the development of generative AI capabilities, the co-development of AI/ML-driven digital transparency safeguards and human explainable evidence frameworks becomes critical.[65] To have the best chance at diminishing the societal impact of digital disinformation in an age of generative AI approaches, human decision-making must move past simple detection and target more holistic solutions.

BOX 14.2 ETHICS IN AI-DRIVEN DEBUNKING

Ethics plays a critical role in AI and debunking misinformation and disinformation, as it guides the design and implementation of AI tools and algorithms that prioritize accuracy, transparency, and fairness in combating false narratives and promoting informed decision-making. Consider the changing role of human decision-makers with the incorporation of AI-driven debunking tools across the spectrum of human only, hybrid human–AI teaming, and fully AI-driven systems. Think critically about the ethical challenges of each model with a partner and share key strengths, weaknesses, and ethical concerns you identify the larger group.

Conclusion

The battle against misinformation and disinformation requires a multi-faceted approach that combines cutting-edge detection tools, evidence-based debunking strategies, and proactive communication tactics. By mastering the art of detection, deconstructing deceitful narratives, and navigating the complex landscape of misinformation, public relations professionals can better protect their organizations' reputations, maintain transparency with stakeholders, and contribute to a more informed and resilient public discourse. As we move forward in this digital era, it is crucial that communications professionals remain vigilant and adapt to the evolving tactics of misinformation agents. By doing so, we can ensure that truth and accuracy prevail, even in the face of increasingly sophisticated falsehoods.

Reflections

1. Which of the four media types (text, images, audio, and video) currently represents the most significant misinformation threat to your key stakeholders? Through which platforms?
2. Have you attempted to integrate human–machine collaborative AI approaches into your communication strategy for monitoring and detecting misinformation, and do you understand their strengths and limitations?
3. How quickly can you respond to misinformation in your organization to minimize its impact?
4. Have you established a proactive communication strategy to counter potential misinformation before it arises?
5. How transparent are you in your communication? Are you providing clear and honest information to the public to build trust?
6. Have you identified and cultivated key third-party influencers who can support and amplify your misinformation response?

Notes

1 Howell, L. "Digital wildfires in a hyperconnected world." *WEF Report*, 2013.
2 Zhou, Xinyi, and Reza Zafarani. "Network-based fake news detection: A pattern-driven approach." *ACM SIGKDD Explorations Newsletter* 21, no. 2 (2019): 48–60.; Aïmeur, Esma, Sabrine Amri, and Gilles Brassard. "Fake news, disinformation and misinformation in social media: A review." *Social Network Analysis and Mining* 13, no. 1 (2023): 30.
3 Ecker, Ullrich K. H., Stephan Lewandowsky, John Cook, Philipp Schmid, Lisa K. Fazio, Nadia Brashier, Panayiota Kendeou, Emily K. Vraga, and Michelle A. Amazeen. "The psychological drivers of misinformation belief and its resistance to correction." *Nature Reviews Psychology* 1, no. 1 (2022): 13–29.
4 Ecker, Ullrich KH, Stephan Lewandowsky, John Cook, Philipp Schmid, Lisa K. Fazio, Nadia Brashier, Panayiota Kendeou, Emily K. Vraga, and Michelle A.

Amazeen. "The psychological drivers of misinformation belief and its resistance to correction." *Nature Reviews Psychology* 1, no. 1 (2022): 13–29.

5 Karinshak, Elise, and Yan Jin. "AI-driven disinformation: a framework for organizational preparation and response." *Journal of Communication Management* 27, no. 4 (2023): 539–562.

6 Uppada, Santosh Kumar, and Parth Patel. "An image and text-based multimodal model for detecting fake news in OSN's." *Journal of Intelligent Information Systems* 61, no. 2 (2023): 367–393.

7 Uppada, Santosh Kumar, and Parth Patel. "An image and text-based multimodal model for detecting fake news in OSN's." *Journal of Intelligent Information Systems* 61, no. 2 (2023): 367–393.

8 Mirza, Shujaat, Labeeba Begum, Liang Niu, Sarah Pardo, Azza Abouzied, Paolo Papotti, and Christina Pöpper. "Tactics, threats & targets: Modeling disinformation and its mitigation." In *ISOC Network and Distributed Systems Security Symposium (NDSS)*, 2023.

9 Uppada, Santosh Kumar, and Parth Patel. "An image and text-based multimodal model for detecting fake news in OSN's." *Journal of Intelligent Information Systems* 61, no. 2 (2023): 367–393.

10 Uppada, Santosh Kumar, and Parth Patel. "An image and text-based multimodal model for detecting fake news in OSN's." *Journal of Intelligent Information Systems* 61, no. 2 (2023): 367–393.

11 Smith, Steven T., Edward K. Kao, Erika D. Mackin, Danelle C. Shah, Olga Simek, and Donald B. Rubin. "Automatic detection of influential actors in disinformation networks." *Proceedings of the National Academy of Sciences* 118, no. 4 (2021): e2011216118.

12 Tsikerdekis, Michail, and Sherali Zeadally. "Misinformation detection using deep learning." *IT Professional* 25, no. 5 (2023): 57–63.

13 Farkas, Johan, and Jannick Schou. "Fake news as a floating signifier: Hegemony, antagonism and the politics of falsehood." *Javnost-The Public* 25, no. 3 (2018): 298–314.

14 Mehta, Amisha M., Brooke F. Liu, Ellen Tyquin, and Lisa Tam. "A process view of crisis misinformation: How public relations professionals detect, manage, and evaluate crisis misinformation." *Public Relations Review* 47, no. 2 (2021): 102040.

15 Asr, Fatemeh Torabi, and Maite Taboada. "The data challenge in misinformation detection: Source reputation vs. content veracity." In *Proceedings of the First Workshop on Fact Extraction and Verification (FEVER)*, pp. 10–15, 2018.

16 Dennis, Alan R., Patricia L. Moravec, and Antino Kim. "Search & verify: Misinformation and source evaluations in internet search results." *Decision Support Systems* (2023): 113976.

17 Shao, Chengcheng, Pik-Mai Hui, Pengshuai Cui, Xinwen Jiang, and Yuxing Peng. "Tracking and characterizing the competition of fact checking and misinformation: case studies." *IEEE Access* 6 (2018): 75327–75341.

18 Nakov, Preslav, David Corney, Maram Hasanain, Firoj Alam, Tamer Elsayed, Alberto Barrón-Cedeño, Paolo Papotti, Shaden Shaar, and Giovanni Da San Martino. "Automated fact-checking for assisting human fact-checkers." *arXiv preprint arXiv:2103.07769* (2021).

19 Uppada, Santosh Kumar, B. S. Ashwin, and B. Sivaselvan. "A novel evolutionary approach-based multimodal model to detect fake news in OSNs using text and metadata." *The Journal of Supercomputing* (2023): 1–32.

20 Wu, Junchao, Shu Yang, Runzhe Zhan, Yulin Yuan, Derek F. Wong, and Lidia S. Chao. "A survey on llm-genrerated text detection: Necessity, methods, and future directions." *arXiv preprint arXiv:2310.14724* (2023).

21 Weber-Wulff, Debora, Alla Anohina-Naumeca, Sonja Bjelobaba, Tomáš Foltýnek, Jean Guerrero-Dib, Olumide Popoola, Petr Šigut, and Lorna Waddington. "Testing of detection tools for AI-generated text." *International Journal for Educational Integrity* 19, no. 1 (2023): 26.

22 Tolosana, Ruben, Ruben Vera-Rodriguez, Julian Fierrez, Aythami Morales, and Javier Ortega-Garcia. "Deepfakes and beyond: A survey of face manipulation and fake detection." *Information Fusion* 64 (2020): 131–148.

23 Marra, Francesco, Diego Gragnaniello, Davide Cozzolino, and Luisa Verdoliva. "Detection of gan-generated fake images over social networks." In *2018 IEEE Conference on Multimedia Information Processing and Retrieval (MIPR)*, pp. 384–389. IEEE, 2018.

24 Corvi, Riccardo, Davide Cozzolino, Giada Zingarini, Giovanni Poggi, Koki Nagano, and Luisa Verdoliva. "On the detection of synthetic images generated by diffusion models." In *ICASSP 2023-2023 IEEE International Conference on Acoustics, Speech and Signal Processing (ICASSP)*, pp. 1–5. IEEE, 2023.

25 Pedreschi, Dino, Fosca Giannotti, Riccardo Guidotti, Anna Monreale, Salvatore Ruggieri, and Franco Turini. "Meaningful explanations of black box AI decision systems." In *Proceedings of the AAAI Conference on Artificial Intelligence*, vol. 33, no. 01, pp. 9780–9784, 2019.

26 Almutairi, Zaynab, and Hebah Elgibreen. "A review of modern audio deepfake detection methods: Challenges and future directions." *Algorithms* 15, no. 5 (2022): 155.

27 Yu, Peipeng, Zhihua Xia, Jianwei Fei, and Yujiang Lu. "A survey on deepfake video detection." *Iet Biometrics* 10, no. 6 (2021): 607–624.

28 Li, Meng, Beibei Liu, Yongjian Hu, Liepiao Zhang, and Shiqi Wang. "Deepfake detection using robust spatial and temporal features from facial landmarks." In *2021 IEEE International Workshop on Biometrics and Forensics (IWBF)*, pp. 1–6. IEEE, 2021.

29 Ganti, Dhanvi. "A novel method for detecting misinformation in videos, utilizing reverse image search, semantic analysis, and sentiment comparison of metadata." *Utilizing Reverse Image Search, Semantic Analysis, and Sentiment Comparison of Metadata (June 5, 2022)* (2022).

30 Horne, Benjamin, and Sibel Adali. "This just in: Fake news packs a lot in title, uses simpler, repetitive content in text body, more similar to satire than real news." In *Proceedings of the International AAAI Conference on Web and Social Media*, vol. 11, no. 1, pp. 759–766, 2017.

31 Lewandowsky, Stephan, Ullrich KH Ecker, Colleen M. Seifert, Norbert Schwarz, and John Cook. "Misinformation and its correction: Continued influence and successful debiasing." *Psychological Science in the Public Interest* 13, no. 3 (2012): 106–131.

32 Mills, Adam J., and Karen Robson. "Brand management in the era of fake news: Narrative response as a strategy to insulate brand value." *Journal of Product & Brand Management* 29, no. 2 (2020): 159–167.; Mills, Colleen. "Experiencing gossip: The foundations for a theory of embedded organizational gossip." *Group & Organization Management* 35, no. 2 (2010): 213–240.

33 DiFonzo, Nicholas, and Prashant Bordia. *Rumor Psychology: Social and Organizational Approaches*. American Psychological Association, 2007.; Lewandowsky, Stephan, Ullrich KH Ecker, Colleen M. Seifert, Norbert Schwarz, and John Cook. "Misinformation and its correction: Continued influence and successful debiasing." *Psychological Science in the Public Interest* 13, no. 3 (2012): 106–131.; Pennycook, Gordon, Tyrone D. Cannon, and David G. Rand. "Prior exposure increases perceived accuracy of fake news." *Journal of Experimental Psychology: General* 147, no. 12 (2018): 1865.

34 Ecker, Ullrich K. H., Stephan Lewandowsky, Briony Swire, and Darren Chang. "Correcting false information in memory: Manipulating the strength of misinformation encoding and its retraction." *Psychonomic Bulletin & Review* 18 (2011): 570–578.

35 Shtulman, Andrew, and Joshua Valcarcel. "Scientific knowledge suppresses but does not supplant earlier intuitions." *Cognition* 124, no. 2 (2012): 209–215.

36 Ecker, Ullrich K. H., Stephan Lewandowsky, John Cook, Philipp Schmid, Lisa K. Fazio, Nadia Brashier, Panayiota Kendeou, Emily K. Vraga, and Michelle A. Amazeen. "The psychological drivers of misinformation belief and its resistance to correction." *Nature Reviews Psychology* 1, no. 1 (2022): 13–29.

37 Bryanov, Kirill, and Victoria Vziatysheva. "Determinants of individuals' belief in fake news: A scoping review determinants of belief in fake news." *PLoS One* 16, no. 6 (2021): e0253717.

38 Nyhan, Brendan, and Jason Reifler. "When corrections fail: The persistence of political misperceptions." *Political Behavior* 32, no. 2 (2010): 303–330.

39 Thaler, Richard H., and Cass R. Sunstein. *Nudge: Improving Decisions about Health, Wealth, and Happiness.* Penguin, 2009.; Lewandowsky, Stephan, Ullrich KH Ecker, Colleen M. Seifert, Norbert Schwarz, and John Cook. "Misinformation and its correction: Continued influence and successful debiasing." *Psychological Science in the Public Interest* 13, no. 3 (2012): 106–131.

40 Johnson, Eric J., and Daniel G. Goldstein. "Defaults and donation decisions." *Transplantation* 78, no. 12 (2004): 1713–1716.

41 Lewandowsky, Stephan, John Cook, Ullrich Ecker, Dolores Albarracín, Panayiota Kendeou, Eryn J. Newman, Gordon Pennycook et al. "The debunking handbook 2020." (2020).

42 Enholm, Ida Merete, Emmanouil Papagiannidis, Patrick Mikalef, and John Krogstie. "Artificial intelligence and business value: A literature review." *Information Systems Frontiers* 24, no. 5 (2022): 1709–1734.

43 Horne, Benjamin D., Mauricio Gruppi, and Sibel Adali. "Trustworthy misinformation mitigation with soft information nudging." In *2019 first IEEE International Conference on Trust, Privacy and Security in Intelligent Systems and Applications (TPS-ISA)*, pp. 245–254. IEEE, 2019.; Horne, Benjamin D., Dorit Nevo, Sibel Adali, Lydia Manikonda, and Clare Arrington. "Tailoring heuristics and timing AI interventions for supporting news veracity assessments." *Computers in Human Behavior Reports* 2 (2020): 100043.; Jia, Chenyan, Alexander Boltz, Angie Zhang, Anqing Chen, and Min Kyung Lee. "Understanding effects of algorithmic vs. Community label on perceived accuracy of hyper-partisan misinformation." *Proceedings of the ACM on Human-Computer Interaction* 6, no. CSCW2 (2022): 1–27.

44 Holzinger, Andreas, Chris Biemann, Constantinos S. Pattichis, and Douglas B. Kell. "What do we need to build explainable AI systems for the medical domain?" *arXiv preprint arXiv:1712.09923* (2017).; Horne, Benjamin D., Dorit Nevo, Sibel Adali, Lydia Manikonda, and Clare Arrington. "Tailoring heuristics and timing AI interventions for supporting news veracity assessments." *Computers in Human Behavior Reports* 2 (2020): 100043.

45 Statista Research Department. (2022). "User-generated internet content per minute 2021." *Statista*, available at: www.statista.com/statistics/195140/new-user-generated-content-uploadedby-users-per-minute/

46 Karinshak, Elise, and Yan Jin. "AI-driven disinformation: A framework for organizational preparation and response." *Journal of Communication Management* 27, no. 4 (2023): 539–562.

47 Schwarz, Norbert, and Madeline Jalbert. "When (fake) news feels true: Intuitions of truth and the acceptance and correction of misinformation." In *The Psychology of Fake News*, pp. 73–89. Routledge, 2020.

48 Ribeiro, Filipe N., Koustuv Saha, Mahmoudreza Babaei, Lucas Henrique, Johnnatan Messias, Fabricio Benevenuto, Oana Goga, Krishna P. Gummadi, and Elissa M.

Redmiles. "On microtargeting socially divisive ads: A case study of russia-linked ad campaigns on facebook." In *Proceedings of the Conference on Fairness, Accountability, and Transparency*, pp. 140–149, 2019.

49 Lewandowsky, Stephan, and Sander Van Der Linden. "Countering misinformation and fake news through inoculation and prebunking." *European Review of Social Psychology* 32, no. 2 (2021): 348–384.; Brady, William J., Julian A. Wills, John T. Jost, Joshua A. Tucker, and Jay J. Van Bavel. "Emotion shapes the diffusion of moralized content in social networks." *Proceedings of the National Academy of Sciences* 114, no. 28 (2017): 7313–7318.

50 Austin, Lucinda, Brooke Fisher Liu, and Yan Jin. "How audiences seek out crisis information: Exploring the social-mediated crisis communication model." *Journal of Applied Communication Research* 40, no. 2 (2012): 188–207.

51 Guthrie, W. Scott, and John Rich. "New technology, big data, and artificial intelligence." In *Social Media and Crisis Communication*, pp. 180–192. Routledge, 2022.; Hurley, B. "How corporate communications can keep up with disinformation attacks: PRNEWS." 2023, available at: www.prnewsonline.com/monitoring-for-disinformation/

52 Liu, Brooke Fisher, Yan Jin, Rowena Briones, and Beth Kuch. "Managing turbulence in the blogosphere: Evaluating the blog-mediated crisis communication model with the American Red Cross." *Journal of Public Relations Research* 24, no. 4 (2012): 353–370.

53 Karinshak, Elise, and Yan Jin. "AI-driven disinformation: A framework for organizational preparation and response." *Journal of Communication Management* 27, no. 4 (2023): 539–562.

54 Kertysova, Katarina. "Artificial intelligence and disinformation: How AI changes the way disinformation is produced, disseminated, and can be countered." *Security and Human Rights* 29, no. 1–4 (2018): 55–81.

55 Lai, Vivian, Samuel Carton, Rajat Bhatnagar, Q. Vera Liao, Yunfeng Zhang, and Chenhao Tan. "Human-ai collaboration via conditional delegation: A case study of content moderation." In *Proceedings of the 2022 CHI Conference on Human Factors in Computing Systems*, pp. 1–18, 2022.

56 Karinshak, Elise, and Yan Jin. "AI-driven disinformation: A framework for organizational preparation and response." *Journal of Communication Management* 27, no. 4 (2023): 539–562.; Pennycook, Gordon, Adam Bear, Evan T. Collins, and David G. Rand. "The implied truth effect: Attaching warnings to a subset of fake news headlines increases perceived accuracy of headlines without warnings." *Management Science* 66, no. 11 (2020): 4944–4957.

57 Jin, Yan, Toni GLA van der Meer, Yen-I. Lee, and Xuerong Lu. "The effects of corrective communication and employee backup on the effectiveness of fighting crisis misinformation." *Public Relations Review* 46, no. 3 (2020): 101910.; Vijaykumar, Santosh, Yan Jin, Daniel Rogerson, Xuerong Lu, Swati Sharma, Anna Maughan, Bianca Fadel, Mariella Silva de Oliveira Costa, Claudia Pagliari, and Daniel Morris. "How shades of truth and age affect responses to COVID-19 (Mis) information: Randomized survey experiment among WhatsApp users in UK and Brazil." *Humanities and Social Sciences Communications* 8, no. 1 (2021).

58 Jin, Yan, Toni G. L. A. van der Meer, Yen-I. Lee, and Xuerong Lu. "The effects of corrective communication and employee backup on the effectiveness of fighting crisis misinformation." *Public Relations Review* 46, no. 3 (2020): 101910.

59 Lewandowsky, Stephan, and Sander Van Der Linden. "Countering misinformation and fake news through inoculation and prebunking." *European Review of Social Psychology* 32, no. 2 (2021): 348–384.

60 Van der Linden, Sander, Anthony Leiserowitz, Seth Rosenthal, and Edward Maibach. "Inoculating the public against misinformation about climate change." *Global Challenges* 1, no. 2 (2017): 1600008.

61 Lewandowsky, Stephan, and Sander Van Der Linden. "Countering misinformation and fake news through inoculation and prebunking." *European Review of Social Psychology* 32, no. 2 (2021): 348–384.

62 Karinshak, Elise, and Yan Jin. "AI-driven disinformation: a framework for organizational preparation and response." *Journal of Communication Management* 27, no. 4 (2023): 539–562.

63 Boman, Courtney D., and Erika J. Schneider. "Finding an antidote: Testing the use of proactive crisis strategies to protect organizations from astroturf attacks." *Public Relations Review* 47, no. 1 (2021): 102004.; Schneider, Erika J., Courtney D. Boman, and Heather Akin. "The amplified crisis: Assessing negative social amplification and source of a crisis response." *Communication Reports* 34, no. 3 (2021): 165–178.

64 Davis, Jason "In a digital world of generative AI detection will not be enough." *Newhouse Impact Journal* 1, no. 1, Article 5 (2024). http://doi.org/10.14305/jn.29960819.2024.1.1.01

65 Yang, Jeongwon, and Regina Luttrell. "Digital misinformation & disinformation: The global war of words." In *The Emerald Handbook of Computer-Mediated Communication and Social Media*, pp. 511–529. Emerald Publishing Limited, 2022.

GLOSSARY

AI hallucination   A phenomenon whereby large language models create nonsensical or inaccurate outputs

AI synthetic personas   Virtual representations generated through artificial intelligence technologies, simulating human characteristics and behaviors to serve specific roles in public relations and communication strategies.

Algorithm(s)   A finite sequence of rigorous instructions, typically used to solve a class of specific problems or to perform a computation. Algorithms are used as specifications for performing calculations and data processing.

Artificial intelligence (AI)   Technologies capable of performing tasks that imitate or replicate human intelligence, often involving learning, reasoning, problem-solving, and decision-making processes.

Augmented reality (AR)   Technology that overlays digital information or virtual elements onto the real-world environment, enhancing the user's perception and interaction with the surroundings.

Authenticity   The quality of being genuine, real, or trustworthy; in the context of public relations, it refers to maintaining truthful and sincere communication with the audience.

Beneficence   An ethical principle that means doing good or contributing to the wellbeing of others

Bias   A systematic error or deviation from the truth in judgment or decision-making, often influenced by personal beliefs, preferences, or stereotypes.

Biased AI   AI systems that result in incorrect outputs/predictions for specific populations and/or discriminatory output/predictions for specific populations.

Black box models   A mathematical or computational model that represents a system or process whereby the inputs and outputs of the system are known, but the underlying algorithms, equations, or processes that transform the inputs into outputs are not visible or understandable.

Bloggers   Individuals who create and publish content, typically in a diary-style format on the internet, expressing personal opinions, experiences, and insights.

Brand ambassadors   Individuals, often influencers or celebrities, who promote and represent a brand, endorsing its products or services to their audience.

Celebrities   Well-known public figures with a significant following and influence.

Chatbots Apps or interfaces that can carry on human-like conversation using natural language understanding (NLU) or natural language processing (NLP) and machine learning (ML).

Communication landscape The overall environment or context in which communication occurs, including the media ecosystem, cultural trends, technological developments, and regulatory frameworks.

Computer-generated imagery (CGI) The creation of visual elements, scenes, or effects using computer graphics, commonly used in movies, video games, and other forms of media.

Concept drift The phenomenon whereby the statistical properties of the target variable change over time, making the predictions less accurate.

Content analysis A research method used for systematically analyzing textual, visual, or audio content by categorizing and interpreting patterns.

Content Creation/generation The process of creating material for various purposes, such as marketing, communication, or entertainment.

Corporate social responsibility (CSR) CSR is a comprehensive concept that integrates various corporate management domains, including business ethics, corporate citizenship, sustainability, stakeholder management, environmental management, and corporate social performance.

Creativity The use of imagination or ideas to create original work.

Crisis An unexpected event that violates stakeholder expectations and generates negative outcomes, such as threatening the organizations reputation and stakeholders' wellbeing. Crises can take many forms depending on their nature, such as a paracrisis, sticky crises, and a scansis.

Crisis communications The strategic messaging that serves to protect the organization and its publics. It involves the strategic dissemination of information during a crisis to maintain relationships with its various stakeholders.

Crisis management The process of preparing for and responding to adverse events that negatively affect stakeholders. It is a systematic process undertaken to prepare for, respond to, and recover from a crisis.

[Critical] digital literacy Digital literacy refers to the ability to use, understand, and evaluate technology to complete a variety of tasks safely and ethically. Critical digital literacy focuses on critiquing and interrogating digital tools to assess their function and impact in civic and professional contexts.

Critical thinking the analysis of facts, observations, and arguments to develop a rational judgment.

Data analysis The process of inspecting, cleansing, transforming, and modeling data to uncover meaningful insights, patterns, or trends.

Data analytics The collection, transformation, and organization of data in order to draw conclusions, make predictions, and drive informed decision making.

Data poisoning A type of attack on machine learning whereby the training data is intentionally manipulated to corrupt the model's output.

Data visualization Data visualization is the graphical representation of information and data by using visual elements like charts, graphs, and maps.

Debunking The process of critically examining and refuting claims, theories, or beliefs that are found to be false, misleading, or lacking in evidence using scientific skepticism, critical thinking, and rigorous testing to identify flaws, inconsistencies, or inaccuracies in a claim or theory.

Deepfake A type of synthetic media that uses artificial intelligence (AI) and machine learning algorithms to create realistic, manipulated, or fabricated audio, video, or image content that appears authentic. Deepfakes are created by swapping faces, voices, or other elements between different media sources.

Deep learning A method of AI that uses combined data from many sources to create understanding of a topic.

DEI-conscious PR approach Involves organizations using public relations to connect with and involve diverse audiences, aligning corporate values, culture, and strategic messaging with varied needs, including those of marginalized communities.

Deontology The study of the nature of duty and obligation in ethics.

Dialogue The final desired outcome for relationship building in certain situations. It is characterized by ongoing communication events, with the purpose of solving a problem or issue whereby both parties are dedicated to listening and shifting behaviors. It often includes high levels of openness, understanding, empathy, risk, commitment, and change.

Dictionaries (in sentiment analysis) Predefined lists of words with associated sentiment values used for analyzing text.

Disinformation the deliberate creation and distribution of false or misleading content with the intent to deceive or manipulate public opinion.

Diversity Refers to the range of personal and group characteristics shared among people, such as race, ethnicity, gender, age, ability, religion, sexual orientation, socioeconomic status, and more.

Diversity communication The organization's communication efforts convey its commitment to diversity, fostering a supportive environment for diverse talents and enhancing organizational performance.

Earned media Publicity gained through non-paid means, such as media coverage, influencer mentions, and word of mouth. AI tools analyze large datasets to identify trends and influencers, helping PR professionals craft pitches that resonate more effectively with journalists and bloggers, thereby enhancing SEO through valuable backlinks and media coverage.

Engagement The desired final outcome for relationship building in certain situations. Engagement is characterized by a series of exchanges in an environment with relationship building potential, whereby both parties are motivated to participate in ongoing communication. This concept is connected to trust, satisfaction, loyalty, and supportive behavioral intentions.

Ethical implications The moral considerations or consequences associated with a particular action, decision, or technology.

Equity Being treated fairly or impartially. It involves promoting justice and fairness in institutional procedures and resource distribution, addressing root causes of societal outcome disparities.

Excellence Theory A general theory of public relations that specifies how public relations makes organizations more effective, how it is organized and managed when it contributes most to organizational effectiveness, the conditions in organizations and their environments that make organizations more effective, and how the monetary value of public relations can be determined.

Fairness Fairness in AI refers to the ethical and unbiased treatment of individuals or groups in the development and deployment of artificial intelligence systems.

Gamification The application of typical elements of game playing (e.g. point scoring, competition with others, rules of play) to other areas of activity, typically as an online marketing technique to encourage engagement with a product or service.

Generative AI Refers to a class of artificial intelligence (AI) algorithms that can create new, original content or data that resembles existing data. These models learn patterns and relationships within large datasets and use this knowledge to generate novel outputs that are often indistinguishable from those created by humans.

GPT-3 (Generative Pre-trained Transformer 3) An advanced language processing model that uses machine learning to generate human-like text and understand natural language.

Hallucinate/hallucination   Used as a metaphor in the context of artificial intelligence to describe a response given by a generative AI system that "went off the rails." Hallucinations can range from inaccurate information (think, for example, the misattribution of an existing article to an existing researcher) to completely non-sensical responses.

Human-in-the-loop   A framework whereby human input is required to guide or improve AI systems.

Hypertargeting   Refers to the ability to deliver advertising content to specific interest-based segments in a network.

Inclusion   The ability to ensure that every individual feels like they belong.

Inclusive climate   A collective commitment to incorporating diverse cultural identities for insights and skills. Individuals, regardless of their backgrounds, receive fair treatment, consideration, recognition, and equal involvement in workplace decision-making.

Influencer marketing   A marketing strategy that involves collaborating with influencers to promote products or services to their audience.

Influencers   Individuals with significant online followings who can affect their audience's opinions and behaviors.

Influencers   A person with the ability to influence potential buyers of a product or service by promoting or recommending the items on social media.

Innovation   The process of introducing new ideas, methods, products, or services that create value or improve existing processes.

Interactivity   The third stage of relationship-building, including at least three exchanges that are related to each other that are sent between the same parties (one-to-one, one-to-many, or many-to many). Messages may be shared synchronously and asynchronously.

Large language model (LLM)   A large language model is a system designed to analyze and process data/text. Its main function is to perform a variety of natural language processing tasks, from generating to editing/revising and translating text. In this way, an LLM falls under the broader category of generative AI. What makes LLM models "large" and powerful is the vast amount of text data on which they are trained and the massive amounts of parameters they contain (think billions – or even trillions – of parameters), all of which influence the prediction outcome. This is also what makes them capable of analyzing and processing not just isolated words but entire sentences and paragraphs. ChatGPT is an example of an LLM.

Latent content   The underlying, implicit meaning or interpretation of a communication or message.

Machine learning (ML)   A subset of artificial intelligence that enables systems to learn and improve from experience without being explicitly programmed.

Macroinfluencers   Influencers with a large following, typically in the hundreds of thousands or millions.

Manifest content   The actual, concrete content or information visible in a communication or message.

Media relations   Managing the relationship between an organization and the media to ensure positive coverage and effective communication of the organization's messages.

Megainfluencers   Influencers with an exceptionally large and widespread influence, with a reach of millions or tens of millions of followers.

Microinfluencers   Influencers with a smaller but highly engaged and niche audience.

Misinformation   False information that is disseminated without harmful intent

Nanoinfluencers   Influencers with a very small but highly specific and loyal follower base.

Natural language processing (NLP)   A branch of AI that enables machines to understand and interpret human language. In SEO, NLP helps search engines understand the context and intent behind search queries, delivering more relevant search results and enabling the creation of more effective and personalized content.

Neoliberalism   A political approach that favors free-market capitalism, deregulation, and reduction in government spending.

Noise (in data)   Irrelevant or meaningless data points or information that can distort or reduce the accuracy of analysis in machine learning.

Non-maleficence   An ethical principal that means to avoid actions that could cause harm to others.

Opinion leaders   Individuals who are considered authorities in a particular field and whose opinions are highly regarded and influential.

Outreach efforts   Outreach efforts refer to activities aimed at reaching out to external stakeholders, such as journalists, influencers, or the public.

Owned media   Refers to content created and controlled by the brand, such as websites, blogs, and newsletters. AI aids in content creation and optimization, ensuring that this content is relevant, engaging, and optimized for search engines to improve organic search rankings and overall visibility.

Paid media   Refers to any form of advertising that involves paying for placement, such as pay-per-click (PPC) campaigns. AI optimizes these strategies by automating bid management, targeting specific audience segments, and personalizing ad content to ensure higher engagement and better ROI.

PESO Model©   Developed by Gini Dietrich, the PESO Model© stands for paid, earned, shared, and owned media. It is an integrated communications model that helps PR professionals create cohesive and strategic campaigns. When combined with AI, the PESO Model© can enhance SEO and SEM strategies by providing a framework for leveraging different types of media to achieve strategic objectives.

Plagiarism   The act of using someone else's work, ideas, or expressions without proper attribution or permission, presenting them as one's own.

Prebunking   A proactive approach to preventing the spread of misinformation, pseudoscience, and false claims by anticipating, identifying, and refuting flawed arguments or theories before they gain widespread acceptance.

Precrisis phase   The stage before a crisis occurs where organizations plan and prepare for an event to occur. A crisis management plan may be developed within this stage to assist in identifying issues advise a public relations professional with message content, source, communication platform strategies, and other guidance to help enact when a crisis occurs.

Predictive analytics   Involves using AI to analyze historical data and identify patterns to predict future trends and behaviors. In PR, predictive analytics can forecast search trends, consumer preferences, and market developments, enabling proactive adjustments to SEO and SEM strategies for optimal results.

Professional practice   The practice refers to the standards, principles, and norms that guide the conduct of individuals within a particular profession or field.

Professional responsibility theory   Based on the public relations professional's dual obligations to serve client organizations and the public interest.

Proportionality   AI should only be used to the extent necessary to accomplish a goal.

Public relations (PR)   The practice of managing and disseminating information from an organization to the public to shape public perception and build relationships. It involves strategic communication processes that build mutually beneficial relationships between organizations and their publics.

Relationship initiation The first stage of relationship building, which is conceptualized as the initial outreach by either a public or an organization. It includes the research that occurs before a relationship is initiated, when both parties are learning about one another and the communication environment.

Relationship management Involves building and maintaining positive relationships with stakeholders, such as journalists, clients, partners, or the public.

Responsible AI Implies the ethical and accountable development and use of artificial intelligence (AI) technologies to benefit society, customers, businesses, and employees.

Responsiveness The second stage of relationship-building, which is characterized by a one-time, first message sent between parties in reaction to an initial message. It can have positive or negative outcomes. Timeliness, relevance, willingness, and ability to respond are key.

Rule-based algorithms Algorithms that apply a set of predefined rules or criteria to sort and analyze data.

Rule-based bot A type of artificial intelligence that generates content including human-like text responses, images, audio, and video based on limited, pre-approved responses from which it is trained.

Scansis The intersection of a crisis and scandal that occurs when an organization engages in offensive behavior. A scansis is socially constructed to evoke moral outrage in stakeholders.

Search engine marketing (SEM) SEM includes paid advertising strategies, such as pay-per-click (PPC) ads, to achieve immediate visibility on search engines. In PR, SEM is used to amplify messages quickly and reach broader audiences by promoting content like press releases or corporate announcements through paid search ads, ensuring that they appear at the top of search results.

Search engine optimization (SEO) The practice of optimizing online content to improve its ranking on search engine results pages (SERPs). This involves keyword research, quality content creation, and technical optimization to ensure that digital content like press releases and blog posts are easily discoverable by search engines like Google. Effective SEO increases the visibility and credibility of PR messages, ensuring they reach the target audience organically.

Sentiment analysis The process of analyzing text or speech to determine the sentiment or opinion expressed.

Sentiments Feelings or emotions expressed towards a particular topic, product, or idea.

Shared media Involves content shared across social media platforms. AI enhances the reach and impact of shared content by predicting which types of content are most likely to be shared and by whom, driving organic traffic and engagement that benefits SEO.

Social listening The process of monitoring digital conversations to understand what customers are saying about a brand or topic online.

Stable diffusion An advanced deep learning AI model that employs diffusion processes to produce high-quality artwork from text prompts.

Stereotypes A fixed and oversimplified concept or idea of someone else.

Strategic communications Plans or approaches used to convey messages effectively to a target audience.

StyleGAN (Style Generative Adversarial Network) A machine learning model used for creating realistic images, including faces and objects.

Synthetic media Media or content that is artificially created or generated using advanced technologies such as artificial intelligence (AI), machine learning (ML), large language models (LLMs), and computer vision, including any combination of synthetic text, deepfakes, AI-generated images, synthetic audio, and video.

To fine-tune Making small adjustments to a machine learning model to improve its accuracy or performance.

To train (in AI) The process of teaching a machine learning model to make predictions or decisions, typically by feeding it data and allowing it to learn from that data.

Unstructured data Data that does not have a predefined format or organization, often text-heavy and including things like emails, social media posts, and articles.

Utilitarianism The doctrine that an action is right insofar as it promotes happiness, and that the greatest happiness of the greatest number should be the guiding principle of conduct.

Virtual influencers AI-generated personas designed to function as influencers, interacting with audiences on digital platforms.

Virtual reality (VR) A computer-generated environment that simulates a realistic or imaginary experience, often experienced through special electronic equipment like VR headsets.

Virtue ethics An approach that treats virtue and character as the primary subjects of ethics, in contrast to other ethical systems that put consequences of voluntary acts, principles or rules of conduct, or obedience to divine authority in the primary role.

Workflow Sequence of tasks or processes involved in completing a project or achieving a goal.

XAI/explainable AI AI systems designed to be transparent, providing clear and understandable explanations of their processes and decisions.

INDEX

For Product Safety Concerns and Information please contact our EU
representative GPSR@taylorandfrancis.com
Taylor & Francis Verlag GmbH, Kaufingerstraße 24, 80331 München, Germany